Assessing the Nuclear Age

Assessing the Nuclear Age

Selections from the *Bulletin of the Atomic Scientists*

Edited by Len Ackland and Steven McGuire

EDUCATIONAL FOUNDATION FOR NUCLEAR SCIENCE
CHICAGO, ILLINOIS

© 1986 by the Bulletin of the Atomic Scientists
Educational Foundation for Nuclear Science
5801 South Kenwood Avenue
Chicago, Illinois 60637
All rights reserved.

Distributed by the University of Chicago Press
Marketing Department
5801 South Ellis Avenue
Chicago, Illinois 60637
UCP order numbers: 03872-6; 03873-4 (paperback)

Book and cover designed by Lisa Grayson.
Typeset in Compugraphic Bem by R&S Media Services.
Printed and bound by George Banta, Inc. in the United States.

Library of Congress CIP no. 85-082511
ISBN 0-941682-07-2
ISBN 0-941682-08-0 (paperback)

Contents

Preface

In October 1984 the directors and editors of the *Bulletin of the Atomic Scientists* and a few interested friends met at the Johnson Foundation's Wingspread Center in Racine, Wisconsin. The purpose of the two-day conference was to consider the *Bulletin*'s mission and to lay out a 10-year plan for this unique magazine, which is dedicated to preventing nuclear war. The 25 conferees agreed that the magazine's core concern can be bolstered by giving more attention to the underlying factors of the arms race and by clarifying the connections among issues such as Third World development, global population trends, regional conflict, and the potential for escalation to nuclear war. And the group reconfirmed that the *Bulletin* should continue to be, as it has been since its founding by concerned scientists in December 1945, a nonpartisan, nontechnical forum for debate and a source of credible information on issues of science and public policy.

On the heels of the Wingspread meeting, the magazine's editorial board and editors met at the *Bulletin*'s offices on the University of Chicago campus to brainstorm about one of the projects agreed upon at the conference—a special 40th-anniversary issue to be published in August 1985 to commemorate the tragic use of nuclear weapons on the populations of Hiroshima and Nagasaki in August 1945. We decided that the special issue should cover a broad range of subjects and should analyze the past and the present in terms of lessons that need to be learned so the world can survive. The next step was to commission articles ranging from reflections by well-known Manhattan Project veterans to suggestions by scholars about future actions. Getting authors to agree to write for the anniversary issue was easy; the difficult part was trying to decide who among the many authoritative natural scientists, social scientists, and other persons comprising the *Bulletin* community should be invited to write articles. In addition, top artists were commissioned to illustrate the articles and to do the cover for the 172-page 40th-anniversary issue.

Assessing the Nuclear Age consists primarily of articles published in the *Bulletin*'s August 1985 anniversary issue. But in preparing this book

x

we decided to delete a few articles and to add a dozen others from recent issues of the magazine in order to enhance coverage of important current topics such as Star Wars, verification of and compliance with arms treaties, and proliferation.

This book, and the 40th-anniversary issue that preceded it, reflect the ideas and labor of many people and organizations. Special thanks go to Arthur Singer of the Alfred P. Sloan Foundation and Rita Goodman of the Johnson Foundation for supporting the *Bulletin* conference at Wingspread. We are also grateful to the Sloan Foundation, the Ruth Mott Fund, the Columbia Foundation, and the George Gund Foundation for grants they made in support of the anniversary issue.

As for the book's contents, we particularly want to thank Bernard Feld, the *Bulletin*'s former editor in chief, for recruiting several of his Manhattan Project colleagues to write articles and for his own contribution. John Holdren, David Holloway, and Deborah Shapley of the magazine's editorial board helped shape the anniversary issue and contacted certain contributors. Editor in chief Harrison Brown was a ready source of ideas for the project. Art director Lisa Grayson did a marvelous job of commissioning illustrations for the issue (which unfortunately were too costly to reproduce in this book) and did the layout and cover for the book. Associate editor Nancy Myers provided a deft hand in the rewriting and editing process, manuscript editor Ruth Grodzins applied her fine editorial polish, and editorial assistant Susan Henking stayed on top of the numerous details that such a project entails. The annotated bibliography was based largely on a much lengthier one compiled by Holdren. General manager Thomas Hazinski supervised the business end of the operation, without which the book could never have been produced. Finally, we wish to thank the *Bulletin*'s board of directors for the encouragement and intellectual contributions they made toward this book. As always, the responsibility for any mistakes in such a project rests with us.

Len Ackland and Steven McGuire
February 1986

Introduction

The guns of World War II were silenced in Europe on May 8, 1945 and in Asia some three months later. During the five and a half years of World War II, some of the most barbarous events in human history took place, on a scale never before experienced. Some 50 million persons lost their lives, including 20 million Russians, five million Germans, two million Japanese, one million British and French, and 300,000 Americans. To this must be added an additional 1.3 million who were killed in the Chinese-Japanese war of 1937–1945.

Cruelty fed upon cruelty, climaxed by the fanatic German effort to eradicate Jews and other "undesirables" from the human species. The Nazis established a vast and highly efficient killing enterprise, resorting to firing squads, gas chambers, crematoriums, starvation, disease, and slave labor camps. By the end of the war some 10 million Jews and others considered "undesirable" for racial or political reasons had been exterminated. This amounted to some 20 percent of all World War II deaths.

By the end of the conflict five additional catastrophes stood out as truly significant in the long history of warfare. Dresden and Hamburg were totally destroyed by a combination of explosions and fires. This horrible planned destruction was undertaken, not because the two cities were important military targets, but rather as attempts to show the Germans that they could not win the war. Related to this monstrous killing of Germans, who for the most part were civilians, Tokyo was virtually destroyed by fire bombs; Hiroshima and Nagasaki were totally destroyed by a new weapon—the atomic bomb.

The extent of killing and destruction that occurred during World War II was unprecedented, but only in small measure due to the development of nuclear weapons. The scientists and engineers who worked on the Manhattan Project, however, realized fully that while a city the size of Dresden could be wiped out by conventional weapons, to do so required an enormous mobilization of air power. By contrast, the same city could be demolished relatively easily with nuclear weapons. Accordingly, it seemed quite plausible to the scientists that a future world war, fought with some 100 megatons of airborne fission bombs, might kill 100 million people and destroy 1,000 cities. Given the proper selection of targets, this could be sufficient to bring modern industrial civilization to a halt.

Such considerations caused the scientists to mount a number of educational campaigns through hastily formed organizations and to engage in vigorous lobbying in Washington. Notable among the newly created institutions were the *Bulletin of the Atomic Scientists*, the Federation of American Scientists, and the Emergency Committee of Atomic Scientists.

The scientific groups clamored for the initiation of discussions leading to international agreements which might make possible the control of the manufacture and use of nuclear weapons. Discussions were started at the United Nations on the basis of proposals put forward by the United States. But it soon became clear that the Soviet Union was opposed at that time to any such agreements. (They were on the verge of developing their own nuclear capability.) Furthermore, strong forces in the United States were also opposed, in the mistaken belief that the United States would be able to maintain its nuclear monopoly for a very long time.

Discussions of controls over nuclear arms virtually ceased following three major technological developments:

The Soviets developed their own nuclear weapons capability—indeed, more rapidly than many knowledgeable people had expected.

The United States and the Soviet Union developed their own versions of the fusion or hydrogen bomb, which increased by another thousandfold the explosive power of the device that destroyed Nagasaki.

Guided ballistic missiles capable of delivering hydrogen bombs with tremendous speed over great distances were developed by both countries (with considerable help from the German experience).

Thus, in a very few years, the killing power of weapons systems had once again been increased dramatically.

Some feeble attempts were made to restart intergovernmental discussions of the control of nuclear arms, but in the face of the massive efforts being made by the two superpowers during the 1950s to increase their nuclear strike forces, these efforts were unsuccessful. For some time the only significant international discussions were held in the private sector, sponsored by a diversity of organizations. Notable among these were the Pugwash Conferences, founded by a number of prominent scientists. The first meeting was held in 1957 at the Pugwash, Nova Scotia, home of the late Cyrus Eaton, industrialist and railroad magnate. At least for a few years, these meetings provided an invaluable communications link between the United States and the Soviet Union through their respective scientific communities. The conferences assuredly played a major role in the creation of the "hotline" between Moscow and Washington, and evidence also suggests that they led eventually to intergovernmental discussions concerning a possible agreement banning nuclear testing in the atmosphere.

During the 1960 U.S. election campaign, a group of scientists proposed the creation of a "peace agency" within the federal government, urging that such a project be made an important element of the Democratic Party platform. This proposal was indeed incorporated into the platform, and shortly after John F. Kennedy's election a modified version was created—the Arms Control and Disarmament Agency. Over the years this agency undertook a number of important research tasks which clarified many critical arms control issues and prepared the United States to engage in arms control and disarmament discussions, should the occasion ever arise. Largely because of political considerations, however, the organization's usefulness has been seriously limited.

In the 1960s and 1970s the technology of delivery systems became increasingly complex. A variety of systems emerged and, even more important, their accuracy improved dramatically. A prime example was the nuclear-powered submarine, capable of carrying large numbers of warheads which could be launched from below the sea's surface and accurately find their way to distant targets. Thus, both the Soviets and the Americans had various delivery systems available, including airplanes and missiles which could be launched from land bases, surface ships, and submarines. The submarines are particularly effective because it is extremely difficult to detect them when they are submerged.

In addition to strategic nuclear weapons systems, tactical systems were designed for battlefield use. These were originally conceived by the United States and NATO forces to compensate for the large numbers of troops available to the Eastern bloc countries in Europe. But eventually such systems became available to both sides.

We now find ourselves locked in an arms race with the Soviets which has gone on for nearly 40 years and has reached the point where there are more than 50,000 nuclear weapons—representing a total yield of about 13,000 megatons—deployed by the United States and the Soviet Union. Remembering that the bomb that obliterated Hiroshima was but 0.01 megaton, we begin to appreciate the enormity of the overkill potential in the hands of the superpowers.

Were one of these nations to launch a preemptive strike against the other, we might expect that the combination of all warheads used might amount to perhaps 5,000 to 10,000 megatons. A 1983 study by the World Health Organization (WHO) concluded that about a billion persons would be killed outright, while an additional billion would suffer injuries from blast, fire, and radiation and could die because most medical personnel would be killed or incapacitated.

These estimates are based upon the conventional theoretical knowledge of the detonation effects of large numbers of megaton-sized nuclear explosives. New calculations suggest, however, that several other effects could increase these numbers substantially. The earlier calculations did not take into account the results of the considerable disruption of the infrastructure, including communications, or the depletion of the ozone layer. But far more important is the recent estimate that nuclear explosions on the scale visualized would have a profound effect upon the opacity of the atmosphere.

Surface explosions would push large quantities of dust into the atmosphere, and to this would be added smoke from forest fires and urban conflagrations. The dust and smoke would greatly decrease the amount of sunlight reaching the earth's surface, particularly in the Northern Hemisphere, where presumably most of the explosions would take place. This would produce dramatic reductions in land-surface temperatures, including the possibility of rapid freezing of those areas under transient patches of smoke. The noncombatant part of the world would face enormous, if not insurmountable, difficulties in maintaining a viable agriculture.

Were the devastation confined to the Northern Hemisphere, the death toll might well approach four billion persons—or about 90 percent of the human population—but it is by no means clear that it would be so confined. Quite possibly, considerable quantities of dust would be transported across the equator, which we have convention-ally considered relatively impenetrable, because of the unusual atmo-spheric circulation patterns in the region.

These findings place the entire issue of nuclear armaments in an entirely new perspective. We should no longer view the end result of U.S.-Soviet madness as simply their own mutual destruction or, at worst, that of the technologically advanced societies. Not only would technological civilization be obliterated; the lives of most people in the developing world would be at stake as well. There would be little hope of rebuilding a new civilization from the ashes of the old, particularly if the 10 percent of humanity living in the Southern Hemisphere were also seriously affected.

The likely effects of a major nuclear war, as predicted in scientific studies, suggest that no group of humans would be so foolhardy as to initiate the first attack, and that mutually assured destruction will remain an effective deterrent for at least another several decades.

Yet the historical record should not make us feel overly confident. Let us look back to the 50 million dead of World War II, to the German extermination camps, to Dresden and Hamburg, to Hiroshima and Nagasaki. Moving forward in time, let us look at the rise of terrorism, at the frequent use of torture, at the widespread application of technological knowledge to sabotage.

Let us look at Lebanon, where a highly cultured society has been reduced to rubble and savagery by ordinary weapons coupled with fanaticism, hatred, and greed. In 1982 Lance Morrow of *Time* magazine eloquently expressed his view of that tragedy:

> If the fate of Lebanon moves us, it is because the country has become a late 20th century fable of the end of civilization. The story of Lebanon carries at least a slight reverberation of every aboriginal myth of the fall from paradise. One feels an eerie premonition and vulnerability before the spectacle. What happened to Lebanon seems both a reversion and a forecast. It is a glimpse of the skull beneath the skin of civilization.

In short, human beings have shown that they are willing to see everything destroyed if they cannot have their own way.

The elimination of nuclear confrontation should have, without question, the highest priority on any agenda aimed at saving our civilization. At the same time we must recognize that the arms race has become such an integral part of our lives—politically, economically, and socially—that it will be extremely difficult to stop, and even more difficult to reverse. But this must be done with all possible dispatch through truly serious negotiations and carefully selected unilateral actions.

Even with all goodwill it will take a long time—perhaps two or three decades—to reach the level of nuclear disarmament necessary to provide nations with a reasonable degree of security. (After all, the buildup of nuclear arms has now gone on for some 40 years.) In the meantime, we must hope that during a serious period of nuclear build-down the threat of massive retaliation will continue to deter the massive use of nuclear weapons.

A nuclear build-down, however, can only be a start, paving the way for bringing some kind of order out of the international anarchy from which the whole world suffers. Clearly, nuclear force would be replaced by substantial conventional military might, and we know from World War II how non-nuclear armed forces can be used to kill and destroy on a vast scale. Therefore we must learn how to contain and eventually eliminate conventional as well as nuclear wars. To this end we must develop a long-term, two-prong approach: first, the creation of truly effective peace-keeping machinery; and second, the gradual elimination of as many basic causes of war as possible—from access to resources and markets, to territorial ambition, to ideological fanaticism.

Most important, we must recognize that our traditional approach to the problem of nuclear build-down has been a failure and seems destined to be a failure for the foreseeable future. Efforts to achieve security simply by attempting to balance numbers of missiles have been tried for decades, without success. We must take a broader view.

The following steps would help pave the way for the creation of effective peace-keeping machinery:

Establishment of a freeze on the production of nuclear materials.

A ban on all future nuclear testing.

An accord on absolute yet minimum nuclear forces in the Soviet Union and the United States which would assure both countries that total destruction would follow an attack by either. These minimal nuclear forces could well take the form of small fleets of nuclear-armed submarines.

Agreement on a time-scale and schedule for reducing nuclear forces to agreed-upon levels.

With such a set of agreements, it might then be possible to arrive at understandings for peace-keeping machinery that would permit the complete elimination of nuclear forces.

What kind of peace-keeping machinery can be made to work? For this purpose the United Nations as presently constituted is ineffective, as are regional structures such as the Organization of American States. Clearly, we have reached the point in the political evolution of our world where international disputes, together with warlike actions such as international terrorism, must be handled through a global legal code backed up by the legal, military, and economic machinery needed to take firm enforcement measures when required.

Although I am not so naive as to suppose that a full-fledged world government can be created in the near future, it should nevertheless be possible for the nations of the world to agree upon a legal code covering the more critical elements of war and peace and to establish the necessary enforcement machinery. We have long passed the point where we can rely upon voluntary controls over critical international questions involving the life and death of nations and people.

Beyond these overriding problems of war and peace, the industrial nations must rapidly come to grips with a multiplicity of issues involving rapid technological and social change. Demographic changes are affecting the size of the labor force, the population of elderly people, and questions of health care. Technological change affects the nature of work, the requirements for workers and, beyond this, the problem of unemployment. In the absence of innovative approaches to the handling of labor and labor benefits, unemployment is likely to become an increasingly difficult matter. Human labor is becoming less and less important in the production of most essential goods and many essential services.

We must, finally, come to grips realistically with the development of the Third World and with the long-term economic and political relationships between the industrial societies and Third World countries. Unless a reasonable degree of economic equity among nations is achieved through a combination of trade and economic assistance, we will see increasing ferment within the poorer countries. Three-fourths of the world's population lives in these countries and that proportion is increasing. Even more significant is the fact that the developing countries collectively spend more of their income on military activities than they spend on public health and education combined. Some are working to acquire nuclear armaments.

Clearly, the Third World must be integral to whatever peace-keeping machinery the world eventually develops. For one of the greatest dangers facing the world is the prospect that a local conflict could escalate into nuclear war.

As we begin to fashion the steps leading toward nuclear peace, it is vital that we keep in mind the history of the past 40 years and possess an unclouded view of present realities and future possibilities. *Assessing the Nuclear Age* is an effort to link the past and the future by providing thoughtful perspectives on a wide range of interrelated subjects.

Harrison Brown

Retrospectives

1

How Well They Meant

Martin J. Sherwin

"History is a very important thing," I.I. Rabi told his audience of physicists at Los Alamos on the fortieth anniversary, in 1983, of that facility's founding, "because by perusal of history you see the greatness and the folly of humanity." And so it was with the Manhattan Project to which many of the finest minds in American physics dedicated themselves. Their first objective was "to save Western civilization" from fascism, by building an atomic bomb ahead of the Germans; their second objective was "to save Western civilization" from the atomic bomb itself, by devising formulas to prevent a nuclear arms race.[1]

As Rabi and others are painfully aware, the ironies associated with those rescue efforts are numerous. But one that has gone almost unnoticed is particularly poignant: all of the ideas currently associated with nuclear weapons derive from those originally conceived by scientists during the war for the purpose of preventing a nuclear arms race afterward. Appropriately, the title of Rabi's Los Alamos speech was: "How Well We Meant."

The Strategic Arms Limitation Talks (SALT) were presaged by Niels Bohr and James Conant in 1944, and then officially proposed in 1946, in the State Department's Acheson-Lilienthal Report, the earliest nuclear arms control proposal. Nuclear intimidation, the psychological premise of nuclear containment, was anticipated in 1945 at the atomic bomb targeting committee meetings in Los Alamos. Limited nuclear

3

war—an idea popularized in 1958 by Henry Kissinger's *Nuclear Weapons and American Foreign Policy* and then adopted in 1980 as Presidential Directive-59 by the Carter Administration—was discussed during the war as an integral part of plans for international control. Deterrence and even the "warning shot" strategy, if not the terms themselves, were implicit in the decisions that led to the destruction of Hiroshima and Nagasaki.

The concept of the atomic bomb as the final arbiter of war was recognized in 1939 with the publication of the discovery of nuclear fission. Every scientist familiar with the physics of this phenomenon understood that in theory a weapon of extraordinary power might be fashioned if the technical requirements could be mastered. To this end scientists enlisted the president's support; they formed committees to study the possibility of an atomic bomb; they lobbied the military; and they conducted experiments. But it was not until the summer of 1941, two-and-a-half years after fission was discovered in Germany, that scientists in England thought of a way to harness the theory to practical technology. In the fall of 1941 an Anglo-American scientific partnership was initiated. Its goal was to beat the Germans in a race for the atomic bomb.

The delay literally terrified the scientists associated with the bomb project. Aware of the weapon's potential and their own desultory start, they reasoned that the Anglo-American effort lagged behind Germany's, perhaps by as much as two-and-a-half years. In their minds the atomic bomb was the *ultimate weapon*; if the Germans developed it first, the Allied cause was lost. Arthur Compton, director of the atomic energy project at the University of Chicago, was so distressed at the slow rate of progress that, in June 1942, he urged a program for researching and developing "countermeasures" against a German atomic bomb. In July J. Robert Oppenheimer wrote despairingly that the war could be lost before answers to the immediate problems under consideration could be found. "What Is Wrong with Us?" was the heading Leo Szilard chose for a memorandum in September criticizing the rate of progress.[2]

Despite the concern expressed at a high-level meeting at the White House in October 1941, the actual development of the bomb had not yet started at the beginning of 1943, and only limited progress had been made in constructing the many necessary facilities. General Leslie Groves was not appointed to head the project until September 17, 1942. The site for the uranium separation plant at Oak Ridge, Tennessee, was acquired only two days later. The land on which the bomb laboratory would be constructed outside Los Alamos, New Mexico, was not even purchased by the government until November, and it was December 1942 before Oppenheimer was appointed director. Enrico Fermi's critical experiment, the first controlled nuclear chain reaction, was completed that same month at the University of Chicago.

Thus, four years after fission was discovered, scientists were not confident that the United States was closing the lead the Germans were assumed to have. A feeling of desperate urgency grew with each passing month, and with it the conviction that, once developed, the bomb would be a decisive factor in the war—a conviction that permeated the entire chain of command. Vannevar Bush and James Conant, the science administrators who oversaw the Manhattan Project, kept President Roosevelt informed of both their colleagues' progress and their fears.

The implications of Bush's ability to communicate directly with the president can hardly be exaggerated. Roosevelt came to accept the scientists' view that the Allies were involved in a two-front war. Not only were there hard enemies on the fields of battle, but in German laboratories there were enemies who posed an even greater danger: scientists who might be first to develop a weapon that could alter the course of the war. This view of the bomb assured that its importance would not be underestimated by policymakers. Indeed, it assured that its value would be exaggerated and that those responsible for the military security of the United States after the war would view it, as Secretary of War Henry L. Stimson did at the Potsdam Conference, as a "badly needed equalizer," as a panacea for any real or imagined deficiencies of U.S. power.[3]

The atomic scientists' view that the bomb could win the war for Germany was easily converted by policy-makers to the idea that it could expedite the winning of the war for the United States. By the spring of 1944 the bomb's successful development appeared likely, but the timing of its completion remained uncertain. January 1945 was a possibility, but a later date—perhaps the summer of that year—appeared more probable.

Under the circumstances there is an irony in the decision to target Japan. Whatever other reasons may have contributed to that still incompletely understood decision, one element was the fear that an atomic attack on Germany might under certain conditions increase the possibility of a retaliatory attack in kind. This embryonic form of nuclear deterrence was expressed early. The May 5, 1943 minutes of a military policy committee meeting note that in a discussion of use of the first bomb "the general view appeared to be that its best point of use would be on a Japanese fleet concentration in the Harbor of Truk [in the Caroline Islands]. General Styer suggested Tokio [*sic*], but it was pointed out that the bomb should be used where, if it failed to go off, it would land in water of sufficient depth to prevent easy salvage." The minutes went on to say: "The Japanese were selected as they would not be so apt to secure knowledge from it as would the Germans."[4]

Two years later, in the spring of 1945, with the Germans on the verge of defeat, confidence replaced caution, and urban centers replaced military targets. While this shift in atomic bomb targets parallels an earlier shift in conventional bombing strategy, it also marks a new appreciation of the atomic bomb as a weapon of psychological intimidation. It was not expected that the destruction and havoc that two atomic bombs might wreak would suddenly break the back of Japan's war machine, but it was hoped that such attacks would shock the Japanese government into discontinuing its hopeless struggle. The selection of targets reflected this intention.

Guided by instructions from Groves, a target committee, composed of Manhattan Project scientists and ordnance specialists, studied the available options and developed criteria for their selection. The report of the committee's second and third meetings, held in Oppenheimer's office at Los Alamos in May 1945, suggests a major concern with the weapon's psychological impact. The minutes record the committee's view that any small, strictly military target should be located in a much larger area subject to blast damage "to avoid undue risks of the weapon being lost due to bad placing of the bomb." The members of the committee agreed, too, that the psychological impression the bomb made was not just a matter of wartime interest. "Two aspects of this," the report states, "are 1) obtaining the greatest psychological effect against Japan and 2) making the initial use sufficiently spectacular *for the importance of the weapon to be internationally recognized* [emphasis added] when publicity on it is released."[5]

The target committee's concern that the full implications of the bomb be recognized internationally reflected a pervasive anxiety among those scientists who had begun to worry about the bomb's role in the postwar world. As an instrument of peace based on the international control of atomic energy, or as an instrument of diplomacy to be used in postwar negotiations, the influence of the weapon depended upon a general recognition that pre-atomic-age calculations had to give way to new realities. If the Japanese did not accept this view, the war might continue; if the Soviets ignored it, the peace would be lost. In this sense the bomb became its own message, and within the context of the war the scientists who participated in the decision to bomb Japan were consumed by a single objective—to transmit in the most dramatic fashion possible the message that the new age required new forms of international organization.

Leo Szilard, who had composed Einstein's famous letter to Roosevelt warning of the military implications of the discovery of fission, was the first to suggest a resolution to the problem of the bomb in the postwar world. Writing to Bush in January 1944, he referred to the potential development of a bomb of even greater power (the hydrogen bomb), and commented that "this weapon will be so powerful that there can be no peace if it is simultaneously in the possession of any two powers unless these two powers are bound by an indissoluble political union." Some type of international control scheme had to be created, he argued, "if necessary by force," to prevent a war that would recreate the dark ages, or worse.[6]

This was not the last time a scientist would suggest the use of military force to achieve security against nuclear uncertainty. The overwhelming sense of hopelessness before the developing of an unprecedented power created an urge to seek assurance against that power being turned upon its inventors. Bound to their task by fear of German progress, and terrified by the consequences of their own success, men of sensibility, culture, and peace were driven to recommend policies that they would find abhorrent in other circumstances.

Like Kurt Vonnegut's Trafalmadorians in Slaughterhouse Five, the scientists could see into the future: a postwar nuclear arms race leading to circumstances that literally could bring about the end of the world. But no one with power to prevent such a catastrophe seemed to recognize that this problem existed. As they worked desperately to build the bomb, scientists who were alert to these issues grasped at schemes to keep its potential destructive force under control.

The first serious attempt to meet this challenge was offered by Niels Bohr, who escaped to England from Nazi-occupied Denmark in September 1943. "Officially and secretly he came to help the technical enterprise," Oppenheimer noted, but "most secretly of all . . . he came to advance his case and his cause." In the broadest sense, Bohr's cause was to ensure that atomic energy "is used to the benefit of all humanity and does not become a menace to civilization." More specifically, he warned that "quite apart from the question of how soon the weapon will be ready for use and what role it may play in the present war," some agreement had to be reached with the Soviet Union about the future control of atomic energy before the bomb was developed.[7]

Bohr's ideas on the international control of atomic energy remain significant today beyond any actual effect they might have had on Anglo-American policy. Arguing for a unilateral initiative, he insisted that the time to prepare for security in the nuclear age was before the bomb's development overwhelmed the possibility of international cooperation. If the bomb was born in secret in the United States, it would be conceived in secret by the Soviets. The only hope for avoiding a nuclear arms race after the war was to create an international-control arrangement before the war ended and before the bomb was tested. A nuclear arsenal was simply too big, in every sense, to be placed on any negotiating table; a weapon in the process of becoming was not.

As a scientist, Bohr apprehended the significance of the new weapon even before it was developed, and he had no doubt that Soviet scientists would also understand its profound implications for the postwar world. He was also certain that they would convey these implications to Stalin, just as scientists in the United States and Great Britain had explained them to Roosevelt and Churchill. Thus the diplomatic problem, as Bohr analyzed it, was not the need to convince Stalin that the atomic bomb was an unprecedented weapon that threatened the life of the world, but the need to assure the Soviet leader that he had nothing to fear from the circumstances of its development.

Roosevelt and Churchill shared neither Bohr's assumptions nor his vision, and perhaps it is too much to expect that they could. Harnessed to the yoke of war, without a scientist's intuitive understanding of the long-range implications of a weapon that did not yet exist, they accepted the bomb as it had been presented to them—as an ultimate weapon. "The suggestion that the world should be informed regarding [the atomic bomb], with a view to an international agreement regarding its control and use, is not accepted," they agreed in September 1944. "The matter should continue to be regarded as of the utmost secrecy."[8]

It was not only Bohr who tried to shed light on the dark shadow the bomb cast across the future. Scientists of a more politically conventional turn of mind, once alerted to the problem, turned to unconventional ideas. James Conant favored "the calculated risk," and to achieve a fair chance of success he was inclined "to talk in terms of concrete and limited objectives." Yet as early as May 1944, as James Hershberg has shown, Conant confronted the problem of the atomic bomb in the postwar world and came to the conclusion that limited objectives were dangerously inadequate. In the long run, he wrote to Bush, "the only hope for humanity is an international commission on atomic energy with free access to all information and right of inspection."⁹

In a memorandum entitled "Some Thoughts on International Control of Atomic Energy," Conant peered into the future and discerned only two alternatives: an atomic arms race and "in the next war destruction of civilization," or "a scheme to remove atomic energy from the field of conflict."¹⁰ To achieve the second alternative Conant proposed 14 points. An association of nations specifically committed to control atomic energy had to be formed, and an international commission on atomic energy, which would include Britain, the United States, the Soviet Union, and perhaps six other nations, had to control all atomic energy work.

The commission would license, finance, and control all research and development work, and all results would be published. Agents of the commission would police the system by frequent inspections of all laboratories, factories, or other relevant facilities, and even if two countries were at war, the inspectors would have the right of entry. The commission was to have its own international air force and an army of 10,000 men to prevent the seizure of supplies. If any nation refused to permit inspections, or interfered with the commission in any other important way, its actions would be "considered an act of war."

But, Conant asked, "what happens if a nation refuses entry of agents to factories etc. or disobeys [the] edicts of [the] commission?" His answer was "war," declared by the other members of the international organization who might, if the commission approved, *use atomic bombs* to bring the renegade nation to heel. This idea of a limited nuclear war to prevent a general conflagration was even extended to the "use of bombs by arsenal guards," if the United States, Canada, or Britain tried to seize the commission's atomic arsenal, which Conant had located in Canada.

By recommending the use of a limited number of atomic bombs to prevent a general nuclear war, Conant succumbed to the temptation that lies across the path of all nuclear arms control efforts. If the desire to rid the world of the potential danger of nuclear war stems from a fear of their destructive potential, then why not use that threat in the service of international security?

Conant believed not only that the bomb was an ideal weapon to shock Japan's leaders into surrender, but that its use was necessary to impress upon the world in general, and on the Soviet government in particular, his vision of the destruction that it could inflict. Assuming "that in another war atomic bombs will be used," he recommended to Stimson that in the present war "the bomb *must be used*" for that was "the only way to awaken the world to the necessity of abolishing war altogether. No technical demonstration . . . could take the place of the actual use with its horrible results." Nor was Conant the only scientist to hold this view. "If the bomb were not used in the present war," Arthur Compton wrote to Stimson in June 1945, "the world would have no adequate warning as to what was to be expected if war should break out again."[11]

A group of scientists at the University of Chicago reasoned quite differently, their analysis flowing from alternative assumptions formulated during the closing months of the war. Far removed from political pressures, and from considerations associated with the policy-making process, they broadcast a prescient warning to a deaf audience: the indiscriminate military use of the atomic bomb would undermine the possibility of achieving the international control of atomic energy.[12]

Early in June 1945, under the chairmanship of the distinguished emigre physicist James Franck, they assembled as the Committee on the Social and Political Implications of the Atomic Bomb. Their central concern was "the conditions under which international control is most probable," and their basic assumption was that the "manner in which this new weapon is introduced to the world will determine in large part the future course of events." They too saw the path from atomic bombs to superbombs with limitless destructive power. They too described the uncertain security that an attempt at monopoly would bring. And they too outlined methods of international control that might be feasible.

Their primary purpose, however, was less to enumerate the dangers of the atomic age than to recommend policies that might circumvent those dangers. The central argument of the report was that a surprise atomic attack against Japan was inadvisable—whether one was optimistic or pessimistic about the possibility of international control. "If we consider international agreement on total prevention of nuclear warfare as the paramount objective, and believe that it can be achieved," they argued, "this kind of introduction [surprise attack] of atomic weapons to the world may easily destroy all our chances of success. Russia, and even allied countries which bear less mistrust of our ways and intentions, as well as neutral countries may be deeply shocked."

They argued against dropping the bomb on a populated area to show its capacity for terror and annihilation. "It may be very difficult to persuade the world that a nation which was capable of secretly preparing and suddenly releasing a weapon as indiscriminate as the [German] rocket bomb and a million times more destructive, is to be trusted in its proclaimed desire to have such weapons abolished by international agreement."

The report also made the converse case for not using the atomic bomb, even "if one takes the pessimistic point of view and discounts the possibility of an effective international control over nuclear weapons at the present time . . . early use of nuclear bombs against Japan becomes even more doubtful—quite independently of any humanitarian considerations. If an international agreement is not concluded immediately after the first use," they reasoned, exhibiting Bohr's sense of timing that was elsewhere lacking, "this will mean a flying start toward an unlimited armaments race. If this race is inevitable, we have every reason to delay its beginning as long as possible in order to increase our head start still further."

The members of the Franck Committee shared a basic assumption with those who had a sanguine view of the results that would flow from using the bomb: an atomic attack against Japan would "shock" the Soviets as well as the Japanese. But their reasoning about the effect of such a shock was very different. Conant, Compton, Truman, Stimson, and Secretary of State James Byrnes shared the view that an undeveloped weapon was not a very useful bargaining counter, a concept that is all too familiar today. They believed that an actual combat demonstration would make a far greater impression on those who needed to be convinced to end the war, and on those who needed to be persuaded that postwar international control of the atomic bomb was in their long-range interest. It was this quest to make an *impression*—the psychological impact of a single bomb dropped from a lone aircraft causing damage equal to that caused by thousands of bombs dropped from hundreds of aircraft—that was the basis for the decisions that led to Hiroshima.

The Franck Committee, however, drew the diametrically opposite conclusion: the more awesome the bomb's demonstrated power, the more likely an arms race. The most important demonstration needed was some means of conveying to Moscow a U.S. commitment not to use the bomb, a commitment that might instill in the Soviets a measure of confidence that the Anglo-American monopoly would not be turned on them, a commitment that might persuade them that the objective of U.S. policy was the neutralization of the atomic bomb. Szilard made this point to Oppenheimer when they saw each other in Washington in June. "Don't you think," Oppenheimer rejoined, "if we tell the Russians what we intend to do and then use the bomb in Japan, the Russians will understand it?" "They'll understand it only too well," was Szilard's prescient reply.[13]

In a sense more complex than originally stated, P.M.S. Blackett's charge "that the dropping of the atomic bombs was not so much the last military act of the second World War, as the first major operation of the cold *diplomatic* war with Russia," contains an essential truth.[14] The scientists and policy-makers who promoted the international control of atomic energy and supported the use of the bomb against Japan never expected that good relations with the Soviet Union would be possible if diplomatic efforts to achieve a nuclear arms control pact were not successful. They never thought that achieving such an agreement would be easy, nor that tough negotiations and a measure of intimidation should be avoided. Hiroshima and Nagasaki were part of that diplomatic strategy. So were the postwar tests at Bikini, held in the summer of 1946, at the same time that Bernard Baruch was presenting the U.S. plan for the international control of atomic energy to the United Nations.

Following a line of reasoning that President Truman stated in January—that "unless Russia is faced with an iron fist and strong language another war is in the making"[15]—Conant believed that atomic diplomacy would serve a useful purpose in bringing about security from atomic war. Speaking at an off-the-record dinner sponsored by the Council on Foreign Relations in New York on April 12, 1946, Truman responded to a question about the relationship between the Bikini tests and the upcoming United Nations Organization's international control conference: "The Russians are more rather than less likely to come to an effective agreement for the control of atomic energy if we keep our strength and continue to produce bombs."[16]

Atomic testing was not the only arrow in Conant's atomic diplomacy quiver; history also had a role. The atomic bombings of Japan were supported by the majority of Americans, but in the aftermath of the war Conant discerned a "spreading accusation that it was entirely unnecessary to use the atomic bomb at all," particularly among those whom he described to Stimson as "verbal minded citizens not so generally influential as they were influential among the coming generations of whom they might be teachers or educators."[17] To combat that view he urged Stimson to write an article on "the decision to drop the bomb," which subsequently appeared under that title in the February 1947 issue of *Harper's* magazine.

If "the propaganda against the use of the atomic bomb had been allowed to grow unchecked," Conant wrote to Stimson after reading a prepublication version of the article, "the strength of our military position by virtue of having the bomb would have been correspondingly weakened," and the chances for international control undermined.[18] "Humanitarian considerations" that led citizens to oppose the strengthening of the U.S. atomic arsenal, in Conant's opinion, were likely to subvert the common effort to achieve an international atomic energy agreement. "I am firmly convinced," he told Stimson, "that the Russians will eventually agree to the American proposals for the establishment of an atomic energy authority of world-wide scope, *provided* they are convinced that we would have the bomb in quantity and would use it without hesitation in another war."[19]

That Conant and those who supported this view were wrong is less a criticism of their logic than of their fundamental assumptions about the nature of the forces underlying the atomic arms race. If the Americans viewed the bomb as an effective instrument of diplomacy and as a weapon to be used "without hesitation in another war," the Soviets could hardly be expected to take a loftier view. Scientific greatness gave way to political folly with the view that the atomic bomb could be used to fashion a solution to its own existence. It is a folly that we continue to live with today. And, to paraphrase Rabi, how well we mean.

1. I.I. Rabi, "How Well We Meant," transcript of Rabi's 1983 talk, Los Alamos National Laboratory Archives (no date).

2. Arthur Compton to Henry Wallace, June 23, 1942, F.D. Roosevelt, President's Secretary's File, Vannevar Bush folder, Roosevelt Library, Hyde Park, N.Y.; Robert Oppenheimer to John Manley, July 14, 1942, Oppenheimer Papers, Box 49, Library of Congress; Martin J. Sherwin, *A World Destroyed* (New York: Vintage Books, 1977), p. 47; Richard G. Hewlett and Oscar B. Anderson, Jr., *The New World, 1939/1946: A History of the United States Atomic Energy Commission, I* (University Park, Pa.: Pennsylvania State University Press, 1962), p. 179.

3. Henry L. Stimson and McGeorge Bundy, *On Active Service in Peace and War* (New York: Harpers, 1947), p. 617.

4. "Policy Meeting, 5/5/43," p. 2, Record Group 77, Manhattan Engineering District Records, Top Secret, folder 23A, National Archives.

5. Derry and Ramsey to Groves, May 12, 1945, MED–TS, Box 3, Target Committee Meetings, folder 5D.2.

6. Szilard to Bush, Jan. 14, 1944, in Gertrude Weiss Szilard and Spencer R. Weart, eds., *Leo Szilard: His Version of the Facts* (Cambridge, Mass.: MIT Press, 1978), p. 163.

7. J. Robert Oppenheimer, "Niels Bohr and Atomic Weapons," *The New York Review of Books,* 3 (Dec. 17, 1966), p. 7. Bohr memorandum, May 8, 1945, Oppenheimer Papers, box 34, Library of Congress; Bohr to Roosevelt, July 3, 1944, Oppenheimer Papers, box 34, Library of Congress.

8. Hyde Park Aide-Memoire, Sept. 18, 1944, President's Map Room papers, Naval Aide's File, box 172-General folder, Franklin Delano Roosevelt Library, reprinted in Sherwin, *A World Destroyed,* p. 284.

9. "The Tough-Minded Idealist," Sept. 23, 1946, *Harvard Alumni Bulletin,* 49, no. 2 (Oct. 12, 1946), quoted in James G. Hershberg, *Ends Versus Means: James B. Conant and American Atomic Policy, 1939–47* (unpublished senior thesis, Harvard College, 1982),

pp. 208–9. See also marginal comment by Conant on a memorandum, Bush to Conant, April 17, 1944, entitled "Shurcliff's memo on Post-War Policies," Atomic Energy Commission Historical Document no. 180, Department of Energy Archives, Energy Research Collection.

10. James Conant, memo dated May 4, 1944, Bush-Conant files, box 9, folder 97, Office of Scientific Research and Development, S-1 Section files, National Archives; reprinted in Hershberg, *Ends Versus Means*, pp. 189–90.

11. James Conant to Grenville Clark, Nov. 8, 1945, Bush Papers, box 27, Conant folder, Library of Congress; Henry Stimson to Raymond Swing, quoting Conant, Feb. 4, 1947, Stimson Papers, Swing folder, Sterling Memorial Library, Yale University; Arthur Holly Compton, *Atomic Quest: A Personal Narrative* (New York: Oxford University Press, 1956), pp. 239–40.

12. The Franck Report is reproduced in Alice Kimball Smith, *A Peril and A Hope: The Atomic Scientists' Movement, 1945–1947* (Chicago: University of Chicago Press, 1965), Appendix B, pp. 560–72.

13. Leo Szilard, "Reminiscences," edited by Gertrude Weiss Szilard and Kathleen R. Winsor, in Donald Fleming and Bernard Bailyn, eds., *The Intellectual Migration: Europe and America, 1930–1960* (Cambridge, Mass.: 1969), p. 128.

14. P.M.S. Blackett, *Fear, War and the Bomb: Military and Political Consequences of Atomic Energy* (New York: Whittlesey House, 1948), p. 139.

15. Harry S. Truman, *Memoirs: Year of Decisions* (Garden City, N.Y.: Doubleday, 1955), pp. 551–52.

16. James Conant, "International Controls of Atomic Energy," April 12, 1946; *Records of Meetings*, vol. XII, July 1945–June 1947, Council on Foreign Relations Archives, New York, quoted in Hershberg, *Ends Versus Means*, p. 157.

17. Stimson to Felix Frankfurter, quoting Conant, Dec. 12, 1946, Stimson Papers, box 154, folder 14.

18. Conant to McGeorge Bundy, Nov. 30, 1946, Stimson Papers, box 154m folder 11.

19. Conant to Stimson, Jan. 22, 1947, Stimson papers, box 154, folder 18.

2

Leaving the Bomb Project

Joseph Rotblat

orking on the Manhattan Project was a traumatic experience. It is not often given to one to participate in the birth of a new era. For some the effect has endured throughout their lives; I am one of those. This essay is not an autobiography; it describes only my involvement in the genesis of the atomic bomb. All extraneous personal elements are left out, but their exclusion does not mean that they are unimportant. Our hopes and fears, our resolutions and actions, are influenced by an infinite number of small events interacting with each other all the time. Because of this, each of us may react differently to the same set of conditions. The experience of every Los Alamite is unique.

At the beginning of 1939, when the news reached me of the discovery of fission, I was working in the Radiological Laboratory in Warsaw. Its director was Ludwik Wertenstein, a pupil of Marie Curie and a pioneer in the science of radioactivity in Poland. Our source of radiation consisted of 30 milligrams of radium in solution; every few days we pumped the accumulated radon into a tube filled with beryllium powder. With this minute neutron source we managed to carry out much research, even competing with Enrico Fermi's prestigious team, then in Rome, in the discovery of radionuclides. Our main achievement was the direct evidence of the inelastic scattering

15

of neutrons; my doctoral thesis was on that subject.

In the earlier experiments on inelastic scattering we used gold as the scatterer. By the end of 1938 I had begun to experiment with uranium, so when I heard of the fission of uranium, it did not take me long to set up an experiment to see whether neutrons are emitted at fission. I soon found that they are—indeed, that more neutrons are emitted than produce fission. From this discovery it was a fairly simple intellectual exercise to envisage a divergent chain reaction with a vast release of energy. The logical sequel was that if this energy were released in a very short time it would result in an explosion of unprecedented power. Many scientists in other countries, doing this type of research, went through a similar thought process, although not necessarily evoking the same reaction.

In my case, my first reflex was to put the whole thing out of my mind, like a person trying to ignore the first symptom of a fatal disease in the hope that it will go away. But the fear gnaws all the same, and my fear was that someone would put the idea into practice. The thought that I myself would do it did not cross my mind, because it was completely alien to me. I was brought up on humanitarian principles. At that time my life was centered on doing "pure" research work, but I always believed that science should be used in the service of mankind. The notion of utilizing my knowledge to produce an awesome weapon of destruction was abhorrent to me.

In my gnawing fear, the "someone" who might put it into practice was precisely defined: German scientists. I had no doubt that the Nazis would not hesitate to use any device, however inhumane, if it gave their doctrine world domination. If so, should one look into the problem to find out whether the fear had a realistic basis? Wrestling with this question was agonizing, and I was therefore glad that another pressing matter gave me an excuse to put it aside.

This other matter was my move to England, where I was to spend a year with Professor James Chadwick in Liverpool, on a grant to work on the cyclotron which was then being completed there. This was my first trip abroad, and the upheaval kept me busy both before the journey in April 1939 and for some time afterward, because I spoke very little English, and it took me a long time to settle down.

Throughout the spring and summer the gnawing went on relentlessly. It intensified with the increasing signs that Germany was getting ready for war. And it became acute when I read an article by S. Flügge in *Naturwissenschaften* mentioning the possibility of nuclear explosives.

Gradually I worked out a rationale for doing research on the feasibility of the bomb. I convinced myself that the only way to stop the

Germans from using it against us would be if we too had the bomb and threatened to retaliate. My scenario never envisaged that we should use it, not even against the Germans. We needed the bomb for the sole purpose of making sure that it would not be used by them: the same argument that is now being used by proponents of the deterrence doctrine.

With the wisdom of hindsight, I can see the folly of the deterrent thesis, quite apart from a few other flaws in my rationalization. For one thing, it would not have worked with a psychopath like Hitler. If he had had the bomb, it is very likely that his last order from the bunker in Berlin would have been to destroy London, even if this were to bring terrible retribution to Germany. Indeed, he would have seen this as a heroic way of going down, in a *Götterdämmerung*.

My thinking at the time required that the feasibility of the atom bomb be established, one way or the other, with the utmost urgency. Yet I could not overcome my scruples. I felt the need to talk it over with someone, but my English was too halting to discuss such a sensitive issue with my colleagues in Liverpool.

In August 1939, having gone to Poland on a personal matter, I took the opportunity to visit Wertenstein and put my dilemma before him. The idea of a nuclear weapon had not occurred to him, but when I showed him my rough calculations he could not find anything scientifically wrong with them. On the moral issue, however, he was unwilling to advise me. He himself would never engage in this type of work, but he would not try to influence me. It had to be left to my own conscience.

The war broke out two days after I returned to Liverpool. Within a few weeks Poland was overrun. The stories that Hitler's military strength was all bluff, that his tanks were painted cardboard, turned out to be wishful thinking. The might of Germany stood revealed, and the whole of our civilization was in mortal peril. My scruples were finally overcome.

By November 1939 my English was good enough for me to give a course of lectures on nuclear physics to the Honors School at Liverpool University, but by then the department's senior research staff had disappeared: they had gone to work on radar and other war projects. I had, therefore, to approach Chadwick directly with an outline of my plan for research on the feasibility of the atom bomb. His response was typically Chadwickian: he just grunted, without letting on whether he had already thought of such a plan. Later I learned that other scientists in the United Kingdom did have the same idea, some of them with similar motivation.

A few days later Chadwick told me to go ahead and gave me two young assistants. One of them presented a problem: he was a Quaker and as such had refused to do war work. He was therefore sent to Liverpool University for academic duties—but was diverted to work with me on the atom bomb! I was not allowed to reveal to him the nature of our research, and I had qualms of conscience about using him in such an unethical way.

The main idea which I put to Chadwick was that for the atom bomb the chain reaction would have to be propagated by fast neutrons; otherwise it would not differ much from a chemical explosive. It was therefore important to measure the fission cross-section for fast neutrons, the energy distribution of fission neutrons, their inelastic scattering, and the proportion of those captured without producing fission. It was also relevant to find out whether stray neutrons might cause a premature start of the reaction, which meant determining the probability of spontaneous fission of uranium.

We built up a small team of young but devoted physicists and used the cyclotron to tackle some of these problems. Later we were joined by Otto Frisch who measured the fast neutron fission cross-section for uranium-235. I had the idea of using plutonium, but we had no means of making it.

As a result of these investigations, we were able to establish that the atom bomb was feasible from the scientific point of view. However, it also became clear that in order to make the bomb a vast technological effort would be required, far exceeding the manpower and industrial potential of wartime Britain. A top-level decision was reached to collaborate with the Americans. And so I found myself eventually in that "wondrous strange" place, Los Alamos.

In March 1944 I experienced a disagreeable shock. At that time I was living with the Chadwicks in their house on the Mesa, before moving later to the "Big House," the quarters for single scientists. General Leslie Groves, when visiting Los Alamos, frequently came to the Chadwicks for dinner and relaxed palaver. During one such conversation Groves said that, of course, the real purpose in making the bomb was to subdue the Soviets. (Whatever his exact words, his real meaning was clear.) Although I had no illusions about the Stalin regime—after all, it was his pact with Hitler that enabled the latter to invade Poland—I felt deeply the sense of betrayal of an ally. Remember, this was said at a time when thousands of Russians were dying every day on the Eastern Front, tying down the Germans and giving the Allies time to prepare for the landing on the continent of Europe. Until then I had thought that our work was to prevent a Nazi victory, and now I was told that the weapon we were preparing was intended for use against the people who were making extreme sacrifices for that very aim.

My concern about the purpose of our work gained substance from conversations with Niels Bohr. He used to come to my room at eight in the morning to listen to the BBC news bulletin. Like myself, he could not stand the U.S. bulletins which urged us every few seconds to purchase a certain laxative! I owned a special radio on which I could receive the BBC World Service. Sometimes Bohr stayed on and talked to me about the social and political implications of the discovery of nuclear energy and of his worry about the dire consequences of a nuclear arms race between East and West which he foresaw.

All this, and the growing evidence that the war in Europe would be over before the bomb project was completed, made my participation in it pointless. If it took the Americans such a long time, then my fear of the Germans being first was groundless.

When it became evident, toward the end of 1944, that the Germans had abandoned their bomb project, the whole purpose of my being in Los Alamos ceased to be, and I asked for permission to leave and return to Britain.

Why did other scientists not make the same decision? Obviously, one would not expect General Groves to wind up the project as soon as Germany was defeated, but there were many scientists for whom the German factor was the main motivation. Why did they not quit when this factor ceased to be?

I was not allowed to discuss this issue with anybody after I declared my intention to leave Los Alamos, but earlier conversations, as well as much later ones, elicited several reasons why the others decided to remain. The most frequent reason given was pure and simple scientific curiosity—the strong urge to find out whether the theoretical calculations and predictions would come true. These scientists felt that only after the test at Alamogordo should they enter into the debate about the use of the bomb.

Others were prepared to put the matter off even longer, persuaded by the argument that many American lives would be saved if the bomb brought a rapid end to the war with Japan. Only when peace was restored would they take a hand in efforts to ensure that the bomb would not be used again. Still others, while agreeing that the project should have been stopped when the German factor ceased to operate, were not willing to take an individual stand because they feared it would adversely affect their future career.

The groups I have just described—scientists with a social conscience—were a minority in the scientific community. The majority were not bothered by moral scruples; they were quite content to leave it to others to decide how their work would be used. Much the same situation exists now in many countries in relation to work on military projects. But it is the morality issue at a time of war that perplexes and worries me most.

Recently I came across a document released under the Freedom of Information Act. It is a letter, dated May 25, 1943, from Robert Oppenheimer to Enrico Fermi, on the military use of radioactive materials, specifically, the poisoning of food with radioactive strontium. The Smyth Report mentions such use as a possible German threat, but Oppenheimer apparently thought the idea worthy of consideration and asked Fermi whether he could produce the strontium without letting too many people into the secret. He went on: "I think we should not attempt a plan unless we can poison food sufficient to kill a half a million men." I am sure that in peacetime these same scientists would have viewed such a plan as barbaric; they would not have contemplated it even for a moment. Yet during the war it was considered quite seriously and, I presume, abandoned only because it was technically infeasible.

After I told Chadwick that I wished to leave the project, he came back to me with very disturbing news. When he conveyed my wish to the intelligence chief at Los Alamos, he was shown a thick dossier on me with highly incriminating evidence. It boiled down to my being a spy: I had arranged with a contact in Santa Fe to return to England and then to be flown to and parachuted onto the part of Poland held by the Soviets, in order to give them the secrets of the atom bomb. The trouble was that within this load of rubbish was a grain of truth. I did indeed meet and converse with a person during my trips to Santa Fe. It was for a purely altruistic purpose, nothing to do with the project, and I had Chadwick's permission for the visits. Nevertheless, it contravened a security regulation, and it made me vulnerable.

Fortunately for me, in their zeal the vigilant agents had included in their reports details of conversations with dates, which were quite easy to refute and to expose as complete fabrications. The chief of intelligence was rather embarrassed by all this and conceded that the dossier was worthless. Nevertheless, he insisted that I not talk to anybody about my reason for leaving the project. We agreed with

Chadwick that the ostensible reason would be a purely personal one: that I was worried about my wife whom I had left in Poland.

And so, on Christmas Eve 1944, I sailed for the United Kingdom, but not without another incident. Before leaving Los Alamos I packed all my documents—research notes as well as correspondence and other records—in a box made for me by my assistant. En route I stayed for a few days with the Chadwicks in Washington. Chadwick personally helped me to put the box on the train to New York. But when I arrived there a few hours later, the box was missing. Nor, despite valiant efforts, was it ever recovered.

The work on the Manhattan Project, as I said at the outset, has had an enduring effect on my life. Indeed, it radically changed my scientific career and the carrying out of my obligations to society.

Work on the atom bomb convinced me that even pure research soon finds applications of one kind or another. If so, I wanted to decide myself how my work should be applied. I chose an aspect of nuclear physics which would definitely be beneficial to humanity: the applications to medicine. Thus I completely changed the direction of my research and spent the rest of my academic career working in a medical college and hospital.

While this gave me personal satisfaction, I was increasingly concerned about the political aspects of the development of nuclear weapons, particularly the hydrogen bomb, about which I knew from Los Alamos. Therefore, I devoted myself both to arousing the scientific community to the danger and to educating the general public on these issues. I was instrumental in setting up the Atomic Scientists Association in the United Kingdom and within its framework organized the Atom Train, a traveling exhibition which explained to the public the good and evil aspects of nuclear energy. Through these activities I came to collaborate with Bertrand Russell. This association led to the foundation of the Pugwash Conferences, where I met again with colleagues from the Manhattan Project, who were also concerned about the threat to mankind that has arisen partly from their work.

After 40 years one question keeps nagging me: have we learned enough not to repeat the mistakes we made then? I am not sure even about myself. Not being an absolute pacifist, I cannot guarantee that I would not behave in the same way, should a similar situation arise. Our concepts of morality seem to get thrown overboard once military action starts. It is, therefore, most important not to allow such a situation to develop. Our prime effort must concentrate on the prevention of nuclear war, because in such a war not only morality but the whole fabric of civilization would disappear. Eventually, however, we must aim at eliminating all kinds of war.

3

Looking back on Los Alamos

Victor F. Weisskopf

T hinking back to those eventful years at Los Alamos, from
1943 to 1945, evokes two opposite feelings. On the one side,
it was a heroic period of our lives, full of the most exciting
problems and achievements. We worked within an international community of the best and most productive scientists in the
world, facing a stupendous task fraught with many unknown ramifica-
tions. All of us widened our intellectual horizons in this stimulating
company that included giants like Niels Bohr and Enrico Fermi.
Lasting bonds were created among us, friendship for our lifetimes.

On the other side, we must be deeply aware of the result of our
work—which was awesome enough at the time, when we saw the
explosion in the desert, and murderous enough when it destroyed
two Japanese cities. The bomb did end the cruel and destructive war
with Japan, but since then it has developed into the greatest danger
that humankind has ever faced, and it threatens more and more to
destroy everything on earth that we consider worth living for.

Two years ago, at a reunion of Los Alamos scientists, I.I. Rabi gave
a talk entitled "How Well We Meant." It certainly expressed our thinking of 40 years ago. Our nation and, indeed, the whole world, faced
the deadly threat of a hateful, cruel regime. Nuclear weapons exclusively in the hands of Hitler would have meant his victory; there was
no other choice but to develop them on our side as fast as possible.
After Hitler's defeat, it turned out that our fears were unfounded; but

by then the weapon was almost ready, and it did help to end the war in Japan, saving many lives, American and Japanese.

Yes, we meant so well. We also did so well and accomplished our mission successfully in spite of the real and imagined obstacles that lay in the way. It was a truly international effort; we worked together with our colleagues from Britain, France, Italy, Denmark, and other countries involved in the fight against German and Japanese aggression.

Much of our success was due to the inspiring influence of Robert Oppenheimer. To quote Rabi again: "He constructed the laboratory from the ground up and made it into the most effective and deadly instrument for the application of science to destruction. At the same time . . . he created an atmosphere of excitement, enthusiasm and high intellectual and moral purpose." Oppenheimer was the ideal leader, involved in every aspect of the work. He appeared out of nowhere when an important discussion took place; he was there, even at three in the morning, when an important experiment reached its critical stage.

Yes, we meant so well. We served our country, and we thought that these powerful new weapons would make wars between great powers unthinkable. Some of us thought that the very existence of these dangerous sources of destructive power would lead to an international administration of military and peaceful applications, ending the age-old tradition of organized mutual mass murder. It was a great and innovative idea, but neither side was yet ready for it.

We were naive, perhaps; we should have known better. True enough. Because the bomb exists we have had no war between great powers for 40 years—an unusually long period. But the great powers have found only one way to sustain this state of affairs—to deploy more and "better" bombs, and more efficient means for their delivery. A few useful but half-hearted steps have been made to stabilize this precarious situation, such as the atmospheric test ban and the ABM Treaty. But even these small steps may soon be modified and weakened, instead of being strengthened and enlarged.

A tragic fate gave those weapons to humanity at a time when two great powers were pitted against each other, by the forces of history, by conflicting ideologies, and by mutual fear. These fears led to ever-escalating arguments—"They did this, therefore we must do that, which they also will do, therefore"—which have brought us today into the craziest arms race in history, where each side has more than 50 times what is needed to destroy all of us, knowing full well—and this is the difference from all previous armament races—that any actual use of those weapons means the annihilation of both sides.

Future generations, if there are any, will regard this as a virulent case of collective mental disease. As long as each of the superpowers is poised in mortal fear that the other will use every opportunity to obstruct and destroy it, there will be no stopping this madness.

In the last two years, more and more people here and abroad have become aware of this tremendous danger. Even the U.S. government has expressed doubts about this way of "coexistence." It has tried to placate the fears of the public by proposing some futuristic space technology intended to protect us from annihilation; but it could at best be achieved, if at all, only after several decades of continuing madness and increasing danger. In the meantime the project will escalate the arms race and extend it into space.

All this is the outcome of our work, or our brainchild, of our achievements: "How well we meant." Can we celebrate our successes and remain silent about the consequences?

In today's world, loaded with nuclear explosives, any use of nuclear bombs is a crime against humanity. Nuclear explosives are not weapons of war. The only purpose they can possibly have is to deter their use by the other side, and for that purpose far fewer are good enough. It is senseless to try to avoid a nuclear war by preparing to wage such a war and to prevail. The old slogan, *Si vis pacem para bellum* (if you want peace prepare for war), carved on a war memorial in my home town of Vienna, might have been true with old-fashioned weapons. Today our only hope is prevention by removing the causes of war.

Our achievement 40 years ago has been the unintended cause of the world's tragic predicament. Therefore, we physicists have a special duty. We must do what we can to reduce the terrible threat that hangs over humanity. And this task is much more difficult than the solution of scientific or technical problems, which requires only creative intelligence and technical ingenuity. To reduce the threat requires political and military insight, an understanding of the psychology of the adversary, a readiness to compromise and, most importantly, a great deal of wisdom. Our efforts must be totally dedicated, on ethical and moral grounds, to making sure that a nuclear war will not, cannot, and must not occur.

We have many reasons to oppose the Soviet regime with its cruel oppressions and expansionist tendencies. But the times are gone when objectionable regimes could be removed by force. World War II was the last occasion when only the United States had the bomb. War between nuclear powers is no longer acceptable. The only hope for change in a repressive regime lies in the decay of its ideology and a gradual movement toward more sensible policies. But this is possible only if we cease to threaten one another.

Confrontation and the threat posed by ever-increasing nuclear arsenals diminish our national security; they increase the fears on each side and the danger of desperate acts. Confrontation and threats must be replaced by increasing interdependence and cooperation between the adversaries in various fields, such as arms control, aid to the Third World, and common scientific projects in space, such as a world accelerator or a lunar laboratory. It can be done; we have had successful collaborations with Soviet science in Antarctica, in the study of fusion reactors, and in other fields.

There are pressing problems facing the whole earth, East and West, apart from nuclear annihilation. One such problem is the increase in carbon dioxide which may lead to meteorological instabilities, such as melting of the ice caps, resulting in vast inundations of coastal regions. Another is atmospheric pollution, which threatens destruction of the world's forests, making many regions unsuited for human habitation. Much research is necessary to understand and prevent these catastrophes, but few resources are allotted for their purpose: military research absorbs most of the needed brain and financial power.

The United States must work with the Soviets in spite of their human rights violations, for noncooperation will not reinstate these rights. Confrontation must be replaced by competition—not in military pursuits, where they can and will do the same as we do— but in economic and social actions and in human affairs. Our aim must not be the destruction of their economy and their system; that would only lead to a war of desperation from their side. We should show them and the rest of the world how one can do better in these fields.

Of course threat and confrontation also come in large measure from the Soviets. We have seen many acts of aggression and noncooperation on their part. The question arises: is there any hope that they will also choose the way of replacing confrontation by cooperation? We don't know. It would be in their interest, and they have always served their own interests.

One thing, however, is certain: they will not do so if we pursue the relentless confrontational stand of today. Matters will get worse, as we can see from today's situation. We can only stop the arms race and turn it around by finding ways of dealing with the Soviets which are to our mutual advantage and which do not threaten their existence.

If that fear subsides, there is a possibility that their policy will also change. Fear has always been an important cause of their aggressive acts.

Forty years ago, "how well we meant," but it did not turn out so well. At that time we did not foresee the consequences of our new and unique work. We did not expect that it would develop into a senseless, deadly arms race. Today we are in a position to know what has come out of our work and to know where it leads. The present policies of both superpowers are on a collision course. We must do everything to bring about a change in the attitude of the American people toward the problems of nuclear war—away from counting weapons, toward eliminating the causes of nuclear war through non-military measures.

This change is already beginning. Questions are asked that were not asked before. There is a strong grassroots movement here and abroad, although recently it has shown some signs of abating. We must attempt to keep it going, to strengthen it. In the past these movements used arguments based mainly on the terrible consequences of a nuclear war. In the future it would be better to concentrate on ways and means to end the confrontation and to arrive at a mutual understanding of how to turn the arms race around. Desperation is unproductive. We need hope and confidence that there are ways out of the deadly dilemma.

Do not condemn demonstrators when their slogans are simplistic or naive; they express people's revulsion against the nuclear arms race. We are a democracy; a change in the people's attitudes will produce a change in the government's policies, and that change may lead to a change in Soviet attitudes. I say, it may, not that it will; but we must never cease to try. We have to find new ways to work with the Soviets.

We did so before. Leo Szilard initiated the Pugwash meetings which led to the atmospheric test ban and the ABM Treaty. The U.S. and Soviet Academies of Sciences hold common discussions on the problems of the danger of nuclear war. But much more must be done along these lines. Our Soviet colleagues, some of whom are very influential, must also take a far more active part in curbing the excesses of the Soviet military-industrial complex. We must never be fatalistic about the inevitability of nuclear war. There *are* ways to avoid the holocaust, and we must never cease to search for them.

If we do not succeed, our century will be remembered by the

unfortunate survivors as the time of preparation for the great catastrophe, and science will be seen as the main culprit. Our century should be remembered as the age in which human beings acquired their deepest insights into the universe and learned to control their martial impulses. Let us hope, strive, and act so that they will.

4

Reflections of a British Participant

Rudolf Peierls

The story of the development of atomic energy started for me, a British scientist, one day in March 1940, when O.R. Frisch asked me, "Suppose one had a large quantity of separated uranium-235, what would happen?" We both knew the Bohr-Wheeler theory of fission and could make a rough guess at the fission cross-section of the light uranium isotope. I had derived a formula for determining the critical size to achieve a self-sustaining chain reaction, in terms of the cross-section and the number of neutrons emitted per fission, which was known approximately. We were surprised that the critical size came out quite small, in pounds instead of the tons one might have guessed.

Next was the question of how far a chain reaction would go before the developing heat would drive the uranium apart. My formula also gave the time scale of the chain reaction, and though we could not get more than a rough estimate, that estimate indicated that a substantial fraction of the uranium would undergo fission.

We were staggered by these findings, because an atom bomb now seemed a practical possibility. We knew that isotope separation on a large scale posed big problems, but the power of the weapon would justify a large effort. In what turned out to be a classic understatement we said to ourselves: "Even if the isotope separation plant costs as much as a battleship, it would be worth it."

Our immediate fear was that the Germans might also have seen

29

the point and might be working on an atom bomb. The thought of this weapon exclusively in Hitler's hands was a nightmare. We wrote a memorandum with our arguments and conclusions, urgently recommending that research on the weapon be started, and that, if it proved feasible, it be developed as a deterrent against a possible German weapon.

The technical part of the memorandum was accompanied by a nontechnical note describing the likely effects, including radioactivity and fallout. We pointed out that since the bomb could probably not be used without killing large numbers of civilians, "this may make it unsuitable as a weapon for use by this country." It might conceivably be used against fleet concentrations, though in a harbor it would still be likely to involve many civilians. We did not spell out the obvious fact that, even in the absence of a German atom bomb, British possession of such a weapon would drastically alter the military balance. It was too early to argue what use of this terrible new weapon would make military sense and be morally justified.

As a result, research work was started under the "MAUD" Committee (a code name), with teams including a group under James Chadwick, in Liverpool, who seemed to have come to conclusions similar to ours, and Francis Simon's group in Oxford starting to study the problem of isotope separation. The committee's report in 1941 led to a government decision to increase the scale of the work, and a new administrative structure, with the meaningless dull-sounding cover name of "Directorate of Tube Alloys," was set up to support it. Harold Urey and G.B. Pegram from Columbia University attended the first meeting of the new committee and reported back in the United States that the British government was taking the project very seriously. This is believed to have influenced the U.S. decision to give their own project high priority.

There was little doubt that the atom bomb could be made, but it was very doubtful that it could be made within a reasonable time in wartime Britain. The possibility of a joint project with the United States was raised very early, but for a long time it did not get anywhere; it is clear now that this was due to political short-sightedness on both sides. Eventually the political problems were settled in conversations between Roosevelt and Churchill and incorporated into the Quebec Agreement of 1943.

After this a number of British scientists were sent to join in the "Manhattan District" of the U.S. Army Engineers, and work in the United Kingdom was closed down, except for some research that could prove useful to the U.S. project. I worked for the first half of

1944 in New York, in contact with the Kellex Corporation, the designers of the Oak Ridge isotope separation plant. From mid-1944 until the end of the war I worked in Los Alamos.

By 1944 our fear of the Germans developing the atom bomb first had abated somewhat. I conducted my own intelligence operation, based on published information. I knew, for example, that each semester the *Physikalische Zeitschrift* printed the physics lecture lists of all German universities. These lists, which would have been difficult to fake, showed that most of the German physicists were in their normal places, lecturing on their normal subjects. There were some exceptions, and these were probably people involved with the atom bomb or other wartime projects. The picture suggested that some research was going on, but no crash program. All the same, one dared not rely on this conclusion, however plausible.

But when the war in Europe ended with the defeat of Nazi Germany, the fear of a German atom bomb was also over. I have been asked many times why I continued working for the project when the bomb was no longer needed as a deterrent, and whether I felt happy about developing a weapon that was going to be used to cause unprecedented destruction and suffering. My answer to this question may differ from that of other scientists, but I believe it is not untypical. The war in the Pacific was still raging, with many people being killed or wounded. The possession of the atom bomb would obviously strengthen the Allies' position enormously. Its use on cities was likely to kill and hurt large numbers of civilians, as Frisch and I had pointed out in the very beginning. At that time we felt that a British government would be willing to use such a weapon only in special circumstances, and I felt that the U.S. military and political leaders likewise would not resort lightly to its use.

It was of course essential that the scientists who understood the physical consequences of an atom bomb explosion and had thought about the implications should explain these ideas to the authorities. This could not be done by every scientist on the project, but we knew that people like Robert Oppenheimer, Enrico Fermi, and Arthur Compton were in touch with the men who would have to make the decisions. I had great faith in my colleagues' depth of understanding and their capacity for simple and clear explanation. The leaders, I felt, were also intelligent men of good will and would try to make wise and humane decisions. In retrospect I have to admit that these views were a little naive.

The thought that the bomb would be used on a city without warning never occurred to me. While an explosion in an empty place would not have been enough—the scene after the Trinity test in Alamogordo did not look impressive to a layman—it could have been dropped on a sparsely inhabited place, perhaps some island, to show its power. Such a demonstration could have been accompanied by the threat to use the bomb in earnest, unless Japan surrendered. It would have killed some people and wrecked some buildings, but this was war, and people were being killed all the time.

This idea, which seemed obvious to me, was apparently never considered by the high-level committees. They did discuss an announced demonstration, in the presence of international observers, but this idea was rejected. The reliability of the mechanical and electronic devices in the bomb had not yet been proved, and failure of the demonstration would have been counterproductive.

I do not want to imply that I regarded any use of an atom bomb in itself as immoral. The number of casualties in Hiroshima was less than in one fire raid on Tokyo or Dresden. It was therefore not the scale of the results that put the atom bomb in a new category, but the ease with which it could be used. Instead of the great effort of staging a massive air raid, a single plane was enough to carry the weapon, and one man's decision to press the release button over one city or another would decide the fate of many thousands of people. It was this ease which created the temptation to use it irresponsibly. One can debate the merits of the decision to drop the first atom bomb on Hiroshima, but few would dispute that the second one on Nagasaki was unnecessary and therefore irresponsible.

The raid on Hiroshima was no more and no less unethical than the raids on Tokyo or on Dresden. It is remarkable how attitudes to strategic air raids on cities changed in the course of World War II. The attitude of outrage at the raids on Guernica and Rotterdam changed to acceptance, and even approval, of large-scale raids on cities. Hiroshima would not have been attacked without the climate of opinion that made the Tokyo and Dresden raids acceptable.

Apart from the effect of the bomb on the war in progress, we were of course aware of the problems of its future consequences. In thinking about the future, however, I had no idea of the tension between East and West which would develop and be a major factor in the atomic-weapons problem. I had no illusions about the nature of the Soviet regime but expected that, as we had managed to fight as Allies in the war, we would also manage to coexist in peace.

But even without a clear idea of who would be potential adversaries, we felt the nature of war had changed. With generous supplies of nuclear weapons, war would acquire such grotesque proportions that any nation would be too frightened to start a war if it was likely to bring in nuclear weapons. That expectation has so far been borne out.

It seemed an attractive idea to create international machinery that would institutionalize the fear of nuclear war and thus prevent it. With many other scientists, I welcomed the ideas on international control of atomic energy put forward in the Acheson-Lilienthal report of March 1946. In the United Kingdom we founded the Atomic Scientists' Association (ASA), which backed the idea of international control.

The ASA was dissolved in 1959 mainly because of weaknesses in its structure, and because the activities of the Pugwash Conferences appeared more promising. Instead of international control, which probably never had a chance, the aim of these conferences was arms control and disarmament.

In spite of some important but minor achievements, there has been no success with disarmament so far, and an insane arms race continues. This arms race is one of the developments I did not foresee at the early stages. Perhaps the scientist who is used to rational arguments makes the mistake of expecting politicians to act rationally.

Everybody accepts the fact that a war cannot be fought with nuclear weapons if both sides possess them, and therefore their only purpose is to act as a deterrent against a nuclear attack by an adversary. This requires an invulnerable retaliatory capacity, sufficient to inflict unacceptable damage on a nuclear aggressor. One can argue about the number of weapons necessary for this, but there is no question that the present stockpiles of the superpowers are vastly greater than needed for this purpose. Why, then, do both sides continue to increase their arsenals and worry if the numbers or the power of their weapons are in some respect inferior to those of the other side? I have heard it said that the weapons count might affect a nation's political will, that is, that they might be more frightened by the threat of a nuclear attack if the enemy had a greater number of weapons, even if it would be suicidal to use them. I find it very hard to believe in the reality of this proposition.

From the point of view of the danger of nuclear war, British nuclear weapons do not seem very important. Since the early 1950s, when the decision was made to create a British nuclear weapon, the purpose it was supposed to serve has varied a great deal, but the policy has not changed. It has always been denied that a substantial role was played by the prestige argument—that is, that nuclear nations could expect to be listened to in international policy debates. One could not of course admit the validity of this argument and at the same time favor nonproliferation, which would dissuade others from becoming nuclear. Yet one cannot help feeling that something like this played a part in the British decision.

The British deterrent is supposed to be independent and available in the event of a conflict in which the United States turned isolationist. The scenario of the Soviet Union, or some other nuclear power, threatening a nuclear attack on the United Kingdom without involving the United States seems hardly likely enough to justify a heavy insurance premium against it. If such insurance is considered worthwhile, it is obviously important to make the deterrent force as invulnerable as possible. This would favor the maximum number of submarines — not necessarily carrying weapons of very great destructive power — rather than the planned Trident system which is very sophisticated and therefore so expensive that the country will be able to afford only a small number of vessels.

The U.S. cruise missiles now being deployed are an addition to the existing excessive overkill capacity and therefore are unnecessary and wasteful. I do not, however, believe that their presence in Britain is harmful; in particular I do not believe that the danger of a nuclear attack on this country is increased by their presence. They are a small factor within the overall insanity of the arms race.

5

Niels Bohr and the Young Scientists

Robert R. Wilson

I t was natural for the students of pre-World War II physics to venerate Niels Bohr as they were learning the new quantum physics. Doubly to venerate him would be more exact, because their teachers, many of whom had worked with Bohr, respected him not only as the leader of the quantum revolution in physics. They also loved him for his deep humanness, as expressed in his philosophical writing and in his efforts on behalf of the refugees from fascism.

This veneration was later to be an important factor in the belief of these students that their work on the nuclear bomb was virtuous — virtuous because Bohr thought it was. It would also motivate them to hold steadfast to his vision of how they should conduct themselves in a postwar atomic world.

I, personally, can only write some anecdotes from my own limited experiences with Bohr. But my reflections may be characteristic of those other once-young scientists who were similarly active during the war, and who were similarly caught up afterward in the young scientists' involvement with the social and political problems presented by nuclear energy. Who was young and who was old? The "young" were those active in scientists' organizations, including the *Bulletin* and the Federation of American Scientists (FAS). The "old," the establishment, were directly involved in governmental planning. ("In" and "out" might have been more apt designations.) Some, of course, were simultaneously young and old.

Bohr came to the University of California in 1936 to give the Hitch-cock lectures. I could attend the lectures, but, as a lowly graduate student, I was desolate that there was no opportunity to meet him. However, my big chance came at a reception for Bohr at International House, where I lived. Chien Shiung Wu (a contemporary student just over from Shanghai) and I dressed in our best and eagerly awaited the moment when we would meet the great man.

Alas, there was no possibility that two bashful students could break through the faculty crowd that surrounded him. Both of us were on the verge of tears and ready to leave when the crowd momentarily dispersed. Seizing Chien Shiung by the hand, I led her up to Bohr and with all the urbanity I could muster said, "May I present a young physics student recently from China." Soon we were chatting away about physics, perhaps a welcome relief for Bohr from the formal conversation of the reception. Transported by the experience, we even imagined that we could understand what Bohr was saying, contrary to his reputation for muttering unintelligibly in his thick Danish accent. Presently he had his beloved pipe out and was patting his pockets fruitlessly in search of pouch and matches. "Here, have some of mine," I said, euphorically passing them over. After all, this was the stuff of friendship!

However superficial that brief meeting, I now felt that I knew Bohr. I read every word of his that I could get my hands on. The human spirit expressed in his writing opened a vision for me, a physics grind, of what a scholar could be—should be.

Near the end of 1940, I joined the uranium project at Princeton University, where I was an instructor. We were to use the Princeton cyclotron to help Enrico Fermi and his colleagues at Columbia University where they were working toward the realization of a nuclear reactor.

Niels Bohr was still in Copenhagen, but we kept hearing gossip about what he was up to. In particular, there was an enigmatic telegram that mentioned "Maud." This was construed to be a code word since no one knew of such a person. As a result, the British project was sometimes referred to as MAUD. It turned out that there really was a Maud, a sometime governess of the Bohr children. My point is that Bohr was regarded as an important leader, even in absentia.

It was only after I went to Los Alamos in 1943 that I really got to know Bohr when, later on, he began his regular visits to the project. Not long after he arrived, J. Robert Oppenheimer (Oppy) brought him down to the cyclotron of which I was in charge. It seems that

"Uncle Nick," as we referred to him, had an idea similar to one I had had earlier about an autocatalytic bomb. I think both ideas provided for wedges of boron (an absorber of neutrons) to be inserted into the bomb. These wedges were to be squeezed out somehow as the bomb exploded, causing the nuclear reaction to go ever more strongly and thus to make a bigger bang.

I explained to Bohr why my idea was no good, and by implication why his idea was also no good. Bohr was not about to be patronized by the likes of me and argued warmly to the contrary. Finally he got a drawing out of his pocket which outlined an experiment he wanted me to do which might prove or disprove his idea. Sanctimoniously I informed him how full the cyclotron schedule was with really important and relevant experiments. Bohr argued. I remained adamant. We would not do his experiment. Bohr argued further: surely there was a technician who might do the experiment? No! These people were important to the war effort.

As Bohr argued on, I finally was horrified to hear myself suggesting cynically that he might want to do the experiment himself. Bohr drew himself up and said, "Young man, do you think I could not do the experiment? Do you not know that I am an experimental physicist? That my doctoral thesis was an experimental problem?" Then he went on to describe in detail his thesis about the measurement of capillary surface tension. "Those results are still definitive," he told me with pride.

Well, we didn't do his experiment, but we did become friends over the course of the discussion. I did sound like a young smart aleck, but in fact I was performing up to my ideal of what Bohr should have expected of me—no less than complete honesty and objectivity. I had yet to learn that this can be done within the veneer of civilized forms and—God help us—compassion. Bohr was compassionate with me then and, I suspect, amused.

Jane, my wife, and I were on good terms with the international group at Los Alamos so we saw much of Bohr at the Fermis', the Rudolf Peierls', the Hans Bethes', the Victor Weisskopfs', and others, in addition to seeing him at the Oppenheimers'. Mostly I remember sitting on the floor in a group of awestruck listeners as Bohr agonized over the kind of world that would result from our grim work on nuclear energy. Actually, much of the conversation was of a playful nature; it scintillated. Jane remembers playing "The Game"— charades—with Bohr—he was rotten at it—and others. "How can I compete with you? You are so clever," he confided to her.

Bohr was far from being specific during those evenings. Rather, he raised questions, created an aura of doubt about the future, of searching for answers. After all, that was the Socratic method he was famous for. I know now what I did not know then: that Bohr was approaching both Roosevelt and Churchill, and that he was under some suspicion and, possibly, surveillance.

Oppy admired and respected Bohr deeply, and spoke to me frequently about his conversations with him. According to Oppy, what Bohr felt most strongly was that nations should not have secrets from one another in the postatomic world and that there should be some kind of international control. Even before coming to help with the early organization of the Los Alamos project, I had argued with Oppy that we should have Soviet physicists at Los Alamos, just as we had the British. Oppy never accepted this and cut off any of my attempts to discuss it, but I think that it was the sort of thing Bohr could and did talk about.

In retrospect, I suppose that Oppy could not afford to compromise himself on that subject with our security people. Others who knew Bohr better than I would also occasionally relay the spirit, if not the actual content, of conversations with him. Bohr was the one person who was consistently concerned with postwar problems. The rest of us seemed just too busy, I regret to say, doing what had to be done to usher in the atomic age. As we later learned, the situation at the "Met Lab" in Chicago was quite different—perhaps because their work was finished sooner. It was there that James Franck and Leo Szilard became the principal initiators of discussions about how our work would affect society.

Perhaps it was my exposure to Bohr that led me in early 1945 to call a meeting in the cyclotron building at Los Alamos on the pretentious subject: "The Impact of the Gadget [bomb] on Civilization." Although Oppy warned me about the possibility of getting into trouble with the security people, he showed up at the meeting. It was evident by then that the Germans would be beaten, and I wanted to raise questions about what our next steps should be.

Eloquent and persuasive as ever, Oppenheimer dominated the meeting. He argued that we should redouble our effort in order to demonstrate the reality of the nuclear bomb, so that the United Nations would be set up in an intelligent manner to deal with the problems presented by this new weapon. Bohr was not at the meeting, nor do I recall his name being brought into the discussion. It is hard to express now the loyalty we felt for Oppy, our leader, and our confidence that he would do the right thing. He was essentially our only contact with the world of Washington. Maybe we had no other choice than to put our trust in him, but in any case, we did. We returned to our work with enthusiasm.

There is a vast difference between a logical possibility, even a logical certainty, and a demonstrated fact. It was not until I directly observed the test explosion on the Jornada del Muerto desert of New Mexico that I had a real, an existential, understanding of what we had been making. There was always a possibility (some thought of it as a probability) that the bomb would fizzle because of some unknown phenomenon.

My first reaction, after being overwhelmed by its very existence, was to feel all my scientific and technical responsibilities literally just slide away: we had done our job. My second reaction, almost simultaneous with the first, was one of horror at what we had done, at what such a bomb could do. As the message of the bomb's actuality sank in deeper and deeper, it became clear that I—that we all—shared the kind of responsibility that Bohr had so perceptively been preaching about. Almost all of us changed gears almost immediately, began to discuss intensely the social dimensions of the problems before us, and began to organize for an expression of our ideas without depending on our technical leaders.

It was no accident that Bohr had faced up to those crucial problems so soon. He was a true citizen of the world. No prewar international meeting of physicists was complete without Bohr. The Soviet physicist Lev Landau and the German physicist Heisenberg both had worked at his institute in Copenhagen. Indeed, Heisenberg said that he tried unsuccessfully to converse with Bohr about the German uranium project in order to get Bohr to understand that the German physicists would not make a bomb. Bohr's Copenhagen institute was the recognized world center of quantum physics, and physicists came there from all over the world. Bohr was respected and loved by all those people as well as by their students. If anyone could, Bohr would have been able to empathize with all countries after the war. Also important, I think, is the fact that he had lived through a scientific revolution, quantum mechanics, which, in different ways, was as violent as that of nuclear energy. It was that kind of transmogrification that we who were mere mortal scientists had to experience at first hand in order to go beyond the physics problems to the vital societal problems. Before that direct experience, we were just small cogs in a gigantic war effort. But Bohr the precursor had at least prepared us with the idealism and the vision of what might be done.

The story of the young physicists and their movement is mainly about the immediate organization of nearly all of the scientists at each of the large wartime laboratories into associations for study and action, and how those were eventually welded into the very effective Federation of American Scientists (FAS). It has been well told, especially in *A Peril and a Hope* by Alice Kimball Smith.

After the war I went to Harvard University as an associate professor. The faculty there was distinguished, to put it mildly, and having spent nearly all of my postdegree work in war research, I felt insecure as I resumed the important business of teaching. No doubt about it, I was the low man on the Harvard totempole. At this time Bohr was scheduled to give a colloquium. The day came. In my lowly state, I wondered if he would even recognize me as we gathered for the ritual precolloquium tea. Bohr was escorted into the crowded hall, took one look around the room, and headed straight to where I was cowering in a corner. He greeted me warmly and then, looking around suspiciously, asked in a loud voice if there was some place more private where we could be alone. "Step into my office," I responded proudly, taking him off as ostentatiously as possible.

Once in my office, Bohr told me that he had especially wanted to talk to me in my role as the chairman of the FAS. He said that he had been much impressed by what we had been doing to insure civilian control of nuclear energy and in pressing for an international atomic energy agency in line with Oppenheimer's ideas. I replied that we in the FAS had only been doing what he had inspired us to do back at Los Alamos. Then he dropped his voice a few decibels and said that he wanted me to carry out a mission for him, so important (his voice falling a few more decibels) that peace in the world depended on it.

I assured him that I was eager to carry out the mission, but would he please speak a little louder so that I could clearly understand what I was to do. Bohr lowered his voice even more. I hitched my chair closer now because I knew that this was genuinely crucial, since it was Bohr's style to give emphasis by lowering his voice—and I could barely hear him at that point. He began to discuss his talks with Churchill and Roosevelt, and went on to further, more fruitful developments. I turned one ear toward him, the better to hear. He started to instruct me on what to do, just as someone knocked at the door and announced that his lecture was to begin. Bohr lowered his voice and continued the instructions—inaudibly.

In desperation, I pressed my ear actually into contact with his lips. Knock, knock, knock. "The lecture Dr. Bohr! The lecture! It's past time." Tears streaming down my face, I pleaded, "For God's sake, man, speak up!" Alas, the instructions had been delivered. Bohr got up and gave himself over to the importunate professor who should have introduced him 15 minutes earlier.

As I followed them into the lecture hall, two emotions were expressed on my face at the same time (complementarity). One was the pride of being a recognized friend of Niels Bohr; the other was the despair of a man who might have saved the world from the arms race if only he had heard. If only he had heard!

Bohr inspired us to look beyond physics to the problems of survival. He imbued us with hope. But there is something we must teach ourselves—to be heard.

6

New Evidence on Truman's Decision

Robert L. Messer

T he use of atomic bombs on Japanese cities at the end of
World War II is one of the most debated and analyzed events
in history. This discussion is not an attempt to explain that
event. Rather, to borrow a phrase from Senator Howard
Baker during the Watergate hearings, the focus is upon what the president knew and when he knew it. My purpose is not to indict President
Truman, but only to clarify his role in a larger process.

The main source of information for such a clarification is not White
House tape recordings, but something very nearly as candid and
revealing—the president's own words. Not just his public statements,
or his own writings on the subject after the fact, but Truman's private
journal and letters written at the time he gave the bombing order.

The recent discovery of this evidence helps us to understand better
at least some aspects of a 40-year-old issue. It reveals, for example,
that contrary to his public justification of the bombings as the only
way to end the war without a costly invasion of Japan, Truman had
already concluded that Japan was about to capitulate. Whether or not
he was correct in this estimate of when the war would end, the fact
that he held this view at the time he made his decision to use the
bomb is clearly set down in his own hand.

This new evidence is not a "smoking gun" that settles the old issue
of why the bomb was used. But it tells us more than we knew before
about the timing of the bombings. It also tells us more than Harry

Truman, for all his famous candor, ever told us.

In his first public statements regarding the use of the bomb, on August 6, 1945, Truman explained that this terrible new weapon represented an American victory in a life-and-death "race against the Germans." It had been dropped on a place called Hiroshima, which the president described as "a military base." It would continue to be used, he said, "until we have completely destroyed Japan's capacity to make war."

Even then there were those, although in a distinct minority, who raised questions about the bombings. What relevance to its use against Japan, they asked, was the fear that Hitler might get the bomb first? Three months before the atomic bombs fell on Japanese cities, Germany had surrendered. Months before that, Allied scientists had concluded that the worst-case scenario, which had prompted the Anglo-American atomic bomb project, was overly pessimistic. The Germans lagged far behind in the race for the bomb. Even more to the point, there had been no serious concern about a Japanese bomb. Was the bomb used then merely "because it was there," to justify its existence and its unprecedented expense?

Regarding the bomb's specific military justification, critics conceded that Hiroshima, as a major port and regional army headquarters, and Nagasaki, with its many war plants, contained legitimate military targets. We now know that those same targets could have been destroyed earlier by the sort of conventional bombing that had leveled just about every important military objective in Japan. In fact, the cities set aside as possible atomic targets were deliberately left "virgin," so as not to obscure the effects of the new weapon. It soon became clear, however, that the radius of destruction of even those first-generation 13- kiloton bombs far exceeded the size of any "military base." Casualty figures varied greatly, but all showed that the overwhelming majority of those killed and wounded were civilians in their homes, not soldiers or war workers on the assembly line. For having reversed the ratio of military and unavoidable or "incidental" civilian deaths, the Hiroshima and Nagasaki bombings were condemned, even at the time, by proponents of the principles of just war as "America's atomic atrocity."[1]

Such moral and religious outrage was confined almost exclusively to those who also had condemned conventional "obliteration" or "terror" bombing of civilians earlier in the war. By 1945 the technology of mass destruction had combined with the doctrine of total war to lower the moral threshold for all but a few dissenters. Many times brighter and hotter, the atomic fireballs over Hiroshima and Nagasaki were nonetheless dimmed when set against the precedents of the firestorms of Hamburg, Dresden, and Tokyo.

The early critics also were at a disadvantage in assailing the broader military, political, and moral justification for the bombings. The bomb was used, said Truman, "to destroy Japan's capacity to make war." Few outside government could then know to what extent that war-making capacity had been destroyed before the use of atomic weapons. Certainly the Japanese surrender within days after Hiroshima and hours after Nagasaki were bombed seemed to leave no doubt in the minds of almost all Americans: This new bomb had ended history's greatest and most destructive war; without it the war might have dragged on for many months, even years.

In announcing the bombings, the president had said that they were carried out in order to "shorten the agony of war" and save "thousands and thousands of American lives." Later he would be more specific, citing the estimated 250,000 Allied casualties expected to result from the planned invasion of Japan. Added to the Allied losses were the estimates of Japanese casualties in a prolonged war. These ranged from 500,000 to five million. Official U.S. estimates of Japanese killed in the atomic attacks totaled about 110,000. Thus, in saving more lives than they took, the atomic bombings were justified as the lesser of two evils.*

At the time few could argue with such logic. Indeed, opinion polls taken immediately after the war showed that for every American who thought the bombs should not have been used (5 percent) more than four times as many (23 percent) were disappointed that more bombs had not been dropped before Japan had a chance to surrender. Predictably, the majority of those polled (54 percent) backed Truman's decision to use just two bombs on cities as the proper and prudent middle course.[2] Of course, none of these people knew then that the entire U.S. nuclear arsenal had been expended in as rapid succession as possible, without waiting for a response to the first of the only two bombs available.

It was not long, however, before critics of the bomb decision got what seemed authoritative support for their contention that Japan was already defeated by the summer of 1945 and that therefore the use of the bomb had been an unnecessary, wanton act. The U.S. Strategic Bombing Survey's official report on the Pacific War appeared less than

---

*After the war Truman said that he had been told that the population of the target cities was about 60,000. Hiroshima's population was in fact more than 350,000 and Nagasaki's about 280,000. Of these, nearly 200,000 were killed and 150,000 injured.

one year after the Hiroshima and Nagasaki bombings and on the eve of a controversial series of atomic tests at Bikini atoll.

The authors of this massive, authoritative study of Japan's war-making capability concluded that "the Hiroshima and Nagasaki atomic bombs did not defeat Japan, nor, by the testimony of the enemy leaders who ended the war, did they persuade Japan to accept unconditional surrender." Rather, the bombs, along with conventional air power, naval blockade, Soviet intervention, and other internal and external pressures acted "jointly and cumulatively" as "lubrication" of a peace-making machinery set in motion months before the atomic attacks. The Survey's analysts concluded that "certainly prior to 31 December 1945 and in all probability prior to 1 November 1945 Japan would have surrendered, even if the atomic bombs had not been dropped, even if Russia had not entered the war, and even if no invasion had been planned or contemplated."[3]

Responding to a resurgence of criticism based upon the Bombing Survey's findings, Truman moved quickly to preempt such second-guessing of his use of the bomb. The point man for the Administration's public counteroffensive was Henry L. Stimson, former secretary of war and a key adviser on atomic matters at the time of the bomb decision. In responding to the president's urging that he "set the record straight" Stimson agreed on the need to get out in front of the issue and "satisfy the doubts of that rather difficult class of the community . . . namely educators and historians."[4]

Sharing this concern about how future historians might judge the bomb decision, Truman lent his full support, during his years in the White House, to Stimson's writings on the subject and other such projects. After retiring to private life, he repeated—in private interviews, public statements, and his two-volume memoirs—that he had always regarded the bomb strictly as a weapon and had no doubt or regret, either at the time or in retrospect, about the necessity or wisdom of its use against Japan. Any speculation about how things might have been done differently was based upon hindsight. Truman frequently cut off any further discussion of the subject with the observation that "any schoolboy's afterthought is worth more than all the generals' forethought."[5]

In his off-the-record comments Truman was more blunt. To a correspondent who had questioned the propriety of the air of celebration surrounding the news of the bombings, the president responded with the observation: "When you have to deal with a beast you have to treat him as a beast." Similarly, Truman had no sympathy for anyone else who might have second thoughts. Even before Robert Oppenheimer publicly confessed to having "known sin" in helping to build the bomb, Truman dismissed him as typical of the "crybaby scientists" who thought they had blood on their hands.

Even years after wartime passions had cooled, Truman remained unapologetic. When in the 1960s the makers of a television documentary suggested that he might travel to Japan as a goodwill gesture, the former president replied in classic Trumanesque language: "I'll go . . . but I won't kiss their ass." Perhaps fortunately for all concerned, the crusty old man never made the proposed trip to Hiroshima. Until his death in 1972, Truman held firm to his original justification for the bombings.[6]

The formulation by Truman, Stimson, and other official or "orthodox" defenders of the bomb decision established the terms of the debate and held the high ground of privileged sources and classified information for many years. That defense rested upon the military necessity and therefore the lesser-of-two-evils morality of the decision. The bomb had been dropped because not to do so risked prolonging the war. By ending the war, the bomb saved lives, American and Japanese. The reason for using it was strictly military—to hasten the surrender of Japan. There had been no ulterior political motives: neither domestic, in justifying a very expensive weapons development project, nor international, in regard to any power other than Japan.

In the emerging Cold War between the United States and the Soviet Union, the last point was perhaps the most important. The term "atomic diplomacy" had first appeared in *Pravda* within weeks after the end of the war. The charge that the Truman Administration was attempting to use the United States' atomic monopoly to intimidate the Soviet Union was picked up by political mavericks in the United States, such as Franklin Roosevelt's former vice-president, Henry Wallace, as well as by influential voices from abroad, such as British Nobel Prize laureate in physics P.M.S. Blackett.

Blackett pointed out that the invasion of Japan, the next major U.S. military action, was not scheduled to begin until November. However, the Soviet Union, under an agreement signed by the Big Three leaders at Yalta early in 1945, was scheduled to enter the war against Japan in August, three months before the planned invasion.

After Germany's defeat, the Soviets represented Japan's last hope for a negotiated peace, and American leaders knew of Japanese peace feelers in Moscow. Why then was there the rush to use the bomb before Moscow dashed Japan's hopes by declaring war? The impact of that major diplomatic and military blow might well have brought about surrender. Why not at least wait to find out?

Blackett concluded that the timing and circumstances of the atomic bombings made sense only as an effort at atomic diplomacy directed at the Soviet Union. He put the "revisionist" case succinctly in his observation that "the dropping of the atomic bomb was not so much the last military act of the second World War, as the first major operation in the cold diplomatic war with Russia now in progress."[7]

The basic elements of the debate over the bomb decision remained essentially unchanged over the years. The revisionist hypothesis, largely deductive and circumstantial, won few converts beyond the left. Twenty years after the bombs fell on Japan, former State Department official-turned-historian Herbert Feis concluded that, even though we can say, with the advantage of hindsight, that the use of atomic bombs at that juncture probably was unnecessary to bring about Japan's surrender before the planned invasion, the decision-makers "ought not to be censured." Although perhaps mistaken, they acted in good faith. They sincerely believed, based upon the best evidence available to them at the time, that using this new weapon was the best, surest, and quickest way to end the war.[8]

Feis and other orthodox defenders of the faith in U.S. leaders dismissed New Left revisionist arguments on grounds of ideological preconceptions, selective use of evidence, and shoddy scholarship. Although in some cases deserved, such criticism of the revisionist challenge could not altogether offset the mounting evidence against the original orthodox defense.

The declassification of government documents and presidential papers, and the release of privately held manuscript sources such as Stimson's private diary forced a revision if not a total refutation of accepted orthodoxy. Drawing upon this newly available primary source material, scholars put forth analyses that were more balanced, more penetrating, and more convincing than either extreme in the previous debate over the bomb.

In the 1970s the work of Martin Sherwin, Barton Bernstein, Gregg Herken, and others revealed the early and continuing connection U.S. leaders made between the bomb and diplomacy. Recent scholarship has stressed the continuity of atomic policy from Roosevelt to Truman. Concerning the motives or objectives of this policy, by the 1980s it was generally accepted that considerations of the bomb's effect on postwar Soviet behavior had been one of several factors contributing to what was in the end a virtually irresistible presumption in favor of using the bomb.[9]

While it is true that dropping the bomb was virtually a foregone conclusion, it does not follow that Truman was, as General Groves described him, merely "a little boy on a toboggan." Dependent upon his advisers and far from a free agent, he was still the ultimate decision-maker. He was the only person who had the final say—not only on whether the bomb would be used at all, but when and how it would be used. With the Soviet Union about to enter the war, the decision not to tell Stalin about the bomb and the decision to drop all the available bombs in advance of Soviet entry take on major implications for our understanding of the overall decision.

Until recently the evidence of Truman's thinking at the moment he gave the order to deliver the bombs was largely circumstantial or indirect. Those "rather difficult" historians Stimson had worried about were able to reconstruct in detail the views of Truman's key advisers. We know, for example, that Truman's secretary of state, James F. Byrnes, wanted to use the bomb to end the war before Moscow "could get in so much on the kill." It is clear from his diary entries at the time that Stimson saw the bomb as the United States' "master card" in dealing, not just with Japan, but with the Soviet Union as well.[10] But there did not seem to be comparable direct evidence about Truman's private thinking on the bomb at the time he made the decision.

The first batch of this new evidence on the bomb decision surfaced in 1979. It had been misfiled among the family records of Truman's press secretary at the Truman presidential library. This sheaf of hand-written notes made up Truman's private journal kept during his trip to the Big Three summit meeting at Potsdam outside Berlin in July 1945.

During that trip Truman first learned of the successful test explosion of a plutonium device in New Mexico, gave the order for the Hiroshima and Nagasaki bombings, and, as he sailed home, received the news that his order had been carried out. The event, he said at the time, was "the greatest thing in history."

Four years after the discovery of Truman's Potsdam diary, a second batch of new evidence of Truman's contemporary thinking on matters relating to the use of the bomb turned up among his widow's private papers. These letters, written during that same Potsdam trip, along with other private correspondence between Bess and Harry Truman had been presumed destroyed years earlier. But they had somehow survived.

Taken together, these two sets of documents shed new light on how

Truman came to grips with an entirely new force in human affairs and how he incorporated his understanding of the bomb into his thoughts about when, how, and on whose terms the war would end.

The first news of the successful test detonation in New Mexico reached Truman on the evening of July 16. The message gave no details about the size of the explosion. Although he makes no explicit reference to the bomb in his diary entry for that date, the news of its existence may have moved him to reflect upon the relation between technology and morality: "I hope for some sort of peace—but I fear that machines are ahead of morals by some centuries and when morals catch up perhaps there'll be no reason for any of it. I hope not. But we are only termites on a planet and maybe when we bore too deeply into the planet there'll [be] a reckoning—who knows?" Elsewhere in this diary, after the bomb's power had been made clear to him,* Truman wondered if this new weapon might "be the fire [of] destruction prophesied in the Euphrates Valley Era, after Noah and his fabulous ark." Such apocalyptic visions, however, did not keep him from using what he recognized was "the most terrible bomb in the history of the world." Perhaps he reassured himself with the observation that "it seems the most terrible thing ever discovered, but it can be made the most useful."

On July 17, still without knowing any details about the bomb test, Truman met for the first time with Stalin. In his diary account of that meeting, he noted that the Soviet leader's agenda items, which included the overthrow of Franco's fascist government in Spain, were "dynamite." To this observation Truman added: "but I have some dynamite too which I'm not exploding now." Whether or not he was thinking of the bomb as his diplomatic dynamite is unclear.

But Truman then makes a very clear statement that goes to the heart of the issue of the bomb's necessity. Referring to the Soviet commitment to declare war on Japan three months after the defeat of Germany, Truman noted Stalin's reaffirmation of the agreement he had made with Roosevelt at Yalta: "He'll [Stalin] be in Jap War on August 15th." To this Truman added: "Fini Japs when that comes about." In these two brief sentences Truman set forth his understanding of how the war would end: Soviet entry into the war would finish the Japanese.

In writing to his wife the following day (July 18), the president underscored the importance of Soviet entry and its impact upon the timing of the war's end. "I've gotten what I came for—Stalin goes to war on August 15 with no strings on it. . . . I'll say that we'll end

---

*A full report, including vivid eye-witness accounts, arrived on the afternoon of July 21.

the war a year sooner now, and think of the kids who won't be killed! That is the important thing."

The implications of these passages from Truman's diary and letters for the orthodox defense of the bomb's use are devastating: if Soviet entry alone would end the war before an invasion of Japan, the use of atomic bombs cannot be justified as the only alternative to that invasion. This does not mean, of course, that having the bomb was not useful. But it does mean that for Truman the end of the war seemed at hand; the issue was no longer when the war would end, but how and on whose terms. If he believed that the war would end with Soviet entry in mid-August, then he must have realized that if the bombs were not used before that date they might well not be used at all.

This relationship between the Soviet entry, the bomb, and the end of the war is set forth in Truman's diary account for July 18. "P[rime] M[inister Churchill] and I ate alone. Discussed Manhattan [the atomic bomb] (it is a success). Decided to tell Stalin about it. Stalin had told P.M. of telegram from Jap emperor asking for peace. Stalin also read his answer to me. It was satisfactory. [I] believe Japs will fold up before Russia comes in. I am sure they will when Manhattan appears over their homeland. I shall inform Stalin about it at an opportune time." Truman apparently believed that by using the bomb the war could be ended even before the Soviet entry. The bomb would shorten the war by days rather than months. Its use would not save hundreds of thousands of lives—but it could save victory for the Americans. The race with the Germans had been won. It was now a race with Soviets.

Unaware of Soviet espionage, Truman assumed that Stalin did not know that such a race was underway. Despite his stated intention to tell Stalin about the bomb at an "opportune" time, Truman—apparently due to the urgings of Churchill and Byrnes—did not inform Stalin even of the bomb's existence, much less of the plans to use it on the eve of a major Soviet military offensive into Manchuria.

We now know that Klaus Fuchs, among others, kept Stalin well informed about progress on the bomb. But at Potsdam Truman believed he had succeeded in keeping Stalin in ignorance by a carefully staged charade, casually mentioning a "new weapon" without giving any details about it or its immediate use. Stalin showed no interest, and Truman was convinced he had fooled "Mr. Russia." The following day the order to deliver both bombs as soon as possible went out from Potsdam.

This cat-and-mouse game between the two leaders was apparently what the president had in mind when, in a letter to his wife at the end of the conference, Truman, an ardent poker player, commented on Stalin's stalling tactics: "He doesn't know it but I have an ace in the hole and another one showing—so unless he has two pairs (and I know he has not) we are sitting all right."

It can be argued that ending the war sooner rather than later, even a few days later, by whatever means at his disposal was Truman's first responsibility. It also can be argued that limiting Soviet expansion in Asia, as a bonus to ending the war as soon as possible, was in the U.S. national interest and therefore also Truman's duty. But the point here is that the president, in publicly justifying his use of the bomb, never made those arguments.

It is in this light that the new evidence, in both the Potsdam diary and letters to his wife, calls for a reevaluation of the old issue: why were the only two bombs available used in rapid succession so soon after testing, and on the eve of the planned Soviet entry into the war? From this unique record, in Truman's own hand, we can understand better how this relatively inexperienced leader, who had only recently first heard the words "atomic bomb," grasped this new technology, and used it as a solution for a multitude of military, political, and diplomatic problems.

The evidence of the Potsdam diary and letters does not close the book on the question why the bomb was dropped. Rather, it opens it to a previously unseen page. What appears there is by no means always clear or consistent. At times it is hard to know what to make of such statements as Truman's diary entry for July 25, in which he expresses his determination to use the bomb "so that military objectives are the target and not women and children." This extraordinary comment follows a very detailed and accurate description of the effects of the bomb test. Perhaps he really did believe that Hiroshima was just a "military base."

Elsewhere in these pages Truman seems to disprove the revisionist contention that he did not want "the Russians" in the war at all. In writing to his wife on July 18, Truman made it clear that his highest priority at the conference was getting the Soviet Union into the war against Japan. Two days later, after a "tough meeting" with Churchill and Stalin, the president noted that he had made his goals "perfectly plain" to both men: "I want the Jap War won and I want 'em both in it."

The dual objectives of assuring Soviet entry while containing Soviet expansion apparently were not contradictory to Truman. As he put it a decade later: "One of the main objectives of the Potsdam Conference [was] to get Russia in as quickly as we could and then to keep Russia out of Japan—and I did it."[11] Although he saw the bomb as useful for ending the war before the Soviets could claim credit for the victory, Truman apparently wasn't ready to rely totally on the bomb until it was proven in combat. This lingering skepticism is revealed in his use of quotation marks in noting, on the same day he gave the bomb order, that "we 'think' we have found the way to cause a disintegration of the atom."

Truman's attitude toward "the Japs" seems clear enough in his diary references to them as "savages, ruthless, merciless and fanatic." Yet to a senator who, after the Hiroshima bombing, had urged continued attacks until the Japanese were brought "groveling to their knees," the president replied: "I can't bring myself to believe that, because they are beasts, we should ourselves act in the same manner." Indeed, after the Nagasaki bombing, Truman reportedly told his cabinet members that there would be no more such attacks because he could not bear the thought of killing "all those kids."[12]

While these new sources, as they relate to Truman's private perspective on the bomb, contribute to our understanding, they remain fragments which by no means complete the mosaic.[13] The point here is not that Truman single-handedly controlled the course of history. Rather, it is that as a major participant in that history his attempt to mold nuclear weapons policy at the beginning of the atomic era contributes to our understanding of an event the meaning and lessons of which, after 40 years, we still seek.

1. Editorial, *Christian Century*, 62 (Aug. 29, 1945), pp. 3–4.

2. "The Fortune Poll," *Fortune* 32 (Dec. 1945), p. 305.

3. "Japan's Struggle to End the War," p. 12, and "Summary Report (Pacific War)," p. 26, both dated July 1, 1946, in David MacIsaac, ed., *The United States Strategic Bombing Survey*, vol. 7 (New York: Garland, 1976).

4. Truman to Henry L. Stimson (Dec. 31, 1946), folder "Atomic Weapons, Use of," Vertical File, Part II, Harry S. Truman Papers, Harry S. Truman Library, Independence, Missouri (hereafter, HSTL); Stimson to Truman, Jan. 7, 1947, quoted in Martin J. Sherwin, *A World Destroyed: The Atomic Bomb and the Grand Alliance* (New York: Knopf, 1975), p. 3.

5. Transcript of press conference (Aug. 14, 1947), folder "Atomic Bomb," Box 4, Eban Ayers Papers, HSTL.

6. Truman to Samuel Cavett (Aug. 11, 1945), folder 692 misc., Official File, Truman Papers, HSTL; Nuell Pharr Davis, *Lawrence and Oppenheimer* (New York: Simon and Schuster, 1968), p. 260; Merle Miller, *Plain Speaking* (New York: Berkley, 1974), p. 248.

7. P.M.S. Blackett, *Fear, War and the Bomb* (New York: Whittlesey House, 1948), p. 139.

8. Herbert Feis, *The Atomic Bomb and the End of World War II* (Princeton, N.J.: Princeton University Press, 1966), p. 200.

9. Sherwin, *A World Destroyed;* Barton J. Bernstein, "Roosevelt, Truman, and the Atomic Bomb, 1941–1945: A Reinterpretation," *Political Science Quarterly* (Spring 1975),

pp. 23–69; Gregg Herken, *The Winning Weapon: The Atomic Bomb in the Cold War, 1945–1950* (New York: Knopf, 1981).

10. Robert L. Messer, *The End of an Alliance: James F. Byrnes, Roosevelt, Truman and the Origins of the Cold War* (Chapel Hill: University of North Carolina Press, 1982), pp. 92, 105.

11. Truman's remark was made in an off-the-record session with staff members preparing his memoirs. The quotation did not appear in the published volumes. (See Acheson Interview, Feb. 17, 1955, a.m., Post Presidential Papers, HSTL, p. 40.)

12. Truman to Senator Richard Russell (Aug. 9, 1945), with attached telegram, Russell to Truman (Aug. 7, 1945), Folder 197, misc., Official File, HSTL; entry for Aug. 10, 1945, in John Morton Blum, ed., *Price of Vision: The Diary of Henry A. Wallace, 1942–1946* (Boston: Houghton Mifflin, 1973), p. 474.

13. The Potsdam diary and correspondence are reprinted in Robert H. Ferrell, ed., *Off the Record: The Private Papers of Harry S. Truman* (New York: Harper and Row, 1980), pp. 48–60; and in Robert H. Ferrell, ed., *Dear Bess: The Letters from Harry to Bess Truman, 1910–1959* (New York: Norton, 1983), pp. 516–23.

7

Japan's Policies since 1945

Toshiyuki Toyoda

The explosion of a uranium bomb over Hiroshima on August 6, 1945, and of a plutonium bomb over Nagasaki three days later gave a tremendous shock to Japan's wartime rulers. After studying the report of the Japanese scientists who surveyed the devastated cities, the leaders realized the extraordinary power of the atomic bomb: a single shot could instantly obliterate an entire city. They moved quickly to surrender in order to avoid a third use of this awesome and inhumane weapon on another Japanese city.

Despite severe wartime control of information, many Japanese citizens, through direct and indirect contact with badly injured survivors, learned of, and were horrified by, the infernos that had reduced Hiroshima and Nagasaki to ashes. Soon after the Allied occupation forces entered Japan, however, a press code was imposed by the General Headquarters of the Allied Powers (GHQ) on September 19, 1945. The press code was putatively intended to promote "public tranquility" and to prevent "mistrust or resentment" of Allied troops, but it was, in fact, specifically used to prohibit publication and dissemination of all reports, commentaries, and treatises on atomic-bomb damages, including even those on medical treatment of bomb-related injuries and illnesses. Thus the Japanese people were denied access to details of the atomic disasters until the signing of the San Francisco Peace Treaty in September 1951 brought an end to press censorship.

Even under restrictive conditions, however, the gravest fear and hatred of the atomic bomb settled deeply in the minds of the Japanese people. Mixed with these feelings, however, were those of gratitude and relief at being liberated from a long, ultra-nationalistic regime, and the bright hope that human beings would not be so foolish as to initiate another war. Many Japanese thought that the advent of the atomic bomb had made warfare between nations intolerable. Indeed, the impact of Hiroshima and Nagasaki led the Japanese public to embrace two grand aspirations: the abolition of all nuclear weapons and the renunciation of war as a sovereign right of the state.

Unfortunately, the succeeding four decades have seen these aspirations gradually weaken, in appearance at least, because of countervailing pressures of international affairs governed by power politics. The majority of the population has shifted from those with bitter war experiences to the postwar generation with no war memories, and this has also, inevitably, vitiated these cherished aspirations.

Thus, while still paying lip service to the long-held hopes, successive governments have moved with increasing vigor away from the original ideal of a nation committed to peace and disarmament. But even so, each time a new nuclear threat has occurred, the deeply rooted antipathy of the Japanese people toward nuclear weapons has revived enough to place considerable restraint on the government's propensity to overcommit the nation to U.S. nuclear strategy.

In contrast to the overall fluctuation of antinuclear fervor, one movement has continued for many years without interruption—the movement seeking specific relief and compensation for the atomic-bomb victims. Yet, after 40 years the efforts have been in vain.

The major premise of the movement is that use of nuclear weaponry is illegal under international law; it constitutes a crime against humanity and an international miscarriage of justice. This is precisely the point of repeated U.N. resolutions—1653 (XVI) of November 24, 1961; 33/71 B of December 14, 1978; and 38/73 G of December 15, 1983— which Japan, to my shame, has voted against or abstained from.

The Japanese people's first postsurrender task was to replace their old constitution. Circumstances surrounding the drafting of the new constitution involved some controversy, particularly regarding negotiations between Japanese lawmakers and the General Headquarters of the occupation forces. Nevertheless, the new constitution was enthusiastically received by the overwhelming majority of the Japanese people. They were strongly impressed by the pacifism expressed in its Preamble and in Article 9, which states in part:

> Aspiring sincerely to an international peace based on justice and order, the Japanese people forever renounce war as a sovereign right of the nation and the threat or use of force as means of settling international disputes.
>
> In order to accomplish [this] aim . . . land, sea, and air forces, as well as other war potential, will never be maintained. The belligerency of the state will not be recognized.

Pacifism's roots in the Quaker and other peace churches are well-known. The renunciation of war in the new Japanese constitution can be traced in part to these early roots. The same is true of other constitutions, promulgated before and after Japan's, which include stated renunciations of war; examples are those of France (1946), Italy (1947), and the Federal Republic of Germany (1949). What makes Japan's constitution unique is its *constitutional pacifism through disarmament*, as clarified in Article 9. In fact, then Prime Minister Shigeru Yoshida asserted before the Diet (parliament), in June 1946, that Article 9 implies rejection of belligerency even for self-defense.

Despite mounting political tensions and the escalating arms race between the United States and the Soviet Union, the Japanese people initially shared with their government the absolute pacifist view. They preferred to devote themselves to developing peaceful industries for survival, along with promotion of the pure sciences. But the situation was drastically changed by a shift in U.S. policy toward Japan when the Korean War broke out in June 1950. The occupation GHQ in July urged the Japanese government to establish the Police Reserve Force (*Keisatsu Yobitai*), embryo of the later paramilitary forces.

Naturally, all Japanese wanted both the earliest possible termination of the occupation and peace settlements with former enemies. But public opinion became divided—one faction insisting on "complete and overall peace," meaning peace treaties with all former enemies, the other urging speedy settlement with the U.S. side of the East-West confrontation. Obviously, the former view was faithful to the spirit of Japan's new constitution, but under strong U.S. pressure Japan chose the latter course, concluding the San Francisco Peace Treaty with the United States on September 8, 1951.

At the same time, the Japan-U.S. Mutual Security Treaty was concluded, bringing Japan under the "nuclear umbrella" of one of the two nuclear superpowers. This arrangement was vitally significant for Japan's future, since it obliged successive Japanese governments to obscure from public scrutiny the contradiction between the nation's constitutional pacificism and its military-oriented partnership with a major nuclear-weapons state.

Still, the constitution prevented Japan from undertaking collective security commitments outside the country, even under the Japan-U.S. Mutual Security Treaty. Moreover, use of military terms such as "army," "navy," and "air force" was taboo; instead, "self-defense forces" was the label given to the paramilitary organization. Article 9 seemed to be bearing some fruit, however limited.

During the occupation, the press code had created an atmosphere that made it virtually impossible for the Japanese to raise their voices openly against nuclear weapons, no matter how uncomfortable they felt about the stupid and dangerous arms race between the nuclear giants. They were also inhibited by their feelings of guilt and responsibility for Japan's wartime collaboration with Nazi Germany and Fascist Italy. And many conscientious Japanese who had survived the war were profoundly remorseful for not having tried, or been able, to halt the march into militarism before and during the war.

When the San Francisco Peace Treaty ended press censorship, a wide range of documents on Hiroshima and Nagasaki appeared. One of these was an anthology of atomic-bomb poems (*Genbaku shishū*) by Hiroshima survivor Sankichi Toge, issued on September 20, 1951. Another, anticipating the end of censorship, was the August 1951 publication of the *Summary of the Survey on A-bomb Damages (Genshi bakudan saigai chōsa hōkokusho, sōkatsuhen)*. Commissioned by the city of Hiroshima soon after the bombing and completed by local scientists in the summer of 1946, it had been previously denied publication permission by the General Headquarters. (The full two-volume report was published in 1953.) Actually, General Headquarters had given permission, on December 8, 1950, to translate into Japanese the U.S. government publication, *The Effects of Atomic Weapons*. The stated purpose of this book, however, was to be a guide for persons engaged in civil defense activity.

In any case, once many Japanese gained access to a considerable amount of scientific data on the Hiroshima and Nagasaki disasters, they began to reflect on the global and historical implications of these events in light of their own heartbreaking experiences. Alarmed by the virulent course of the U.S.-Soviet nuclear arms race, informed and concerned Japanese could foresee the ominous consequences. They wanted to speak out internationally, but were hesitant to do so because of their status as citizens of a defeated nation.

Then a shocking incident roused the Japanese out of their reticence. Twenty-three Japanese crewmen on board the tuna fishing vessel "Lucky Dragon No. 5" (*Daigo Fukuryū Maru*) suffered badly from radioactive fallout from the hydrogen-bomb test conducted by the United States on Bikini Atoll in the Marshall Islands on March 1, 1954. One of the crewmen, Aikichi Kuboyama, died six months later. Tuna on the ship's deck were badly contaminated. Yet at the time of the test explosion, "Lucky Dragon No. 5" was well outside the danger zone indicated by the United States.

After this incident, Japanese scientists measured the radiation contamination of various materials, including fish caught in Japan's coastal waters, air in its urban areas, and vegetables grown on its islands. Considerable amounts of radiation were detected in all samples, without exception; the scientists could even identify several nuclides specifically from the Bikini explosion. Until this time most Japanese had abhorred nuclear weapons and denounced their use in war; but it had not occurred to them that even tests posed radiation hazards to widely dispersed populations, including their own.

An aroused public responded in great numbers to a grass-roots movement against atomic and hydrogen bomb testing, a movement initiated as a signature campaign by a women's group in the Suginami ward of Tokyo. Eventually 20 million signatures were collected, as the movement swelled to nationwide proportions. Its ultimate goal, of course, was the abolition of nuclear weapons, but its immediate, urgent objective was a ban on nuclear-weapons tests. The movement led to the First World Conference against Atomic and Hydrogen Bombs, held in Hiroshima from August 6 to 8, 1955. It also exerted considerable influence on the enactment, in 1963, of the multilateral Partial Test-Ban Treaty, banning nuclear tests in the atmosphere, in outer space, and under water.

Regrettably, the nationwide movement was split, in August 1964, by the involvement of political parties, which disputed whether the test ban should apply to *any* country or only to *some* countries. Despite sustained efforts by many concerned persons for over 20 years, substantial reunification of the antinuclear movement has not yet been achieved. However, the movement to win relief and compensation for A-bomb and H-bomb victims has throughout this period played a valuable role as a binding agent of the divided groups. It is also of some significance that the Tokyo District Court, in a December 7, 1963 ruling on the bomb victims' demand for compensation for damages, held that the atomic bombings were illegal under international law, although the right to press claims against the state was not recognized.

Just when the tide of antinuclear sentiment was high—in the summer of 1954—Japan's Defense Agency was established and the law creating the Self-Defense Forces (SDF) was promulgated. The National Security Forces (*Hōantai*), successor to the initial Police Reserve Force (*Keisatsu Yobitai*), were expanded to form the Land, Maritime, and Air Self-Defense Forces; their duties were restricted to defending the nation against external attack. A majority of Japanese constitutional specialists assert that the law is unconstitutional, but successive governments have treated the SDF's existence as an accepted fact.

The SDF has steadily expanded under strong U.S. pressure and now ranks eighth in the world in terms of military power. The "defense budget" (a euphemism for military expenditures) has been increasing at a much higher annual rate—6.5 percent in 1983; 6.6 percent in 1984; 6.9 percent in 1985—than the expenditures in the general account—1.4 percent in 1983; 0.5 percent in 1984; 3.7 percent in 1985. Japan's defense budget for fiscal 1984 totalled 2,934 billion yen, over two-thirds of which went to repay loans for purchasing advanced weapons systems from the United States. For example, the Defense Agency's Mid-Term Perspective, defining the defense program for fiscal 1981–1985, lists 72 P-3C Orion antisubmarine aircraft, which can carry the Harpoon antiship cruise missile with one nuclear warhead. If the existing 10 P-2Js are added, the SDF's squadron of antisubmarine aircraft is second only to that of the United States.

This example is typical of the current SDF. Its equipment and operational manuals are almost entirely incorporated within the U.S. military forces deployed in the Asia-Pacific region. Indeed, the Japanese Navy played a professional role in the joint exercises called RIMPAC, conducted in May and June of 1984. The present Self-Defense Forces have, in fact, developed far beyond the "exclusively defensive defense" (*senshu bōei*) claimed repeatedly by the government of Japan. In the United States, say Japanese officials, persistent voices condemn Japan's "free ride" in mutual defense obligations and urge Japan, as a member of the Western bloc, to strengthen significantly the SDF's military capability.

Japanese industries in various fields have developed remarkably through constant technological innovation. And although their products are oriented to peaceful uses, many can be utilized as crucial parts of sophisticated weapons systems. Moreover, the high quality and relatively low cost of Japanese industrial products have precipitated some conflicts in foreign trade, particularly with the United States. Overlooking, intentionally or not, the fact that Japanese industrial success stems from devotion to peaceful instead of military ventures, some influential U.S. politicians complain about Japanese laxity in security matters—and then urge Japan to buy as many U.S. weapons as possible. Indeed, the temptation to commit enormous resources to the research and development of sophisticated weapons systems is strong throughout the world, and Japan may ultimately succumb to it.

To suppress this tendency at home, the Miki cabinet in November 1976 placed a 1 percent ceiling on the ratio of defense expenditure to gross national product, and subsequent governments have adhered to this policy. Despite resistance by opposition parties, however, current Prime Minister Nakasone has refused to maintain this ceiling. This was made clear after he returned from a meeting with President Reagan in Los Angeles in January 1985. In this connection it should be noted that if the NATO formula is used to calculate Japan's defense budget—that is, to include pensions for retired military personnel—then the ratio of defense cost to GNP has already reached 1.5 percent in fiscal 1985. Furthermore, Japan spends about $1 billion annually to accommodate U.S. forces in Japan. On a per-capita basis, this exceeds comparable expenses shouldered by West Germany.

Okinawa, largest of the southernmost Ryūkyū chain of Japan's islands, remained under U.S. administration for many years after the San Francisco Peace Treaty because of its vital importance to U.S. nuclear strategy in the Asia-Pacific region. There were many U.S. military bases on other islands, but the United States tried to conceal the nuclear capabilities of these bases from the notice, much less the scrutiny, of antinuclear Japanese citizens. Okinawa, however, was a different case. The United States openly utilized the island as a cornerstone of its nuclear strategy, installing launchers for Mace nuclear missiles and other facilities for strategic bombers.

On Japan's main islands people had long felt guilt toward the Okinawans, tragic victims of the bloody battle of Okinawa in World War II, and thus ardently wished for the return of the island to Japanese administration. Along with this wish was another: to have no nuclear weapons there. So the Japanese were eager to get Okinawa back *without* nuclear weapons facilities. Successive governments tried to persuade the Japanese people to accept reliance upon the nuclear deterrence offered by the United States. But government leaders could not wholly ignore the public's firm rejection of nuclear weapons. Thus, when the reversion of Okinawa became a hot issue in 1971, then Prime Minister Eisaku Satō felt obliged to promise that he would ask the United States to return a nuclear-free Okinawa.

The Japanese Diet then adopted what is known as the Three Non-

Nuclear Principles: not to possess, produce, or permit the introduction of nuclear weapons into Japan. The government since then has had to acknowledge, perhaps reluctantly, these principles as constituting one of the nation's most important policies. It is, however, not easy to implement the three principles, especially the third one, because the United States adheres to its policy of neither confirming nor denying the presence of nuclear warheads on board its naval vessels calling at Japanese ports, or in aircraft landing in Japan. That being the case, the Japanese government should refuse to allow port calls by U.S. warships or landings by U.S. aircraft known to have nuclear capabilities. New Zealand's Prime Minister David Lange did this, with the strong support of his people.

The Three Non-Nuclear Principles are unquestionably in accord with Japan's constitutional pacifism, and in substantive contradiction to the doctrine of nuclear deterrence. Thus, we Japanese have frequently been told that we suffer from a "nuclear allergy," or that the nuclear issue is still a "taboo" in Japan. Although the terms sound somewhat pejorative, many Japanese believe that, far from being abnormal, their "nuclear allergy" and "nuclear taboo" are sure signs of sanity in an age of nuclear madness.

The doctrine of nuclear deterrence is pernicious and fallacious, yet supposedly reasonable people in the nuclear-weapons states, and especially the superpowers, still take it to be a "realistic" basis for living with nuclear weapons, even though the credibility of deterrence has steadily declined with the development of "destabilizing weapons." In spite of sustained efforts by Japanese scientists to inform the Japanese public about the dangers of the arms race, which has been accelerated by the deterrence doctrine, the fact remains that many citizens, and the younger generation in particular, seem strangely apathetic toward this vital issue. They murmur hopelessly about the futility of trying to impede the present fierce arms race of the nuclear giants.

The constitution of Japan and the Three Non-Nuclear Principles have prevented the Self-Defense Forces from being armed with nuclear weapons. But they are equipped with many advanced weapons systems, such as 138 F-15 Eagles, and the Harpoon antiship cruise missiles on at least 47 vessels, as well as the P-3C Orions. This weaponry is to supplement the "limited availability of the U.S. forces in the East Asia and Pacific region," while the United States plans "to base F-16 Fighting Falcons at Misawa Air Base in Japan" (this according to the "Annual Report to the Congress," by Secretary of Defense Caspar W. Weinberger, Fiscal Year 1985).

Japan's close military cooperation with the U.S. nuclear strategy in the Asia-Pacific region can be seen also in the fact that crucial facilities of C³I (command, control, communication, and intelligence) are located in Japan. These facilities are connected with NORAD and SAC, and thus are part of the WWMCCS (World-Wide Military Command and Control System).

In 1981, immediately after Ronald Reagan was inaugurated, he announced an extensive increase in U.S. naval forces, stressing the growing military threat of the Soviet Navy and the deployment of SS-20 missiles in Siberia. Then the U.S. Navy decided to deploy 3,994 Tomahawk sea-launched cruise missiles over a 10-year period, starting in 1984. It is said that many of these have been loaded onto U.S. vessels cruising in the Northwest Pacific area, including the Sea of Japan.

Deployment of Tomahawk missiles near Japan has reactivated the seemingly stagnant antinuclear movement among Japanese citizens, although, as noted above, nationwide unification of the grass-roots movements has yet to be achieved. If the Three Non-Nuclear Principles are taken literally, it should not be difficult to refuse port calls by U.S. vessels loaded with, or capable of loading, Tomahawk missiles. Many Japanese, however, realize that nuclear confrontation between the United States and the Soviet Union has now shifted from Europe to the Asia-Pacific region, and Japan is caught in the middle.

Faced with this grave situation, over 100 leading Japanese representing various fields issued an appeal in June 1984 proposing *Five* Non-Nuclear Principles: not to possess, produce, or permit introduction of nuclear weapons; not to allow Japan to be used as a base from which to launch a nuclear attack; and to strive for global nuclear disarmament. Within the definition of nuclear weapons systems are included the command, control, and communication facilities indispensable to the movements of nuclear submarines deployed in waters surrounding Japan. The appeal further states:

> The governments of Japan and the United States have heretofore stood on the principle that American forces stationed in Japan will not be directly deployed in combat operations overseas. However, insofar as vessels loaded with Tomahawk cruise missiles have the capability of making direct nuclear strikes from Japanese ports, it is natural to deny port calls from this perspective, too. The government should therefore stick firmly to the position of not allowing Japan to be used as a forward base for offensive strikes.

Since Nakasone became prime minister in December 1982, Japan's security policy has been deeply, and unprecedentedly, involved in U.S. worldwide military strategy, as promoted by President Reagan. As a typical example, the Japanese government, on November 8, 1983, exchanged official letters with the United States in connection with "Provision of Weapons Technology to the United States," substantially intensifying and deepening the previous military collaboration. This has officially opened a way for participation by Japanese scientists and engineers in U.S. military research and development where Japan's high technology is clearly needed.

This trend seems to have been amplified, according to Nakasone's testimony before the Diet last February. In addition to support for Reagan's Strategic Defense Initiative (SDI), he expressed willingness to send Japanese scientists and engineers to work with SDI groups if so requested by the United States. Although many conscientious media figures have repeatedly reported the severe criticisms of SDI by American scientists and world-renowned statesmen, Nakasone stresses the need for the Western bloc to counter the Soviet threat with such high-technology wizardry.

Japan is now at a turning point in its security policy. Like many Western countries, Japan faces various social and economic difficulties, particularly the growing social burden of an aging society. Nakasone's repeatedly declared interest, however, is in liquidating the results of postwar politics while he is in office. This means, implicitly, revision of the constitution and other institutions of education and social welfare. Thus a dangerous symptom in Japan's course has become plainly visible: the ideal of the welfare state is fading as Japan turns increasingly toward military-oriented nationalism. It is a miniature mirror-image of the United States under Reagan's leadership. Indeed, Nakasone is proud of the "Ron-Yasu" intimacy and claims to have ushered in an unprecedented partnership with the United States. But is flattery the proper role of a good friend?

The Japanese know the reality of nuclear war more profoundly than other peoples and can, from experience, infer the horrible consequences of the arms race. We should abandon the delusion that development of military technology increases national security — a view clearly discredited by the postwar history of the arms race. As the only nation to have suffered nuclear disaster, what Japan needs to do is to recover our special influence on all nations, including the United States, and thus to urge every country to pursue deliberate nonmilitaristic policies toward the abolition of nuclear weapons.

8

Forty Years of Muddling Through

Bernard T. Feld

On August 6 and 9, 1945, two nuclear weapons annihilated two Japanese cities—respectively, Hiroshima and Nagasaki—and a major fraction of their populations. At the time these were the only nuclear weapons in existence, and, fortunately, the war was over before any more became available.

It has been argued that the dramatically visible effects of this first use of nuclear weapons in warfare were so frightening that they have inhibited any tendencies to accept such weapons into "normal" military arsenals and operational doctrines. I strongly hope that this is the case. But I would also maintain (parenthetically) that the same effect would have been achieved—and at a much lower human and moral cost— by only one weapon and, particularly, by its detonation over a target that was both unpopulated and highly visible. A number of such targets were available. One possibility might have been an explosion at the head of Tokyo Bay, far enough from land so that the radiation would have been nonlethal and the shock wave, while felt, would not have been intense enough to cause appreciable damage.

Be that as it may, the bombs were used in 1945, and no bomb has been exploded in a conflict (although hundreds have been exploded in weapons tests) since Nagasaki. This is true despite a number of serious international crises in which the possible use of a nuclear weapon was certainly contemplated by one or more of the parties involved, among them the Korean War (1953), the Berlin blockade

(1959), the Cuban missile crisis (1962), and the battle of Khe Sanh during the Vietnam War (1968).

But the fact that we have managed to get through 40 years without another nuclear disaster is no guarantee that we can continue in this relatively happy state. Indeed, indications are that the dangers of nuclear weapons use are increasing, monotonically, year by year, to the extent—at least in my view—that it is quite likely that a nuclear weapon will again be used in a conflict before the end of this century. This relatively pessimistic outlook stems mainly from three clearly observable tendencies:

The number of nuclear-weapons-capable nations is increasing from year to year. This number is already well beyond (by a factor of two or three) the six nations that have publicly demonstrated their nuclear capability by carrying out at least one nuclear test explosion—the United States, the Soviet Union, the United Kingdom, France, China, and India. I would be highly astonished if the military establishments in almost all the relatively technically advanced nations have not carried out all the necessary tests—short of an actual nuclear detonation—required to enable the rapid assembly of one or more nuclear weapons, once the political go-ahead is given and they are provided with the requisite 10-to-20 kilograms of plutonium or highly enriched uranium.

There has been evident erosion, among the non-nuclear nations, of their conviction that continued adherence to the nuclear Non-Proliferation Treaty (NPT) of 1970 remains in their interest. On the one hand, it is painfully obvious that one of the major NPT incentives—Article VI, which requires that the "superpowers" rapidly reach agreements to limit and reduce their nuclear arsenals—has not materialized. Furthermore, the continuing development and testing of increasingly sophisticated weapons over a fantastic range of strengths—from nuclear mines to people-killing but property-preserving neutron bombs to multimegaton city-busters—make it hard to maintain the thesis that these are nonusable weapons.

There is also the related "keeping up with the Joneses" syndrome: If China and India have them, Pakistan must certainly not be left out. If Israel develops (or is suspected of having) a capability, can Egypt permit itself to fall behind? Should Iraq be less capable in the nuclear area than Iran?

Finally, the rapidly spreading technology of nuclear power is building up, in those nations that are embarking upon such programs, both the technical capabilities and many of the materials and facilities required for nuclear weapons production. Unfortunately, this aspect of nuclear weapons proliferation is greatly exacerbated by the lively competition among the nuclear entrepreneurs in the capitalist developed nations to sell reactors in the Third World. This competition leads many to "sweeten the deal" by providing auxiliary facilities such as reprocessing plants. How can we expect the developing nations to resist such tempting deals?

All of these factors indicate the precarious state of the so-called non-proliferation regime, but where are we left with respect to getting through the next 40 years intact? In a rather precarious position, I'm afraid. As far as the danger of a direct nuclear confrontation between the superpowers is concerned, I believe that this remains a rather unlikely possibility. The leaders of the Soviet Union and the United States are well aware of the devastating consequences for both sides that would follow upon the first use of a nuclear weapon by either opponent. However, such realization by no means excludes the possibility that one or the other would be drawn—by accident, inadvertence, miscalculation, or sheer stupidity—into a nuclear showdown in which the fatal button would be pressed.

Heads of great powers have been known in the past to show frightening lapses of judgment; and this possibility becomes increasingly worrisome as we approach the time when many nations, or even nongovernmental (for example, terrorist) groups may be able to gain control over the ingredients of a crude nuclear bomb. Remember that the detonation of 10 kilograms of plutonium, with even the ridiculously low efficiency of one-tenth of a percent, would release the equivalent of 200 tons of TNT, that is, several carloads of high explosives. Think of the effects of such an explosion in the center of a busy city!

The answer to these dangers lies, of course, in the eventual elimination of nuclear weapons and—to the extent that nuclear power is required for the progress and well-being of peoples—the strict control of plutonium and enriched uranium to insure that they cannot be fabricated into weapons. Highly enriched uranium does not present a great problem right now. Such stocks can be "denatured" by mixing them with enough ordinary uranium to reduce the uranium-235 concentration to, say, around 20 percent or less—a high enough level to permit its use in all types of nuclear power reactors, even those moderated and cooled by ordinary water.

The denaturing of plutonium, however, presents greater difficulties. The isotopes heavier than the reactor-produced plutonium-239 isotope (that is, 240 and 241) also undergo fission on the absorption of fast neutrons, so that their presence does not greatly increase the "critical mass" for a plutonium detonation. Mixing with other "unpleasant" constituents—for example, a strong gamma-ray emitter which would

make its handling under ordinary circumstances extremely hazardous
—would only raise the level of technical sophistication required in
the use of straightforward chemical techniques for its repurification.

It may be expected that, in the future, groups—whether governmental or terrorist—which are intent on acquiring a small number
of nuclear weapons will be able to recruit the necessary technological
skills (all of which are thoroughly described in the open literature).

Eventually, and probably within our 40-year context, the development of high-power tunable lasers will make universally available a
potent laser-isotope-separation capability. Such a development could
well place nuclear bombs in the hands of the most lunatic fringes of
various irredentist or "liberation" groups unless the major technological
powers—particularly the United States and the Soviet Union—start
now to develop the necessary international measures to maintain effective controls over the source materials required for bombs.

Given the state of East-West relations, it is unlikely that the cooperation necessary to avert proliferation will come about, short of some
tragic incident that will propel the antagonists into realization of their
common interests in curbing the nuclear genie. An admittedly optimistic scenario might envision the destruction of some fair-sized city in
a terrorist extortion attempt, whereupon the U.S. president and the
Soviet premier will get on the "hot line" and agree that it is necessary
to take joint action to disarm the perpetrators and insure that there
will be no repetition of the event.

Meanwhile, we in the West must begin to take weapons proliferation
problems much more seriously. The Soviets are far ahead of us in this
respect. While they have exported a great deal of nuclear energy technology, together with power and research reactors, to nations within
their economic sphere, they have insisted on one very simple provision:
the fuel elements, at all times, belong to the Soviet Union. Fabrication
and reprocessing facilities are exclusively located in the Soviet Union.
The fabricated fuel elements are brought to and installed in the reactors
by Soviet technicians. And they are removed by these technicians,
when their useful reactor lifetime is over, to be returned to the Soviet
Union for reprocessing and refabrication.

Assuming that the nuclear supplier nations in the West could reach
the necessary political accommodations, such a solution would be
entirely feasible. We could still maintain a healthy capitalistic competition for the sale of reactors and fuel services, but the fuel would belong
to the supplier countries. It would be handled and transported under
close control, with whatever precautions are necessary to insure non-

diversion. The enriched uranium and plutonium not in current use would be stored in very safe locations, behind stone walls and barbed-wire barriers, under guard, lock, and key—very much in the way we handle, transfer, and store gold. (One could call this the "Fort Knox Solution.") After all, plutonium is more valuable than gold or platinum —and far more lethal.

But the handling and storage of fissile materials is but one aspect of the problem and—at least for the immediate future—not the most urgent. There are already between 30 and 50 thousand nuclear weapons; most, but by no means all, are in the hands of the super-powers. Eventually these must be eliminated, their fissionable cores safely stored, and eventually consumed. One possibility would be for power production. Or would it be better to transport them by rocket into the sun?

How can we safely get from here to there? The problem, of course, is to avoid the outbreak of *any* nuclear conflict, since the probability is always unacceptably high that the first use of a nuclear weapon will rapidly escalate into universal nuclear destruction. Somehow, we must develop and propagate the concept that nuclear weapons are simply not usable weapons, under any circumstances; that the first use of a nuclear weapon may well signal the ultimate catastrophe. We must construct an effective firebreak against the use of any nuclear bomb in any kind of conflict. Whether we try to define such nuclear-weapons use as "limited," "winnable," or "acceptable," these terms are all meaningless and deceptive when applied to nuclear war.

Nor can the consequences of nuclear war between the superpowers be significantly diminished through the medium of "civil defense." All programs envisaged under this rubric—whether they involve the individual shelters promoted by U.S. authorities, or massive community-shelter programs said to be prevalent in the Soviet Union —are absurd. The foolishness of T.K. Jones's recommendation—to pack a few shovelsful of dirt over a cellar door covering a shallow ditch (grave)—has been widely recognized. And the Soviet humor magazine, *Krokodil*, published a cartoon showing a citizen crawling along a Moscow street, covered by a white bed sheet, while the civil defense sirens are blasting their warning. Asked by a running com-patriot to explain his behavior, he replied: "I'm just following instruc-tions; we have been told that, when the alarm goes off, we must behave in such a way as not to spread panic!"

There is now almost universal recognition that civil defense measures are not only useless, economically wasteful, and misleading, but also positively dangerous, insofar as they may convey the impression that the nation pursuing such a program is preparing to launch a surprise or preemptive nuclear attack on the other side. (Civil defense would be seen as calculated to mitigate the effect of any surviving retaliatory forces available to the victim of the attack.) Hence, active civil defense is now generally understood to be a destabilizing factor in the superpower nuclear arms confrontation.

The essential first step in the elimination of the possibility of nuclear war is, in my view, the acceptance by the nuclear weapons states — eventually by all states — of a universal *no-first-use* arrangement. I would, in the long run, prefer a *no-use* agreement; but at least for the foreseeable future political realities seem to require the maintenance of nuclear deterrent forces and their associated doctrines of retaliation in kind. Such deterrence, however, could be maintained at levels far short of the present "overkill" capabilities that guarantee total "mutual assured destruction" (MAD) if ever the system should break down.

I am convinced that such an arrangement, arrived at today, would greatly enhance the security of all nations concerned. Furthermore, it would facilitate, indeed encourage, the dismantling of those particularly destabilizing systems that are clearly intended for a preemptive first strike and, in times of crisis, are subject to the "use 'em or lose 'em" syndrome. Furthermore, it would be an arrangement requiring no complicated or intrusive verification measures; in a sense, no-first-use is the ultimate in self-verifiable agreements.

It is frequently argued that such a no-first-use agreement is entirely declaratory; that it would be impossible to maintain in a situation where a nuclear-capable nation finds itself with its back against the wall, convinced that its national survival depends on the "defensive" use of a nuclear bomb. In this regard, I would again emphasize the "delegitimization" argument. It may take time, but if such an arrangement could be maintained over a few decades, we would finally arrive at a condition where, no longer depending on nuclear weapons, all nations would be willing to eliminate them completely, to ban them forever under an agreement that would also provide for sufficient verification to provide assurance of compliance.

Lest this idea be dismissed as hopelessly utopian, let me recall the Geneva Protocol of 1925 — essentially a no-first-use agreement with regard to chemical and bacteriological (biological) weapons. With very few exceptions — one or two alleged instances in Third World conflicts, the U.S. use of herbicides in Vietnam, a possible use of chemicals by the Soviets in Afghanistan — the Protocol has been religiously adhered to. Finally, in 1972, it evolved into the Biological Weapons

Convention, which completely prohibits the development, production, and stockpiling of bacteriological weapons and provides for their destruction, an agreement which is now adhered to by well over 100 nations. Furthermore, in 1983, when all U.S. and Soviet arms control talks were broken off, a comparable convention covering chemical weapons was tantalizingly close to agreement.

All of this indicates that a no-first-use agreement can be an extremely fruitful arms control approach. Nor does one need to be absolute about it: an agreement is already in force, covering the first-use of nuclear weapons against nations that foreswear the acquisition, deployment, or storage of such weapons on their territories. This pact has been an essential supportive element of the Non-Proliferation Treaty. Such partial arrangements can provide useful impetus for the eventual achievement of a complete no-first-use agreement and, ultimately, for a universal non-use agreement relating to nuclear weapons.

Clearly, there is no dearth of possibilities for "getting the ball rolling" on arms control. Nor do we have to depend on the pitifully slow negotiating process. As Ambassador George Kennan eloquently put it in his speech of acceptance of the 1982 Albert Einstein Peace Prize, an American president could, with complete impunity as to its military or strategic implications, announce the unilateral reduction of U.S. nuclear forces and delivery systems by a substantial fraction—even up to 50 percent.

This would be not only possible, but also politically effective, if accompanied by an invitation to the Soviets stating that, were they to follow suit within some specified, reasonable interval, we would be prepared to take reasonable further steps toward reduction and limitations. Nor would there be any problem in verifying, with the requisite accuracy, their acceptance of our invitation. We can already observe, thanks to our satellite capabilities, the construction of any new shack on the Siberian tundra, and this is only part of our ubiquitous verification capabilities.

The achievement of effective and drastic arms control and disarmament progress is no longer a technical problem; it is, today, entirely a political one. Whether, in light of the ongoing technological arms race, especially in relation to space, this situation will continue to prevail very much longer is open to some dispute.

Continuing pursuit of the illusory "Star Wars" capability would certainly undermine the present "open skies" situation—one that is more a result of parallel technical advances on both sides than of any diplomatic acumen on either side. The most important aspect of today's standoff in military space capabilities is the obvious fact that neither we nor the Soviets are capable of attaining any significant military advantage in this area. Why not, then, acknowledge our mutual need to remove space from the arena of military confrontation?

One thing is certain: given the political will on both sides, arrangements could be arrived at today that would effectively remove the Damoclean sword of nuclear disaster under which we have all been living for so long. If we can only muster the political courage to take these necessary steps, the coming 40 years could go down in history as a new Age of Enlightenment.

9

The Technological Imperative

Hans A. Bethe

The industrial revolution, and hence our present material well-being, was founded on technology. In its early days and for two centuries thereafter it was important to develop everything that was technologically possible. Now there are so many possibilities that choices must be made. In the civilian economy, these choices are generally made by the marketplace.

In war, likewise, technological superiority has counted since ancient times. There are many examples in previous wars, but most impressive was World War II. The Allies' superiority in radar was decisive, both in averting disaster and in ultimate victory.

World War II ended with Hiroshima and Nagasaki. Albert Einstein summed up the situation after the atomic bombs had been dropped: "Everything has changed, except human thinking."

For a brief period, the U.S. government's thinking did change. President Harry Truman in 1946 appointed a committee chaired by David Lilienthal to explore the possibilities of international control of all activities related to atomic weapons and atomic power. When the positive report of this committee was endorsed by then Undersecretary of State Dean Acheson, President Truman proposed, through Bernard Baruch, that the United Nations establish an international control agency. The Soviet Union, having worked on military applications of nuclear fission since 1943, turned down the proposal.

After this, however, human thinking returned to the pre-Hiroshima

patterns. The atomic bomb was incorporated into our arsenal as if
it were just another weapon. The Air Force built squadrons of bombers
equipped with atomic bombs, so that soon there were hundreds of
them. No thought was given to the demonstrable fact that just one
atomic bomb was enough to devastate a city.

For several years the United States had a monopoly in atomic
weapons. Then in 1949 the Soviets developed and tested their own.
The test was detected by U.S. planes equipped to pick up any radioactive debris that might be in the air. Many scientists (and others) had
expected that the Soviets would, sooner or later, develop an atomic
weapon. For instance, in 1945 Fred Seitz and I published an article
saying that "a determined country will be able to develop an atomic
weapon in 5 years." As a matter of fact, it took the Soviets only four.

A number of American scientists felt in 1949 that it was necessary
to stay ahead of the Soviets and, to this end, that the United States
should develop the hydrogen bomb. They found willing ears in Congress and in some parts of the Administration. President Truman was
bombarded with arguments on both sides of the question, but the
decisive news, which moved him to approve the development of the
H-bomb, was the discovery of the treason of Klaus Fuchs. When it
was shown that Fuchs had given the Soviets most of the information
he had about various parts of the Manhattan Project—including
whatever knowledge then existed about the possibility of hydrogen
bombs—Truman decided that it had become a technological imperative
for the United States to go ahead with the development of the vastly
more powerful weapon.

It soon became apparent that this task was not nearly as easy as
had been anticipated; the methods which had previously been considered simply were not promising. A new method had to be found,
and it was Edward Teller who devised one in the spring of 1951. As
is well known, that method was successfully tested in November 1952.
The Soviets tested a preliminary device in August 1953, and a more
developed one at the end of 1955. It is a matter of controversy whether
they would have developed an H-bomb if we had not done so.

Was Truman's decision really a technological imperative? What if
his decision had been in the negative and then the Soviets had confronted us with a test of their own H-bomb? A possible solution was
suggested just before our test in 1952, and was taken up again in 1983
by McGeorge Bundy in the *New York Review of Books*. We could have
announced that we would do the research leading to an H-bomb but
would not test it. A hydrogen bomb (in contrast to an atomic bomb)

is sufficiently complicated that nobody would consider adding it to the weapons stockpile without first testing it. And any test of an H-bomb in the atmosphere will be detected around the world.

An announcement of this kind would have led to two possibilities: either the world would have been spared this most devastating weapon, or some other country might have tested an H-bomb. Had such a test occurred, the United States would quickly have followed suit. We would then have been ready to develop the H-bomb as a weapon; and because of our great technological capacity, we probably would have obtained the ready-to-use weapon earlier than other countries. So it would have been possible for us to avoid this escalation in the arms race.

There would have been problems with this alternative path, one of them being the morale of the weapons laboratories. It is very discouraging to spend two or three years on the development of a completely new concept, and then to find that the concept could not even be tested, let alone be accepted into the U.S. weapons arsenal. I know this disappointment well, having worked at both a weapons laboratory and an industrial laboratory concerned with development of missiles. When the missile designed by the industrial laboratory was rejected by the Air Force in favor of that developed by another company, it was a most discouraging blow. However, if we wish to escape the vicious cycle of ever-increasing armaments, we have to find a way to make weapons laboratories operate without the certainty that what they develop will actually be used.

The next important step in the armaments race was the intercontinental ballistic missile. The Soviets were the first to test such a missile in 1957. Their test of an ICBM was soon followed by Sputnik, the first artificial satellite. We made a frantic effort to catch up, and I think that in this case it was indeed justified to feel a technological imperative. But then there was the question of how many we should deploy. Then Secretary of Defense Robert McNamara decided on 1,000, in keeping with the existing number of bombing planes and atomic bombs. Soon we found out through our intelligence satellites that the Soviets had deployed only a very few ICBMs. Knowing this, it would have been sensible for us to reduce the number of ICBMs to around 200, which might have mitigated the arms race in missiles. But once we had installed 1,000, it was obvious that the Soviets would follow their technological imperative and build a similar number.

The first ICBMs carried a single warhead. This made for a rather stable balance: If either the Soviet Union or the United States were to attempt a first strike by attacking the other country's ICBM silos, the attacking nation could at best expect to destroy one of the other country's ICBMs for every one of its own. In fact, since surely not all of them would hit their targets, making a first strike would actually be a disadvantage in the case of two evenly matched adversaries.

This "happy" stability was disturbed by the Soviets' technological imperative which led them to develop anti-ballistic-missile (ABM) systems. "We can hit a fly in space," said Khrushchev, and an ABM system was deployed around Moscow. In response, the United States developed penetration aids (decoys, chaff, and so on) and increased the number of its ICBMs targeted on Moscow, thus negating the protection given by the ABM.

But U.S. designers were sure they could do better; they could put several warheads on one missile. In this way, the Soviets could not tell whether the swarm of objects coming at Moscow or some other target was one warhead and many decoys, or whether it contained perhaps several warheads, all of which had to be engaged by their ABMs. With this argument, MIRVing (multiple independently targeted reentry vehicles) was sold to U.S. decision-makers—and its development became a technological imperative.

Fairly soon thereafter, in 1972, the ABM Treaty was concluded. In it the Soviet Union and the United States agreed that neither of them would build more than two ABM systems and that each of these systems would be limited in the number of anti-ballistic-missiles. Once that treaty was concluded, the United States would have been well advised to give up MIRVs. In fact, the Arms Control and Disarmament Agency warned that if we proceeded with building MIRVs the Soviets would follow suit, and they were much better equipped to do so because their missiles were much heavier than ours and could therefore take a larger number of MIRVs. But no serious attempt was made to prohibit MIRVs by means of a treaty with the Soviet Union.

Once we—and the Soviets—had MIRVs, there was no longer any strategic stability in the ICBM system. A potential aggressor could, with just a few of his missiles, wipe out a large number of the opponent's silos. Thus the development and installation of MIRVs was another example of the technological imperative being followed without regard for the consequences. MIRVs reduced the security of both sides because a first-strike counterforce attack was now, in principle, possible. In fact, many U.S. strategic planners in the early 1980s feared that our missile silos had become vulnerable to a Soviet attack, and they spoke of a "window of vulnerability." However, the Scowcroft Commission, appointed by President Reagan in 1983, concluded that while our ICBMs might indeed become vulnerable one had to consider the whole triad of our strategic weapons: missile-carrying submarines remained invulnerable, and therefore a Soviet first strike against our silos would still not disarm us.

The technological imperative is again upon us. In the last years much progress has been made in such areas as heat-seeking missiles, electro-optics, lasers (including X-ray lasers), and computers. On the basis of this progress, many claims have been made by scientists and engineers that a defense against missiles is now possible. Persuaded by these claims, President Reagan, on March 23, 1983, launched his Strategic Defense Initiative (SDI), popularly known as "Star Wars." The intention of this project is to intercept ballistic missiles before they reach their targets and thus gradually eliminate the threat of nuclear weapons carried by such missiles. Unfortunately, I and most of my colleagues who have looked into this problem are convinced that none of the proposed systems will work as advertised. They can, in fact, be defeated easily by countermeasures which will cost much less than it will cost to develop SDI. The technological imperative, however, is strong; our government feels that we must use this new technology in an attempt to reduce the threat of nuclear war. On the other hand, the Soviet Union has announced that it considers the project a threat to them, and therefore, unless negotiations can convince the Soviets to the contrary, SDI will lead to a new escalation in offensive weapons rather than to a decrease.

One of the pressures for developing the Strategic Defense Initiative comes from the weapons laboratories. Having recognized that there is little more to be done in improving offensive weapons, they are enthusiastic advocates of defensive weapons. And in this advocacy, they are finding a very receptive government.

An argument which is sometimes made is that the devellopment of weapons technology is needed to stay ahead in technology as such and that it will have a beneficial influence on peacetime technology. This surely has been the case in some instances, such as radar, which is now an essential navigation aid for commercial shipping and airlines. Likewise, the development of satellites has brought great civilian benefits. But today military technology demands such enormously sophisticated devices that it is highly unlikely that they will benefit the civilian economy to a substantial degree. On the contrary, the diversion of much scientific and engineering talent to military inventions has impoverished our civilian technology to a considerable extent. One reason for the great superiority of Japanese civilian technology in many fields is that the Japanese do not need to worry about military problems. I think that the redirection of engineering talents to civilian problems could very strongly benefit our own economy.

Whenever the technological imperative calls for new military devices, we should think very carefully about whether this particular development will contribute to the security of the United States and the world. In the case of MIRV it is clear that it did the opposite. I still consider the H-bomb a calamity. However, the nuclear submarine, whose "technological imperative" I did not recognize at the beginning of its development, has proved to be the best defense we have: ballistic-missile-launching submarines are the most invulnerable of our strategic weapons.

Preliminary considerations of the possible effects of new weapons systems should ideally take place at the level of the weapons laboratory. But the most important place for careful consideration of the possible effects of such systems is, of course, at the government level. A highly qualified group for such deliberations used to be the President's Science Advisory Committee. The ad hoc commissions appointed by President Reagan can also function well, provided their conclusions are not conditioned by previous decisions. Whatever group deliberates on the worth of a new weapons system should show restraint and should not lightly follow the technological imperative.

Atomic Culture

1

The Heyday of Myth and Cliché

Spencer R. Weart

"IT IS AN ATOMIC bomb. It is a harnessing of the basic power of the universe. The force from which the sun draws its power has been loosed against those who brought war to the Far East,"[1] President Truman's announcement struck the world with a mental shock comparable to the bomb itself exploding over Hiroshima. People could understand the news only in terms of what they already had in their heads, their hard-won stock of experience and ideas.

In fact there was no real experience, no carefully worked out set of ideas, to deal with the new weapon—yet when Truman said "atomic bomb," the world public immediately associated the news with certain long-established images which held important personal meanings for almost everyone. Nothing that happened afterward would greatly alter the way most people viewed the weapon.

Already for decades journalists had been writing articles about the fantastic energies hidden within the atom, and Truman's words about harnessing "the basic power of the universe" sounded like a 1930s newspaper Sunday supplement column. That was no accident. Truman had taken his statement from a committee chaired by his secretary of war, who adapted it from a draft forwarded by General Leslie Groves, who got it from a veteran newspaper reporter, William Laurence.[2]

Groves, having foreseen the need for such pronouncements, had carefully selected Laurence and then introduced him to the secrets of the Manhattan Project. The journalist had grown up with a conviction that science could give humanity unimaginable powers, akin to the powers of God himself. Already greatly impressed by prewar ideas about atomic energy, he could be expected to exclaim with awe and enthusiasm about the prodigies of Groves's project. Indeed, from the outset Laurence found the Project, as he said, a story comparable to the Second Coming of Christ. His awestruck feelings colored the draft statement he wrote for Truman, two months before the first bomb test and almost three months before the destruction of Hiroshima — that is, well before anyone had actually experienced what a nuclear weapon could do.

Laurence wrote a number of other reports before the bombing of Hiroshima, and on August 6, 1945 the War Department gave these to the press. Day after day newspapers talked on page one about "the great bomb, which harnesses the power of the universe." Otherwise the world had few facts to go on, and what little news did emerge seemed only to confirm that scientists had loosed something from beyond the mortal sphere. Reports from planes flying over Hiroshima and then Nagasaki told of square miles aflame, hidden by smoke. From the Japanese radio came cries of atrocity and stories of mangled corpses scattered everywhere. An American newsreel that went out swiftly to movie theaters exclaimed that Hiroshima was "pulverized," almost "wiped off the earth." It was "hellfire," cried the narrator, "violence described by eyewitnesses as Doomsday itself!" The newsreel said again and again that what scientists had harnessed was "cosmic power."[3]

By that time physicists were already beginning to suspect that nuclear forces are neither more nor less basic to the universe than are more familiar electrical forces, and that a release of nuclear energy is cosmic only in the same sense that the burning of a match is. But in 1945 not even scientists denied that there was something supremely mysterious, majestic, almost divine, in any manifestation of atomic energy. That was what scientists themselves had said from the outset.

The beginning was at the turn of the century, when radioactive changes within the cores of atoms, accompanied by a release of energy, were first understood by Ernest Rutherford and Frederick Soddy. Soddy in particular was immensely impressed; he told Rutherford that they had found something that went far beyond anything previously discovered. Soddy said it was nothing less than the secret of "transmutation"—a word that already meant a lot to him.[4]

What did transmutation signify? Soddy had been reading up on the history of chemistry, was fascinated by the visionary quest of ancient alchemists for the philosophers' stone that could transmute metals, and immediately compared his nuclear science discoveries with the transmutation that the alchemists had sought. The nonscientific press took up the idea with flamboyant enthusiasm, until even the level-headed Rutherford was speaking of nuclear physicists as the "new alchemists." But whenever the word "transmutation" was spoken it evoked resonances, echoing from unsuspected corridors in the public consciousness. For transmutation was at the center of a complex cluster of images that can be traced back to the earliest times. The imagery was not just a matter of getting rich through turning lead into gold. Beyond that it included a traditional symbolism, addressing the most important human ideas.

Soddy and others who studied the history of alchemy found that transmutation could mean not only chemical change but spiritual change. Alchemists saw the transmutation of base substances into gold as secondary, an aid and symbol for the transmutation of the soul. In their crucibles, substances were supposed to die and be reborn, undergoing a descent into corruption and putrefaction before they would, perhaps, be transformed. This could be a symbol for the agonizing descent into darkness that is necessary, many have believed, for any great psychological or spiritual transformation. It was a peril-ous process, for not everyone emerged from corruption. That was one reason why alchemists kept their craft a secret, forbidden to the profane. In short, the symbol of transmutation traditionally called to mind great human themes, important to everyone from childhood on: dangerous forbidden secrets and death itself; rebirth and transcendence.

Students of comparative mythology have found that this theme has a significance beyond the individual, corresponding with cosmic and social cycles. The descent of matter into decay parallels a coming time of chaos, a time in which evil will triumph, humanity will be victim-ized by wars and disasters, and in the extreme the entire universe will be destroyed. In Western culture this theme took form as a fear of Armageddon. Beyond that could come the millenium, all of society purified by fire and transmuted into perfection, into what was called — by no coincidence — the "Golden Age." In sum, there is abundant evidence that the moment the idea of transmutation is brought for-ward, we must deal with an ancient, associated symbolism involving personal and social transformation, hopes for the greatest conceivable things, and an array of possible dangers, up to and including the end of the world.[5]

By the nineteenth century these themes had become separated, surviving only as fragments scattered in various areas of modern culture. For example, ideas of an end of the world were taken up by astronomers in terms of an explosion of the sun and the like; ideas of a golden future age became associated with promises of scientific progress; ideas of forbidden secrets and magical working through corruption toward rebirth became associated with Frankenstein's monster and the golem. But after 1901 something unexpected happened. All the old ideas began to coalesce again around the original symbol of transmutation—or rather, around the new transmutation that involved atomic energy.

Scarcely a year after the discovery of radioactive transmutation, Soddy told the public that the energy locked within atoms was so great that the earth must be regarded as a storehouse of explosives. A man who could unleash this energy, he said, "could destroy the earth if he chose." Rutherford thought of the possibility of a chain reaction that would spread uncontrollably from atom to atom, and soon anyone who read the newspapers was familiar with his idea that "some fool in a laboratory might blow up the universe unawares."[6]

The idea was perpetuated over the next decades as noted scientists like Walther Nernst and Frédéric Joliot-Curie announced, in well-publicized speeches, that nuclear experiments might indeed provoke a chain reaction that would turn the planet into a new sun. The idea made little sense scientifically, for if the world really were so unstable, random radioactive combinations would long since have set off the disintegration. But the idea had a fascination that made even scientists hesitate. A few reporters and science fiction writers proposed that a foolish or wicked scientist might destroy not just the planet but the entire universe.

The stories that would be heard in later decades—the warnings that civilization or perhaps all life on earth might end through nuclear weapons—were not ideas that emerged as the number of actual bombs increased. If anything, the scenarios of the late twentieth century would be less apocalyptic than what Soddy and Rutherford offered at the century's beginning, drawing on ideas far older still.

Like these apocalyptic fears, gorgeous millennial hopes did not grow up along with atomic energy but attached themselves to it from the beginning. Soddy for example pointed out in 1909 that the energy in a few pounds of radioactive matter such as uranium could drive a steamship across the Atlantic. This example of scientific wonder-working was repeated by almost everyone who wrote about atomic energy during the following generation. For Soddy himself the tireless ship was only a prosaic beginning, for he insisted in a widely read book that "A race which would transmute matter . . . could transform a desert continent, thaw the frozen poles, and make the whole world one smiling Garden of Eden." This was, he hinted, exactly the sort of idea that he had met in his readings about medieval alchemy.[7]

By the 1930s it was a cliché that atomic energy might someday bring about an industrial revolution, a golden age of plenty. Of course, there was also the prospect of weapons, what H.G. Wells in 1913 was the first to call "atomic bombs."[8] Readers of science fiction stories and newspaper science columns became familiar with remarks about cities or entire civilizations smashed by such weapons. But many felt that if such all-powerful weapons were ever built, the human race would have to foreswear war, and therefore the atomic golden age would enjoy not only prosperity but peace. Thus to most people in the 1930s the prospect that scientists might eventually release atomic energy seemed—at least on the surface—a cause for hope.

Beneath the surface less attractive images were stirring. Doubts about the ability of scientists to use their discoveries wisely reached a huge audience mainly through fiction, stories of the mad scientist, such as Frankenstein, who meddled in forbidden secrets. Atomic energy was often mentioned in this connection. People were especially struck by the fact that atomic radiation can cause disease or cure it, and can bring about monstrous mutations. The irradiated giant insects of the 1950s horror movies and antinuclear cartoons of the 1970s were scarcely in evidence yet. Fiction writers concentrated on something more obviously derived from myths of transmutation: the alteration of human beings.

After Boris Karloff became famous in his role as Frankenstein's monster, for example, Universal Studios next cast him in the role of scientist. In a laboratory lashed by thunderstorms, he trespassed upon strange secrets and made amazing discoveries with atomic rays, meaning to work wonders for the benefit of humanity. But the scientist accidentally irradiated himself, began to glow in the dark, went mad, and lurched off on a murderous rampage. In his quest for transformation, he had lost control and become stuck at the nadir. Specifically, Karloff was transformed not just into an ordinary monster but into a creature overcome by, and embodying, atomic forces of virtually supernatural peril.[9]

Thus by the end of the 1930s, for most of the public, atomic energy had come to represent *more important things*. It was not just a plain property of matter; it stood for uncanny power that could transform the flesh and spirit. It was not just a potential source of weapons and industrial power; it stood for the coming of the end of the world or a Golden Age. Almost nobody noticed that beneath the surface of mad scientist movies, Buck Rogers comics and Sunday supplement articles, atomic energy was becoming a symbol for one of the most important of all themes: human control over the cosmic forces of death and life.

After August 6, 1945 this idea of mastering cosmic power—or perhaps, like Karloff, being mastered by it— popped up everywhere at once. The official American and British government statements, prepared in advance, dwelled on the need to control the dreadful discovery, while newspapers and radio announcers exclaimed over the incredible forces that scientists had "harnessed" or "unleashed."[10]

Was atomic energy itself a sort of monster? Certainly the War Department's report on the Trinity test of July 1945, the first description of an atomic explosion to reach the press, suggested a scene right out of the 1930s Universal Studios horror films: "Darkening heavens, pouring forth rain and lightning immediately up to the zero hour," set the stage for the towering atomic cloud. That was an exaggeration, for in fact the storm had passed hours before the test began. But a *New York Times* writer on August 7 caught the underlying image: "The experiment," he wrote, "was seen against a wild background where rain poured in torrents, and lightning pierced the sky up to the zero hour." Everyone, from reporters to statesmen, sounded like Universal scriptwriters, explaining that scientists had tampered with the unknown and released a forbidden secret.[11]

The new force was soon personalized. There were not many atomic bombs in all the talk during the next years; everyone spoke of *the* atomic bomb, or simply the Bomb, capitalized like a mythical deity. Cartoonists drew muscular genies escaping from bottles or brutal giants labelled "atomic power," looming over hapless scientists or politicians. The imagery could be more explicit: H.V. Kaltenborn, the mellow-voiced NBC radio pundit, larded his broadcast on August 6 with all the drama of secrets and awful powers. "For all we know," he concluded in hushed tones, "we have created a Frankenstein." This became a favorite term, heard everywhere from street corners to the U.S. Senate.[12]

I could parade endless examples of the old clichés that the new bombs dredged up, but instead I will defer to an authority. Mr. Arbuthnot, the fictional creation of humorist Frank Sullivan, in 1946 admitted that he was the leading "cliché expert" on the atom. No question could stump him. For example, he was asked:

Q. Where do we stand, Mr. Arbuthnot?

A: At the threshold of a new era. . . . Will civilization survive? Harness.

Q. Harness, Mr. Arbuthnot?

A. Harness and unleash. You had better learn to use those two words, my boy, if you expect to talk about the atom.

The cliché expert could also say just what had been harnessed, or unleashed: "The hidden forces of the universe. Vast . . . that's another word you'd better keep at hand." Mr. Arbuthnot easily identified whose stone atomic energy was: the philosophers' stone; and whose dream: the alchemists' dream; and, of course, whose monster. This virtuoso of the banal had no trouble summarizing the excited talk of 1945. After all, he could have given exactly the same answers a decade or two earlier.[13]

Mr. Arbuthnot, and the real-life cliché experts who staffed newspapers, magazines and radio networks worldwide, agreed that the central symbol was humanity standing at a crossroads. As the *Woman's Home Companion* put it a few years later, the choice was between "Paradise or Doomsday." If humanity took the correct road, we would soon come to the golden age promised in earlier years. Laurence told a huge radio audience that with the new energy, "We can turn deserts into blooming gardens. We can air condition the jungles and make the arctic wastes livable . . . and we can lick disease." And of course atoms would drive ships across the ocean with only a little fuel—"a lump the size of a pea," said Mr. Arbuthnot: "The pea is the accepted vegetable in these explanations."[14]

Atomic bombs themselves mightily strengthened the old idea that nuclear energy could almost automatically solve every social problem, including war. Two bombs had apparently ended the war against Japan all by themselves. In mid-1945 most people had expected the fighting to go on for many more bloody months, and now atomic bombs seemed to have forestalled that as if by a stroke of magic. Americans in particular were heartily pleased with the new triumph of Yankee know-how, although British, French, Russians, and even Germans and Japanese were anxious to point out that discoveries by their scientists had also played a part. An uneducated Virginia farmer spoke a common American feeling: "When the bomb fell, we had peace. . . . I never was so proud of something in my life as I was when it fell."[15]

Yet even the farmer admitted worrying about what would happen if other nations learned the secret of making atomic bombs. When newspapers, including the sober *New York Times,* editorialized that atomic energy could make the world "a paradise," they automatically noticed the other way leading from the crossroads: we might eventually "blow ourselves and perhaps the planet itself to drifting dust." This was not merely fear of the destruction of cities, or of civilization, or even of all human life, though such talk was common enough. That old bugbear, the runaway chain reaction which could explode a planet, also cropped up everywhere. A prominent U.S. senator voiced the worry that fission might turn the earth into a new sun, and two 1947 movies repeated the thought in passing. A poll found that a quarter of all Americans thought it likely that atom-smashing experiments would someday destroy the entire world.[16]

A few cultists and crackpots, in America and elsewhere, began to speak of apocalypse. Atomic bombs, they held, proved that the end foretold in biblical revelation was on its way. There had always been a few people preparing for doomsday, but from 1945 on the most sober leaders, from presidents to popes, spoke in language that evoked such thoughts. As sociologist Edward Shils remarked, atomic bombs made a bridge across which apocalyptic fantasies, marching from their refuge among fringe groups, invaded all of society.[17]

Armageddon or Golden Age: either way the message was that atomic energy was so far beyond anything humanity could imagine that the matter must be dealt with in an altogether new way. Standing at the fateful crossroads, surely people could be persuaded to take the path toward miraculous new life rather than utter death? Hardly anyone observed that there might be other paths lying between the two highways—obscure and confusing trails that struck cross-country to a future where atomic energy would neither annihilate nor redeem us.

In the years after 1945 there would never be much real experience to set against the imagery of apocalypse. Photographs and eyewitness accounts arrived from Hiroshima, but these only reinforced the view that atomic energy was capable of doing almost anything. And in any case, hydrogen bombs soon followed, a thousand times mightier than fission weapons, and it became plain that the events in Japan had been closer to what other cities had experienced in World War II fire-bombings than to what a nation might expect in a future war.

The world's good fortune in escaping modern nuclear war had one unfortunate effect: when the public tried to see nuclear energy, there was little to look at except the usual archaic myths. From 1945 into the 1980s very few people saw atomic energy as a physical fact, something that might be handled with much the same commonsense methods as facts about oil reserves or chemical poisons. Most of us persisted in approaching the subject instead with feelings of awe and terror, little different from what we might feel if confronted with a mad scientist's monster or a divine apocalypse. We have relied on strange ideas and imagery, only loosely connected with reality, that have swayed people's thinking since the days of alchemy.

1. *New York Times,* Aug. 7, 1945, p. 4.

2. Interview of William L. Laurence by Louis M. Starr, 1956–57, Columbia University Library, New York; Laurence, "Tentative Draft of Radio Address by President Truman" (May 17, 1945), file 4; Groves to Chief of Staff (Aug. 6, 1945), file 5B; "Top Secret" correspondence of the Manhattan Engineer District, RG 77 and microfilm 1108, National Archives, Washington, D.C.

3. "Atom Bomb," Paramount newsreel (Aug. 1945), text courtesy of Public Information Office, Argonne National Laboratory, Argonne, Illinois.

4. Muriel Howorth, *Pioneer Research on the Atom: The Life Story of Frederick Soddy* (London: New World, 1958), pp. 83–84; Soddy to Rutherford (Aug. 7, 1903), Rutherford correspondence, Cambridge, microfilms at Archives for History of Quantum Physics repositories including Niels Bohr Library, American Institute of Physics, New York City.

5. Mircea Eliade, *The Forge and the Crucible: The Origins and Structure of Alchemy* (New York: Harper and Row, 1962).

6. F. Soddy, "Some Recent Advances in Radioactivity," *Contemporary Review,* 83 (May 1905): pp. 708–20; W.C.D. Whetham to Rutherford, July 26, 1903, Rutherford correspondence.

7. F. Soddy, "The Energy of Radium," *Harper's Monthly,* 120 (Dec. 1909), p. 56; *The Interpretation of Radium* (London: Murray, 3d ed., 1912), p. 251.

8. H.G. Wells, "The World Set Free: A Story of Mankind," *English Review* (1913–1914).

9. *The Invisible Ray,* released by Universal Studios (1936).

10. For example, Lyle Van, NBC News (Aug. 6, 1945), recording R78: 0344, Museum of Broadcasting, New York City.

11. War Department release, in Henry D. Smyth, *Atomic Energy for Military Purposes* (Princeton, N.J.: Princeton University Press, 1946); *New York Times,* Aug. 7, 1945, p. 1.

12. H.V. Kaltenborn, NBC radio (Aug. 6, 1945), R78:0345, Museum of Broadcasting.

13. Frank Sullivan, "The Cliché Expert Testifies on the Atom," in *A Rock in Every Snowball* (Boston: Little, Brown, 1946), pp. 28–36.

14. William L. Laurence, "Paradise or Doomsday?" *Woman's Home Companion,* 75 (May 1948), pp. 32ff; Laurence on "The Quick and the Dead" (NBC radio and RCA Victor Records, 1950); Sullivan, op. cit., p.31.

15. Leonard S. Cottrell, Jr., and Sylvia Eberhart, *American Opinion on World Affairs in the Atomic Age* (Princeton, N.J.: Princeton University Press, 1948; reprinted New York: Greenwood, 1969), p. 67.

16. *New York Times,* Aug. 18, 1945, p. 10; Senator Richard Russell, quoted in Harry S. Hall, *Congressional Attitudes towards Atomic Energy* (New York: Arno, 1979), pp. 44–45; *The Beginning of the End* (Metro-Goldwyn-Mayer film, 1947); *A Matter of Life and Death* (*Stairway to Heaven*) (Janus, 1947).

17. Edward A. Shils, *The Torment of Secrecy: The Background and Consequences of American Security Policies* (Glencoe, Ill.: Free Press, 1956), p. 71.

2

Lost in Space

Alan P. Lightman

M y first face-to-face meeting with scientists working on space weapons happened on a visit to the Hudson Institute in January 1979. Jimmy Carter was still in the White House, and Ronald Reagan's "Star Wars" speech was more than four years down the road.

After strolling across the serene and spacious grounds of the Institute, which is nestled in a bucolic setting overlooking the Hudson River, I was led into the cozy office of a physicist who could scarcely wait to tell me about new developments in "particle beam" weapons, to be stationed aboard orbiting satellites in space. After a vivid description of intense beams piercing earthward from above, he excitedly showed me some artists' sketches of what the things might look like and, as I recall, even had a papier-mâché model, which he let me hold briefly. For a moment I got caught up in the air of derring-do and wondered what Santa might bring *me* next year.

That childlike and visceral attraction to the new generation of nuclear weapons in space is real, dangerous, and seldom discussed. The technical issues, on the other hand, have received a lot of attention. To summarize briefly, there is a growing consensus among most weapons experts that a space-based ballistic missile defense system is probably not workable for another 20 years and, even if eventually deployed, would be costly and destabilizing. In the words of Hans Bethe, the needed technologies are "far beyond the state of the art."

While countermeasures, like decoys and hardened boosters, appear abundant and relatively cheap, the price of a working system would be staggering. To aim a defensive laser beam at the soft parts of a missile thousand of miles away requires the angular resolution of the upcoming (and peaceable) space telescope, which runs to a billion dollars. One hundred ballistic missile defense satellites would be needed to give adequate coverage of the Soviet Union, adding up to at least several hundred billion dollars, not to mention the incalculable cost of a new arms race likely to follow.

Once operational, an effective space-based system, in unison with offensive weapons, could give the deployer a first-strike capability, inviting preemptive attack by the other side. The high vulnerability of such a system further encourages attack. And any orbiting weapon in space, offensive or defensive, threatens the surveillance and communications satellites used since the early 1960s and considered vital for national security. All of the above arguments apply whether the ballistic missile defense system is nuclear or not. A nuclear space-based ballistic missile defense system would, in addition, violate the 1967 Outer Space Treaty and the 1972 Anti-Ballistic Missile Treaty. When it comes to nuclear weapons, all agreements between the United States and the Soviets seem especially precious. These are a few of the technical worries.

Technical issues aside, however, the glamor of Star Wars still shimmers and beckons. Millions of us, children and grownups alike, saw the movie and were mesmerized by images of death-dealing laser rays, sleek aircraft shooting it out in space, and handsome young men battling the forces of evil. These heady visions seep into the unconscious and resonate with the leftover daydreams of little boys. The space age is here at last, and no one—teacher or businessman or senator —wants to be left behind. "Seize the high ground before the Russians do" is a familiar bugle call from the Air Force, which established its Space Command in 1982.

Scientists are needed to work on these things and scientists, as C.P. Snow has reminded us, are not much different from other people. The team of fighter jocks immortalized in Tom Wolfe's *The Right Stuff* seem to have been curiously reincarnated in the dozen or so young physicists "pushing back the edge" in space weapons design in "O Group" at Lawrence Livermore National Laboratory.

Profiled in William Broad's book *Star Warriors,* these intellectual test pilots are mostly in their twenties and are all male. They inhabit a world of empty Coke bottles and all-night bouts with top-secret research and share an admiring respect for each other's brain power. A "right stuff" ethic flourishes in all areas of science. But in O-group this is combined with the glamor of space, the thrill of inventing new kinds of nuclear weapons, and youthful idealism.

Says O-group physicist Lawrence West, age 28, "We can try to negotiate treaties and things like that. But one thing I can do personally, without having to wait for arms control, is to develop the technology to eliminate them myself, to eliminate offensive nuclear weapons." What more dangerous creature than the inexperienced macho, armed here with pencil and paper? Chuck Yeager, Gordon Cooper, and John Glenn all prided themselves on hanging their hides over the edge. How much hide-hanging has been done and can be done by the fellows of O-Group? None has seen a nuclear explosion. Since the 1963 Test Ban Treaty, there haven't been any, above ground. Even the few old men of my generation, in their mid-thirties, were born after World War II, after Hiroshima and Nagasaki, and learned about the Manhattan Project from books.

A related motive to watch closely is the love of technology for its own sake: from greeting cards that sing Happy Birthday when opened to F-15s that turn corners at greater acceleration than pilots can endure. In theoretical physicists, this translates into pursuit of intellectually interesting problems—wherever they lead. As West says proudly, "The number of new weapon designs is limited only by one's creativity." Compare Robert Oppenheimer's comment 30 years ago: "When you see something that is technically sweet you go ahead and do it and you argue about what to do about it only after you have had your technical sweetness."

It is difficult to find fault with the argument that basic research in space weapons should continue. We had better at least find out what the laws of physics allow. Most likely the Soviets will. And it is conceivable, as the Harvard Nuclear Study Group and Freeman Dyson have suggested, that our security in the long term might best be served by replacing our current nuclear strategy of mutually assured destruction with one of defense, possibly from space.

Research should continue—but soberly, with both feet on the ground. Earthbound ICBMs, waiting silent and preprogrammed in their Midwest silos, are dreamlike enough. Weapons orbiting in space dissolve almost completely into a mist of make-believe.

Sirens of the unconscious call us to Star Wars: glamor, novelty, childhood fantasies, macho power, technical narcissism. It would seem wise to bring these psychological motives into daylight, to attach as much importance to them as to the technical issues. The weapons themselves are unthinking, but their creation and deployment spring from the human mind.

3

A View from the Weapons Labs

Michael M. May

To understand and appraise the role of the nuclear weapons laboratories we must examine the historical and policy context in which they operate. Within this context, it is clear that the U.S. and Soviet governments have recognized that nuclear war would yield either side nothing but overwhelming destruction. Yet, under the world political system that both have inherited, such a war remains a possibility. No one can be sure that the crises and conflicts that might generate it can all be foreseen and averted.

In response, the two countries have evolved somewhat similar pragmatic approaches to the problem of avoiding nuclear war and the circumstances that might lead to it. These approaches consist, in the main, of maintaining invulnerable nuclear forces sufficient to deny the possibility of meaningful victory to the attacker under any circumstances, while acting cautiously where the opponent's vital interests are perceived to lie.[1]

Both sides have been firm in demarcating and defending these areas of vital interest: at times, wisely; at times, as in Eastern Europe, with tragic consequences. Both sides have learned to recognize these areas. Yet it is in the very process of demarcating these areas that we have come closest to war; and it is in the process of limiting their (very different) geographical and ideological expansionism that the two sides have exercised the most caution.

As pursued by the two nations rather than as advocated by some of its supporters, arms control has been a part of the cautious approach to matters involving vital interests adopted by the United States and the Soviet Union. The weapons systems banned or limited, and the areas of deployment denied, have been those which, in the view of both governments, contributed little to additional deterrence, but which had the potential for worsening the relationship and for taking money needed for other uses.

The purpose of arms control, apart from propaganda, is to avoid mistakes, political as well as military, rather than to change the basic relationship of cautious, armed deterrence. Avoiding mistakes is perhaps the single most important precondition to avoiding a war that nobody wants, so arms control is a necessary ingredient of such a policy.

The policy described has the advantage of recognizing nuclear weapons and international relationships for what they are, but it is not ethically or intellectually satisfying to many people. For one thing, it does not by itself improve the international system under which we all live, a system which has historically been dangerously unreliable. For another, it does little to assuage the feelings of those to whom nuclear weapons have become symbols of what they deem wrong with our civilization—symbols of human talents dangerously misused and corrupted.

I share the first objection and have attempted elsewhere to make some preliminary suggestions about it.[2] The second objection lies, I believe, at the root of disagreements about the proper role of scientists, and specifically of weapons laboratory scientists.

Nuclear weapons are both symbols and pieces of hardware. Their role as symbols is what matters to most people, including scientists, most of the time. Nuclear weapons symbolize different things to different people. To some, as we have noted, they symbolize misspent talents and dangerously obsolete institutions. Others, including myself, have a less apocalyptic view of the modern world. But no one's view of nuclear weapons is free of misgivings.

To most people in the U.S. and Soviet defense establishments, and probably to most U.S. and Soviet citizens, the weapons symbolize an ultimate recourse, one that everyone hopes will never be used, but which the governments see, rightly or wrongly, as necessary to discharge the very responsibilities which their citizens lay upon them. At the same time, they symbolize, to many of the same people, a dangerous and irrational arms race.

Weapons laboratory scientists share to various degrees these and other perceptions of nuclear weapons and support a variety of policy initiatives. In addition, however, they are faced with nuclear weapons as pieces of hardware to an extent very few others are.

From the hardware point of view, the laboratories' nuclear warhead designs must contribute to or make possible the survivability of strategic systems. This requirement has led and continues to lead to changes in order to develop new and less vulnerable missiles as well as to improve the operability, safety, and other factors of the systems. Old missiles and warheads are retired as new ones are deployed. Much of the improvement in strategic survivability has hinged on new warhead designs from the laboratories. Similar requirements come from tactical deployments. Compatibility with survivable deployments, operability, better safety and security, and so on provide the objectives for the laboratories' work.

Weapons hardware suffers from the same difficulties as other hardware. The materials used are chemically and radiologically active. The components degrade. Sometimes they can be replaced without nuclear tests, sometimes not. Sometimes the effects of stockpile aging are sudden and surprising. With or without testing, much laboratory work goes to maintaining the stockpile.

The laboratories devote much effort to finding out whether nuclear explosives can be put to significantly different military uses. Strategic defensive uses are a recent case in point. The laboratories also investigate new or overlooked nuclear effects. Nuclear winter, which was of course discovered elsewhere, as well as new radiobiological efficiencies for neutrons, are recent examples of such effects, while radioactive rainout is an earlier example.

Finally, the laboratories maintain continuing investigations of the underlying technologies necessary to design and evaluate nuclear weapons. As do most applied sciences, nuclear weapons design generates the need to understand aspects of physics, chemistry, and engineering that have not been previously investigated.

The laboratories carry out nuclear testing programs for all the reasons that scientists might expect: to verify the adequacy of changes in design, to investigate new concepts, to measure fundamental physical quantities, and, in cooperation with the Defense Nuclear Agency, to measure nuclear effects. Again, the special conditions under which nuclear test measurements are made cause the laboratories to develop new instrumentation and measurement techniques. These hardware-related activities are what Congress, the executive branch, and most citizens expect the laboratories to do. They do not fit neatly into any one symbolic or strategic role.

Thus, the changes in nuclear weapons and the nuclear tests that made submarine-launched nuclear missiles possible extended the arms race, but made deterrent forces far more survivable against attack. The changes and tests that made MIRVs possible made first strikes against fixed ICBMs more effective, but they also made ABM systems less effective and helped pave the way for the ABM Treaty of 1972. The changes and the nuclear tests that might make strategic defenses possible could be used to help deterrence, but they could also be used to help an aggressor. A tested, reliable stockpile can serve both deterrer and first-striker.

Because U.S. weapons laboratory personnel are not government employees, present and former laboratory personnel can be found on various sides of the debates over defense and arms control policies, a situation which is not replicated in any other country, Western or Eastern. Nuclear weapons laboratory employees have stated that there was no evidence that the Soviet Union was cheating on the threshold nuclear test ban;[3] have supported the comprehensive nuclear test ban;[4] have opposed systems in the course of deployment;[5] and have, of course, also taken positions more favorable to defense efforts. Valuable as this ability to participate in the public debate is, it does not relieve laboratory scientists of the responsibility to make the conclusions that must be drawn from the hardware aspects of nuclear weapons as plain as possible.

From the hardware point of view, more nuclear tests are needed rather than fewer. The number and kinds of tests permitted result from a political compromise which may be wise or unwise, but which in any case has hardware-related costs, as Herbert F. York, a former laboratory director who is a strong advocate of the comprehensive nuclear test ban and of nuclear disarmament, has stated.[6] These costs must be pointed out even to audiences which are predisposed politically to favor test bans. Also from the hardware point of view, it is the laboratories' job to propose new alternatives for discharging military missions. This is sometimes welcomed by the military services, sometimes opposed by them. It may be said of this activity that the laboratories are driving the "qualitative arms race."

But what is this qualitative arms race? If it is a process of replacing older systems by new ones which will do a better job of strategic deterrence, or of tactical deterrence in Europe, or of strategic defense — assuming this to be a desirable addition to our posture — then we accepted that process when we decided to accept armed deterrence in the first place. We can hope to cut numbers of weapons systems to a minimum and avoid deployments that will not add to deterrence or defense; but we cannot hope to avoid technical change, nor can we expect that the laboratories will not play a role in this change.

Many misgivings about the laboratories' role in the defense establishment stem from a belief that, while deterrence may be necessary, the United States and the Soviet Union have far too much in the way of nuclear weaponry for the needs of that task. The excess, it is thought, detracts from both countries' security.

The present dimensions of the nuclear deterrent were established at times when the two sides were repeatedly and dangerously testing each other in areas such as Berlin, Cuba, the Middle East: areas where the two sides considered that they had major interests. Thus, it became important to deter both conventional and nuclear options for changing the status quo by force in these areas.

In the estimate of most people who have participated in this aspect of government on both sides, the need is to avoid war of any kind, as well as crises serious enough to make war a plausible alternative, and not just to deter nuclear attacks on homelands.[7] Once crises or conventional wars become so severe that either side has reason to think the other might strike it, much of the stability of deterrence is lost.

Thus nuclear weapons, in concert with other arms, should provide a sort of extended deterrent, the cautionary impact of which must be felt before crises are reached. At the same time, they must not provoke or exacerbate crises. As a result, neither cutbacks nor increases in hardware will lead automatically to a safer situation. We must look carefully at the interplay of arms decisions with the institutions involved if we want to enhance safety.

Nuclear weapons were bound to come. Our physics world and our political world would have conspired to bring them about, if not at Alamogordo and Hiroshima, then elsewhere. Robert Oppenheimer and company were not any more responsible than anyone else for bringing in the atomic age. We all build atomic bombs, as we all build the institutions that demand them.

How will improvement come? The fundamental goal is the attainment of a more widespread realization that security exists only if it is shared by those we regard as our enemies. Weapons hardware restrictions play a role in bringing this goal about, but weapons hardware also provides the spur to make progress. The laboratories' role in this process is unlikely to please every part of the political spectrum. It must be guided by the centrist compromise which the country has chosen and which I think is the only sensible route.

1. For a clear presentation of the goals of U.S. strategic capability, see Harold Brown, Department of Defense, "Annual Report for Fiscal Year 1980," pp. 74 ff.

2. Michael May, "The U.S.-Soviet Approach to Nuclear Weapons," *International Security*, 9, no. 4 (Spring 1985).

3. Gerald E. Marsh, "No Evidence of Cheating," *Bulletin* (March 1983), p. 4.

4. Hugh E. DeWitt, "Labs Drive the Arms Race," *Bulletin* (Nov. 1984), pp. 40–42.

5. John D. Immele, "A Missile Deal for Europe — and Beyond," *Washington Post* (Jan. 13, 1984), p. A23.

6. Herbert York, "Nuclear Weapon Test Bans," in *Arms Control in Transition, Proceedings of the Livermore Arms Control Conference* (Boulder, Colorado: Westview Press, 1983), pp. 71–78.

7. For further discussions see G. Allison, A. Carnesale, J. Nye, eds., *Hawks, Doves, and Owls: An Agenda for Avoiding Nuclear War* (New York: W.W. Norton, 1985). This point was also made by Konstantin Chernenko (*Pravda*, March 3, 1984), one of a number of similar statements by Soviet leaders over many years. For a general examination of Soviet views about the uses of military power in the nuclear age, see David Holloway, *The Soviet Union and the Arms Race,* (New Haven, Conn.: Yale University Press, 1983).

4

Labs Drive the Arms Race

Hugh E. DeWitt

For 27 years I have been a physicist on the staff of the Lawrence Livermore National Laboratory, one of the two U.S. weapons design laboratories. From this vantage point I have reached the conclusion that the scientists in these laboratories are a major force in driving and perpetuating the nuclear arms race.

Behind this driving force and its great influence on national policy decisions is a strong belief held by many members of the laboratories' management structures that high technology can provide safety and national security in a dangerous world. Coupled with this belief that technological solutions are paramount over political solutions is a high degree of enthusiasm for possible new technologies that will supposedly keep the United States militarily ahead of the Soviet Union. The consequence of this faith in technology is that weapons scientists have had great influence with every Administration since World War II. A respected senior American statesman, George Kennan, has stated:

> Over all these years the competition in the development of nuclear weaponry has proceeded steadily, relentlessly, without the faintest regard for all these warning voices. We have gone on piling weapon upon weapon, missile upon missile, new levels of destructiveness upon old ones. . . . And the result is that today we have achieved, we and the Russians together, in numbers of these devices, in their means of delivery, and above all their destructiveness, levels of

redundancy of such grotesque dimensions as to defy rational understanding.[1]

Kennan's statement can be understood better when one realizes how powerful and influential the nuclear weapons establishment is in this country. And the Soviet nuclear establishment may well be equally influential with the top Soviet leaders.

Inside the weapons laboratories even the most enthusiastic nuclear bomb designers often express a belief in "deterrence" as the main purpose of nuclear weapons development. One hears such statements as: "We design and build these weapons so that they will never be used." Yet if this view is a basic credo for many weapons scientists, managerial sentiment in the laboratories appears to be that there are never enough designs of nuclear weapons for deterrence.

The laboratories have devised, designed, lobbied for, and developed an incredible array of strategic and tactical nuclear warheads, ranging from multimegaton monsters to small nuclear landmines that can be carried on the back of one infantry soldier. Yet in spite of the mature state of nuclear weapons technology, the managers see no end to their work. There are always new designs to be developed and tested for new delivery systems; old weapons designs to be modernized; and possible new ideas for weapons technology to be researched and developed over many years, such as the nuclear-pumped X-ray laser as a potential defense against enemy missiles. Thus in the name of deterrence the weapons laboratories feel impelled to continue indefinitely the design of new weapons, unimpeded by any restrictive nuclear arms control treaties. And the runaway arms race between the superpowers continues with no foreseeable letup.

My own conclusions, after many years in the weapons establishment, are quite contrary to the general attitudes found at the top levels of the laboratories. I believe that if the danger of nuclear war is to be reduced and national security improved, then political agreements between the nuclear powers are more conducive to safety than uninhibited technological competition. Specifically, a number of constructive steps can be taken:

Ratification at last of a number of useful arms control treaties of recent years, such as SALT II and the Threshold Test Ban Treaty of 1974.

Resumption of negotiations toward an end to nuclear weapons testing, resulting in either a Comprehensive Test Ban Treaty, or at least a threshold treaty that prohibits explosions of more than one or two kilotons.

Serious negotiations as soon as possible to ban further development of anti-satellite weapons. This very dangerous new technology can be stopped now; in a couple of years it will be too late.

The proposed massive new strategic defense initiative — the "Star Wars" program described by President Reagan in his March 23, 1983 speech — should be stopped now so as to prevent a major new round of the arms race in space.

Existing arms control treaties, such as the 1972 Anti-Ballistic Missile Treaty, should be reaffirmed and strengthened.

An end to nuclear weapons testing is the central point. The unratified Threshold Test Ban Treaty, which limits underground tests to not more than 150 kilotons, has not been a serious restriction, since there are a number of proven bomb designs in the megaton range, and the weapons laboratories have apparently not yet felt any urgent need for further tests in that category. The threat of a complete end to nuclear testing posed by a Comprehensive Test Ban Treaty is another matter,[2] and the labs have a 25-year record of strong opposition to such an agreement.[3]

An end to nuclear testing, whether by a comprehensive treaty or a very low threshold treaty, would effectively stop the development of new varieties of current nuclear weapons, as it is unlikely that a new bomb design would be stockpiled without adequate explosive testing.

The cessation of nuclear testing by the two superpowers is also the most reasonable way to put political pressure on smaller nations not to develop their own nuclear arsenals. Further proliferation of nuclear weapons seems likely unless the superpowers can agree to end the testing and development of the already huge stockpiles of sophisticated nuclear weapons.

Another reason for putting an end to nuclear testing is that it would prevent the development of such bizarre concepts as the directed energy weapons intended as part of Reagan's Star Wars proposals. And finally, a comprehensive test ban would strengthen the fragile base of existing arms control treaties and perhaps lead to a political climate that would make it possible to negotiate agreements leading to reductions of the present bloated nuclear arsenals.

The weapons laboratories' opposition to a real nuclear test ban is based on what the Soviets might do in the future and on the perceived need for further testing in order to maintain and modernize our own arsenal. The fear of clandestine Soviet weapons activities after a test ban leads naturally to complex questions of adequate treaty verification. But the possible yield of nuclear explosions that might be masked by testing underground is in the range of a few kilotons. Indeed, seismologists Lynn Sykes and Jack Evernden argue that with an array of unmanned seismometers in the Soviet Union it is now possible to detect all explosions tamped in hard rock down to a small fraction of a kiloton.[4]

Even if the Soviets do try to cheat by continuing a clandestine testing program in cavities, the biggest bomb they can hope to hide successfully is only about five kilotons. Furthermore, recent work indicates that even decoupled (muffled) explosions can be detected by using higher frequency seismic waves.[5] Seismological detection is now good enough to make verification of a realistic nuclear test ban treaty no longer a serious problem.

The other class of argument used by the weapons laboratories to oppose an end to nuclear testing is the fear that without such testing the United States' weapons stockpile will be unreliable. Hence, our deterrent capability would decline. One part of this argument is that since nuclear warheads degrade chemically, after, say, 15 to 20 years, they must be replaced by remanufactured copies of the original proven designs. But because of the sophistication and complexity of modern nuclear weapons design, there is no certainty that the copy will work satisfactorily. But some weapons experts deny the need for proof testing. Norris Bradbury, Carson Mark, and Richard Garwin wrote to President Carter in 1978 in support of a comprehensive test-ban treaty: "It has been rare to the point of non-existence for a problem revealed by the sampling and inspection program to require a *nuclear* test for its resolution."[6]

Weapons laboratory spokesmen also fear that, in the event of a real test-ban treaty, weapons design experts now employed in the two U.S. weapons laboratories will move to other, more interesting jobs. It has even been suggested that nuclear testing must continue, if only to provide exciting work to keep these experts happy in the laboratories and thus insure maintenance of a reliable U.S. stockpile. To me, such arguments are suspect and even self-serving. The laboratories oppose a comprehensive test ban because they want to continue nuclear weapons development—to refine existing designs and do research in exciting new areas such as the X-ray laser.

Nuclear weapons technology for many years has been a mature technology. Current designs of fission and thermonuclear weapons are reaching the limits of what is possible. Thus the labs are looking eagerly toward major new weapons concepts, intended ultimately for use in space against Soviet missile attack. Indeed, the new ideas for at least the nuclear portion of Star Wars all originated at Livermore.

As simply a research effort into possibilities for creating directed energy devices, the program might be reasonably harmless. The Star Wars program, however, was announced with great fanfare by President

Reagan, the proposals have now been blessed by the Defense Department's Fletcher Panel, and a budget of $26 billion has been proposed for the coming five years. This is already a massive program with its own momentum, and the weapons laboratories will benefit greatly if it continues.

There are consequences beyond a possible enormous waste of money. The Livermore Laboratory is already said to have successfully tested the X-ray laser pumped by underground nuclear explosions.[7] If this work continues, and the device looks like a potential weapon against Soviet missiles and satellites, it will ultimately have to be tested in space rather than underground in Nevada. Such testing will violate the 1967 Space Treaty and the 1972 ABM Treaty. Thus the drive to develop even "defensive" nuclear weapons for use in space will almost certainly lead to the abrogation of the ABM Treaty.

At that point the fragile structure of today's arms control treaties is likely to disintegrate completely. The Soviets will certainly not stand still while the Americans develop a nuclear shield in addition to maintaining their present large offensive nuclear capability. In a few years the Soviets can be expected to follow with the same kind of "defensive" program. Furthermore, they will make every effort to upgrade in quantity and quality their own offensive weapons and to work out the many methods that can foil our defense. This space race will eventuate in some kind of parity both in offensive nuclear weapons that are known to work and in defensive nuclear weapons of questionable utility. The existing arms control treaties are the likely first victims of this next level of the arms race.

The incredible expense of the proposed Star Wars weapons will be extremely damaging to the economies of both countries, and this is not likely to foster trust and cooperation between the superpowers. I find this prospect of an arms race in space very frightening because it can easily increase the risk of a nuclear war while failing to provide the protection to civilians set forth by President Reagan.

For all of these reasons, the enthusiasm of the weapons laboratories for both old and new nuclear weapons technology should be curbed by the United States' political leaders. The Americans and the Soviets would be much better off now if in 1963 Kennedy and Khrushchev had negotiated a complete ban on all nuclear explosions. A test ban in this decade would still be of great help in reducing the danger to the world. The scientists in the weapons laboratories may sincerely believe that their products will protect us. Instead, they may kill us all.

1. George Kennan, "How to Break the Nuclear Impasse: A Modest Proposal," *New York Review of Books* (July 16, 1981).

2. Hugh E. DeWitt, "Debate on a Comprehensive Nuclear Weapons Test Ban: Pro," *Physics Today* (Aug. 1983), p. 24.

3. Glenn Seaborg, *Kennedy, Khrushchev, and the Test Ban* (Berkeley: University of California Press, 1981).

4. L. Sykes and J. Evernden, *Scientific American* (Oct. 1982), p. 47.

5. J.F. Evernden, C.B. Archambeau, E. Cranswick, "An Up-Dated Evaluation of Seismic Decoupling," report presented at a Verification Conference, MIT (Feb. 1–3, 1984).

6. Nicholas Wade, "Defense Scientists Differ on Nuclear Stockpile Testing," *Science*, 201 (Sept. 22, 1978), p. 1105.

7. Clarence A. Robinson, Jr., "Advance Made on High-Energy Laser," *Aviation Week and Space Technology (AWSP)*, (Feb. 23, 1981), pp. 25–27; "Panel Urges Defense Technology Advances, *AWSP* (Oct. 17, 1983), pp. 16–18; "Study Urges Exploiting of Technologies," *AWSP* (Oct. 24, 1983), pp. 50–57; "Shuttle May Aid in Space Weapons Test," *AWSP* (Oct. 31, 1983), pp. 74–78.

5

Nuclear Power

David J. Rose

C ivilian nuclear electric power today is both successful and unsuccessful, in ways that are astonishingly different from many expectations of only a decade ago. In the United States, for example, with one-third of the world's installed nuclear power capacity, many reactors are running well; some have recently come into service almost on time and almost within budget. However, many others have been canceled or are now likely to be canceled, far over budget and long delayed. And the projections made in the late 1960s for 1,000 gigawatts (one GW is a billion watts) of installed capacity by the year 2000 have been revised drastically downward. The 1985 projections are for 125 GW or less by the end of the century.

Elsewhere, however, nuclear power is in less trouble than in the United States. Plants have been built recently in Japan in only five to six years, much more rapidly than before, and nuclear power is considered a major supply option. The Japanese expect to have 31 GW installed by the early 1990s to provide 25 percent of the country's electric power. France, which has little domestic coal, has a firm policy of replacing oil-fired plants with nuclear ones and expects to have 57 GW by the early 1990s, although this perhaps exceeds domestic needs temporarily. Canada, Finland, West Germany, Spain, Sweden, Switzerland, the Soviet Union, and the United Kingdom all have successful nuclear programs, not all without controversy and some temporarily overbuilt, but none in so much difficulty as the U.S. program. Korea and Taiwan spend larger fractions of their gross national products on nuclear power than do any other countries.

There are several global reasons for the problems in the U.S. nuclear power industry. The primary one is the slowdown in electric power growth, caused to some extent by the slowdown in economic growth but mainly a result of conservation. Electric power use, which was increasing at a rate of 7 percent each year between 1900 and 1970, has suddenly slowed to an uncertain 2 to 3 percent increase. In addition, nuclear power plants have become intrinsically much more expensive with the passage of time and increasing complexity. Finally, the period of high interest rates and inflation, centering around the year 1980, was particularly disadvantageous to nuclear power. High capital costs and the slow construction of nuclear plants (even when the construction was managed efficiently) made many of them targets for cancellation, as their payback time receded beyond the horizon of economic attractiveness. Finance and escalation charges made up half the cost of many nuclear power plants—a burden far in excess of that falling on other generating options.

While these factors affected the nuclear power industry worldwide, others were more peculiar to the United States:

Many electric utility companies underestimated the level of technological sophistication and complexity associated with nuclear power. Few of them employed nuclear engineers with advanced degrees before the mid-1970s. Operators were not trained to understand the plant thoroughly enough to handle more than one problem at a time. This was a major factor in the Three Mile Island accident.

Lack of coordination affected the industry technically. For example, steam generators corroded because the water-quality requirements of the generators conflicted with those of the reactors.

The interactions among utilities, vendors, and architect/engineers were often less than satisfactory. These interactions are simplified in Japan and Korea, where the vendor is usually the designer and builder as well, and the utilities make every effort to cooperate.

Increasingly cumbersome regulations served the interests of neither proponents nor opponents of nuclear power. As accountability was prescribed in increasingly rigid regulations, the industry itself took less responsibility. In general, when the function of promotion is separated completely from the regulatory one and the two sides become adversaries, instabilities develop as one side comes to dominate the other. If neither side "wins," unresolved issues are passed up to higher and less well-informed levels, or to the courts, where the two sides are either forced together again, or arbitrary decisions are made, under less than ideal circumstances.

Public distrust of nuclear power played a significant role, though not as decisive as is often imagined. Public skepticism regarding costs, the need for plants, and the disposal of nuclear waste was legitimate. But the demands for absolute safety and concerns about the environmental hazards associated with normal operation were unwarranted. Many groups, both industrial and governmental, understood little about how to respond to such criticisms—a failing that undermined the public acceptance that is necessary for any technology.

This combination of circumstances multiplied the uncertainties surrounding nuclear power to an extent that was intolerable to the electric utility sector, which by its nature has to think about 40-year investments. As a result the U.S. nuclear power industry fell on hard times, and part of it is on the verge of collapse.

Increasing electrification worldwide affects the future of nuclear power and its alternatives. The portion of U.S. primary energy devoted to electric power generation has risen from 25 percent in the early 1970s to 35 percent at present. In Korea and Taiwan it exceeds 30 percent, and in Canada and Japan it is closer to 40 percent. The Organization for Economic Cooperation and Development (OECD) estimates that the total OECD primary energy fraction so allocated will exceed 45 percent during the 1990s.

The convenience of electric power is one reason for this increase. It is also better matched to most new technologies, is environmentally clean at the point of use, and is technologically superior in many applications. Many new or prospective supply options, besides nuclear, are electric: wind, geothermal, and photovoltaic, for example. Coal's future seems tied to electricity as well.

While conservation is still the best option, on the supply side coal is the principal alternative to nuclear power for thermal-cycle electric power generation. Global supplies are adequate for a few centuries at projected rates of use. In some favored locations, such as plants situated at the mouths of mines, coal-fired power will be cheaper than that from even the most efficiently built nuclear plants. However, in Japan, for instance, coal energy is significantly more expensive than nuclear energy.

Except for global carbon dioxide, the problems with coal can be overcome, though at a price. Consider acid rain, which, according to the National Research Council, results principally from sulphur in coal. The Economic Commission of Europe adopted the Convention on Long-Range Transboundary Air Pollution in 1979, aimed principally at acid rain. In 1984 most members, including Canada and the Soviet Union but not the United States or the United Kingdom, pledged to cut sulphur emissions 30 percent by 1993. If coal consumption were to double, in order to decrease acidity by that amount, a nearly threefold reduction of sulphur emissions per unit of energy would be required. That would present a substantial challenge to coal technologies, surely leading to widespread adoption of coal-cleaning techniques, and probably to fluidized bed burners, which burn the coal with a mixture of inert material to reduce gaseous and particulate pollutants.

Opinions about the environmental and accident hazards of nuclear power seem to be changing. The Three Mile Island accident appears to show that nuclear reactors are more sturdy than previously believed. Various estimates now downgrade the public hazard from potential accidents—moderately, according to a report of the American Physical Society to be published in the *Review of Modern Physics*, or substantially, according to a September 1984 report of the American Nuclear Society. The economic risk of reactor accidents (or even serious malfunctions), however, is enormous and daunting to electric utilities.

The disposal of nuclear waste presents special problems. Almost all the associated hazards disappear after a few centuries, a period short enough to assure the geologic integrity of a waste repository. The residue of radioactivity that lingers on for millennia, however, makes the selection of a site for a satisfactory repository considerably more difficult, though still possible. It was the failure of the former U.S. Atomic Energy Commission to address this problem early on, as well as the Commission's apparent insensitivity to public concern, that so inflamed public debate on this issue that it remains controversial, despite professional consensus that the problem of nuclear waste disposal is technologically resolved.

Waste disposal programs were begun, stopped, and changed by various administrations until Congress passed the Nuclear Waste Policy Act of 1982, which ordered permanent repositories to be built according to a set schedule, with permanent disposal to begin in 1998. That deadline is unlikely to be met. Meanwhile, growing public alarm about the careless handling of hazardous and toxic chemical waste is likely to affect perceptions of the relative risks associated with nuclear waste disposal.

The option of not reprocessing spent fuel, but entombing it as it is, is becoming more attractive. Uranium resources are sufficient to fuel all conventional light-water reactors until at least the third decade of the twenty-first century, because of slower growth in demands as well as new finds, especially in Canada and Australia. Thus the incentive to develop and deploy breeder reactors declines, with the U.S. program being restructured for the long term, and Japan's schedule for initial breeder deployment being moved from the 1990s to 2010 or later. The European Superphénix reactor will probably be commercialized very slowly.

The cost of reprocessing is also high—about $700 per kilogram at present. In addition, fuel fabrication with plutonium is more expensive than with enriched virgin uranium. Uranium costs, which now stand at about $50 per kilogram, would have to reach $300 per kilogram in order to make a plutonium economy at all attractive, an unlikely prospect for many decades.

Since permanent disposal of unreprocessed spent fuel breaks the principal connection between nuclear power and nuclear weapons, this decision would be favorable to nonproliferation. In the meantime, however, the degree of connection between the two is the responsibility of the governments concerned. Certainly, an ongoing nuclear power program provides some expertise applicable to a weapons program and makes it easier for a government to decide for weapons, even if that had not been the original intention. But it would be foolish to build a multi-billion-dollar civilian program in order to provide cover for a small, clandestine weapons program that could have been built for perhaps $100 million. To be sure, not all governments are rational, but these governments would probably proceed with a weapons program whether there was a civilian program or not.

Two approaches have evolved to reactor development for the 1990s and beyond, when the slow, steady growth of electric power worldwide is likely to stimulate interest in nuclear systems.

The more conventional and shorter-term approach attempts to solve the problems of light-water reactors, which have been developed too quickly, especially in larger sizes, and under the false assumption that they would always be economically advantageous. Japan, in partnership principally with the United States, has taken the lead in developing advanced versions of pressurized-water reactors and boiling-water reactors. The early phases of development, now complete, rearranged equipment within the containment shell, improved access, solved some piping problems, and improved rod drives, steam generators, and so forth. The final phase, extending through the 1980s, will improve capability, lengthen the fuel cycle, speed up and improve the maintenance and refueling operations, reduce construction time, and improve equipment to reduce occupational radiation exposure.

There is a substantive debate about high-temperature gas reactors, especially regarding the "pebble-bed" designs. The fuel is embedded in graphite balls about five centimeters in diameter, which are dropped into the reacting bed of balls inside the pressure vessel; flowing helium removes the heat. Balls are removed at the bottom, tested individually, then either reinserted or sent to spent-fuel storage. Such reactors can withstand coolant losses, overheating, and other events better than light-water reactors. Single-phase flow (instead of two-phase flow with water and steam) simplifies analysis. West Germany is in the lead with gas reactors; a small research reactor there has been running well with on-line refueling for more than a decade, and a 300-megawatt reactor was 99 percent complete in March 1985.

With the technological dominance shifting to Japan and Germany through these developments, the United States might have to import reactors from abroad in the 1990s. One can also speculate that if the United States had not developed light-water reactors for submarines, higher-temperature gas-cooled reactors might be the winners today.

The longer-term approach builds on the fact of slower nuclear growth, which leaves room not only for this new generation of reactors, but also for a succeeding one, even more fuel-efficient, more resistant to damage under unusual conditions, perhaps gas-cooled, and smaller. None of these relatively new options, however, will come into service before about the year 2000. If the technologies prove worthy, they will be installed over the following 20 years and will last 40 years per unit, or until about the year 2060. The stakes in such ventures are enormous. Even with electricity use growing at only 1 percent per year, the electric power bill in the United States between 1985 and 2060 would exceed 14 trillion 1985 dollars, much of it relating to the choices between nuclear and non-nuclear power, and the type of nuclear power.

The trend to smaller reactors bears watching; new opinions have been forming in recent years. Slower growth favors smaller power plants, especially where the electric power companies are private and relatively small, as in the United States. The topic figured prominently earlier this year in the program of the Fifth Pacific Basin Nuclear Conference in Seoul, Korea, and the U.S. industry was reported to agree that smaller reactors will likely be the first step in any nuclear revival in the United States.

Civilian nuclear power will, in the long run, be a major supply option, certainly for electricity, and also possibly for industrial heat. The qualified acceptance and good performance of nuclear power in some places demonstrate that it is not an impossible technology. With other long-term energy options so limited, and encumbered with economic, material, or environmental problems, the present nuclear power growing pains will surely not continue without resolution.

6

Flaws in the Non-Proliferation Treaty

Paul Leventhal

The Treaty on the Non-Proliferation of Nuclear Weapons has the twin objectives of stopping the further spread of nuclear weapons and ending the nuclear arms race on the one hand, and promoting peaceful uses of atomic energy on the other. In quantitative and symbolic terms the NPT is a huge success. More than two-thirds of the world's nations have signed on, making this the most popular arms control agreement on earth. Not a single nation has declared itself to be a nuclear-weapons state beyond the original five members of the "nuclear club" who qualified for weapons status under the terms of the Treaty itself: the United States, the Soviet Union, the United Kingdom, France, and China.

No party to the Treaty has exercised the permitted option to drop out, and none has been found by the International Atomic Energy Agency (IAEA) to have diverted nuclear material from civil to weapons purposes. Nor has any party been known to have violated NPT prohibitions on developing or assisting other nations to develop nuclear weapons.

Treaty enthusiasts credit the NPT and the IAEA with being the principal reasons that dire predictions, by President Kennedy and others, of dozens of nuclear-armed nations emerging by the 1980s have not been fulfilled. And all the while, they point out, the Treaty's nuclear-assistance and safeguards provisions have been instrumental in the development of peaceful nuclear power and research programs around the world.

In qualitative and substantive terms, however, the NPT is not cause for enthusiasm. It is a flawed instrument that has helped to fashion a nuclearized world so potentially perilous as to prompt dismay if not despair.

One-third of the world's nations have not signed the Treaty, including two of the original nuclear-weapons states, France and China, and several states suspected of building the bomb or being close enough to taste it: Argentina, Brazil, India, Israel, Pakistan, and South Africa. Each country in the latter group, with the possible exception of Israel, has received substantial commercial assistance from nuclear suppliers who are party to the Treaty, much of it directly significant to weapons production. Yet, the suppliers are not in technical violation of the NPT, which is interpreted to permit its parties to trade with nonparties so long as the items received are dedicated to peaceful purposes and subject to IAEA inspections. Such trade, however, contributes to the development in non–NPT nations of nuclear capabilities that can be applied to weapons development in indigenous facilities which are off-limits to IAEA inspectors.

The pursuit of nuclear weapons has not been limited to non–NPT nations. One NPT party, Libya, has been trying to buy a bomb for years; two others, Iran and Iraq, appear ready to develop one as soon as they stop fighting each other. Two other Treaty members, South Korea and Taiwan, terminated nuclear-weapons programs only under strong pressure from the United States.

The greatest danger, however, is "latent" proliferation. This is the acquisition of materials and capabilities required for making weapons by way of peaceful power and research programs made possible by acceptance of the NPT or, in the case of non–NPT nations, by acceptance of IAEA safeguards. The weapons-usable materials are plutonium, a waste product of reactors, which becomes an explosive after it is separated from spent fuel in a reprocessing plant; and highly enriched uranium, an explosive produced in an enrichment plant and used as fuel in many research reactors and in some demonstration nuclear power plants. These were the materials used in the Nagasaki and Hiroshima bombs respectively. NPT parties with major nuclear power and research programs are coming to possess or have access to these materials in quantities large enough to build many atomic bombs, all without violating treaty commitments or without ever needing to consider whether to drop out of the Treaty.

Projected amounts of commercial separated plutonium are staggering and soon will dwarf that in the superpowers' weapons stocks. Between them the superpowers have about 50,000 nuclear weapons, representing a combined stockpile of about 200 metric tons of plutonium. But within the next decade, if current reprocessing plans proceed, more explosive plutonium will have been separated from the spent fuel of commercial nuclear power plants than now exists in the U.S. and Soviet weapons stocks, according to projections by David Albright of Princeton University and the Federation of American Scientists. By the year 2000, separated plutonium in the commercial sector is projected to reach 400 tons. This is twice the amount in the current weapons stocks. An additional 1,000 tons of plutonium will be contained in spent fuel awaiting reprocessing; if separated, it would comprise enough explosive material for an additional 125,000 weapons.

This plutonium is intended for use as fuel in conventional and breeder reactors; if diverted by nations or stolen by terrorists, however, it can be used in bombs. The likelihood of such diversion or theft increases in proportion to the amounts of material produced, transported, and used. A similar danger exists with regard to the other nuclear-weapons material—highly enriched uranium—which is used throughout the world, albeit in smaller quantities, to fuel many research reactors.

The NPT is blind to the weapons potential of these materials so long as they are dedicated to peaceful purposes and subject to IAEA audits and inspections. But the IAEA, long defended by nuclear advocates as having an effective safeguards system, is now widely acknowledged to lack the technical means and the political power to detect and give timely warning of diversions of explosive nuclear materials from peaceful to weapons programs. Further, the IAEA was, by design, never given international police authority to prevent such diversions, even though Article III of the Treaty calls for the application of IAEA safeguards "with a view to preventing diversion of nuclear energy from peaceful uses."

The underlying proliferation dilemma, then, is the current trend toward accumulation of vast stores of weapons-usable materials by dozens of nations throughout the world, under the cloak of legitimacy provided by the NPT and IAEA safeguards. Most nations with major nuclear programs are not likely to violate solemn treaty and safeguards obligations by diverting civilian materials to secret weapons programs, but there are a few in unstable regions that may (indeed might already have done so). Most significant, there remains the possibility of wholesale conversion of national nuclear stockpiles into weapons at a time of regional or global crisis. There is also the growing danger of theft of nuclear explosive materials by terrorists.

Fortunately, some time remains to prevent world commerce in vast quantities of nuclear explosive materials. Most commercial reprocessing has taken place in France and Britain. Although some 60 tons of plutonium have been separated worldwide (including in Belgium, West Germany, India, Japan, and the United States), more than 90 percent of it remains in France and Britain. Fully four-fifths of spent fuel from modern power plants remains unreprocessed. Reprocessing is not a necessary step in nuclear-waste management because spent fuel can be disposed of without removing the plutonium. As for highly enriched uranium, most research reactors can now be modified to replace this explosive fuel with newly developed lower-enriched fuels not suitable for weapons.

Given what is known today about the inadequacy of IAEA safeguards, and of the NPT regime as a whole, to cope with today's vast quantities of nuclear explosive materials, it would be prudent to reconsider early assumptions about trade in explosive materials and in the technologies needed to produce them—*before* thousands of tons of these materials are created and injected into world commerce. Certainly the slowdown in nuclear power development, the adverse economics of plutonium in relation to plentiful and cheap nonexplosive uranium fuel, and delays in development of the plutonium-fueled breeder reactor all point to a final opportunity to consider the proliferation implications of industry's continuing commitment to reprocessing and use of plutonium.

Unfortunately, preoccupation with escalation of the superpowers' arms race ("vertical" proliferation) diverted the attention and resources of the review conference away from longer-term but no less dangerous problems of "horizontal" proliferation.

The 1985 NPT Review Conference, as in 1980 and to a lesser degree in 1975, was dominated by Third World charges that the United States and the Soviet Union have failed to keep their end of the basic NPT bargain: the obligation contained in Article VI "to pursue negotiations in good faith" toward ending the nuclear arms race "at an early date," and toward nuclear and general disarmament. This is one of two fundamental trade-off arrangements in the Treaty—the legal basis for the obligation of the parties not possessing nuclear weapons to abstain from building them. The other such arrangement, contained in Article IV, involves a guarantee of full access to peaceful nuclear technology to parties in return for their no-weapons pledge. Article IV also requires that assurances of nuclear assistance to Treaty parties be "in conformity with" Article I and II prohibitions on the giving or receiving of any assistance in making weapons. It is hard to understand, therefore, how commerce in weapons-usable plutonium and uranium can be regarded as conforming to the letter or the spirit of the Treaty.

The Review Conference has been widely regarded as a diplomatic success for having reached a consensus on Article VI issues after a near-deadlock over the refusal of the United States to embrace a comprehensive test ban as a fundamental commitment to arms control. The conference, however, was a nonproliferation failure for having neglected plutonium issues entirely (a proposal underscoring "the importance of minimising stocks of separated plutonium" was rejected) and for giving lip service to the need for strengthening and widening the scope of IAEA safeguards.

The Treaty is flawed not only because it has not held the superpowers accountable for the continued growth in their nuclear arsenals; it has also failed to hold the commercial nuclear supplier nations (the United States, the Soviet Union, France, West Germany, Canada, and Switzerland) accountable for the incipient spread of weapons-grade materials throughout the world. The Treaty is at risk of becoming irrelevant to the very arms control problems it was intended to address and prevent.

The NPT's defects take a number of forms:

First, the Treaty is crafted in such a way that its measure of nuclear proliferation, as spelled out in its prohibitions, is in terms of explosions and acquisition of explosive devices, rather than the basic ingredients of proliferation— the explosive materials themselves, separated plutonium and highly enriched uranium.

Thus, the Treaty bars transferring or acquiring nuclear explosive devices (or exploding them), but does not bar nuclear explosive materials so long as the materials are dedicated for "peaceful" purposes and placed under "safeguards." Similarly, the Treaty does not restrict— indeed, it promotes— transfers of spent-fuel reprocessing and uranium-enrichment technologies needed to produce these materials. Separate supplier agreements require safeguards and call for restraint on such dangerous transfers, but do not bar them.

The NPT is outdated in its choice of devices over materials as the proliferation target of choice. Public display or explosion of a device is the last way a nation is likely to proliferate, because of the obvious political liabilities and military risks. Further, most of the basic knowledge and engineering skills for building a bomb are no longer classified and are available throughout the world. The principal obstacle to making bombs is obtaining the necessary material. Ironically, the Treaty makes it easy to surmount that obstacle by legitimating these materials and whetting appetites for them in the industrial and developing worlds.

Second, the IAEA inspections and audits required by the Treaty are unequal to the task of safeguarding ton quantities of materials that can be used by the pound to make nuclear weapons. But even if the safeguards deter sneak diversions, there remains the latent proliferation problem; the plutonium equivalent of hundreds of thousands of nuclear weapons worldwide will be temptingly close at hand if current plans proceed to reprocess power reactor spent fuel.

Third, the Treaty requires parties not possessing nuclear weapons to place all their nuclear activities under IAEA safeguards ("full-scope safeguards") as a means of verifying that there are no diversions to clandestine weapons production facilities. But the NPT does not obligate suppliers who are party to it to require nonparties to accept full-scope IAEA safeguards as a basic condition of supply. This puts nonparties at a relative advantage to NPT parties and serves as a disincentive for nonparties to join the Treaty—a situation that violates both the spirit and the letter of the Treaty.

Fourth, the Treaty is silent (and the IAEA has only advisory responsibility) regarding physical protection of nuclear materials against theft by terrorists, either from facilities or in transit. An international convention has been negotiated to establish minimum standards for nations in guarding international shipments of nuclear materials, but for lack of signatories the convention has not come into force, and it is in any case widely regarded as inadequate to meet a credible terrorist threat.

The basic response of industry and governments to these gross inadequacies is to downplay the proliferation dangers of plutonium and highly enriched uranium, as well as the inability of the IAEA to safeguard them. Secret military production facilities, not safeguarded civilian plants, are seen as the likely source of weapons. Use of the materials is defended with claims that their benefit, as essential power and research reactor fuels, far outweighs their proliferation risks. Another argument is that it is too late and politically impossible to persuade such energy-short nations as France, West Germany, and Japan to give up their reprocessing plans. Suggestions that allies cooperate in foregoing plutonium and ensuring supplies of nonexplosive uranium from a global resource now estimated by the IAEA and the Organization for Economic Cooperation and Development to be as high as 20 million tons (5,000 tons are needed to fuel one power reactor over its 30-year life) are dismissed as unfeasible and idealistic. For plutonium to become economical, the price of uranium would have to increase to $150 per pound, compared to its present price of about $20.

Criticism of the use of nuclear explosive materials as uneconomical and dangerous, and as imposing an unbearable burden on the IAEA, are glibly dismissed by nuclear advocates not only as extremist and "antinuclear" but also as belying a secret agenda to shut down the nuclear industry. Expressions of concern about the danger of nuclear terrorism are also often regarded as antinuclear agitation and too dangerous to discuss publicly.

Serious efforts should be made to come to grips with the obvious linkage between the vertical and horizontal growth of nuclear arsenals, and to put a stop to both the rapid accumulation of nuclear explosive materials and to the *laissez-faire* attitude toward unsafeguarded nuclear activities. Otherwise, the Treaty on the Non-Proliferation of Nuclear Weapons will become irrelevant to the very objective spelled out in its name. And a terrified world may soon find that a nonproliferation treaty in name only is not worth the paper it is written on.

7

North-South Issues and East-West Confrontation

John P. Holdren

It is clear that the future course of history will be determined by the rates at which people breed and die, by the rapidity with which nonrenewable resources are consumed, by the extent and speed with which agricultural production can be improved, by the rate at which the underdeveloped areas can industrialize, by the rapidity with which we are able to develop new resources, as well as by the extent to which we succeed in avoiding future wars. All of these factors are interlocked.—Harrison Brown, *The Challenge of Man's Future,* 1954

The division of mankind threatens it with destruction. Civilization is imperiled by: a universal thermonuclear war; catastrophic hunger for most of mankind; stupefaction from the narcotic of "mass culture"; bureaucratic dogmatism, a spreading of mass myths that put entire peoples and continents under the power of cruel and treacherous demagogues; and destruction or degeneration from the unforseeable consequences of swift changes in the conditions of life on our planet. In the face of these perils, any action increasing the division of mankind, any preaching of the incompatibility of world ideologies and nations is madness and a crime. Only universal cooperation . . . will preserve civilization.—Andrei Sakharov, *Progress, Coexistence, and Intellectual Freedom,* 1968

E ver since the simultaneous beginnings of the nuclear era and the U.S.-Soviet confrontation 40 years ago, perceptive scientists (and others) on both sides have pointed out that averting global catastrophe depends not only on sensible management of East-West relations, but also on the reduction of the North-South disparity in material well-being that leaves three-quarters of the world's population to divide up one-quarter of the economic product. Indeed, that the global prospects for a stable and durable peace depend on alleviating the sources of tension between North and South as well as on constraining the competition between East and West seems so obvious as to be beyond dispute.

Yet despite the apparent logic of the connection, and notwithstanding the testimonials to its importance offered by such distinguished international panels as the Brandt and Palme Commissions,[1] much of the "expert" debate on international security proceeds on the premise that the East-West relationship is the principal problem and that North-South issues are separable and secondary. How valid has this premise been—as an explanatory principle or as a basis for priorities and policies —over the past four decades? How valid is it likely to be in the future?

NUCLEAR HARDWARE

The premise of the primacy of the East-West relationship in governing the prospects for averting a major nuclear war is largely rooted in the overwhelming concentration of the "hardware" of nuclear war in U.S. and Soviet hands. The combined nuclear arsenals of the United States and the Soviet Union comprise perhaps 50,000 nuclear bombs and warheads; all other countries together probably have fewer than a tenth as many, and the greater part of these belong to Great Britain and France—themselves participants in the "central" East-West confrontation.

Unquestionably, the numbers and characteristics of the great bulk of these nuclear weapons and their delivery systems have been governed by the action-reaction dynamic of the U.S.-Soviet nuclear arms race itself. To the extent that these numbers and characteristics—and those of the systems of command and control that would govern the wartime use or non-use of these weapons—are themselves important determinants of the probability and consequences of major nuclear war, the preoccupation of most analysts with the East-West dimension of the nuclear confrontation has been justified.

On the other hand, the era in which decisions about the great bulk of the world's nuclear forces have been made by the United States and the Soviet Union, reacting only to one another, may soon be over. Negotiations concerning U.S. and Soviet nuclear weapons in and around Europe already have been complicated by the existence of British and French nuclear forces, not least because of the substantial numerical increases planned for both of these "small" nuclear arsenals over the next few years. China's plans for expanding its nuclear arsenal are less clear, but the potential for a further complication of the East-West nuclear calculus obviously is present.

There is still another complication in prospect: the proliferation of nuclear weapons to additional countries in the South. Perhaps because proliferation has proceeded more slowly so far than many feared, it is now widely underrated as a potential contributor to the threat of general nuclear war. Unfortunately, there is much reason to think that the "nuclear club" is on the verge of a rather sudden and sizable expansion.[2] This prospect is due in part to the conspicuous failure of the United States and the Soviet Union to curb their own nuclear arms race, despite their obligations to do so under Article VI of the Non-Proliferation Treaty, and in part to their less obvious but no less damaging failure to collaborate effectively to slow the spread of the technical ingredients of nuclear-weapons capabilities.

Against the prospect of increased horizontal proliferation in the late 1980s and 1990s, some commentators offer the consolation that small powers with small nuclear arsenals are likely to use them only against each other. I am neither much consoled by this possible restriction nor persuaded that small-power use of small nuclear arsenals would not provide the tinder for global conflagration. It is all too easy to think of ways the latter syndrome could occur: the use of a small number of nuclear weapons against a superpower in a way that obscures the source of the attack; the increased chance of superpower involvement in any conflict once nuclear weapons have been used; the increased chance that the superpowers, if drawn into a conflict, will use their own nuclear weapons should the initial participants use such weapons; and the increasing probable extent and severity of a nuclear war as the number of targets for preemptive attack, represented by nuclear-armed potential adversaries, proliferates.

Further proliferation also can be expected to have deleterious feedbacks on the major-power arms race itself. Specifically, proliferation increases the diversity of contingencies with which the major powers think they and their nuclear forces might have to cope, thus serving as a rationale (or an excuse) for further increases in the types and numbers of nuclear weapons they possess. At best, proliferation tends to put a rising "floor" under the possibility of deep cuts in the nuclear arsenals of medium-sized nuclear powers and, in turn, those of the superpowers. These nations will, after all, wish to maintain the gaps between their own nuclear-weapons capabilities and those of "lesser" powers—precisely to preserve their "major power" or "superpower" status.

CAUSES OF CONFLICT

The characteristics of the world's nuclear arsenals obviously have something to do with the chances of a nuclear war and the severity of such a war if it occurs, but it would be a mistake to suppose that these "hardware" characteristics are the only important factors, or even the main ones. To think sensibly about the chances of nuclear war and the means of preventing one, it is essential to look not only at the arsenals but also at the sources of hostility that have led to the acquisition of such weapons and at the ways in which crises capable of converting that hostility into armed conflict might materialize and escalate.

The root of the East-West problem, of course, is the adversarial relationship of the United States and the Soviet Union, a long-standing and perhaps inevitable competition with ideological, economic, and military components. Most relevant for our concern with the relation of East-West to North-South issues, however, is that an important part of this competition is influence with other countries, each superpower being acutely interested in maintaining or increasing its own international influence while limiting or diminishing that of its adversary. Inasmuch as the United States and the Soviet Union both define their most vital interests of this type in terms of influence with their respective West European and East European allies, it is widely believed that the boundary between Eastern and Western Europe is the most likely locus for the outbreak of major conflict.

Maybe; but maybe not. Certainly, as we are often reminded, Central Europe contains the largest concentration of military forces on the planet. Yet that has been true for 40 years, during which time there have been crises and near-crises—Berlin twice, Hungary, Czechoslovakia, Poland—but no armed conflict between East and West. In the same period, there have been some 200 armed conflicts in the South, many of them genuinely international (that is, engaging the organized military forces of two or more countries) and an appalling number involving direct or indirect participation by the United States or the Soviet Union.

This record provides some support for the proposition that the greatest danger may lie not at the intersection of the most vital and long-established interests of the two sides — Central Europe—where a more-or-less stable status quo has long prevailed, but at the somewhat unstable and therefore tempting periphery—the South—where large parcels of the currency of geopolitical influence are still, in the eyes of the superpowers, "up for grabs." The main motivations for superpower involvement on this periphery vary: protection or denial of access to resources (the Middle East, Southern Africa?); support or isolation of a distant ally bound by strong cultural or historical ties (Israel, the Philippines); extracting or twisting a thorn in the backside of one side or the other (Cuba, Afghanistan); or simply generalized expansion or containment of spheres of geopolitical influence (Korea, Vietnam, the Horn of Africa, Central America). But the motivations are perhaps not so important as the overall pattern: the most ambitious and unpredictable military adventures of the superpowers, the main manifestations of their proclivity for adversary-baiting and generalized risk-taking, and hence the greatest dangers of miscalculation and unintended escalation, have occurred in the South.

It can be argued, of course, that the South has simply been an arena in which the primary East–West conflict is played out, and that a "general settlement" of the East–West issue is not only a necessary but also a sufficient condition for sharply reducing the danger of major war arising in or over the South. This argument for the primacy of the East–West dimension of the potential for major conflict may have been valid for the first half or even three-quarters of the four-decade period since World War II, but it is by now a misleading oversimplification and is becoming more so year by year.

The present and future reality is one of diminishing superpower capacity to control events in the South, without any sign, however, that either one has the inclination or even the option to respond to this trend by pulling back. The diminishing capacity for superpower control is partly the result of the increase, especially over the past two decades, in the economic and military power of many Third World states, accompanied by a corresponding increase in the confidence and assertiveness of these countries, including their willingness to intervene militarily in the affairs of their neighbors.[3] Decreased control and predictability for the superpowers have come also from increasing interpenetration, over the same period, of their respective spheres of involvement.

The growth of the military capabilities of the South, of course, has been greatly facilitated by massive arms transfers from the superpowers and other Northern countries, to a value of about $200 billion (in 1981 dollars) between 1973 and 1982 alone.[4] These weapons flows are cherished on the supplier side for their contributions to trade balances, defense-industry profitability, and stabilization (or destabilization) of regional power balances. But they have been multiply pernicious in their long-term effects on the interests of Northern suppliers and Southern recipients alike.

They have enhanced the destructiveness of whatever conflicts occur in the South — without any noticeable deterrent effect as a redeeming feature. They have diverted scarce capital from compelling social needs in the importing countries, thereby impeding the alleviation of the widespread poverty that is one of the main factors in the continuing potential for regional instability and violence. And they have contributed to a vicious circle in which the Northern suppliers, seeing their capacity to control events in the South eroded by the increasingly powerful arsenals the arms transfers have produced, then attempt to compensate by means of expensive and provocative buildups in their own capabilities to project overpowering military force at great distances.

Even the pleasant, if hypothetical, possibility that the superpowers might yet come to their senses and constrict drastically the southward flow of military hardware is rapidly losing relevance. For in this respect, as in others, matters are moving out of the North's control. By the early 1980s, South-South arms transfers originating from such supplier countries as China, North and South Korea, and Brazil were growing at a dizzying rate.

SUPERPOWER REACTIONS TO THE DANGER

While the evidence for diminishing superpower capacity to control, or even to predict, events in the South seems compelling, there is not much sign that the superpowers have noticed. Far from any tendency toward what might be regarded as a prudent degree of disengagement, both the United States and the Soviet Union have been displaying an increased proclivity to intervene. Both their actions over the past few years and the evolution of their military capabilities point to this conclusion.

The superpowers' disinclination to pull back is understandable, if not entirely praiseworthy. They continue to view the South as an arena in which to compete for influence, where any vacuum left by one is likely to be filled by the other. They are linked to countries of the South by a web of political commitments, military agreements (including those governing the use of important bases), financial ties, trade relationships, and — mainly on the U.S. side — real and perceived resource dependencies.

For better or for worse, then, no substantial degree of disengagement is likely. But the impracticality of withdrawal combined with the erosion of predictability and control constitutes an increasing threat to the prospects for keeping crises in the South from becoming East-West crises, these crises from becoming conflicts, and the conflicts from escalating out of control. Where instability in the South may once have represented a potential opportunity for one superpower or the other to increase its own influence and diminish its adversary's, this game has now become hazardous out of proportion to the possible gains. The danger is all too great that a war engaging the superpowers could arise via their involvement in a conflict in the South that escalates beyond their intentions or control.

One class of responses to this danger consists of East-West efforts toward *crisis prevention.* Such measures include agreed "codes of conduct" governing superpower interventions in the South, negotiated restraints on North-South arms transfers, and provision for superpower consultation to head off impending crises.[5] A second class of responses consists of *crisis management,* which includes such mechanisms as the Moscow-Washington "hotline" and upgraded versions of it, jointly operated crisis-control centers, and other measures to try to prevent crises from growing into major conflicts.[6]

Both approaches obviously have merit and need to be pursued. It should be noticed, however, that both—at least in the forms that have been most analyzed and discussed—address the problem mainly as an *East-West* conflict in which the South just happens to provide the arena.

Roots of tension in the predicament of the South

This paradigm of the primacy of East-West interaction in governing the potential for major conflict arising from the South is more and more a part of the problem rather than of the solution. It is leading analysts and policy-makers alike to underrate the growing importance of sources of tension and conflict inherent in conditions in the South, and in the nature of North-South relations per se, as determinants of the prospects for avoiding major war. Refinements in "rules of conduct" accepted by the superpowers, and improvements in the crisis-communication capabilities available to them, desirable as these developments would be, cannot cope with major increases in the rate and intensity of South-South and North-South confrontations. Such increases are all too possible if the problems of the South—and their exacerbation by a combination of perverse actions and inaction by the North—continue to be neglected while the capacity of countries in the South to vent their frustrations and pursue their ambitions with military force grows.

The most fundamental problem is poverty, manifested in chronic shortages of the material ingredients of a decent existence. This condition in varying degrees afflicts half to two-thirds of the five billion people now alive.[7] It surely is the dominant source of frustration and latent social instability on the planet, despite strong competition from other forms of oppression of human rights. That anything like the present distribution of the world's economic output —the poorest three-quarters of the population sharing only one-quarter of the economic pie—could serve as the long-term basis for a stable geopolitical equilibrium is simply inconceivable.

The problem of poverty is interwoven with and greatly compounded by the accelerating degradation of the bio-geophysical environment.[8] By this I mean not only the widespread presence of high concentrations of pollutants harmful to human health, but also the increasingly pervasive disruption of geophysical and ecological systems essential to human welfare—deforestation, erosion, salinization, acidification, desertification, human-induced climatic change.

The burdens of both of these classes of impacts—the disease effects of pollution and the disruption of environmental systems that are the basis of carrying capacity—are borne disproportionately by the poor. The filthiest rural water supplies and the most polluted urban air are found in the South, as is the grossest carelessness in the handling of industrial toxic substances. The most severe air-pollution problem in the world, judged by the product of pollutant concentration times the number of people at risk, is the exposure of half a billion or more women and children to staggering concentrations of particulate matter and hydrocarbons from the combustion of traditional cooking fuels (wood, dung, crop wastes) in Third World village huts.[9] And discovering who is most at risk from deforestation, erosion, and desertification is as easy as watching the telecasts from the Sahel on the evening news.

The North is not solely responsible for these problems, of course, but neither is it wholly blameless. Our sins are of both commission and omission. We have exported our dirtiest industries to the South and called it development. We have countenanced the destruction of vast tracts of tropical rainforest to panel our kitchens and package our hamburgers. And we continue to account for the great bulk of the most threatening human influence on the global climatological system, through our 80 percent share of carbon-dioxide-producing fossil-fuel combustion. The possible consequences over the next few decades include disruptions of world agriculture that could multiply the Sahel famine a hundredfold.

More important, however, is what we have failed to do. Far from mobilizing a serious effort to combat Southern poverty, we have failed even *to comprehend the magnitude of the task.* Part of that lack of comprehension is the failure to grasp that many of the productive technologies from which the prosperity of the North has been derived are themselves not sustainable. They have been based on one-time geophysical windfalls and on progressive erosion of the environmental underpinnings of the long-term carrying capacity of the planet.

Converting even present levels of economic production to a sustainable basis is likely to be very costly. Indeed, much of the rising cost of energy over the past 15 years can be understood in just these terms. The economic difficulties engendered thereby in North and South alike, the reaction of the North to its share of these difficulties by adopting increasingly protectionist policies and by reducing already minuscule programs of development assistance, and the resulting increase in that part of the economic burden borne by the South all serve as unsettling signs of further difficulties ahead.[10]

THE PROSPECTS

The negative implications of this situation for peace are all too clear. Continuing failure to mount the massive efforts needed to overcome the interlinked economic and environmental problems of North and South can only result in massive frustration, despair, and social and political instability that may prove impossible to confine short of major war.

Still, there is a positive implication. It is often remarked that a rivalry like that between East and West can only be overcome by the appearance of a common enemy—a mutual threat so serious as to compel cooperation in defeating it. The Nazi menace was such a problem, but the cooperation needed to defeat it was relatively short-lived. Many have argued that nuclear weapons in themselves constitute a common enemy, but somehow the threat these weapons pose has so far proven too abstract to compel East-West cooperation.

Is it possible that the challenge of providing a decent material existence for the world's population, sustainably and affordably, is big enough, concrete enough, and threatening enough—given the probable consequences of failure in an increasingly nuclear-armed and interconnected world —to compel the cooperation of East and West, North and South in working to solve it?

Harrison Brown had by 1954 understood the problem and the need for massive cooperation to solve it. Andrei Sakharov had reached the same conclusion by 1968. The signs are much more obvious in 1985; perhaps decision-makers in East and West will recognize them yet.

---

1. Independent Commission on International Development Issues (Willy Brandt, chairman), *North-South· A Program for Survival* (Cambridge, Mass.: MIT Press, 1980); Independent Commission on Disarmament and Security Issues (Olof Palme, chair-

man), *Common Security: A Blueprint for Survival* (New York: Simon and Schuster, 1982).

2. Leonard S. Spector, "Nuclear Proliferation: The Pace Quickens," *Bulletin* (Jan. 1985), p. 11.

3. See Neil Macfarlane, *Intervention and Regional Security,* Adelphi Paper 196 (London: International Institute for Strategic Studies, Spring 1985).

4. U.S. Arms Control and Disarmament Agency, *World Military Expenditures and Arms Transfers 1972–82* (Washington, D.C.: Government Printing Office, April 1984).

5. For analysis of such approaches see Alexander George, *Managing U.S.-Soviet Rivalry: Problems of Crisis Prevention* (Boulder, Col.: Westview Press, 1983).

6. See, for example, William Langer Ury and Richard Smoke, *Beyond the Hotline: Controlling a Nuclear Crisis* (Cambridge, Mass.: Nuclear Negotiation Project of the Harvard Law School, 1984).

7. World Bank, *World Development Report 1984* (New York: Oxford, 1984).

8. Paul R. Ehrlich, Anne H. Ehrlich, John P. Holdren, *Ecoscience: Population, Resources, Environment* (San Francisco: W.H. Freeman, 1977); Lester R. Brown, et al., *State of the World 1985* (New York: Norton, 1985).

9. Kirk R. Smith, A.L. Aggarwal, R.M. Dave, "Air Pollution and Rural Biomass Fuels in Developing Countries," *Atmospheric Environment,* vol. 17 (1983), pp. 2343–62.

10. John P. Holdren, "Energy and the Human Predicament," in Kirk R. Smith, Freidun Fesharaki, John P. Holdren, *Earth and the Human Future: Essays in Honor of Harrison Brown* (Boulder, Colo.: Westview, 1986).

The Arms Race

1

Lessons of the Arms Race

David Holloway

On July 24, 1945, after one of the formal sessions of the Potsdam Conference, President Truman approached Premier Stalin and (as Truman later wrote in his memoirs) "remarked casually" to him that "we had a weapon of unusual destructive power." Stalin replied that "he was glad to hear of it and hoped we would make 'good use of it against the Japanese.'"[1]

British Prime Minister Churchill, who had watched this exchange intently from a few feet away, was, like Truman, convinced that Stalin had not grasped the significance of the president's remark. But they were both wrong, for we now know from Soviet sources that Stalin was aware that Truman had the atomic bomb in mind, and that he had initiated a small Soviet atomic bomb project at the end of 1942.

This exchange between Truman and Stalin took place eight days after the Trinity test at Alamogordo, and less than two weeks before the dropping of the atomic bomb on Hiroshima. Stalin regarded the development and use of the atomic bomb by the United States as a challenge to which an immediate response was required. In August 1945 he took the first steps to convert the relatively small Soviet atomic project into a crash program, under the overall direction of Lavrenti Beria, the head of the Soviet police empire.

This history is of more than commemorative interest, for it may teach us something about the present. The Reagan Administration's Strategic Defense Initiative (SDI), for example, is sometimes compared to the Manhattan Project or the Apollo Project. But there is an important difference, because the scientists and engineers who developed the first atomic bomb and put the first man on the moon were pitting their wits against nature, whereas those who want to develop an effective anti-ballistic-missile (ABM) system are pitting their wits against an opponent who might do his utmost to render their efforts useless. Precisely for this reason, the perspectives of the Soviet leaders have to be taken into account in assessing the likely effect of the SDI on the U.S.-Soviet strategic relationship.

Stalin's decision to build the atomic bomb was based on a number of premises. The most obvious was that the new bomb, with its unprecedented destructive power, was a weapon of immense military significance. The Soviet Union, unlike the United States and Britain, had not conducted a significant strategic bombing campaign during the war with Germany. But the very destructiveness of the bomb, which had been so dramatically demonstrated in Japan, made it clear that, irrespective of military doctrine, it would play a significant part in any future war.

The Soviet leader apparently believed that his country would find itself at war once again within 15 to 20 years. He said as much to Yugoslav Party leader Milovan Djilas in April 1945. And he made the same point obliquely in February 1946 when he spoke of needing at least three Five Year Plans to prepare the country "against any and all contingencies."[2] This was not idle talk on Stalin's part, for in the months after the end of World War II he initiated large-scale programs to develop long-range rockets, jet propulsion, and radar, as well as the program to build the bomb.

Stalin was afraid that the United States, by virtue of its atomic monopoly, would be able to use "atomic diplomacy" to put political pressure on the Soviet Union. Alexander Werth, who was a correspondent for the London *Sunday Times* in the Soviet Union during the war, wrote that Hiroshima had "an acutely depressing effect on everybody," and that "some Russian pessimists . . . dismally remarked that Russia's desperately hard victory over Germany was "now 'as good as wasted.'"[3] The British and U.S. ambassadors reported to their governments about Moscow's reaction in much the same terms: the atomic bomb had come as a shock and threatened to deprive the Soviet victory of much of its value.

There is little reason to doubt this assessment of Stalin's view of the bomb. The victory over Germany had given him control over half of Europe and had thereby enhanced Soviet security and power.

Now, however, the new balance of power was upset by this immensely powerful weapon, which the United States alone possessed. In mid-August of 1945 Stalin summoned Igor Kurchatov, the scientific director of the Soviet atomic project, and told him that "Hiroshima has shaken the whole world."[4] Stalin now wanted the atomic bomb as soon as possible.

The decision to launch a crash program was also rooted in a deep-seated urge to demonstrate that the economy and technology of the Soviet Union were as powerful as those of the United States. In the late 1920s the Communist Party had adopted the slogan of "catching up and overtaking the economically and technologically advanced capitalist powers," and this slogan was once again invoked at the end of the war with Germany. The atomic bomb was the most potent symbol of a new kind of scientific and technological strength, and therefore something that the Soviet Union had to acquire as quickly as possible.

The first Soviet atomic bomb test took place in August 1949, four years after the launching of the crash program. Washington was surprised by the speed with which this had happened. In spite of the devastation caused by the war, Stalin had mobilized resources to eliminate the U.S. "atomic monopoly."

Under Khrushchev the Soviet armed forces went through a "revolution in military affairs" (to use the Soviet phrase) in which military doctrine and organization were completely overhauled in response to the development of nuclear weapons.

Khrushchev believed that peaceful coexistence could last indefinitely between states with different social systems. But he thought also that another world war was not impossible and had to be prepared for. If there were such a war, he said, it would begin with missile strikes deep into the enemy interior and end with the collapse of capitalism, because people would understand that "capitalism is the source that breeds wars and would no longer tolerate that system which brings sufferings and disasters to mankind."[5]

Khrushchev may have thought this a convincing basis for confidence in victory, but the military were not impressed. In 1962 Marshal Sokolovskii, who had been chief of the General Staff from 1952 to 1960, wrote in his famous *Military Strategy* that "victory in a nuclear war will not come by itself. It must be thoroughly prepared and provided for."[6] Sokolovskii tried in this book to answer the question: If there is a nuclear war with the United States, how should the Soviet Union fight it, and what forces would it need?

In 1960 Khrushchev boasted that the Soviet Union led the United States in missile development and that it would hold on to that lead until there was disarmament. By October 1964, however, when Khrushchev was removed from office, the Soviet Union lagged four-to-one behind the United States in strategic missiles. Much of official Washington believed that the Soviet Union would not try to catch up. Secretary of Defense Robert McNamara went so far as to say, in April 1965, that the Soviet Union had dropped out of the quantitative arms race.

This judgment proved to be seriously wrong, for the Soviets refused to acquiesce in strategic inferiority and built up their offensive forces, attaining rough parity with the United States by the early 1970s. The origins of this buildup cannot be identified as precisely as the decision to build the atomic bomb. It may indeed have resulted from a series of decisions, some taken when Khrushchev was still in power, others after his fall. But the determination to match the United States, like the decision to build the atomic bomb, was based on various considerations:

Inferiority in strategic offensive missiles did not satisfy the requirements for waging war, as these were understood by the Soviet General Staff. Sokolovskii had argued that the state should aim for superiority over its potential enemies. He had defined military strategy in the nuclear age as the "strategy of deep rocket-nuclear strikes in combination with actions by all services of the Armed Forces, with the aim of simultaneously striking and destroying the economic potential and the Armed Forces on the whole depth of the enemy's territory in order to attain the objectives of war in a short time."[7] This required a large strategic force that could strike a wide variety of targets. The military did not want Soviet security to depend solely on the capacity to retaliate against U.S. cities; they wanted to be able to destroy U.S. forces and war-making potential in the event of war. There was thus a strong military rationale for the expansion of strategic offensive forces.

The Soviet leaders also believed that large military forces were needed to support their foreign policy. Khrushchev had tried to cut Soviet forces, and at the same time to use "missile diplomacy" to make foreign policy gains. He failed, however, to make the gains he hoped for, and in the process he precipitated the Cuban missile crisis. His policy was condemned for forcing the Soviet Union to choose between risky adventures and passivity in the face of Western military power. His successors seem to have drawn the conclusion that his policy had lacked adequate military backing.

The decision to build up Soviet strategic forces was influenced also by the symbolic importance these forces had as the outward and visible sign of the power of the state. Brezhnev and his colleagues were not willing to resign themselves to second place in the symbolism of greatness. They may have hoped in the mid-1960s, as they were to do in the 1970s, that strategic parity would bring the Soviet Union economic and political benefits in its relationship with the West. They later claimed that growing Soviet military power provided the basis for détente.

In the late 1960s the Soviet Union began to build an ABM system around Moscow. ABM fitted well into the Soviet conception of military strategy and appealed to a Soviet desire to base its security on its own efforts, and not to let it depend on mutual deterrence. But in 1972, for reasons that are difficult to examine in detail, the Soviet Union signed the ABM Treaty with the United States. As early as 1966 and 1967 there were signs of Soviet doubt about ABM technology. The Soviet leaders evidently feared that an ABM race with the United States would leave them worse off. They were aware, moreover, that if one side deployed defensive systems, the other could respond by expanding or upgrading its offensive forces—for example, by deploying multiple warheads.

A growing belief in the deterrent effect of its offensive forces may also have contributed to the Soviet decision to sign the ABM Treaty. In 1983 Marshal Nikolai Ogarkov, then chief of the General Staff, wrote that 20 years earlier (about the time of the Cuban missile crisis) the United States could have counted "to some extent" on a first strike.[8] By the late 1960s that was no longer so.

The ABM Treaty did ratify a situation in which both the Soviet Union and the United States were vulnerable to massive and destructive retaliatory strikes, no matter who struck first. Soviet leaders have recognized that this is so. Brezhnev declared more than once that it would be suicidal to start a nuclear war and that parity, not superiority, was the goal of Soviet policy. But at the same time Soviet leaders do not regard military strategy as redundant: nuclear war would be a catastrophe, and the first aim of policy must be to prevent it; but a nuclear war may happen and must therefore be planned for. Nuclear weapons are seen both as agents of potential catastrophe and as instruments of war.

This continuing interest in military strategy has aroused fears that the Soviet Union might try to break out of the relationship of mutual deterrence, perhaps by deploying a nationwide ABM system. This fear has been fueled by the steady Soviet research and development effort in ABM technologies. Though extensive and in some cases questionable from the point of view of Treaty compliance, this effort does not point unequivocally to a Soviet intention to deploy a nationwide system and may be directed to other goals: to provide defenses in areas not covered by the Treaty; as a hedge against U.S. breakout; to explore new technologies that might change the balance between the offense and the defense.

Whatever Soviet goals may be, President Reagan's "Star Wars" speech of March 23, 1983, introduced a dramatic new element into the U.S.-Soviet relationship. The immediate Soviet reaction was to accuse the United States of wishing to deny the Soviet Union the capacity to retaliate in the event of a U.S. attack. Andropov claimed that this was a bid "to disarm the Soviet Union in the face of the U.S. nuclear threat," and said that this scheme would lead to a race in offensive as well as defensive systems.[9]

Andropov, Chernenko, and Gorbachev all have defined the SDI as a challenge they must meet, and they have a number of options available. They can expand or upgrade their offensive forces or try to develop weapons that would destroy the defensive system. They could also field their own ABM system—either a conventional system of the kind now deployed around Moscow or one based on new technologies. Evgeni Velikhov, director of the Kurchatov Institute of Atomic Energy, has said that he would recommend countermeasures but not deployment of an ABM system, on the grounds that it would not be effective.[10] The choice of options gives the Soviet Union the chance to adapt its response to the economic and technological constraints under which it may have to operate.

Nevertheless, if the United States deploys an ABM system, the pressures on the Soviet Union to do likewise will be considerable. Existing restraints on Soviet activity would be gone, since the fear of provoking the United States would already have become reality. Concern about the vulnerability of its offensive forces might lead the Soviet Union to deploy defenses of its own, in order to insure that as many offensive missiles as possible survive for retaliation against the defense (though it could adopt other measures to enhance survivability too).

The Soviet Union is likely to fear (as it has in the past) that any military edge would translate into diplomatic advantage and enable the United States to exert political pressure. Moreover, a U.S. system—or even tests directed toward the development of such a system—would be taken as a sign of the strength of U.S. science and technology. The Soviet Union might fear a loss of status if it did not match the U.S. effort. The Soviet Union has not resisted this kind of challenge before and is perhaps unlikely to do so this time.

Yet the Soviet Union seems anxious to avoid an all-out competition in this area and has returned to arms control negotiations in the hope of stopping the SDI. But agreement in Geneva will be difficult to achieve because the two sides have very different conceptions of the relationship between defensive and offensive systems. The United States wants to reduce offensive forces during the ABM research and development process and then to make an agreed transition to the deployment of defenses. The Soviet Union, on the other hand, has made it clear that unless there is an agreement to stop the SDI there can be no reductions in offensive systems.

Unless something is done to reconcile the positions of the two sides, either unilaterally or by negotiation, the likely effect of the SDI will be to fuel the arms race, make arms control impossible, and lead not to an escape from mutual deterrence, but to a deterrent relationship that may be even more fraught with uncertainty and suspicion than the existing one.

The strategic defense initiative has been interpreted by Soviet leaders as a challenge to their security. The history of Soviet nuclear weapons policy shows that they have accepted such challenges in the past and have surprised the West by the determination and speed with which they have responded to them. Soviet policy has been deeply rooted in the urge to compete with the United States and guided by the belief that any inferiority would have harmful military and political consequences.

The history of the arms race is much more complex than I have suggested here, for it has involved Soviet challenges to the United States as well as U.S. challenges to the Soviet Union. Moreover, the ABM Treaty shows that in the past both sides have been ready to close off some areas of the strategic arms competition and to keep it under some kind of control.

Nevertheless, the Soviet atomic bomb and strategic missile decisions are relevant to any attempt to understand the likely consequences of the SDI, for they show the Soviet determination to compete with the United States. The Reagan Administration's approach to strategic defense seems almost designed to evoke just this kind of atavistic response from the Soviet Union, rather than to elicit Soviet cooperation in controlling and restraining the arms race.

1. Harry S. Truman, *1945: Year of Decision* (New York: Doubleday, 1965), p. 458.
2. Election speech, Feb. 9, 1946, in I.V. Stalin, *Sochineniia*, vol. 3, 1946–1953, Robert H. McNeal, ed. (Stanford, Cal.: The Hoover Institution, 1967), p. 20.
3. Alexander Werth, *Russia at War 1941–1945* (London: Pan Books, 1965), p. 925.
4. Quoted by A. Lavrent'eva in 'Stroitel novogo mira', *V mire knig*, 9 (1970), p. 4.
5. *Pravda*, Jan. 15, 1960.

6. V.D. Sokolovskii, *Voennaia Strategiia* (Moscow: Voenizdat, 1962), p. 237.

7. Ibid., p. 16.

8. *Krasnaia Zvezda*, Sept. 23, 1983.

9. *Pravda,* March 27, 1983.

10. Interviews, Radio Moscow (May 23 and 25, 1984), *Foreign Broadcast Information Service* (June 6, 1984), USSR International Affairs, pp. AA9, AA11.

2

Soviet Decision Making on Defense

Jerry F. Hough

The process by which the Soviet Union has made its military and defense decisions over the years has been extremely complex. At one extreme, some purely military decisions have been monopolized by military officials and a few Politburo members who have jealously guarded their prerogatives against outside involvement to an extent quite unknown in the United States. At the other extreme, the nature of the socialist economy has produced more severe civilian-military conflicts than found in the West, thus forcing more explicit priority choices.

As a result, many Soviet defense decisions have required civilian involvement and have been subject to a degree of civilian influence also quite unknown in the United States. We must therefore be very careful in generalizing about the Soviet defense policy process. A generalization that may be true for one part of the process may be quite inaccurate for another. In practice, the power of the military in defense decision-making as a whole has often been severely exaggerated in the West.

The Soviet socialist economic system has a number of features that affect its defense policy-making process in ways that are counterintuitive to Americans who make assumptions based on their own system. If these features are not kept clearly in mind, an American may read the U.S. experience into the Soviet Union's and be seriously misled

The first difference between the two nations is that much clearer choices must be made in the Soviet Union with respect to investment, defense, and consumption. It may well be that the higher long-term rates of growth in Japan and Germany, compared with those of the United States and Great Britain, seem to indicate that high defense expenditures tend to retard rates of growth, but that conclusion is controversial. Certainly in the short run, high defense expenditures can create demand that stimulates growth if the economy is slack. In the United States it also provides visible employment in individual congressional districts and leads politicians to support specific projects as being economically useful on a micro-level, whatever the overall consequences of high defense expenditures.

In the Soviet Union, by contrast, expenditures, capital investment in various sectors of the economy, and consumption are included within the plan. This plan provides not only for overall expenditure levels for each category, but also specific allocations of concrete supplies—such as coal, steel, and machinery—for every ministry and factory. As in any budgetary process, each unit is always asking for more inputs, and the planners are forced to choose among requests and to allocate less than is said to be absolutely indispensable. As a result, the conflicts and trade-offs between defense and nondefense investment become painfully explicit: decisions must be made.

This conflict between defense and investment is neither a hypothetical nor a new one. In the late 1920s, Marshal Tukhachevsky strongly advocated an increase in military spending and in the size of the armed forces to meet a current foreign threat, while Stalin saw the danger in long-range terms and insisted that priority be given to investment instead of defense. In his famous 1931 speech about the need to maintain tempo Stalin said: "We lag [behind] the advanced countries by 50 to 100 years. We must make up this distance in 10 years. Either we do this or they crush us." This seems to have been an argument for the maintenance of high rates of investment at the expense of defense and for the proposition that the threat was a decade away. The apparent Kirov-Ordzhonikidze opposition to Stalin in 1933–1934 was probably the military-industrial complex insisting that the rise of Hitler and of Japanese militarism required a readjustment in this priority.

Similarly, on a more local basis, the immediate beneficiaries of defense expenditures are far more restricted politically in the Soviet Union than in the United States. Specific industries and plants may benefit from defense expenditures, but in a full-employment economy that is not propelled by demand it cannot be argued that defense expenditures are needed to prevent unemployment in certain communities. Moreover, the absence of competitive elections and a meaningful legislature reduces the leverage that local interests have in the political process.

A second difference in the defense policy processes of the United States and the Soviet Union produced by their respective economic systems centers on the relationship of the military and the defense industry. In the United States, defense industry administrators are judged on the basis of profit, and profit is determined on a cost-plus basis. If the military wants a complicated and sophisticated weapon—and officers do seem much attracted to such weapons—then the defense industry is generally charmed. The higher the cost of the weapon, the bigger the profit. Moreover, a sophisticated weapon may have a larger export market, and government-financed defense on the frontier of technology may be transferable to civilian products. It is no accident that the United States takes the lead in computers and aircraft.

This incentive structure has an impact on the military-defense industry relationship. So long as the U.S. military is willing to pay, either directly or through the acceptance of inflated costs, it can ensure that most conflicts between it and the defense industry can be resolved in its favor. And with weapons officers moving into postretirement jobs in the industry, yet another mechanism exists to produce a smooth adjustment of conflicts of interests, with the military winning on product choice and design and the defense industry on the economics of weaponry.

In the Soviet Union, however, defense industry manufacturers are judged not by profit, even cost-plus profit, but by whether they have fulfilled a predetermined plan. Since plan fulfillment depends more on the nature of the original plan than on the manager's performance, the manager fights for as easy a plan as possible. Complicated or radically new weapons increase the danger of production problems and delays; hence the manager—and the ministry—strongly prefer old weapons to new ones. Moreover, if militarily financed research has a civilian payoff, that intensifies the disaster for the industrialist. If the planners forced the manager to employ the technology in some way in next year's projects, the plan would have a complicated civilian item that also might have bugs and thus complicate plan fulfillment.

Hence, if the military is looking at a foreign weapon based on advanced technology and wants a comparable one—either because of a real perception of threat or simply because they too want the most modern "toys"—the inevitable result is a major conflict of interest with the defense industry. A significant amount of information about the military-defense industry conflict is available only for the years 1939 to 1941, since the immediate prewar and the wartime periods are the only ones since the Civil War on which extensive memoirs and biographical literature have been permitted publication. This literature is filled with discussions of fierce conflicts on airplanes, tanks, and artillery—conflicts that often held up decisions on weapons production.[1]

Because a bureaucratic mechanism was needed to resolve these conflicts, a Council of Defense was established which brought top civilians (as well as civilian staff) into the defense policy-making process in the most detailed manner.[2] It is quite likely that the resolution of military-defense industry conflicts is still the primary role of the Defense Council today.[3]

The complexity of the Soviet defense policy process and the secrecy surrounding it in the postwar period make generalizations difficult and risky. In broadest perspective, however, the major feature of the process in this era has been the dominance of the defense industry over the military. The major development of the last 15 years has been the growing challenge to the defense industry from two opposite sources: the military, and the scholars and diplomats who are concerned with strategic questions.

The strength of the defense industry vis-à-vis other actors in the process derives historically from several different factors:

The industry has had a strong monopoly. There are no competitive factories to which the military can turn if it is dissatisfied with the existing choice of products. Moreover, the weapons designers are subordinate to the defense industry and, not surprisingly, have developed an incremental approach to weapons improvement that is in the interest of their superiors. The military can complain—and in certain cases has won—but the initiative is in the hands of the defense industry, and that is always inherently the dominant position.

Persons coming out of the defense industry, but not the military, have been key members of the political elite. Stalin believed in engineering education as the proper preparation for the political elite, and he took deliberate steps to create such an elite.[4] Incentives were created to attract the best young men—at first men in their mid-twenties, already out of school—into heavy industry and defense industry institutes. In the wake of the Great Purge these men were thrust to the top. (The late Minister of Defense Dmitrii Ustinov, for one, became commissar of the Armaments Industry in 1941 at the age of 33.)

The relative status of the defense industry and the military at the end of the Stalin period was well illustrated by the composition of the enlarged Party Presidium (as the Politburo was then called) elected in 1952. There were 25 voting members and 12 candidates, not one of whom was a military man, if one excludes Marshal Klement Voroshilov — an old crony of Stalin who was working on cultural matters and was in any case about to be liquidated. Five full members and two candidates were heavy industry and defense industry administrators; another seven full members and three candidates were engineers from such industries who had moved into political work. Nikolai Bulganin, an industrial administrator in the 1920s, supervised the military for Stalin and was in charge of the defense industry as well.

When Khrushchev became party secretary in 1953, he relied on Bulganin as his number-two man, even making him chairman of the Council of Ministers in 1955. From 1956 to 1960, one of Khrushchev's closest lieutenants, Leonid Brezhnev (who had a background in ferrous metallurgy engineering) served as Central Committee secretary for military affairs, the defense industry, and the crucial rocket and space programs. In the last years of his rule, Khrushchev moved Ustinov from the post of top defense industry administrator to that of chairman of the Supreme Economic Council.

Brezhnev in turn made Andrei Kirilenko, an aviation industry engineer, his Central Committee secretary for personnel and his heir apparent. Ustinov was Central Committee secretary for the military and the defense industry, and in 1976 became minister of defense. The practice of promoting men with an early defense industry and heavy industry background into top political posts continued. At the end of Brezhnev's life, the Politburo also included Nikolai Tikhonov, a former steel industry administrator; Grigorii Romanov, from the shipbuilding industry; Vladimir Shcherbitsky, from the ferrous metallurgy industry; and Dinmukhamed Kunaev, from the nonferrous metallurgy industry.

Not surprisingly, political leaders with such a background have tended to favor the defense industry in its conflict with the military and the civilian defense theorists. The growth in Soviet weapons procurement stopped in the mid-1970s, but production continued at the same level. As a number of Western scholars have noted, Soviet weapons have usually been simple types that the defense industry has an incentive to produce rather than more complex models, and generally only incremental changes have been introduced. No strong pressure has been applied to catch up with U.S. designs. Over 20 years after the United States introduced a solid-fuel ICBM in the Minuteman, the Soviet Union still has not developed a successful one of its own unless the SS-25 proves itself. Even the enormously counterproductive military secrecy may reflect the defense industry's desire to prevent discussion of its weapons as much as it reflects pressure from the military sector.

In real rather than formalistic terms, the upper-level policy process on defense questions basically remained much the same from the mid-1960s until the mid-1980s, whatever surface changes may have occurred. Ustinov was essentially the dominant force in it, whether he served as Central Committee secretary or minister of defense. After 1976 he was formally in charge only of the military, but in reality he ruled the defense industry as well, at least until the summer of 1983 when Andropov began undercutting his authority with the election of a second defense specialist, Grigorii Romanov, to the Politburo. Symptomatic of Ustinov's strength was the appointment of his college classmate and longtime personal assistant, Igor Dmitriev, as head of the defense industry department of the Central Committee when the old head died in 1981.

Beneath Ustinov's dominance, however, two important long-term developments were occurring. First, the disarmament process was legitimating—even requiring—the creation of a large corps of civilian diplomats and scholars who were experts on strategic questions. Westerners have often been skeptical of the significance of this development because of an assumption that these men have no access to classified Soviet data and therefore to the development of the Soviet position. This assumption is based on an erroneous interpretation of a remark by Marshal Ogarkov some 12 years ago at a SALT I negotiating session,[5] and on the reluctance of Soviet civilians to confirm to foreigners that they have access to classified data, because such an acknowledgement is in itself a violation of security.

Clearly, however, many of the civilians have had over 15 years of experience in the field, and their number has become substantial.[6] In the 1970s there was a single disarmament section of 10 men within the international-organizations department of the Ministry of Foreign Affairs.[7] Today, working directly on disarmament are over half of the 50 to 60 officials of the Ministry's international-organizations department, six in its disarmament section of the U.S. department, and a number of individual officials within its European departments. And there are many more who have worked in this sphere before moving to other posts.

Ministry officials insist that there is no network of firmly established interagency committees, but that the delegation to a disarmament conference—which, of course, includes representatives of all interested institutions—becomes the "base organization" for working out the Soviet proposals. Consequently, the delegation includes quite responsible officials, with, for example, the Ministry's deputy head of the U.S. department for disarmament serving as deputy to the head of the SALT II delegation.

The extent to which scholars are drawn into the drafting of Soviet proposals is less clear, but it is obvious from the literature that they write tirelessly on the role of force, on the degree of the threat, on the priority to be given disarmament. Unlike the situation in the United States, where a large percentage of civilian theorists are directly or indirectly financed by the Defense Department, the Soviet scholars are financially independent of the military. In this respect, the military's jealousy in guarding its information has prevented the creation of a dependent group of civilian intellectuals and has seriously harmed the military's interests. The vast majority working on strategic and disarmament questions take a strongly prodisarmament posture and struggle to modify the old Soviet image of an inherent antagonism between the United States and the Soviet Union.

The civilians' impact is hard to assess. The Soviet Union did not, in fact, increase defense expenditures in the face of the massive U.S. buildup beginning in 1977, and it is unlikely that arguments for this response came from the military and the defense industry. Soviet arms control proposals have become increasingly forthcoming; indeed, Andropov's offer on the SS-20s was almost startling. (In the mid-1970s the West had accepted as equitable a situation in which the Soviet Union had 650 SS-4s and SS-5s balancing the British and French missiles and U.S. airplanes. With the installation of SS-20s, the Soviets permitted the number of warheads on SS-4s and SS-20s to rise to some 950. However, Andropov eventually offered to cut back to 360 warheads, requiring no reduction in the original Western forces, only a willingness to forego future deployments. Nearly 600 warheads were to be dismantled without a quid quo pro, and the remaining number would be nearly 300 below the Soviet level of the mid-1970s.) This development, too, is unlikely to have been the result of military pressure, so the influence of diplomats and scholars on Soviet thinking and policy may be far greater than we have assumed.

Nevertheless, while the Brezhnev-Ustinov-Gromyko generation dominated the Politburo, the Soviets did not take the kinds of actions that might really have made a difference in the West—for example, a reduction in secrecy and a more open approach. The real question is whether the civilian intellectuals have affected the thinking of the men in their fifties who are coming to dominate the Politburo. Lord Keynes once spoke about so-called practical men being the prisoners of some defunct economist, and it certainly is true that the most decisive influences on a person's thinking come fairly early in life. We will know whether the scholarly debates of the last two decades have really had an impact when we learn which scholars—defunct or not so defunct— have captured Gorbachev's mind.

The second major development in the Soviet defense policy process has been the articulation of dissatisfaction by a leading military spokesman, Marshal Nikolai Ogarkov. In a series of statements, culminating in a frank interview in *Red Star* on May 9, 1984, Ogarkov asserted flatly that nuclear weapons are all but unusable; that a disarming first strike on command-and-control installations or opposing rockets is impossible since a crushing retaliation is unstoppable (so much for the Soviet propaganda theme about the Pershing II); that the limited use of nuclear weapons is impossible because a limited nuclear war will escalate; and that the all-out use of nuclear weapons is suicidal. He not only drew the obvious conclusion that conventional weapons and "weapons based on new physical principles" are consequently crucial in the military equation, but he also painted the gloomiest picture of U.S. technological advances in these realms. By quoting Engels to the effect that nothing so depends on the economy as the military, he clearly implied what the nature of the problem was from the Soviet point of view.

Ogarkov's interview was remarkable. General Secretary Chernenko seemed strongly opposed to economic reform, and any criticism of the defense industry's ability to meet the U.S. challenge was a direct thrust at Ogarkov's superior, Ustinov, who had been a central defense industry administrator for 40 years, and the key administrator for 25. Ustinov's statements showed real testiness on the issue —"The defense industry is capable of producing any weapon"—and the tension between the two men was noticeable in the press.[8]

Why, then, did Ogarkov think that he could get away with these public statements? When he was removed, why was he not dismissed from all his responsibilities, as Marshal Zhukov was in 1957, instead of being given a major new role and permitted to republish his statements about nuclear war (but not the implications about conventional weapons) almost verbatim in a propaganda journal for the troops?[9] The inescapable conclusion is that he must have support somewhere high in the Politburo.

The real significance of Ogarkov's statement is that he is essentially right. Because nuclear weapons are basically unusable, the Soviet technological lag threatens a major window of vulnerability for the Soviet Union in the 1990s and early twenty-first century as the new generation of Western conventional weapons is assimilated and as China modernizes. With computerized "smart" shells and the like, Soviet tanks are likely to become as obsolete as the cavalry.

If the United States is having trouble finding personnel to handle *its* advanced technology, what will the Soviet Union do, even if it does computerize its military but has to use Uzbek peasants, who have never seen a computer, to run it? While some of the older military men such as Minister of Defense Sokolov still seem to think in World War II terms, the younger generation of military personnel must understand the problem. Their anger at a defense industry that cannot keep up with the West will grow, and a military that becomes convinced that the civilians are destroying the nation's capacity to defend itself becomes more than a mere interest-group claimant in the budgetary process.

The real question for the present and the future is whether Ustinov's death and Gorbachev's accession to power will fundamentally change the balance of forces in the Soviet defense process. It is too early to be certain, but the likely answer is yes.

The Ogarkov case is a flash of lightning that illuminates the scene not only for us, but also for the Soviet leadership. The significance of generational change in the Politburo is not simply that men with more modern views may come to power; even more important is the fact that men of the Gorbachev generation have a different time perspective on the future. Brezhnev's and Chernenko's worries did not extend past the mid-1980s, and there was no sign of important political trouble within that period. Gorbachev, however, will only be 69 in the year 2000, and there are signs of enormous trouble on that time horizon. If the Soviet Union does not begin to solve the problem of technological lag, it faces the prospect of real political instability. The threat will come from the military, if from nowhere else.

To meet the various potential dangers posed by the technological lag, Gorbachev must undertake a very difficult economic reform, and for this he badly needs a foreign threat. Yet, like Stalin in 1928, he also needs to put money into long-term investment such as computers and electronics, and into military research-and-development rather than into old-line readiness or weapons such as tanks.

The Ogarkov arguments give him the case to make about the long-term threat. The arguments of the civilian theorists about the nature of military force and the stability of the nuclear balance give him the

152   *Jerry F. Hough*

case he needs to play down the short-term threat. In his acceptance speech, Gorbachev hinted at a doctrine of sufficiency and massive retaliation, and this is the intelligent position for him to take.

For all these reasons it is quite possible that the long battle against the dominance of the defense industry and its assumptions will finally begin to have an impact. That the Soviet elite chose a lawyer rather than an engineer as their leader; that they chose the best-educated Politburo member, with only six years' work in Moscow; and that they picked a man 15 years younger than the average age of other Politburo members, all suggest that there is widespread understanding of a need for fundamental change—and not only in economic reform. But whether this will really prove to be true is for a future anniversary issue of the *Bulletin* to discuss.

1. See Jerry F. Hough, "The Historical Legacy in Soviet Weapons Development," in Jiri Valenta and William C. Potter, eds., *Soviet Decisionmaking for National Security* (London: George Allen & Unwin, 1984), pp. 87–115.

2. Ibid., pp. 88–91 and 106; Ellen Jones, "The Defense Council in Soviet Leadership Decision-Making," Kennan Institute Occasional Paper no. 188 (Washington, D.C.).

3. Most sources attribute the responsibility for resolving such disputes to the Military-Industrial Commission of the Council of Ministers, chaired by the country's top defense-industry official, Leonid Smirnov. It is unlikely, however, that he would be allowed to resolve disputes between himself and the military, but if so, the defense industry's power is even greater than suggested here.

4. Sheila Fitzpatrick, "Stalin and the Making of the New Elite," *Slavic Review*, 38, no. 3 (1979), pp. 377–402.

5. Raymond L. Garthoff, "The Soviet Military and SALT," in Valenta and Potter, op. cit., p. 153.

6. Arkady N. Shevchenko, *Breaking with Moscow* (New York: Alfred A. Knopf, 1985), pp. 78–79, 82–84, 96.

7. See Marshall D. Shulman, "SALT and the Soviet Union," in Mason Willrich and John B. Rhinelander, eds., *SALT: The Moscow Agreements and Beyond* (New York: The Free Press/Macmillan, 1974), pp. 101–21.

8. Georg Weickhardt, "Ustinov vs. Ogarkov," *Problems of Communism* (Jan.-Feb. 1985), pp. 77–82.

9. N. Ogarkov, "Merknushchaia slava sovetskogo oruzhiia," *Kommunist vooruzhennykh sil*, no. 21 (Nov. 1984), p. 26.

3

U.S. and Soviet Security Perspectives

John Steinbruner

The sense of tension in U.S.-Soviet relations has been eased by the opening of arms control negotiations in Geneva, by the succession of a personable Soviet leader who has reaffirmed commitment to détente, and by the November 1985 summit meeting. These public events are also reflected in the details of diplomatic procedure where both sides have been making plausible efforts to convey constructive intentions. That is a distinct improvement over the recent past.

On the substance of security policy, however, the two countries remain in sharp contention, and their respective weapons programs are nearing points of irreversible damage to existing arms control arrangements. An enduring improvement in relations will require fundamental compromise on the deployment of strategic weapons.

With political debate in the Western alliance increasingly focused on the theory of missile defense, the immediate weapons development issues that most seriously affect the future of security have largely escaped attention. For example, because of the severe problems of verification they present, submarine-based cruise missile deployments, now being initiated by both countries, are likely to preclude a meaningful ceiling on strategic weapons deployments—heretofore the central means of regulating those deployments. Moreover, if it so chooses, the Soviet Union can readily compound this problem by instituting an effectively concealed deployment of land-mobile

ICBMs, an option that for reasons of geography and of practical realities would be quite difficult for the United States to match. Even more serious, the U.S. strategic defense initiative (SDI, or "Star Wars") and the Soviet reaction to it will predictably create, on both sides, the weapons and organizational units for dedicated antisatellite missions and will thereby threaten space assets critical to the safe and stable management of both strategic establishments.

Urgent as these weapons development issues are, however, and important as they may be for any diplomatic compromise, they are not the core of the problem. They are specific manifestations of a disparity in security perspectives, deeply rooted in differences between the two political systems. Each side understands both the present balance of security and its historical evolution very differently. Compromise is very likely to require some narrowing of these differences.

In the United States, security policy emerges from a deliberately divided government and a highly participatory political process. Clarity of purpose and consistency of action necessarily depend upon underlying attitudes that are widely enough accepted to allow independent institutions to act in concert. Since policy assumptions that enjoy broad consensus are critically important for coherent government operation, naturally enough they are staunchly defended once they are established. It is a strength of the American system that its dominant security perspectives rest on firm conviction and that they facilitate internal political decisions. It is a vulnerability that these perspectives are highly resistant to adjustment and are particularly insensitive to Soviet views.

We generally discount our military strength and exalt our political intentions. In our domestic political discussion, we presume that the immediate fighting capabilities of the United States are quite moderate compared with our security needs and that the fundamental objectives of our policy are unquestionably peaceful. So firmly planted are these beliefs that we treat them as universally apparent, dismissing any doubts that the Soviet Union expresses as hostile propaganda not worth serious attention. We are currently undertaking a comprehensive modernization of our strategic weapons arsenal and despite the rhetoric of defense, the emphasis is on the improvement and extension of offensive systems. We are also sustaining a surge in overall military spending unprecedented in peacetime. And as we do these things, prevailing political opinion in the United States remains confident that they are justifiable responses to past Soviet actions.

We impute to the Soviet Union highly coherent and directly hostile purposes that logically justify and politically mobilize stark U.S. reactions. Soviet actions are usually interpreted as manifestations of a deliberate intention to oppose some important U.S. interest, or to pursue a clear Soviet interest at our expense. The simplest form of this analysis relies on a single word—expansionism—to weave a wide variety of events into a systematic, easily perceived, and, of course, highly objectionable pattern. More sophisticated variants analyze Soviet actions in terms of the details of their immediate context but still use the same type of logic: Soviet objections to the U.S. strategic defense initiative, for example, are widely held to be a political tactic designed to sow dissension in the Atlantic alliance. Such facile interpretation of the Soviet position relieves the burden of more discriminating judgment.

We have an institutionalized aversion to hard choices. A reluctance to acknowledge the necessity of making painful decisions is a universal human tendency, but it is powerfully reinforced in any democratic political process. No political leader aware of popular opinion will readily admit that important objectives cannot be simultaneously achieved. Thus we are introducing six new offensive strategic systems while promoting arms control arrangements that would sharply reduce the level of strategic weapons deployments. Prevailing American opinion sees no contradiction and indeed insists that the one provides incentive for the other.

These attitudes and actions, in a context of intense distrust, present an unavoidable conflict between the most fundamental objectives of U.S. foreign policy. The Soviet Union now possesses the physical capacity to annihilate the United States as an organized society, and history has burdened us with reasons to fear an underlying inclination to do so should a safe opportunity arise. With basic survival at stake, we maintain an annihilating capability of our own that is a compelling deterrent to deliberate attack but does unavoidably risk a war arising out of inadvertent or uncontrollable interactions of the opposing military forces. At the same time, the Soviet Union represents the principal contrast to our form of economic and political organization.

A defense of the most central values of American society continuously produces sharp opposition to Soviet policy on a variety of immediate issues. Although no single one of these issues could plausibly provide the motive for a deliberate war, in combination they certainly make war more likely than it would otherwise be by providing the context for a potentially uncontrollable crisis. We continuously balance survival and political principle in dealing with the Soviet Union, but we are extremely averse to admitting that fact and hence to accepting any arrangement that formalizes it.

These features of the U.S. perspective have made compromise with the Soviet Union very difficult to achieve. Though there are 12 major treaties, with associated protocols and interpretive statements, that directly affect the disposition of the U.S. and Soviet strategic arsenals, the last three—the 1979 SALT II Treaty, the 1974 Threshold Test Ban Treaty, and the 1976 Treaty on Underground Nuclear Explosions for Peaceful Purposes—have not been ratified.[1] Even more important, the central underlying principle—an agreed determination of equal security—has not been established.

The principle of equality has generally been recognized among diplomats as the only realistic basis for stable regulation of the U.S.-Soviet relationship; and implicit in the intricate details of the treaties is a very simple and very fundamental political deal that for nearly two decades representatives of the two countries have been attempting to strike. The impetus for the deal is the central technical problem that plagues any U.S.-Soviet agreement: the fact that their respective security requirements are strikingly different.

The United States is isolated from the prospect of invasion, and long-range bombardment by nuclear weapons is the only direct military threat of serious proportions. The Soviet Union does not even remotely possess the forces required to seize and hold territory in the continental United States, and neither does any other nation. The United States is supported by an alliance of spontaneously loyal nations whose combined economic and technical capacities far exceed those of the Soviet Union and its allies. Our allies, however, are geographically vulnerable to invasion and by themselves would not be capable of preventing it. U.S. forces are therefore deployed on the borders of the Soviet alliance countries to protect our allies and, indirectly, ourselves. The structure of our military forces reflects these circumstances, with substantial reliance on mobile operations and technical sophistication.

The Soviet Union, by contrast, must contend not only with the prospect of nuclear bombardment but also, conceivably, with invasion from Europe or Asia and potentially significant harassment from the Middle East. Soviet allies are not nearly as spontaneously loyal or as economically capable as those of the United States. A heavy emphasis on land armies and a strong regional concentration of forces emerges from these circumstances.

These disparities in the geographic positions of the United States and the Soviet Union, in the nature of their respective alliances, and in the composition of their respective military forces defy any explicit equation, since any given weapon or any given level of its deployment has substantially different military significance for the two sides. Accordingly, by the early 1970s, when both sides had come to acknowledge a mutual interest in controlling military confrontation, U.S. and Soviet negotiators settled on an arrangement, embodied in the SALT I treaty in 1972. They agreed to accept the overall balance of security then prevailing as an equitable baseline from which to proceed, very gradually, toward a more precisely defined equality of position.

It was an understanding to call two wholes equal even though few of their parts could be matched. It required acceptance of existing disparities but imposed a rule that future changes would have to be balanced, with neither side seeking any major additional advantage. Equality was to be a starting point and a signpost, rather than the map of an ultimate destination.

The logic for such an arrangement did not lie in strategic analysis, though it has been defended in those terms. It is quite apparent, for example, that a rationally stabilized balance of strategic weapons, conceding retaliation but denying preemption, would not have allowed multiple-warhead missiles. Nor was the arrangement inspired by much reflection on domestic politics, at least in the United States. In restricting only future decisions while allowing existing and emerging weapons programs to continue, it foreordained that the effects of restraint would be invisible to most of the observing public. Furthermore, the SALT I Treaty would be followed by ostentatious increases in the number of Soviet weapons as multiple-warhead missiles were introduced into Soviet forces. Controversy was bound to follow. Rather than from strategy or politics, the arrangement emerged from the fundamentals of adversarial diplomacy. An arbitrary but nonetheless plausible assertion of equality and the rule of balanced evolution were the first steps necessary to ease two intensely hostile and very dangerous opponents into some stable order.

The U.S. political system, however, is not organized to make political deals of such a general nature in the absence of a life-threatening crisis. Indeed, as protection against tyranny, it is specifically designed to make decisions of that scope difficult. The fundamental compromise implicit in SALT I could not be immediately internalized in the United States. In fact, it was not even articulated without protective qualifications meant to deflect domestic opposition.

American political discussion focused primarily on treaty specifics and quickly generated pressures to define equity in terms of immediate weapons inventories and political events. Moreover, as debate proceeded and irritants in U.S.-Soviet political relations accumulated, a classic dynamic of U.S. politics began to take effect. Opponents of compromise with the Soviet Union acted more forcefully and more skilfully than its proponents—the familiar story of an organized, intensely committed minority dominating a more diffuse, more tepid majority. They evoked fears of specific Soviet advantages—in heavy ICBMs, theater-range missiles, conventional ground-force formations —and anger over Soviet actions in the Middle East, Angola, Afghanistan, and Poland in order to reinforce opposition to political support for the compromise.

In this process the broader dimensions of U.S. interest were obscured. As the 1970s progressed, prevailing American opinion took little notice of the fact that net security circumstances were running distinctly to the advantage of the United States, most notably because of the dramatic shift in Chinese policy and the more gradual political and economic evolution occurring in Eastern Europe.

Thirteen years after SALT I was ratified, the compromise it reflected has not been established within the U.S. political system, and the indirect signals of intention emanating from our statements and actions are bound to seem more negative than positive. So far we have honored the terms of the 1972 ABM Treaty, but Reagan's strategic defense initiative clearly projects its ultimate abrogation and thus violates the spirit of the agreement.

We have also complied with the offensive force limitations in the SALT I protocol and the SALT II Treaty, but we have refused to ratify the latter, and in developing two new ICBMs—MX and Midgetman —we are clearly anticipating a major loosening of its restrictions. In deploying medium-range missiles in Europe we have precluded an extension of the protocol to the SALT II Treaty, mooted Soviet insistence that the protocol was integral to the whole, and violated the implicit rule of not initiating a major unilateral change in the 1972 baseline conditions. We have initiated deployment of nuclear-armed cruise missiles at sea without attempting any negotiated restrictions— also an implicit rejection of restraint on unilateral initiatives.

An important fact of security is that prevailing U.S. perspectives are not shared by the Soviet Union. However firmly we reject the validity of Soviet views, it is imprudent to deny either their sincerity or their practical significance.

In recent years Soviet leaders have repeatedly expressed fears that U.S. strategic programs are designed to provide the capacity to initiate attack on Soviet strategic forces in the event of war, with sufficient success to establish some meaningful form of military victory. The spearhead of this capacity, in Soviet estimation, is the Pershing II missile now being deployed in Western Europe. The relatively short flight-time of this missile, its extreme accuracy, its earth-penetrating warhead, the numbers planned for deployment, and the possibility for tightly controlled operational coordination from land-based installations are all seen as indications of an intention to attack the command structure of Soviet forces located primarily in Western parts of the Soviet Union. Soviet military analysts have long recognized the central command system as the most critical target for an effective preemptive attack.

Further, because of the enhanced accuracy and yield of their warheads, the MX and the projected Trident II SLBM (submarine-launched ballistic missile) are seen as the workhorses of this emerging U.S. preemptive capability. Once incorporated into U.S. forces, these systems, combined with the recently improved Minuteman III, would provide well over 5,000 individual warheads capable of attacking hardened installations in the Soviet Union—enough to threaten the entire Soviet ICBM force if the advertised performance of the new U.S. missiles is taken at face value.

The strategic defense initiative now being promoted in the United States is seen by the Soviets not as fundamental to a shift to a defensive posture, as President Reagan proclaimed it to be, but rather as a supplement to the capacity for offensive preemption. It confirms the implied logic of the U.S. program. In explicit Soviet estimates of the matter, foreseeable defensive technology offers very poor prospects for defending against Soviet offensive weapons that are fired first and are made operationally optimal to negate the defense. These prospects are so poor, in fact, that it would be irrational to pursue a truly defensive mission under that expectation. The prospective technology, however, potentially could defend against a greatly diminished, uncoordinated Soviet offensive force attempting to retaliate after a U.S. preemptive strike.[2]

This Soviet projection of a highly threatening U.S. strategic weapons posture is matched by a correspondingly grim assessment of U.S. political intentions, derived from experience with arms control negotiations. Not only the polemicists but also the professional Soviet diplomats and analysts appear to have settled on a pessimistic account of this experience. They emphasize that the U.S. political system has failed to ratify the past three arms control agreements; that principal figures in the Administration have repeatedly expressed contempt not only for those specific agreements but also for arms control in general; that the United States has entered new negotiations only in response to external public pressure; and that U.S. arms control proposals have been designed to be unacceptable to the Soviet Union. The U.S. arms control positions, they argue, would reduce the allowed levels of strategic weapons primarily in areas where the Soviets currently enjoy numerical advantages—land-based and medium-range ballistic missiles. Moreover, the U.S. position does not envisage restrictions on weapons modernization. In the Soviet view, the perceived development of a U.S. preemptive-strike capability involves weapons modernization programs rather than increases in deployed force levels. Therefore, restraints on weapons modernization must accompany any force reduction agreement that could be accepted by the Soviet Union. Otherwise, the suggested force reduction would simply make the imputed U.S. preemptive strike easier to accomplish.

Moreover, though they are less explicit on the point, it is apparent that Soviet leaders do not perceive the "relentless momentum" in their own military programs that has been repeatedly asserted by U.S. officials. The planning decisions that gave rise to the Soviet offensive weapons surge of the mid-1970s were made in the early to mid-1960s, and much of the effort to implement them was undertaken in the late 1960s. Otherwise, the actual weapons could not have appeared when they did. Similarly, it is apparent that in the wake of the 1972 arms control agreement, Soviet planners introduced relatively few new initiatives involving strategic weapons *deployments* (as distinct from research and development programs), and the process of implementing Soviet strategic weapons programs moderated considerably.

This dynamic in the Soviet system has recently been reflected in retrospective assessments of Soviet military spending: The United States originally estimated that Soviet defense expenditures had grown throughout the 1970s at the rate of 4 percent per year—roughly twice that of the Soviet economy as a whole—but accumulated data have forced a revision of those estimates. From 1977 through 1981, it now appears, Soviet military expenditures probably grew at or below the 2 percent rate that prevailed in the general economy, and in the aggregate Soviet military procurement—expenditures for new weapons deployments—did not grow at all. Since the Soviets did increase their investment (including research and development) in some new weapons categories during this period, the fact that overall military procurement remained constant is due largely to a relative decline in investment for strategic offensive weapons during the course of the 1970s.[3]

The actual capacity of Soviet strategic offensive forces grew considerably as a result of earlier investments, but growth was not sustained. As is the case with U.S. forces, Soviet strategic forces remain today well below the full elaboration that arms control arrangements would allow: approximately 8,500 strategic warheads in mid-1984 as compared with the nearly 18,000 ballistic-missile and cruise-missile warheads that would be legal under the SALT II Treaty. Moreover, throughout the 1970s, as Soviet investment was being restricted, the United States added more strategic warheads to its forces than the Soviets did to theirs.[4] In the Soviet perception, that was hardly relentless momentum or systematic intimidation.

It is impossible for Western observers to guess with any confidence what the detailed nature of political divisions within the Soviet Union might be. But it is reasonable to suppose that the diminishing rate of investment in Soviet strategic forces investment during the past decade has become controversial. It does not require clairvoyance to imagine that there must be a body of opinion disputing the wisdom or adequacy of their allocation of effort and demanding a surge in Soviet strategic investment to match that of the United States. In the absence of definitive evidence either way, that reaction should be considered far more likely to ensue than capitulation to the perceived pressure of U.S. weapons programs. In fact, official U.S. assessments of Soviet military programs are already detecting the early stages of new cruise missile deployments on submarines and the introduction of the SS-X-25 as a land-mobile ICBM.[5] These are strong hints of a new phase in Soviet strategic development.

U.S.-Soviet security relations have almost certainly come to a point of fundamental change, but the ultimate outcome is still to be determined. The tragedy of weapons programs that significantly degrade the security of both sides could readily occur and indeed appears to be the most likely result of current policies. Highly constructive outcomes are also possible if timely decisions are made to reach fundamental compromise.

The technical design of compromise is not difficult. It involves a balance between restraints on weapons modernization (the primary commitment of the Soviet Union) and force reductions (the primary commitment of the United States) which could be implemented in a variety of ways. The outcome turns more on political will than on technical design. For that reason it is important for both sides to reexamine their fundamental attitudes and to adjust the bias in their security perspectives.

1. U.S. Arms Control and Disarmament Agency, "Arms Control and Disarmament Agreements," 1982 edition (Washington, D.C.: 1982).

2. For Soviet views on the strategic defense initiative see R.Z. Sagdeyev, A.A. Kokoshin, and others, "A Space-Based Anti-Missile System with Directed Energy Weapons: Strategic, Legal, and Political Implications," (Moscow: Institute of Space Research, Soviet Academy of Sciences, 1984).

3. Richard F. Kaufman, "Causes for the Slowdown in Soviet Defense," *Soviet Economy,* vol. 1 (1985).

4. Raymond L. Garthoff, *Perspectives on the Strategic Balance* (Washington, D.C.: Brookings Institution, 1983), p. 8.

5. Defense Department, *Soviet Military Power 1985* (Washington, D.C.: Government Printing Office, 1985).

4

Attacks on Star Wars Critics a Diversion

Frank von Hippel

The December 1984 issue of *Commentary* contained an article, "The War Against 'Star Wars,'" by Dartmouth College astrophysicist Robert Jastrow, which attacks two technical critiques of President Reagan's Strategic Defense Initiative (SDI). One of the critiques had been written by a group organized under the auspices of the Union of Concerned Scientists (UCS) and the other by Ashton Carter for the congressional Office of Technology Assessment (OTA).[1]

The *Wall Street Journal* immediately picked up Jastrow's attack, in a December 10 editorial, "Politicized Science," which attacked the UCS and OTA reports as "less than scientific." The editorial ended with a note of concern: "It would be a shame . . . if the President fails to realize that his plan is supported by men such as Mr. Jastrow who have studied the problem carefully and scientifically." In fact, Jastrow had not himself done any scientific studies but was merely reporting somewhat breathlessly the criticisms of the UCS and OTA reports by anonymous "experts" at Lawrence Livermore and Los Alamos Laboratories.

The UCS group and Carter responded with letters to the editor of the *Wall Street Journal* published on January 2. A storm of letters supporting the editorial was then published in the January 17 edition. These included letters from: Lieutenant General James A. Abrahamson, the director of the SDI organization; C. Paul Robinson, the principal associate director of Los Alamos National Laboratory; and Lowell

Wood, the head of the X-ray laser group at Livermore National Laboratory.

At the technical level, the principal focus of the criticisms of the UCS report★ was a calculation of the number of laser battle-stations that would be required in orbit to destroy Soviet ICBMs during "boost phase," the period of up to five minutes after launch while the rocket engine is still burning and before the multiple warheads and decoys are released. According to the *Wall Street Journal*, the original UCS estimate was 2,400 battle-stations, but "defense experts at Los Alamos say only 80 to 100 will do. The initial UCS error would make the difference between estimating a defense cost of say $50 billion and estimating at $1 trillion or more."

At the political level, the issue is the credibility of the technical critics of Star Wars. During the 1968–1972 debate over the anti-ballistic-missile system proposed by the Johnson and Nixon Administrations, two of the principal contributors to the current UCS report, Richard Garwin and Hans Bethe, helped to turn the scientific community against the proposed system, largely by showing in a *Scientific American* article how vulnerable it would be to countermeasures.[2]

Obviously, both sides of the new Star Wars debate remember this history. One side hopes to repeat Garwin and Bethe's success in having an impact on the policy debate with a technical assessment of the Star Wars proposal. On the other side, advocates of the SDI, whose leaders include advocates of the Johnson-Nixon ABM system such as Jastrow and Edward Teller, hope to render the critics ineffective by attacking their credibility.

The UCS group described a hypothetical battle station equipped with a hydrogen-fluoride laser producing a beam of infrared (2.7 micron) radiation with a power of 25 million watts. This beam would be aimed by a perfect (10-meter diameter) mirror able to focus the beam on a spot with a diameter of less than a meter at a distance of 3,000 kilometers with an intensity sufficient to burn through the shell of a booster within about seven seconds.

★I discuss here only the debate over the UCS report because the public discussion has tended to focus on it. However, on May 8, 1984, Abrahamson distributed to the press a set of criticisms of the OTA report. This was followed, on June 4, by a letter from Deputy Secretary of Defense William H. Taft IV to OTA Director John Gibbons, demanding that the OTA withdraw Carter's report. The OTA issued a sharp rebuttal to Abrahamson's list of criticisms and, on July 13, after having the OTA report reviewed by three high-level defense experts, Gibbons turned down Taft's request. The Defense Department does not appear to have pursued the matter further.

The number of such battle stations required to destroy all the Soviet ICBMs—assuming that they were all launched at the same time—would depend upon a number of factors:

the total number of Soviet ICBMs—assumed by the UCS group in their original March 1984 report to be the current number, 1,400;[3]

the duration of the boost phase—assumed to be 100 seconds;

the average distance between the battle-station and the booster—assumed to be 3,000 kilometers;

the distribution of the silos—assumed to be the same as the current distribution;

the distribution of the satellites in orbit—approximated as uniform; and

the "slew-and-settle" time required to move the laser beam from one target to another—assumed to be zero.

Some of these assumptions were generous. For example, the Soviets could increase the number of their ICBMs or deploy relatively inexpensive decoys that would mimic ICBMs during their boost phase. They could concentrate their missile silos in a single area, thus minimizing the number of battle-stations within range at any one time. "Fast-burn" boosters could be developed that cut the duration of the boost phase to 50 seconds. And the slew-and-settle time required to focus a 10-meter diameter mirror on a moving booster 1,000 kilometers away would not be negligible.

However, approximations made in the original UCS calculations were decidedly ungenerous. Most significantly:

the battle-satellites could be placed into orbits which would increase their relative density at the latitudes of the Soviet missile fields by a factor of almost three;

as the density of the battle-satellites increased, the average distance between battle-satellites and targets would decrease.

Similarly crude approximations seem to have been made in the original Los Alamos calculations, and both groups quickly refined their work. By the time the UCS report appeared in book form and, in a shortened version, in *Scientific American* a few months later, *all* its key assumptions were generous to the Star Wars concept, and the estimated number of battle-satellites had been reduced to 300.

In a new analytical paper,[4] however, Garwin has highlighted this generosity by pointing out that, were the Soviet Union to deploy 3,000 small, 40-second burn-time boosters in a region of 1,000 kilometers or less in diameter, and if the slew-and-settle time of the laser mirror were as slow as one-half second, the calculated number of battle-satellites would spring to 1,500. The Soviets would thus be forcing the United States to deploy an extra billion-dollar satellite for every few million-dollar boosters which they deployed—hardly an advantageous exchange for the United States.

It should be emphasized that the hypothetical system being debated by the UCS group and its critics was not an officially proposed design. Although such specific designs have been proposed by small groups of Star Wars enthusiasts, the enormous $26 billion budget that has thus far been requested is only for the first five years of a 10-year exploratory research program.

In the absence of a specific design, the critics have had either to postulate their own—and run the risk of being criticized, as the UCS group was, for ungenerous assumptions—or offer criticisms that would apply to any space-based system. At this stage, the more general criticisms are much more important.

Perhaps the most fundamental technical objection to any Star Wars system would be its susceptibility to countermeasures. Indeed, this point is at the core of the UCS-OTA critique of the Star Wars proposal —just as it was at the core of the Garwin-Bethe critique of the ABM system proposed 15 years ago. From this perspective, the attempts of Star Wars advocates to focus on the details of the earliest version of the UCS calculations of the number of battle-satellites in the absence of countermeasures must be seen as a diversion. McGeorge Bundy, George Kennan, Robert McNamara, and Gerard Smith have made this point particularly well: the "inevitable Soviet reaction is studiously neglected by Secretary Weinberger when he argues in defense of Star Wars that today's skeptics are as wrong as those who said we could never get to the moon. The effort to get to the moon was not complicated by the presence of an adversary. A platoon of hostile moon-men with axes could have made it a disaster."[5]

Consider, for example, the battle-satellites' vulnerability to attack. The Star Wars program puts much emphasis on such orbiting satellites because, after the boost phase, the deployment of multiple warheads and decoys could make the defense problem virtually impossible, and almost all boost-phase schemes require battle-satellites. (Only one directed-energy beam weapon has been proposed that would be light enough to be "popped-up" into space *after* Soviet ICBM launch had been detected. This is the nuclear-explosion-powered X-ray laser. However, as both the UCS and OTA reports point out, the X-rays from this weapon could not penetrate far into the atmosphere and a "fast-burn" booster could be designed to release its warheads below this level.)

A fundamental weakness of all ballistic-missile-defense schemes involving orbiting battle-satellites is that the satellites would be much more vulnerable to attack than their targets. Unlike the boosters, which would be available for destruction for only about a minute at an unpredictable time, the battle-satellites would be at predictable locations in predictable orbits. These billion-dollar machines could therefore easily be destroyed by ground-based lasers or something as simple as a cloud of small metal pellets put into a counter-rotating orbit. (Because of their high closing-speed, such pellets would carry hundreds of times as much energy as an equivalent weight of bullets.) Of course, one could at great expense transport thousands of tons of armor to each battle station, but then how could the sensors see and the lasers fire? In any case, this example shows how one simple countermeasure could either incapacitate a battle station or greatly increase its complexity and cost.

Other countermeasures could neutralize a defensive system without destroying it. For example, Jastrow has proposed a relatively low-cost but easy-to-counter design in an article in the *New York Times Magazine,* written in collaboration with Zbigniew Brzezinski, President Carter's national security advisor, and Max Kampelman, President Reagan's arms control negotiator.[6] The proposed scheme would involve two layers: the first would consist of 100 satellites each carrying 150 interceptor rockets similar to that currently being developed for the U.S. antisatellite system. Those few satellites within range would attack Soviet ballistic missiles during their boost phase. As the UCS group has pointed out, however, a "fast-burn" booster that completed its burn within the atmosphere would also be an effective countermeasure to this system. The infrared sensors of the homing interceptor warheads would be blinded by friction heat as soon as they entered the atmosphere. The second layer of Jastrow's proposed system would be made up of 5,000 ground-based rockets, each of which could intercept a warhead (or decoy) above the atmosphere as it approached its target.

At a political level, there are equally fundamental objections to the Star Wars proposal. Perhaps most importantly, whether or not any Star Wars system was intended to serve only defensive purposes, the other side would not see it as such. And, in fact, such a system makes much more sense as an adjunct to a first-strike capability than as a shield from a first strike. Because of its inevitable vulnerability, a Star Wars-type system would be fairly easy to neutralize at the beginning of a highly orchestrated first strike. But, in the face of a disorganized retaliatory strike by an unprepared victim of a surprise attack, it might be more effective. The Star Wars system would therefore tend to destabilize the balance of terror by increasing the advantages of a first strike. The fact that the Star Wars program has been launched at the same time that the United States is embarking on a huge buildup of exactly the types of accurate ballistic missile warheads that would be most useful in a first strike must be particularly disturbing to Soviet strategic analysts. Indeed, Yuri Andropov said as much four days after President Reagan's original Star Wars speech:

> The strategic offensive forces of the United States will continue to be developed and upgraded at full tilt and along quite a definite line at that, namely that of acquiring a first strike capability. Under these conditions the intention to secure itself the possibility of destroying with the help of ABM defenses the corresponding strategic systems of the other side, that is of rendering it unable of dealing a retaliatory strike, is a bid to disarm the Soviet Union in the face of the U.S. nuclear threat.[7]

The Soviet Union will do whatever is required to prevent the United States from rendering it incapable of launching a retaliatory strike. And, in view of the fact that only one percent or so of the current Soviet nuclear arsenal could obliterate U.S. urban society, the United States could not possibly unilaterally eliminate its mutual hostage relationship with the Soviet Union. The United States can, however, unilaterally launch a defense-offense arms race which, in addition to wasting the skills of tens of thousands of scientists and engineers, would induce enormous uncertainty and paranoia among worst-case analysts on both sides. Staving off such a defense-offense arms race was, of course, the major achievement of the 1972 ABM Treaty.

The debate over the credibility of the Star Wars critics therefore masks a much more important debate—between those who, knowingly or not, are attempting to launch a far more virulent new phase of the nuclear arms race and those who are trying to provide the insight that would allow the United States and the Soviet Union to avoid this danger.

    1. John Tirman, ed., *The Fallacy of Star Wars* (New York: Vintage Books, 1984), based on studies conducted by a group co-chaired by Richard L. Garwin, Kurt Gottfried, and Henry W. Kendall. See also the article-length version, Hans A. Bethe, Richard L. Garwin, Kurt Gottfried, and Henry W. Kendall, "Space-Based Ballistic-Missile Defense," *Scientific American* (Oct. 1984). Ashton Carter, *Directed Energy Missile Defense in Space* (Washington, D.C.: Office of Technology Assessment, 1984).
    2. Richard L. Garwin and Hans A. Bethe, "Anti-Ballistic-Missile Systems," *Scientific American* (March 1968).
    3. *Space-Based Missile Defense* (Cambridge, Mass.: Union of Concerned Scientists, March 1984).

4. "Missile-Killing Potential of Satellite Constellations," draft, Richard L. Garwin, Jan. 2, 1985.

5. McGeorge Bundy, George F. Kennan, Robert S. McNamara, and Gerard Smith, "The President's Choice: Star Wars or Arms Control," *Foreign Affairs* (Winter 1984), p. 264.

6. Zbigniew Brzezinski, Robert Jastrow, and Max M. Kampelman, "Search for Security: The Case for the Strategic Defense Initiative," *New York Times Magazine*, Jan. 27, 1985.

7. Sidney D. Drell, Phillip J. Farley, David Holloway, *The Reagan Strategic Defense Initiative: A Technical, Political, and Arms Control Assessment* (Stanford, Calif.: Center for International Security and Arms Control, 1984), p. 105.

5

Star Wars Bad Even If It Works

Charles L. Glaser

Almost everyone across the political spectrum believes that the United States would be safer if protected by highly effective defenses against nuclear attack. Disagreement focuses on whether such defenses are possible, not on whether they are desirable.[1] Indeed, the technical feasibility of defenses has encountered serious, if not crippling, criticism, which is probably why the desirability of effective ballistic missile defense (BMD) has received little attention.[2]

No one, however, can prove that nearly impenetrable defenses will never be developed. Thus, because they are assumed to be desirable, the search for them will continue. The Strategic Defense Initiative, the BMD research and development program initiated by President Reagan's "Star Wars" speech, is evidence of such continuing interest.

Nevertheless, we should not assume that a world in which nearly impenetrable defenses were deployed would be safer than the current one. In fact, such a defensive situation would not be clearly preferable to our current mutual assured destruction situation even if we make the best case for defense by assuming that it is technically achievable, does not require enormous economic costs, and avoids creation of asymmetries in the superpowers' capabilities that could provide incentives for preventive attack and encourage adventurous, crisis-provoking behavior.

Would the United States not be more secure if both it and the Soviet Union were nearly invulnerable to nuclear attack? The answer, if we are willing to assume that defenses would remain impenetrable, is probably yes. But we do not live in a static world and consequently must consider both the possibility and the probability of changes in Soviet forces which would reduce U.S. security. The robustness of U.S. forces is a measure of the sensitivity of U.S. security to changes in Soviet forces, and the robustness of Soviet forces indicates the sensitivity of Soviet security to changes in U.S. forces.[3] All other things being equal, the more easily U.S. security could be jeopardized by changes in Soviet forces, the less desirable the nuclear situation.

Nuclear situations in which defenses significantly reduce the vulnerability of cities, populations, and other value targets, such as industrial plants, would lack robustness for two interrelated reasons:

A situation in which both superpowers deployed nearly impenetrable defenses would be extremely sensitive to even small improvements in one country's ability to penetrate its adversary's defense. For example, if both countries had impenetrable defenses, then acquiring the ability to penetrate the adversary's defense with 10 warheads would provide the potential for enormous destruction. The country that first acquired even a small capability to penetrate the adversary's defense would have attained an important coercive advantage; it could threaten nuclear attack with impunity since effective retaliation would be impossible given the adversary's inability to penetrate its own defense. Recognizing that the adversary is likely to acquire a similar capability could create pressure to reap the benefits of the strategic advantage quickly. This time-pressure would be especially strong if the advantage could be used to prevent the adversary from acquiring the capability to penetrate one's own defense.

The general conclusion to be drawn from this example is that the lower the vulnerability of cities and other value targets in a given nuclear situation, the smaller the change in vulnerability that is required to gain an advantage. In terms of defenses, the smaller the number of warheads that could penetrate a country's defense, the more sensitive its security would be to offensive changes that reduced its defense's effectiveness.

By contrast, when both superpowers possess redundant assured-destruction capabilities, as they do today, the addition of tens or hundreds or even thousands of warheads would not significantly alter the nuclear situation. The probability of gaining a strategic advantage is thus extremely low, especially when both superpowers are aware of and react to changes in the other's nuclear force.

The technical difficulty of gaining a strategic advantage by changing the capability of attacking value targets depends upon the type, size, and number of changes required to achieve it. Whether the status quo is an assured-destruction situation or a defensive situation determines the type of change. In assured-destruction situations robustness depends upon the difficulty of reducing the adversary's offensive threat. In defensive situations, on the other hand, robustness depends upon both the difficulty of further reducing the adversary's offensive threat and the difficulty of penetrating his defense.

Assessing the relative difficulty of penetrating a specific defensive system with an offensive system or of defeating a specific offensive system with a defensive system is beyond the scope of this paper. But a general point about defenses should be noted. Even if defenses that were perfect against currently deployed offenses were developed, experts believe that the task of developing offensive countermeasures would be relatively easy.[4] The defense would have to be able to overcome the full range of possible countermeasures in order to remain effective. Thus, development of effective defenses against a competitive threat may always be more difficult than developing offenses that can penetrate them.

The size of the change required to gain a strategic advantage also affects the technical difficulty of achieving it. A defense that must reduce a given offensive threat by a large amount is harder to build than one that must reduce the same offensive threat by a small amount. Similarly, it would be harder to build a new offensive system which must be able to penetrate the adversary's defense with many weapons than one that had to penetrate the same defense with only a few weapons. Even taking into account the likely asymmetry between offense and defense mentioned above, it is not possible to say with certainty whether the changes required to gain an advantage in an assured-destruction situation would be easier or harder to achieve than those required in a defensive situation. The size of the requisite change, however, would be larger in the former situation; thus, gaining an advantage will tend to be more difficult.

The number of force changes required to achieve an advantage depends upon the diversity of the adversary's forces. The larger the number of changes required, all else being equal, the harder the advantage will be to obtain. In assured-destruction situations, guaranteeing the ability to destroy large numbers of the adversary's targets of value is the strategic requirement. Diversification of offensive forces helps to ensure the continuing achievement of this objective by increasing the number of defensive changes that are required before the adversary could eliminate one's assured-destruction capability. For example, an offensive force which could annihilate the adversary with either airplanes and cruise missiles or ballistic missiles requires that the adversary develop two highly effective types of defense. The difficulty of defending against all offensive threats determines the technological feasibility of reducing vulnerability to attack.

By contrast, a nuclear situation in which one's own defenses have significantly reduced the vulnerability of cities and other value targets requires the maintenance of a low level of vulnerability, which the adversary's ability to diversify offensive forces makes more difficult. Each offensive threat must be defended against, and the adversary's ability to defeat any of the defenses would be sufficient to make maintenance of low vulnerability impossible. Thus, for what could be called "structural" reasons, defensive situations could not be made as resistant to change as assured-destruction situations.

Lack of robustness would not be so dangerous if the United States and the Soviet Union had no incentives to try to alter the nuclear situation. Creation of a political environment in which the superpowers chose not to attempt to gain a strategic advantage would reduce the need to make the nuclear situation resistant to change. But in a world of impenetrable or nearly impenetrable defenses, nations would feel tremendous pressure to try to defeat the adversary's defenses. Because nothing would guarantee that one's defenses would not be degraded, even a country that did not want to gain an advantage would feel compelled to acquire additional strategic capabilities, including an improvement of its defense to offset anticipated improvements in the adversary's offense. In addition, there would probably be a strong urge to improve its offense as a hedge against the possible inability to offset, with improved defenses, the adversary's enhanced offense. One's adversary, however, could not be confident that these strategic programs were intended only to maintain equal capability. Consequently, even if both countries would prefer to remain in a world of impenetrable defense, an interactive competition threatening to reduce the defenses' effectiveness would likely ensue.

Thus, conditions of reduced vulnerability would make a political environment in which cooperation was possible far more difficult to establish than would conditions of assured destruction.[5] And, given our limited success in negotiating strategic arms control treaties when both superpowers have redundant assured destruction capabilities, the prospects for cooperation offer little reason for optimism. The hope that defenses could lead to reductions in offensive forces is misplaced.

Situations in which defenses eliminated large retaliatory capabilities would thus suffer a lack of robustness. The incentives and pressures that both the United States and the Soviet Union would feel not to cooperate and to increase the other's vulnerability would increase the danger of such situations.

ADDITIONAL PROBLEMS WITH HIGHLY EFFECTIVE DEFENSES

Conventional wars. Impenetrable or nearly impenetrable defenses could increase the probability of superpower conventional wars. Today's nuclear forces greatly increase the potential costs of any direct U.S.-Soviet military confrontation and therefore contribute to the deterrence of conventional war. Impenetrable defenses would eliminate this contribution. Although strategic analysts disagree about which features of the superpowers' extensive survivable strategic arsenals are most critical for deterrence of conventional war, few, if any, believe that the existing arsenals do not contribute at all to deterrence of conventional war.

Extremely effective defenses, assuming that they would remain effective, might be in the United States' security interest despite the greater probability of conventional war. That greater probability, however, does mean that an important trade-off must be considered: global conventional wars, as World Wars I and II demonstrated, can be extremely destructive. The evaluation of this trade-off would involve many factors, including estimates of the probability of nuclear and conventional wars with and without defenses, estimates of the size and costs of these wars, and the availability of options for reducing the probability and costs of conventional war. This short discussion can only call attention to this trade-off, not resolve it.

Uncertainty. The effectiveness of U.S. defenses would be uncertain, and even small uncertainties would be highly significant. In addition to the uncertainties inherent in the operations of complex systems, the defenses' effectiveness would be uncertain due to the severe limits on possible testing. The defense could not be tested against a full-scale attack or against Soviet offenses. And while estimates could be made of effectiveness against deployed Soviet offensive forces, reasonable questions would always arise about Soviet penetration aids which could quickly be added to their offensive force.

With the large offensive forces which are currently deployed, a small difference in the percentage of penetrating weapons would translate into a large difference in destructive potential. The uncertainties involved with a defense which was in fact impenetrable probably would be large enough to leave the United States unsure about whether it was vulnerable to an annihilating attack by the Soviet Union.

Due to the uncertainties, neither the United States nor the Soviet Union would ever feel adequately defended. Even without uncertainties, some would always argue that the United States needed additional defenses to improve its protection against Soviet attacks and as a hedge against Soviet offensive breakthroughs. These arguments would be stronger than those about the inadequacy of today's offensive forces, since defensive capability would start to become redundant only after the defenses were clearly impenetrable. The existence of uncertainties would be likely to result in unrelenting requests for additional defenses, yet fulfilling these requests would yield little satisfaction and add little to the public's sense of security.

Uncertainty would also create fears that the Soviet Union had a superior defensive capability. Prudent military analysis could require assessing uncertainties in favor of Soviet defense and against U.S. defense. As a result, if the United States and the Soviet Union had comparable defensive capabilities, U.S. defenses would not provide confidence that the United States was maintaining a strategic nuclear balance and would likely be judged inferior, thus contributing to demands for improving defensive capabilities.

Allies. Any comprehensive analysis of defensive situations must consider the reactions of U.S. allies and the implications for their security.[6] One issue of great importance to them, the effect of defenses on the probability of conventional war, has already been raised. If strategic defense were believed to increase that probability, then tremendous resistance from the United States' European allies should be anticipated. Conventional wars in Europe are expected to be so costly that to many Europeans they are barely less unacceptable than nuclear wars. The vulnerability of allies to nuclear attack would be another concern. A policy that drastically reduces U.S. vulnerability to nuclear attack while leaving European and other allies highly vulnerable cannot be attractive from their perspective. A third concern would be the effect of defenses on the independent French and British deterrent capabilities. A very effective but not completely impenetrable Soviet defense would leave the United States with a modest retaliatory capability, but it would drastically reduce the value of the French and British European deterrents.

Suitcase bombs. The ability to defend effectively against ballistic missiles, cruise missiles, and bombers could greatly increase the importance of clandestinely delivered nuclear weapons, which could be placed on Soviet ships and commercial airplanes or carried into the United States by Soviet agents. Of course, such deliveries are possible today, but they are not of great importance due to the Soviets' large

STAR WARS BAD EVEN IF IT WORKS

ballistic missile and air-breathing threats.

These alternative forms of delivery would not necessarily render defense useless. The Soviet ability to deliver weapons clandestinely in a crisis might be severely limited; hiding weapons before a crisis would be risky unless early detection were impossible; and the damage from clandestine attacks might be less extensive than the destruction that is possible now, without defenses. Still, the observation that defense against today's most important delivery systems would not eliminate vulnerability to nuclear attack raises basic issues about strategic defense: Against what threats must the United States be able to defend? How would a partial defense, that is, against standard delivery systems, affect the nuclear threat? How would highly effective or impenetrable defense against standard delivery systems affect the political and military uses of nuclear weapons?

Strategic defense and the prospect of invulnerability to nuclear attack have undeniable appeal. But no one should be romantic or unrealistic about the world that would result from highly effective defenses—strategic defense cannot return us to a prenuclear world. Defensive situations have not been studied as carefully or extensively as assured-destruction situations. There is, however, no reason to believe that the former would be either less complex or easier to manage than the latter. A world in which both superpowers have effective defenses might not be preferable to today's redundant assured-destruction situation.

Any serious policy for deploying defenses must address the dangers that would result from the difficulty of maintaining the defensive situation. No defensive situation could be extremely robust. The most robust ones will require superpower cooperation. This brings to the forefront the issue of U.S.-Soviet relations in a defensive world. Statements by President Reagan have suggested that effective defenses would eliminate the need for offensive weapons,[7] an outcome not impossible, but extremely unlikely.

A more realistic assessment is that deploying defenses would lead to an intense offensive and defensive nuclear weapons competition between the superpowers and to tense, strained relations. We should expect arms control agreements to limit or reduce offensive nuclear forces to be difficult, if not impossible, to negotiate. Careful thought should be given to whether a cooperative relationship between the superpowers would be possible in a defensive situation, and to whether pressures for confrontation could be kept low. If, as I believe, these would not be possible, then the prospects for improving security by shifting to a world of effective defenses must be judged especially gloomy.

No evidence indicates that the U.S. decision to pursue highly effective defenses was based upon a complete analysis of defensive situations. Unfortunately, the deployment of effective defenses by the superpowers is far less attractive than proponents suggest. Even on the most optimistic assumptions, defensive situations might not be more secure than assured-destruction situations; and the more likely outcomes would make the United States far less secure than today.

Without the possibility of an outcome clearly preferable to our current situation, there is no good reason to invest enormous resources in strategic defense and to risk creating a more dangerous world. The arguments for not dramatically altering the nuclear status quo are much stronger than those favoring strategic defense. Until a convincing argument is presented for such a fundamental change in U.S. nuclear policy, the United States should restrain its enthusiasm and funding for strategic defense, attempt to repair the damage that is likely to have occurred in Soviet understanding of U.S. nuclear weapons policy, and pursue a prudent policy of offensive weapons acquisition and arms control.

1. See Union of Concerned Scientists, *Space-Based Missile Defense* (Cambridge, Mass.: 1983), p. 71.

2. See, for example, Ashton Carter, *Directed Energy Missile Defense in Space* (Washington, D.C.: Government Printing Office, 1984); Sidney S. Drell, Philip J. Farley, and David Holloway, "Preserving the ABM Treaty: A Critique of the Reagan Strategic Defense Initiative," *International Security* (Fall 1984), pp. 51–91; and Union of Concerned Scientists, *Space-Based Missile Defense.*

3. I have chosen to use "robustness" to avoid the confusion that surrounds the standard term "arms race stability." Arms race stability brings to mind at least two issues related to, but conceptually distinct from, robustness.

First, arms race stability is often considered an indicator of the likelihood and/or intensity of arms races that will occur in a specific nuclear situation. Arms races, however, can occur for a variety of reasons only peripherally related to the effect of building nuclear forces on the adversary's security. Consequently, arms races can occur in highly robust nuclear situations, as has occurred in our current redundant and diversified assured-destruction situation.

Second, arms race stability can connote a belief that arms races cause wars—a theoretical issue on which there is substantial disagreement. But one can assert that the probability of war depends upon the robustness of the nuclear situation without believing that, in general, arms races cause wars. Robustness does not imply that the process of competitive armament itself leads to war. Rather, assuming a force buildup takes place either competitively or unilaterally, a war is more likely when the initial nuclear situation is less robust.

4. See Carter, op. cit., pp. 69–70.

5. See Robert Jervis, "Cooperation Under the Security Dilemma," *World Politics*, 30, no. 2 (Jan. 1978), pp. 167–214.

6. David S. Yost, "Ballistic Missile Defense and the Atlantic Alliance," *International Security*, 7, no. 2 (Fall 1982), pp. 154–58.

7. *New York Times*, March 30, 1983, p. 14.

6

Politics, Technology, and the Test Ban

Jack F. Evernden

olitical concerns for many years have been the ruling consideration in negotiating test ban treaties, even though many have claimed technical considerations to be paramount. In fact, the technical problems have been basically solved by seismology under a long-standing national program to achieve the capability to detect and identify underground explosions and to estimate their yields.

A small segment of seismology has gained such importance that presidents, secretaries of state, premiers, foreign ministers, and ambassadors hold forth eloquently on their understandings or misunderstandings of the subject. These politically motivated assertions, however, have little to do with the relevant science. What is frightening is that national policy has been based on whether seismologists can or cannot identify the seismic waves of earthquakes and explosions at some arbitrarily selected small magnitude level, rather than on the enormity of the potential catastrophe if nuclear weaponry is not contained.

Even if we once believed that technical considerations were of ruling importance in attaining a comprehensive or a low-threshold test ban, that belief is no longer tenable. Technical understanding of the seismological aspects of monitoring such treaties is now essentially complete, and we know that a low-threshold treaty can be successfully monitored. This knowledge extends to detection of the seismic signals of explosions, to identification of those signals as the product of underground explosions rather than earthquakes, and to establishment of the yield of the explosion within factors of certainty relevant to meaningful monitoring. What is more, there is every indication that the required monitoring network could be established and maintained within parameters acceptable to the Soviet Union.

L.R. Sykes and I published, in 1982, a detailed discussion that covers the range of techniques used to identify a seismic source, based upon location, depth of focus, and the spectral composition of the elastic energy radiated from it.[1] Refinement of these techniques in recent years has disposed of lingering concerns over the possibility of "decoupling," or muffling, explosions by setting them off in large cavities, as well as the possibility of "hiding" an explosion in the reverberations of a distant earthquake.

An elastic body like the earth supports two types of seismic waves propagating throughout its body as well as two types propagating over its surface. Three of the four types of waves are present in a simple explosion; all four are generated by earthquakes and most explosions. However, major differences in the radiated waves of each type persist. The patterns of waves radiated by an explosion are radially symmetric, while earthquake patterns are much more asymmetric than those of nearly all explosions, earthquake asymmetry being associated with the movement of two sides of a fault along which strain is released. More importantly, the relative levels of the different types of waves and their amplitude in relation to frequency are predictable and easily observed functions of the type of seismic activity.

Shifting the monitoring network's attention to higher frequency levels than originally proposed has solved a number of problems. Since the decoupling (muffling) effect decreases at high frequencies, monitoring these frequencies makes it possible to detect even low-yield, fully decoupled nuclear explosions. The differences between earthquake and explosion wave patterns at high frequencies also make it possible to distinguish between those two events even if they are recorded simultaneously. This totally eliminates the possibility of hiding the seismic waves of a nuclear explosion in those of an earthquake.

Two questions about the use of these discriminants need to be asked. First, their effective use to detect and distinguish small-magnitude explosions and earthquakes requires detection of frequencies of as high as 30 hertz at distances of a few hundred kilometers. Do the critical waves propagate to such distances in terrains found in most of the Soviet Union? Data available for regions geophysically analogous to most of the Soviet Union, such as the eastern United States, demonstrate that they do. The other question is whether such waves are detectable in the presence of ambient levels of microseismic, high-frequency background noise. Again, the answer is affirmative.

The route to our present verification capability has had some tragic twists and turns. In the late 1950s seismologists proposed criteria for discriminating between nuclear explosions and earthquakes, based on the absence of one of the four wave types in the explosion patterns. The demonstration that some earthquake-associated wave patterns were indeed detectable in some nuclear explosions cast doubt on the verification capability, and President Kennedy was persuaded to drop his insistence on a comprehensive test ban.

Unfortunately, seismologists failed to garner the obvious explanation from the available data: that explosions set off in earth formations where some strain is already present may trigger minor earthquakes, with all the associated wave patterns. Data adequate to demonstrate the validity of the criteria currently used for identifying underground nuclear explosions were available before Kennedy's decision. In fact, the first demonstrations of the validity of most of these criteria, though taking place after ratification of the Limited Test-Ban Treaty of 1963, were based upon data which predated that agreement. Scientific neglect must be blamed in this case for denying the world the one and only real chance it has yet had for negotiation of a treaty banning all nuclear explosions.

Has there ever been support for a comprehensive test ban within the U.S. government since the Kennedy presidency? During the last two decades of nearly continuous negotiations on such a ban by the multinational Committee on Disarmament in Geneva, both political and technical personnel in the U.S. delegations have understood that the intent of our participation was to thwart any progress on a comprehensive test ban by that Committee. Chairman Lewis Strauss of the Atomic Energy Commission protested a test cessation as a "very fateful step."[2] Recent testimony before the Subcommittee on Intelligence and Military Application of Nuclear Energy of the House Armed Services Committee expressed concern over "stockpile aging" and "modification of warheads for new military requirements," as well as the potential attrition of skilled designers that cessation of testing would bring about.[3]

In the mid-1960s, while employed by the Department of Defense, I was asked to advise on the technical content of a letter, written for the signatures of the Joint Chiefs of Staff, withdrawing their previous support for a verifiable comprehensive test ban. It had just been convincingly demonstrated for the first time that there were indeed seismological techniques that could distinguish between the seismic waves of explosions and those of earthquakes, and that there was every reason to believe that these techniques would work for smaller events than had yet been investigated. The Chiefs, obviously, had been willing to support a treaty as long as it was thought that seismologists would be incapable of monitoring it. When that shield was removed, the truth was revealed: that they were then, and would remain, opposed to a comprehensive test ban.

Over the years, each advance in seismological verification has been deprecated by those high in the U.S. government. The Defense Department did not dispute testimony in the early 1970s that a network fundamentally acceptable to the Soviets could be built to monitor Soviet explosions as small as one kiloton. Instead, the director of Defense Research and Engineering insisted that monitoring to a quarter of a kiloton would be required for national security.

A rational answer to the question of how low a threshold monitoring capability is required should be constrained by these considerations:

Development of strategic nuclear weapons requires tests in the five-to-ten kiloton range.

The specified level must not create an unbalanced risk for the parties of the treaty.

The specified level must be enforceable but must not create the basis for interminable irrelevant arguments.

The first condition would be met by a network of about 25 stations within the Soviet Union, plus 15 or so surrounding that country, and a complementary network within the United States. Such a network could easily monitor a treaty within a one-kiloton limit—well below the levels required for the development of strategic weapons.

Secondly, weapons laboratories are concerned that signing an unenforceable comprehensive test ban treaty could create an unbalanced risk, as in the following scenario: we observe the letter of the treaty and allow our key personnel to drift away to stimulating research in other fields, while our determined adversaries keep their laboratories going by conducting low-yield tests, below the detection threshold of the monitoring network. After the treaty has been in force for, say, 10 years, the Soviets abrogate the treaty on some pretext and resume the arms race with a great advantage in weapons design.

With respect to the third condition, seismologists know of no certain way to distinguish the seismic waves of a several-ton tamped (placed in solid rock) explosion from those of a low-yield, fully decoupled nuclear explosion. Thus, even given a capability to detect and identify as an explosion the signal of a subkiloton decoupled explosion, one could not distinguish it from the plethora of small industrial explosions taking place frequently within the Soviet Union. Placement of the treaty threshold too far below that required for security purposes would only lead to endless confrontation over irrelevancies.

All of these considerations suggest that a low-threshold treaty, establishing a one-kiloton level, would be preferable to an outright ban of all testing. The difference between this level and the five-to-ten kiloton testing required for weapons development is so great that any confusion about a yield near the threshold would not come close to jeopardizing national security. In the other direction, a fully decoupled one-kiloton explosion generates a signal comparable to that of a five-ton tamped explosion. Most industrial explosions are below this level, and those above it are generally distributed charges designed to break and move rock. The monitoring network could identify most of these, although an occasional Standing Consultative Commission meeting would be required to clarify particular events. Finally, with such a level of testing permitted, all parties could maintain the integrity of their laboratories.

It would seem advisable to include provisions in the treaty which restrict low-yield tests to a single site and forbid decoupled explosions. These provisions would not guarantee compliance but would greatly decrease the scope for dispute on technical matters.

If it is true, as Noel Gayler and others have repeatedly claimed, that there is no potential military use for theater nuclear weapons, which use low-yield warheads, a one-kiloton threshold treaty would effectively constitute a comprehensive test ban.

The U.S. government has long insisted that on-site inspections be part of a comprehensive test ban treaty. By the time the early round of negotiations, which began under Eisenhower, ended during the Kennedy years, the Soviets had agreed to three annual inspections. But the United States was adamant that seven were necessary. During the most recent round of talks, which began and ended during the Carter Administration, the United States, the Soviet Union, and the United Kingdom agreed in principle to a type of on-site inspection different from the mandatory ones previously discussed. According to the trilateral report submitted in 1980 to the Committee on Disarmament in Geneva, in the event of a seismic disturbance of questionable origin in one of the three countries, the other party could "challenge" the source of the disturbance and request an inspection. By providing detailed arguments about why an inspection was necessary, the challenging side could not easily be refused.

Yet while negotiators shifted the terms of on-site inspections, seismologists also had learned how to do the monitoring in a manner acceptable to the Soviets. Moreover, it was demonstrated in elaborate Defense Department testimony to Congress in the early 1970s, that there is no way to obtain useful information through on-site inspections even if the Soviets agreed to them. It should be noted that the Soviet refusal to accept on-site inspections is at least as irrational as the U.S. insistence on them. One cannot help but speculate that if the Soviets ever agreed to them, on-site inspections would never be heard of again.

The Reagan Administration has tried harder than any other to convince the American public of the dangers of arms control treaties and of Soviet misbehavior. However, since the invention of the bomb, nearly all U.S. administrations, Democratic or Republican, have consistently cast serious doubt on the verifiability of a comprehensive test ban treaty, even while asserting support for such an agreement. Only after leaving office did President Eisenhower realize, and declare, that his greatest mistake was in failing to negotiate a comprehensive test ban.

The Carter Administration, after obtaining Soviet agreement to a remarkable treaty draft during the trilateral discussions in Geneva, aborted further measures to complete an accord. Administration officials were afraid that under a test ban something might go wrong and give the Soviets an unspecifiable but critical advantage. Carter, according to Harold Agnew, then director of Los Alamos National Laboratory, had every intention of going ahead with a ban until Agnew and Roger Batzel, at that time head of Livermore National Laboratory, spent a mere two hours talking with him and "turned him around."⁴

It is now clear that nearly all men in positions of responsibility will build yet another generation of nuclear warheads rather than make any move toward nuclear restraint. As Richard Garwin puts it, "Time after time our national security choices have been misdirected by false argument, concealed assumptions and hidden agendas, and . . . some of the best options have been ruthlessly suppressed."⁵

There is no technical obstacle to negotiation of a verifiable test ban treaty. But the implementation of a rational solution to a political problem is vastly more difficult than finding that solution. If we are to save ourselves, we and the Soviets must learn that our differences arise out of mutual fear and mutual isolation, out of historical processes which have so colored and warped the perceptions of all of us that we accept utter nonsense as revealed truth. For the sake of ourselves and our children, we must strive to approach each other through accommodation and understanding rather than through confrontation and misunderstanding.

1. L.R. Sykes and J.F. Evernden, "The Verification of a Comprehensive Nuclear Test Ban," *Scientific American* (Oct. 1982), pp. 47–55. See also L. Sykes, J. Evernden, and Ines Cifuentes, "Seismic Methods for Verifying Nuclear Test Bans," in D.W. Hafemeister and D. Schroeer, eds., *Physics, Technology and the Nuclear Arms Race* (New York: American Institute of Physics, 1983); J.F. Evernden and C.B. Archambeau, "Seismic Discrimination of Earthquakes and Explosions," in Kosta Tsipis, Penny Janeway, and David Hafemeister, eds., *Technical Means of Verification* (Elmsford, New York: Pergamon, 1986).

2. A. Greb and W. Heckrotte, "The Long History: The Test Ban Debate," *Bulletin* (Aug.-Sept. 1983), p. 37.

3. Ibid., p. 40.

4. Interview with Harold Agnew, *Los Alamos Science Magazine* (Summer-Fall 1981), p. 154.

5. R. Garwin, "Who Proposes, Who Disposes, Who Pays?" *Bulletin* (June-July 1983), p. 11.

7

Technology Won't Solve Verification Problems

Michael Krepon

According to the conventional wisdom, verification will be a major hang-up for new arms control agreements. Verification is "getting virtually impossible as a new generation of nuclear missiles becomes smaller and more mobile," says *U.S. News and World Report*. "The verification problem is becoming increasingly acute, given the mobility of the new systems and the opportunities for rapid reloading and covert deployment," warns Zbigniew Brzezinski, President Carter's national security adviser. "As a consequence, it is realistic to conclude that for both political and technological reasons, the chances of a truly comprehensive agreement, which can be reliably verified, are rapidly fading." Helmut Sonnenfeld, an official in the Nixon and Ford Administrations agrees: "I don't think broad, verifiable arms control agreements are 'doable,' but that doesn't mean we shouldn't try to do useful things at the margins."

These dire predictions will become true if future administrations make the mistake of demanding technological solutions for difficult monitoring problems. But verification problems, like the broader national security concerns of which they are a part, are rarely amenable to technical fixes. Verification problems, however, are amenable to solutions when negotiating partners agree to cooperate.

The arms control community has long warned against deployment of cruise missiles because of the increased security problems they present and because of verification difficulties. Mobile missiles pose less

189

of a monitoring challenge as long as both sides act according to habit, deploying mobile forces in predictable ways. (The U.S. government, for example, has tracked the deployment of Soviet SS-20 missiles with great precision since they were first introduced in 1977.) Nevertheless, mobile missiles are more difficult to monitor than silos, especially during times of crisis or changed deployment practices.

Since warnings against the introduction of hard-to-monitor missiles have not been heeded, their deployment leaves U.S. and Soviet political leaders with essentially three choices:

They can set verification standards so exacting as to foreclose the possibility of new agreements.

They can choose partial agreements covering only those forces whose deployments can be counted precisely.

They can choose comprehensive agreements covering deployed forces, despite difficulties in verification.

The first choice makes little sense. Security on both sides will be impaired by an uncontrolled competition in nuclear forces. And security does not improve when nuclear weapons capabilities are harder for both sides to track. Thus, despite difficulties in monitoring new weapons systems, the search for arms control will become more, not less, of a political and economic imperative for Washington and Moscow.

Partial agreements which avoid sticky monitoring problems offer short-term appeal and long-term headaches. Whenever some nuclear forces are controlled by agreement and others are not, the focus of competition naturally shifts to uncontrolled areas, as can be seen from both the SALT I and II experiences.

After the SALT I Interim Agreement set a limit on missile launchers, but not on the number of warheads they could carry, each side proceeded to deploy MIRVs in a way that made both feel less secure. According to some SALT critics, the Interim Agreement is to blame for the appearance of such large numbers of destabilizing, MIRVed missiles. By this logic, one might just as well blame weekends for causing rain. The real responsibility lies with leaders in both countries who were unwilling to forego MIRVs in the negotiations leading up to the Agreement.

The SALT II agreement finally placed limits on MIRVed missile launchers, but did not set substantive limits on cruise missiles. A familiar pattern has ensued, with each country producing several varieties of new cruise missiles that can only complicate and expand defense requirements for both. New arms control agreements which provide only partial coverage of nuclear forces able to strike each other's territory simply invite a repeat of this track record.

Faced with these unattractive options, comprehensive agreements limiting deployed forces offer clear benefits to both the United States and the Soviet Union, despite their accompanying verification difficulties. Leaders on both sides can include mobile and cruise missiles in comprehensive agreements by supplementing their technical surveillance capabilities with "cooperative measures" and "counting rules" to ease verification problems.

A cooperative measure may be either voluntary or negotiated. Its purpose is to enhance the other side's ability to verify compliance with the provisions of an agreement. Cooperative measures in the unratified SALT II agreement include data exchanges on deployed forces, advance notification of certain missile flight tests, and pledges not to conceal information deliberately—such as using encrypted telemetry during flight tests—whenever such practices impede verification of compliance with an agreement's provisions.

The attitude of negotiating partners toward each other is clearly critical to successful negotiation and implementation of cooperative measures. If prior agreements are not ratified, follow-on negotiations break down, and future intentions toward treaty obligations are in doubt, neither side will be inclined to be very cooperative. Thus it is no surprise that there have been SALT II compliance problems relating to cooperative measures and that, in the forum created by SALT to handle implementation questions, the Reagan Administration has had little leverage to alter Soviet practices. Conversely, when both sides return to serious negotiations and assuage concerns over each other's intentions, it is reasonable to expect better implementation of cooperative measures negotiated earlier, as well as useful additions to them.

A wide variety of cooperative measures could be devised to ease difficult monitoring problems for mobile and cruise missiles. Production facilities could be designated and data exchanged on monthly production rates. Tamper-proof, unattended remote sensors placed outside production facilities could monitor the movement of missiles from production lines to final assembly locations, which could also be designated. Such transfers could take place on a timetable that allows confirmation by photoreconnaissance satellites. Another set of cooperative measures might be required to simplify the process of monitoring land-based missile deployments, such as designating deployment areas and prohibiting deployments beyond their boundaries.

Taken together, these kinds of cooperative measures could provide effective solutions to land-based-missile monitoring problems without the need for on-site inspections of sensitive production facilities — a step neither side is likely to accept. But such cooperative measures will remain hypothetical as long as both sides trade charges of noncompliance and negotiating in bad faith.

Counting rules, like cooperative measures, can ease near-insoluble monitoring tasks by providing useful bookkeeping solutions where technical solutions are not possible. How many nuclear warheads are actually located atop missiles housed in silos or submarines? Neither side knows with any precision, yet both sides were still able to assign warhead numbers to each missile type in SALT II, based on technical observations during flight tests.

Counting rules were also devised for aircraft carrying air-launched cruise missiles (ALCMs). If these were flight-tested or deployed on a certain type of aircraft, then all aircraft of that type, unless otherwise modified, would fall within agreed limitations. Again, in a cooperative political relationship, it is possible to envisage how such rules can be extended to limit ALCMs and sea-launched cruise missiles for different kinds of aircraft and ships.

Both sides, for example, could agree on numbers of "weapon stations" for sea-launched cruise missiles available on different classes of submarines and ships, a subset of which could be designated as nuclear-armed cruise missile stations. A simpler alternative is to designate ships or planes carrying cruise missiles as MIRVed platforms. Every ship or aircraft of each class or type from which long-range cruise missiles have been either flight-tested or deployed would be included within agreed limitations on MIRVed systems. The object would be to provide disincentives to substantial deployments of cruise missiles, while maintaining important limitations on MIRVed ballistic missiles.

There is always a risk that the Kremlin will not comply with limitations governing weapons systems that are relatively easy to conceal. Properly devised counting rules can impose their own penalties for cheating, however. If the Soviets secretly deploy a greater number of nuclear-armed, sea-launched cruise missiles than allowed, they would degrade a ship's ability to carry out conventional missions. With cruise missiles, there are also built-in safeguards against Soviet cheating or "breakout" from agreed limitations. If evidence appears of systematic noncompliance, the Pentagon can respond with counterdeployments on the wide variety of available ground-, air- and sea-based platforms.

With open production lines for cruise missiles, many appropriate countermeasures are possible.

These solutions will still be unsatisfactory to those who believe that even with approximately 15,000 deployed nuclear weapons available to each side, missile reloads and refires can be the critical factor in determining the outcome of a protracted nuclear war. From this perspective, arms control agreements make sense only if they cover total missile inventories as well as launchers. The Reagan Administration adopted this approach in its opening START and INF (intermediate-range nuclear force) negotiating positions—an approach that presumably would require continuing on-site inspections of military warehouses and production facilities. Yet even with on-site inspections, stockpile limitation agreements are harder to monitor than the SALT I and II agreements on deployed forces, which Reagan Administration officials claimed were unverifiable.

If President Reagan is serious about strategic arms control, he will drop the idea of on-site inspections and inventory limits for offensive nuclear forces. At this stage in the arms race, there is no need to set such unrealistic standards. There is also no need for the arms control community to express pessimism on verification questions.

Numerous solutions to monitoring problems are possible. All that is required is a modest amount of imagination and common sense, once political leaders in Washington and Moscow decide to reach accords. The resulting agreements will rely heavily on cooperative measures and counting rules for verification. Such limitations will not provide exact numbers for each side's nuclear weapons, but they will be far better—and less risky—than any of the current alternatives.

8

Nuclear Infrastructure

William M. Arkin and Richard W. Fieldhouse

The superpowers have embarked on programs to expand their nuclear forces that arms control has done little to curtail. Neither side shows much inclination to accept limits on qualitative and quantitative improvements. But arms control's failure has had one positive result: it has drawn attention to the worldwide nuclear infrastructure and the diplomatic relations that support it. Arms control, in a deeper sense of the term, is no longer understood to be a mere technical management issue: it has become a basic issue of international security and national sovereignty.

From prohibitions on weapons deployments and port visits to declarations of "nuclear-free" zones, the nuclear system is under attack. The new campaign—often referred to as a "nuclear allergy"—has emerged as a desperate attempt to restrain the arbitrary powers of nuclear warmaking. The attempts of governments and citizen movements all over the world to rein in the nuclear powers are the most significant new arms control developments of the nuclear era.

At first, restraints on nuclear weapons in the form of "nuclear-weapons-free zones" were mostly symbolic. The new scope of activity, though, demonstrates that these nuclear-free initiatives have moved into the real world. Local groups around the world question and analyze the role of military bases in their area. Overseas maneuvers and exercises, once treated as routine, are scrutinized and have become highly politicized. Proposals for nuclear-free zones have emerged in virtually every region of the world.

The scope of antinuclear activity is vast. Greece has pledged to remove U.S. nuclear weapons and bases from its soil by 1989. New Zealand declared itself a nuclear-free zone and banned U.S. nuclear weapons and nuclear-powered ships from its waters. Spain and Canada succeeded in having U.S. nuclear warheads removed from their soil in 1979 and 1984, respectively. The Netherlands is debating a process to reduce its nuclear "tasks" within NATO. Norway and Denmark halted their national funding for U.S. nuclear missile bases in Europe. Third World countries such as Egypt, Sri Lanka, and India prohibit nuclear ships in their territorial waters. Even Soviet allies have expressed displeasure about the superpower nuclear prerogatives. Romania stated in 1981 that it would not accept Soviet missiles. And Bulgaria denies that it bases Soviet nuclear weapons on its soil in peacetime.

The common thread that ties these actions together is the refusal to aid and abet the arms race and to be a link in the nuclear infrastructure. Fear of being a nuclear target stands out in antinuclear statements and literature, but beneath that fear lies a much more powerful conviction: the growing belief of citizens, parliaments, and governments that they are being used, and in many cases deceived, to perpetuate a system that does not serve the interests of peace and increasingly threatens to bring war.

The new activism, in contrast to the old which only considered the physical presence of warheads, is not simplistic: it focuses increasingly on the overall infrastructure that supports the weapons. Weapons are only one part of the nuclear infrastructure, a complex made up of thousands of obscure research, testing, electronic, and command facilities. Virtually every military laboratory, test range, military base, warning radar, and communications transmitter contributes in some way to preparations for nuclear warfare. Military exercises and maneuvers, communications, surveillance, and testing keep the system alive.

Command, control, communications, and intelligence (C^3I) systems —the nervous system of the nuclear arsenals—are what give the superpowers confidence that they can fight and win a nuclear war. "If deterrence fails," the Air Force says, "the C^3 system must then provide the necessary information, command facilities, and communications to prosecute a nuclear war effectively."[1] Because of this delusion —especially dangerous to allies who host C^3I systems but have little or no influence on the plans, policies, or decisions to go to war—C^3I facilities increasingly provoke citizen coalitions to mobilize against them. Nuclear weapons-testing ranges and antisubmarine warfare technology are examples of programs that increasingly spark public debate because of the role they play in the arms race.

The nuclear infrastructure has gained attention because it is mysterious and dangerous. But it is not passive. Most operations that the military justifies on the basis of "preparedness" are seen by the other side as provocative. Scientific research, information gathering, and early-warning surveillance are part of a qualitative arms race. The superior ability to detect and target the enemy's forces, to hide and communicate with one's own, and to control military operations, have become more important than the weapons themselves. The means to chart the battlefields of nuclear war and the peacetime military operations to prepare for it—observatories, electronic and technical facilities, oceanographic laboratories, and satellites—are integral parts of the military forces of the nuclear era.

Nuclear-free movements that hope to lessen the probabilities and possibilities of warfare have begun to focus on the infrastructure, but only at a surface level so far. Eight of the 16 NATO members (Canada, Norway, Denmark, Luxembourg, Spain, Portugal, Iceland, and France) prohibit peacetime deployments of U.S. nuclear warheads on their soil, and other close allies, notably Japan, also maintain restrictions. But the tentacles of the infrastructure are so obscure that many countries still do not fully understand their contribution and participation in the arms race. Dozens of non-nuclear countries and territories that maintain relations with a superpower house a part of its infrastructure.

At present, the United States stores nuclear warheads in eight foreign countries (Belgium, Greece, Italy, the Netherlands, South Korea, Turkey, West Germany, and the United Kingdom), the Soviet Union in four (Czechoslovakia, East Germany, Hungary, and Poland), and the United Kingdom in one (West Germany). At one time, U.S. nuclear weapons were also stored in Canada, France, Greenland, Libya, Morocco, Okinawa, the Philippines, Spain, Taiwan, and Thailand. But 65 nations and territories house facilities of the nuclear infrastructure: the United States has nuclear-related facilities in 40 foreign countries and territories, the Soviet Union in 11, Britain in 12, and France in nine.[2]

The main flaw in existing nuclear-free policies or nuclear-free-zone proposals is that they set up a system whereby non-nuclear means nothing but the absence of nuclear warheads, while the infrastructure is ignored. In the 1950s and 1960s when nuclear weapons were large and difficult to transport or assemble, the mere restriction of warheads might have made sense as an arms control initiative. But today warheads are small and lightweight and require minimal preparation and upkeep. Virtually every ship and airplane available to the nuclear powers can carry them anywhere on earth, as long as the intelligence, targeting, basing, training, and communications infrastructure is in place to support them. This fact has two effects, the first of which undermines public control in allied countries—indeed national sovereignty—in a direct way, the second of which undermines it more insidiously.

The process of making nuclear weapons smaller and easier to handle over the years now allows weapons to be moved quickly to overseas locations where their peacetime deployment would be inconvenient or controversial. Bureaucratic requirements for nuclear weapons security overseas and the difficulty of maintaining special agreements with host nations influence where nuclear weapons are stationed in peacetime. But the military has long-standing plans, approved by the president, to base nuclear warheads in countries that do not have them in peacetime. Eight nations are currently earmarked to receive these nuclear weapons in crisis or wartime: Bermuda (a British colony), Canada, Iceland, Puerto Rico (a territory of the United States), the Azores (a Portuguese territory), the Philippines, Spain, and the British island of Diego Garcia in the Indian Ocean.[3]

None of the governments of these eight nations were informed of any U.S. plans or authorizations to deploy nuclear weapons in their nations. The plans and preparations to deploy them in Puerto Rico make a mockery of the Latin American Nuclear-Free-Zone Treaty (the Treaty of Tlatelolco) which the United States signed in 1967 and extended to Puerto Rico in 1979. Plans to deploy nuclear weapons in Canada, Iceland, and Spain are an affront to the non-nuclear policies of those countries.

After the plans had been revealed in the Canadian press last January, Lord Carrington, the secretary general of NATO, stated in Toronto that the United States should consult its allies when drawing up contingency plans for deployment of weapons and not leave consultation until times of crisis. "I think it's a good idea if countries are consulted while the contingency planning is going on," he told the *Toronto Globe and Mail* (January 24, 1985). Retired Admiral Robert Falls, former chief of Canada's defense staff, and chairman of the NATO Military Committee from 1980 to 1983, told *Maclean's* magazine (January 28, 1985): "The United States has a moral obligation to consult us when using our territory for something as emotional as nuclear weapons. It is an immoral attitude to make plans without consulting the countries involved."

Falls also revealed in the *Globe and Mail* on January 15, 1985, that U.S. nuclear deployment plans had never been discussed in the councils of NATO: "The implication is they're saying, 'To hell with you little guys, Icelanders, Bermudans, Canadians, we're going to do it anyway.'" As an editorial stated: "There could hardly be a worse example of nuclear planning. The United States has devised a scenario which seems calculated to worry its allies while it delights its adversaries."

The fact that Canada, Iceland, Puerto Rico, and Spain restrict nuclear weapons deployment partly explains why such preparations would be kept secret. The Nuclear Weapons Deployment Plan was not even adequately "coordinated" with the State Department, in spite of the obvious implications such contingency planning has for U.S. foreign relations. These plans are perhaps the most vivid reminders that the nuclear infrastructure is autonomous and impervious to political control.

The second, more insidious effect of the infrastructure's flexibility and pervasiveness is that, even without secret plans to put warheads on a given country's soil, the country can be wired into controlling, launching, and targeting the weapons. Japan, a staunch non-nuclear country, contains a system of U.S. bases that directly serve preparations for nuclear war. Although the United States does not station nuclear warheads in Japan in peacetime, the nuclear infrastructure there comprises 28 facilities which direct nuclear operations, supply or refuel nuclear forces, target them, or communicate with them. The Japanese government turns a blind eye to this nuclear infrastructure—which has been extensively written about in Japan—and does not officially perceive the U.S. presence as a violation of Japan's non-nuclear policies. Other non-nuclear countries (Canada, Denmark, Iceland, Norway, and Spain) also contain these kinds of facilities, whose role in nuclear warfighting is more complicated, but as important as the actual warheads.

When New Zealand first sought to enforce its new non-nuclear policy by refusing to allow a U.S. destroyer to make a port call unless the United States pledged that it was not carrying nuclear weapons, the U.S. government was more concerned about the precedent this would set for countries like Japan than about the merits of the New Zealand case. According to the *New York Times:* "The Reagan Administration said a firm American response was needed . . . to demonstrate that allies could not impose limits on the movements of American military forces and get off 'cost-free.' A senior official said the United States, to deter other allied countries from following New Zealand's example, was examining [a number of ways of retaliating]."[4]

The standard device to avoid dealing with such dissatisfaction among allies is to "neither confirm nor deny" the presence of nuclear weapons. This policy evolved, according to one congressional report, as a result of the political controversy the weapons cause rather than the need to protect the information from a potential enemy:

> The U.S. Government security policy regarding nuclear weapons locations is that it will neither confirm nor deny the existence or location of U.S. nuclear weapons located anywhere. In part, this is at the request of the nations where the weapons are deployed, since in most nations the existence of U.S. nuclear weapons within their borders is a difficult internal political issue. Thus they generally have requested that the United States not declassify the fact that U.S. nuclear weapons are located in their specific nation—even though the evidence that they are there is obvious and generally known by their population.[5]

Morton Halperin, former assistant secretary of defense for systems analysis, told Congress in 1974 that the "neither confirm nor deny" policy

> developed initially in a period in which nuclear weapons were looked upon with [a] kind of mysticism as something very different . . . and in which we were not going to talk about where these weapons are. It was a natural outgrowth of that and from the fear . . . particularly in the Navy . . . that if the word got out there were nuclear weapons in Germany or on Okinawa or other places, you might have domestic opposition in those countries to the stationing of the weapons which would make it impossible to continue to store them there. . . . When I was in the Pentagon [the policy] was not susceptible to review. . . . It was well understood that the feelings of the military services [were] such that one opened this subject at one's peril and without any chance of success in changing it.[6]

The secrecy practices of the nuclear powers can serve, as in the case of New Zealand, to sour foreign relations and alienate allies from U.S. policy. Secrecy also prevents the public—and the Congress—from understanding military force structure and policy. And because the technology of the nuclear infrastructure is often arcane, and its military roles inscrutable, links between civilian and military assets, between ordinary military and nuclear operations, and between scientific research and nuclear weapons are diffuse, protean, and difficult to understand.

Moreover, secrecy, when added to bureaucratic compartmentalization and separation of geographic jurisdictions, prevents the military from having a comprehensive view and inhibits communication among governmental agencies. The Treaty of Tlatelolco is perhaps the best case in point. The Treaty was designed to restrict the kind of deployment plans the United States has for Puerto Rico. Yet the Treaty did not lead to any revision of actual U.S. military plans. The U.S. government did indicate that it had considered the Treaty's effect on military operations, stating that "nuclear weapons transit or transport operations [in the Treaty Zone]" were not affected by the Treaty. But signing the Treaty (and its protocols on Puerto Rico) had no effect on actual plans. In fact, the evidence collected so far indicates that no guidance was provided to U.S. military forces, by either the Defense Department or the State Department, to ensure their compliance with the provisions of the Treaty.

Nuclear-free nations like Iceland, Canada, and Spain now also face a new dilemma. The Nuclear Weapons Deployment Plan, secret until publicized late last year, and the ongoing nuclear infrastructure ignore their policies. The U.S. government employs secrecy as its defense in the fear that any restrictions on its nuclear weapons policies might become an epidemic and that its freedom to operate around the world might be threatened. Already, New Zealand, in contrast to other nominally nuclear-free countries such as Denmark, Japan, and Norway, has shown its determination to make the United States respect the policies of its host nation.

The superpowers already view the nuclear-free trend as a threat. Apprehensive that calls for control could someday lead to limits on their military options, they counter the proposals with ominous incantations: vital interests are at stake, threats in the region are growing, non-nuclear status would make it impossible to defend, allies will be thrust out from under the "nuclear umbrella." But their preparations for war have weakened their credibility, especially where foreign governments are involved. Every day, through training, reconnaissance, and exercises, the nuclear infrastructure makes dry runs of nuclear war. Nuclear-free countries have already begun to realize, however crudely in some instances, that "protection" by this infrastructure entails provocation and high-risk operations. Citizen movements and governments focusing on the nuclear infrastructure could become a third force in arms control.

1. Senate Armed Services Committee, *Department of Defense Authorization for Appropriations for Fiscal 1984: Hearings,* part 2, 98th Cong., 1st sess., p. 886.

202 *William M. Arkin and Richard W. Fieldhouse*

2. William M. Arkin and Richard W. Fieldhouse, *Nuclear Battlefields: Global Links in the Arms Race* (Cambridge, Mass.: Ballinger, 1985).

3. William M. Arkin, "Contingency Overseas Deployment of Nuclear Weapons: A Report," unpublished (Washington, D.C.: Institute for Policy Studies, 1985).

4. Bernard Gwertzman, "U.S. Plans Actions to Answer Rebuff by New Zealand," *New York Times*, Feb. 6, 1985.

5. U.S. Congress, Joint Committee on Atomic Energy, "Development, Use, and Control of Nuclear Energy for the Common Defense and Security and for Peaceful Purposes," 1st annual report to Congress, June 30, 1975.

6. Senate Foreign Relations Committee, *Nuclear Weapons and Foreign Policy: Hearings*, 93d Cong., 2d sess., 1974, p. 36.

9

Nuclear Crisis Management

David A. Hamburg and Alexander L. George

These remarks are offered in the hope that the scientific outlook can contribute to long-term problem-solving with respect to U.S.-Soviet conflict. Several broad approaches occur to us: The two countries might improve upon their arms control negotiations; develop better crisis management; find ways to prevent crises (this assumes no fundamental bettering of U.S.-Soviet relations); gradually change the basic nature of their relationship; and work toward the improvement of world conditions, especially in areas of potential conflict.

We will focus on two of these approaches—crisis management and crisis prevention—with a view to making a concrete proposal. But first, the intrinsic perils of crisis situations must be understood.

In a crisis, political leaders operate under certain familiar cognitive limits on rationality: incomplete information about the situation; inadequate knowledge of the relation between objectives and possible means for achieving them so that the leader cannot predict with confidence the consequences of choosing a given course of action; and difficulty in formulating a single criterion for use in choosing the best available option. In such a setting, strategies for dealing with cognitive complexity and uncertainty become essential.

For the decision-maker, these situations typically pose diverse problems which cannot readily be reconciled. National leaders must consider their national interests. They must also often weigh the interests of their political parties and of various special interest groups and must cope with various personal concerns such as the safety of their own families and their sense of worth as persons.

One difficult task of great practical importance is the appraisal of the situation from another nation's perspective. The desirability of protecting the self-respect and dignity of leaders and people on both sides deserves emphasis. Traditional concepts of "victory" are largely obsolete and misleading, so great ingenuity is required to find areas of mutual accommodation that can constitute "victory" for *both* sides.

There are several additional characteristics of crises that make such experiences highly stressful for leaders and their advisers. For one thing, an international crisis typically entails a strong threat to major values and interests that high officials are responsible for safeguarding. For another, the crisis often comes as a surprise to policymakers: even crises that have been anticipated to some extent can have a shock effect, insofar as they present new and unforeseen features. Also, crises often require quick decisions. The short response time typical of international crises imposes an additional psychological burden on decision-makers.

Finally, stress is generated by the cumulative emotional strain and physical fatigue that an international crisis imposes on top policymakers and their staffs. The demands on one's energies and emotions are intense; at the same time, opportunities for rest and recuperation are limited.

Stress is known to affect a variety of biological and psychological functions. We are interested here in its effects on the types of complex cognitive tasks associated with foreign policy decision-making. The following is a brief summary of major effects that have been noted in laboratory and field research in the psychobiology of stress on individuals and groups.

Impaired attention and perception: This means that aspects of the crisis situation may well escape scrutiny; conflicting values are likely to be overlooked; the range of perceived alternatives is apt to narrow, but not necessarily to the best alternatives; and the search for relevant information and options tends to be dominated by past experience, with a tendency to fall back on familiar past solutions, whether or not they are appropriate in the present situation.

Increased cognitive rigidity: This entails impaired ability to improvise and reduced creativity; less receptivity to information that challenges existing beliefs; increased stereotypic thinking; and decreased tolerance for ambiguity, which results in a tendency to cut off information search and evaluation and to make decisions prematurely.

Shifting the burden to the opponent: This approach permits the belief that one's own options are quite limited and that only the other side has it within its power to prevent an impending disaster.

Thus, if only from the psychobiological point of view, effective crisis management is exceedingly difficult to achieve. Moreover, scholars have carefully examined a series of modern crises, and certain concrete findings have emerged. For example, the ability to terminate such diplomatic confrontations as the Berlin Wall and the Cuban missile crisis without war has required that one or both sides either modify the diplomatic objectives they are pursuing in a crisis situation — that is, be willing to settle for less — or limit the means they employ for this purpose.

More specifically, it has been found that successful crisis management requires that each side maintain top-level civilian control over military options: any alerts, deployments, and low-level actions as well as the selection and timing of military moves. The tempo and momentum of military movements may have to be deliberately slowed down and pauses created. The goal would be to provide enough time for the opponents to exchange diplomatic signals and communications and to give each side adequate time to assess the situation, make decisions, and respond to proposals.

This means that movements of military forces must be carefully coordinated with diplomatic actions as part of an integrated strategy for terminating the crisis acceptably without war. Also, military movements, as well as threats intended to signal resolve, must be consistent with one's limited diplomatic objectives. In short, bluffing is dangerous and likely to lead to escalation.

Conversely, opponents should avoid military moves and threats that give the impression that one side is about to resort to large-scale warfare, thereby forcing the other to consider preemption. Diplomatic-military options should be chosen that signal, or are consistent with, a desire to negotiate a way out of the crisis rather than to seek a military solution. And they should leave the opposing side a way out of the crisis that is compatible with its fundamental interests.

These are difficult requirements for U.S. and Soviet policy-makers to meet in tense, often unexpected, rapidly developing confrontations. Mere awareness of these requirements and a desire to meet them by no means insures that they will be, or can be, effectively implemented.

Also, successful crisis management depends upon the ability of the two sides to communicate effectively with each other. Not only are reliable, speedy channels of communication necessary, but the two sides must avoid misperception of the substance of the communications.

Given these stringent requirements for successfully managing crises, it is remarkable that the two superpowers have managed thus far to work their way out of the tense diplomatic confrontations which have arisen since the end of World War II. The fear of a thermonuclear holocaust is undoubtedly the major factor in this success. But lately the hostile rhetoric and the destructive power of weaponry on both sides have reached an all-time high.

Can the superpowers, regardless of mutual distrust and competition, recognize that it is profoundly in their national interests to find ways to move back to a more respectful distance from the brink of ultimate shared disaster? In short, can we negotiate effective understanding and guidelines for crisis prevention?

In the early 1970s a superpower experiment in cooperation for crisis prevention proved abortive. The Basic Principles Agreement, signed by President Nixon and General Secretary Brezhnev at their first summit meeting in Moscow in 1972, was a constructive first step. But it did not provide explicit norms of restraint or specific guidelines for prevention. Rather, the principles were viewed by each side as a vehicle for imposing constraints on the other's foreign policy but not on its own.

Additional reflection suggests the need to go beyond such general principles to seek more specific ways in which the superpowers can cooperate to regulate and control their competition in different areas of the world:

by agreeing on explicit rules of engagement;

by relying upon tacit norms and patterns of restraint which emerge from past experience;

by improvising ad hoc ground rules for controlling the possibility of escalation once they have entered into competition in a given locale; and

by placing greater reliance on regional actors to define ground rules limiting superpower involvement in an unstable third-area situation.

We also stress that superpower cooperation in crisis prevention and the development of norms, rules, and procedures for this purpose can be independent of a collaborative overall relationship of the kind envisaged at the high point of détente; this is possible even if the relationship remains strained and highly competitive. At the same time, if a charter for a more moderate form of competitive relationship can be agreed upon, the scope and procedures for cooperation in crisis prevention could be enlarged.

Crisis prevention should be viewed as an objective, not as a strategy.

Clarity on this point is essential because there is no single strategy for preventing U.S.-Soviet crises. What is needed is a *repertoire of strategies,* coupled with skill in diagnosing situations of potential crisis and in adopting an appropriate strategy for each case.

Indeed, U.S.-Soviet global rivalry can be moderated through the adoption by each country of unilateral policies that do not require the other nation's cooperation; through third-party initiatives undertaken with a view to moderating or resolving conflicts in areas where the superpowers are already involved; and through bilateral U.S.-Soviet cooperation, which may be pursued via several modalities.

Initiatives by third parties can play an increasingly important role in avoiding, moderating, or eliminating the involvement of the United States or the Soviet Union in third areas. Not only the United Nations, but regional associations and blocs—the Organization of African Unity or the Association of South East Asian Nations—as well as individual states exercising regional influence, such as Mexico and the Caribbean countries, can mediate local conflicts and engage in preventive diplomacy. Regional associations can establish ground rules which attempt to limit the use of force in disputes among members and to regulate and limit superpower involvement.

With respect to bilateral arrangements between the superpowers, it is particularly disappointing that during the high point of détente the United States and the Soviet Union did not undertake to engage in regular diplomatic consultations to develop, if possible, a variety of *specific* crisis prevention understandings tailored to particular countries and regions. Such understandings could include, for example, U.S.-Soviet agreements *not* to compete in certain areas and arrangements for some form of cooperation in managing the danger of escalation when competing in a given locale.

U.S.-Soviet competition, direct or through allies or proxies, always carries with it the danger of escalation. To be sure, escalation can be avoided if either side chooses not to become engaged or withdraws from competition in a particular locale.

The United States, for example, evidently decided after World War II not to compete with the Soviet Union for influence in Finland. It has continued to accept "Finlandization" there, which permits the Finns to retain independence in domestic affairs in return for avoiding foreign policies that might be considered unfriendly to the Soviet Union. For its part, and for whatever reasons, the Soviet Union has sometimes avoided competing in parts of the Third World.

The superpowers can also agree not to compete in a given region or country. They can accomplish this by adopting practices resorted to

by the European powers in the eighteenth and nineteenth centuries —
the era of classical diplomacy. Thus President Kennedy and Premier
Khrushchev agreed on the neutralization of Laos in 1962. Earlier, in
1955, the United States and the Soviet Union signed the Austrian
State Treaty, which ended the occupation and division of Austria,
returning independence and sovereignty to that country along with
its formal neutralization.

One must recognize that the superpowers are unlikely to accept
general rules applying equally in *all* regions. Rules of engagement
designed for a specific area or type of situation might prove to be
more acceptable and workable, since such specific "rules" can take
into account the relative interests of the superpowers, which vary from
region to region.

Situations involving areas of "high interest symmetry" (that is, where
both superpowers have major interests), for instance, offer some promise here. A circumstance of this kind emerged during World War
II when Roosevelt, Stalin, and Churchill foresaw that competition for
advantage in filling the power vacuum in Central Europe, once Hitler
was defeated, might well result in dangerous conflict. Accordingly,
the Allied leaders mapped out zones of occupation for their respective
armies and set up procedures and rules for collective decision-making
and joint administration of occupied Germany.

For this area the Allies adopted what might be appropriately regarded as an explicit crisis prevention regime. Similarly, one might regard
the Four Power Agreement on the status of West Berlin in 1971 as
an effort to agree upon rules of engagement (and accommodation)
in a region of "high interest symmetry."

Other specific crisis prevention measures which serve to illustrate
our approach include suggestions to strengthen the "hotline" by adding
audio, video, or facsimile links and proposals to create a facility, jointly
staffed by the United States and the Soviet Union, to anticipate and
ward off crises and otherwise contribute to a reduced risk of nuclear
war. A useful model of the latter is the Standing Consultative
Commission (SCC) established under the Salt I agreements, but it
might be preferable to have a joint center comprised of components
in Moscow and Washington that were linked together via appropriate
communication facilities.

A principal function of the SCC is to consider questions of compliance with the agreements, and to abet this purpose the superpowers
have voluntarily committed themselves to supply the necessary information. In practice, the SCC has developed into a low-key, professional, and confidential forum. By most accounts, it has worked well

for more than 10 years, even during times of considerable strain in U.S.-Soviet relations.

With the limited example of the SCC in mind, we support recent proposals for the establishment of a joint U.S.-Soviet nuclear risk control center designed to carry out four valuable functions:

It could serve to facilitate communications between the U.S. and Soviet military staffs during world crises and conceivably could be used to forewarn an opponent of one's own military activities, thereby avoiding the risks that are associated with surprises and ambiguous behavior. The center could also be used after the political resolution of a crisis to negotiate details of military activity that would be reassuring. Such a facility might be particularly useful in the event of either the threat, or the actuality, of a nuclear detonation by a third party.

A nuclear management center could be especially helpful in averting nuclear confrontations. During periods of accelerating political and military tensions which typically lead to crises, the center could arrange exchanges of information about military activities along with appropriate explanations. It could also provide opportunities to question representatives of the other side about unannounced activities detected by intelligence systems, thus greatly increasing the chances for resolution of the situation short of a confrontation.

During normal times, a nuclear risk management center could serve as an exchange for various types of information that could build confidence between the superpowers. It could, for example, become headquarters for a continuing dialogue between the military staffs of both sides on issues of nuclear doctrine and deterrence. It could facilitate regular meetings between defense ministers, chiefs of staff, and lower-ranking counterparts. It could provide the mechanism and physical location for prior notification of certain kinds of weapons tests and strategic exercises. It could serve as a forum in which each side could raise questions about the other's military activities, forces, and facilities, in accordance with carefully specified ground rules. In sum, it could serve as an expanded SCC, where questions of compliance with the full range of arms control agreements might be raised and discussed.

Finally, a nuclear risk management center might be used jointly by the United States and the Soviet Union to consider and plan for contingencies involving the acquisition or detonation of nuclear weapons by terrorist groups or other third parties. It could serve as an information exchange in the event of an unexplained nuclear detonation, where each side could inform the other of missing weapons or critical components. It could also project the developmental activities of potential proliferators and facilitate discussion of nuclear safeguards and the possibility of providing them to other nations.

This proposal is offered in the belief that the spirit of science — international, analytic, objective — can and must be brought to bear on the crucial problem of nuclear conflict. In an unprecedented effort to transcend the traditional boundaries of discipline and nationality, science must develop a deeper understanding of large-scale conflict and its resolution. And we must create effective institutions and policies for that purpose.

10

Strategic Confusion, with or without Nuclear Winter

Theodore A. Postol

For most of human existence, the sun was intuitively understood to rotate around the earth, which itself was located at the center of the universe. Not until the sixteenth century did a few people recognize that this "intuitively obvious" belief was false. The implications of an equally profound discovery are yet to be fully comprehended, and its impact may yet have been only partially felt.

In 1945 it was shown that the runaway multiplication of neutrons in a piece of fissionable material could be made to continue long enough for a nuclear explosion to occur. The energy was so great, and was released in such a short time, that for an instant the temperature at the center of the explosion was many times higher than that at the sun's center. Thus a tool that could in effect deliver pieces of the sun's interior to the earth's surface was added to the traditional tools of warfare.

Now, the discovery of a possible nuclear winter effect reminds us that nuclear war would have vast, unimaginable consequences. U.S. nuclear policy, which emphasizes deterrence of war, inherently recognizes that extraordinary levels of destruction would result from a nuclear conflict. But this policy does not recognize that massive uncertainties also would accompany such destruction and would profoundly affect our ability to control escalation if deterrence fails.

Rather, U.S. policy treats nuclear warfare as if it were a chess game between two reasoning, informed adversaries, both of whom understand and agree to play by the rules of the game. The adversaries are presumed to be able to make careful decisions of momentous importance, despite the likelihood of severe limitations of time and detailed information. Escalation control is presumed, despite the fact that both adversaries would have to maintain communications over fragile and easily disrupted data links to vulnerable and diverse forces, each of which faces enemy forces capable of nearly instantaneous weapon delivery and unprecedented firepower.

The threat of a nuclear winter effect may not, as some have argued, confront U.S. nuclear policy with issues more problematic than those it already fails to address. Instead, it may add only one more element to the many that are ignored by a policy that offers little or no consistent practical guidance for either military planning or diplomatic negotiations.

This policy does not, for example, provide answers to vital questions such as how many weapons we really need to meet the country's various military objectives and whether an arms control treaty limiting us to 1,000 warheads would allow us to plan for all the military contingencies of concern to our leadership, or do we really require 20,000? If national policy is to provide guidance on how to deal with nuclear planning uncertainties—whether from threats of nuclear winter or political and military requirements for contingency planning—an expanded and revised policy must incorporate two significant observations:

The entire structure of current U.S. nuclear policy is beset by misconceptions and problematic and contradictory features. The policy does not adequately emphasize the role of uncertainty in military planning; the scale of risks and consequences in the use, or the threat of use, of nuclear weapons; the unpredictability of warfare; the dangers of requiring decisive action where time and information are inadequate. Since the objectives and intellectual framework of the current policy are so unclear, there is no way to determine how the discovery or refined understanding of a nuclear winter, or other nuclear effects, will further modify its structure.

Many nuclear weapons effects—in addition to nuclear winter—are not well understood and could have major military planning and national policy implications. Experience with nuclear effects that were either not fully appreciated (dust, fratricide, silo-failure mechanisms) or not even initially recognized (electromagnetic pulse, glassification of nuclear dust in aircraft engines, fallout) has repeatedly demonstrated the complexity of nuclear environments. Even if a nuclear winter effect did not exist, our changing understanding of many nuclear effects could also result in drastic changes in military planning and the concept of deterrence.

For example, experience with volcanic dust clouds after the Mount St. Helens and Galunggung (in Indonesia) eruptions suggests that under certain conditions relatively low concentrations of very fine dust, such as that raised by nuclear explosions, can cause severe damage to airplane engines perhaps five to 10 hours after a large-scale attack. Dust from nuclear debris clouds could, in the immediate hours after an attack, present a serious hazard to airborne command posts and radio relays, bombers and tankers, and cruise missiles.

In addition, very high radiation levels would be associated with the dust—possibly even high enough to affect the performance of avionics equipment. The implications for military planning are numerous. The U.S. airborne communications relay system, the Post-Attack Command and Control System, has the mission of maintaining communications by line-of-sight radio transmissions between aircraft. Because these aircraft can loiter at about 30,000 feet, they can directly communicate with each other by ultra-high-frequency radio. Radioactive dust spreading from nuclear detonations could present a major hazard to these aircraft and their crews.

Dust raised over the Soviet Union by U.S. SLBM and ICBM attacks could also persist long enough to threaten U.S. cruise missiles and bombers. This would, of course, depend on unpredictable weather conditions and the nature and scale of attack. Of course, Soviet interceptors and other air defense elements may also have difficulty operating in this environment.

STRATEGIC IMPLICATIONS OF NUCLEAR WINTER

Current U.S. defense strategy requires that its nuclear forces have the ability to destroy a large fraction of Soviet urban areas and industry, as well as a wide variety of military targets and to retaliate at any level of conflict in a deliberate and selective way. This strategy aims to deter the Soviets by creating unacceptable levels of danger and uncertainty—a policy objective supposedly achieved by providing U.S. leadership with flexible nuclear systems and military options. Thus, political leadership is equipped with military tools that can be used to deny the Soviets any advantage at any level of conflict, as Secretary of Defense Caspar Weinberger stated in his fiscal year 1985 report:

If deterrence should fail, we cannot predict the nature of a Soviet nuclear strike nor ensure with any certainty that what might begin as a limited Soviet attack would remain confined to that level. We must plan for flexibility in our forces and in our options for response, so that we might terminate the conflict on terms favorable to the forces of freedom, and reestablish deterrence at the lowest possible level of violence, thus avoiding further destruction. Of course, this concept of seeking to enhance deterrence and to limit the level of destruction by having flexible and enduring forces is not new. It has been squarely in the mainstream of American strategic thinking for over two decades.

While many questions can be raised about current U.S. nuclear strategy independent of the threat of a nuclear winter effect, that particular effect raises three broad classes of strategic and military questions:

Does it alter the foundation of the U.S.-Soviet deterrent relationship?

Does it raise questions about the U.S. ability to implement policy objectives?

Are there quantitative or qualitative threshold effects that could seriously constrict the range of possible limited nuclear options that could be credibly used as threats against Soviet aggression?

On the question of mutual assured destruction, it should be noted that at present the scale and consequences of nuclear winter effects are highly uncertain, even for massive urban/industrial attacks. And if the effect does occur, massive attacks on cities would be not only homicidal but also suicidal. Only a very small fraction of both U.S. and Soviet forces could destroy the other's cities so that either country could readily retaliate against the other's cities in almost any imaginable circumstance. Nevertheless, the United States could possibly build nuclear forces capable of threatening the destruction of Soviet cities while limiting nuclear winter effects.

If the ability to continue to threaten the destruction of Soviet society remains an important objective of U.S. nuclear force planning, and the credibility of this threat is judged to be degraded by the possible consequences of a nuclear winter, the technical means to carry out the threat may already be available to both superpowers. A small supplement of strategic warheads of today's standard yields could make the U.S. nuclear arsenal very effective in accomplishing essentially all the strategic military missions now contemplated and could probably also be used in many applications not usually contemplated now —quite possibly without causing a nuclear winter effect. I want to emphasize that I do not advocate the acquisition of the kinds of forces described in the approach to nuclear planning outlined below.

Although the consequences of either a one-kiloton or a 100-kiloton attack on Washington, D.C. could hardly be considered limited, the latter is much more unambiguously so. Depending on variabilities like height of burst, visibility and weather, the 100-kiloton attack could be expected to destroy an area of from 14 to 40 square miles. Most of this area would not be destroyed by blast effects but would instead be consumed in the ensuing mass fires. According to the estimates of R.P. Turco and his coauthors, the detonation of 1,000 such weapons against similarly large, combustible targets could result in fires of such an extent and intensity that the smoke generated by them would sufficiently modify the atmosphere to cause a climatic catastrophe within days.* Hence, an attack involving 1,000 or so such warheads against Soviet urban/industrial targets would either be suicidal or cause serious damage to the United States, its allies, and most or all nonparticipating countries of the world, even if the Soviets did not retaliate. It might therefore be argued that the security of the United States and its allies could be enhanced if urban/industrial targets could be attacked without precipitating a nuclear winter.

By the end of this century, ballistic missiles could be capable of even greater accuracy than the very considerable accuracy available today. Very low-yield weapons could then be used to attack almost any target of military or industrial interest. This would subject an area of about one square mile to enough heat from the fireball of a two-kiloton air-burst that fires would be likely.

But if the attacking nuclear weapon employs a one-kiloton earth-penetrating warhead, the range of severe blast effects could be reduced by about half, and the area within which the fireball would ignite fires would be reduced to less than a hundredth of a square mile, or less than a thousandth of that which might be set on fire by a single 100-kiloton weapon. If one thousand 100-kiloton weapons falling on cities would cause a climatic catastrophe, then, it might be argued, a million of the smaller weapons would now be required to achieve that effect. Violent explosions, however, often initiate many fires due to static electric discharge from collapsing walls, or from ruptured electrical or gas lines. If not extinguished, these fires can do very extensive damage in a target area.

Similarly, one may have very high confidence that fires resulting from the earth-penetrator attacks could not be fought. Since these weapons penetrate into the ground and then detonate, the fallout they

---

*R.P. Turco, et al., "Nuclear Winter: Global Consequences of Multiple Nuclear Explosions," *Science*, 222, no. 4630 (Dec. 23, 1983), pp. 1283–92. For more recent work on the effects of smoke and dust on global circulation patterns, see S.L. Thompson et al., "Global Climatic Consequences of Nuclear War: Simulations with Three Dimensional Models," *Ambio*, 13, no. 4 (1984).

create is in the form of very large particles which fall very close to the area of the blast. The area immediately surrounding the detonation point would have radiation levels perhaps as high as 10,000 rads per hour, delivering a lethal dose every three to four minutes to those foolish enough to attempt to fight the fires.

The many scattered fires initiated in this manner, however, might differ from those initiated in the single flash of a 100-kiloton weapon. The smoke from them might not easily rise to high altitudes, a necessary condition to induce a nuclear winter effect. In addition, the debris clouds following the one-kiloton detonations might also not provide a large upward-moving chimney of air through which burning debris could send its smoke to high altitudes, another possible mechanism for smoke injection to high altitudes. Thus, the smoke from many separate fires might be confined to low altitudes, where scavenging and atmospheric mixing would remove it rapidly, with minimal impact on the global climate. This, of course, is speculation, not assertion.

This type of attack also features extremely intense but very local fallout. The detonation of the one-kiloton earth-penetrating warhead would result in an intensely radioactive debris cloud highly lethal or injurious to those downwind who could not escape or find shelter. In fact, very high levels of fallout could occur as far as five or 10 miles downwind of the target area. However, that debris would not get lifted to very high altitudes and would therefore not be carried far enough to become a worldwide threat. Hence this fallout would not result in a delayed threat against the attacker.

An attack of many such one-kiloton earth-penetrating weapons could selectively destroy water supplies, power stations, rail and highway junctures, even major hospitals or food storage sites. The result, within days, would be tens to hundreds of millions of casualties from massive thirst, starvation, and exposure, followed by the dissolution of the adversary's society.

Thus, I have postulated a force capable of destroying Soviet or American society, which, if used, might not induce a global environmental catastrophe. The acquisition of such forces, however, would resolve none of the profound and imponderable dilemmas that we confront today: the overwhelming threat of uncontrolled escalation, the unimaginable weight of any execution decision, and massive retaliation guaranteeing destruction of the attacking society.

PLANNING WITHOUT NUCLEAR WINTER

If, however, the postulation of a nuclear winter is wrong, the policy and planning issues of U.S. national nuclear policy still cannot be addressed with minor adjustments. The many technical requirements made of our current strategy raise questions that are perhaps considerably more fundamental and serious than even those posed by unambiguous threats of nuclear winter or other nuclear phenomena.

Current strategy treats nuclear warfare as a chess game between two reasoning, informed adversaries, who understand and agree to the rules of the game. For this model to apply, two assumptions that apply in chess must also apply in nuclear warfare: both players can execute and absorb a wide range of limited and general nuclear attacks, and both can recognize and assess the objectives of these attacks and respond in a measured and graduated way with appropriate counterattacks.

If questions of irrationality are put aside, this model of nuclear conflict could not plausibly represent reality without the following technical capabilities:

Both the United States and the Soviet Union must be able to absorb a limited attack from the other without losing the ability to respond in a controlled and limited manner.

Both sides would need astonishingly capable warning, surveillance and communications systems to provide information on the scale, size and success of attacks and counterattacks.

U.S. and Soviet command authorities and their nuclear forces, as well as the warning, surveillance and communications systems, would have to survive throughout the conflict.

The warning, surveillance, and communications systems of both superpowers would have to be relatively free from any disruption or serious degradation throughout all stages of an escalating nuclear exchange.

The last-resort ability to threaten the adversary's society with destruction must exist and be credible.

Clearly, a most remarkable set of technical capabilities would be required before such a strategy could have any hope of being implementable. Those who must plan military options and make the decision to use nuclear weapons will still face uncertainties as profound as those that confront us today: Is the reliability of the systems really what the engineers believe it to be? Will the attack deal a sufficiently mortal blow to the enemy to allow us to avoid destruction? Many argue that it is naive to expect nuclear policy to be militarily rational, that political and bureaucratic needs and objectives are the real stimulus behind weapons procurement programs. But such an attitude guarantees a decreased incentive for sound military planning. Although political considerations in national military planning are no doubt of great importance, these must be carefully and systematically weighed against the risks and costs that could follow from a political misjudgment or an escalating series of uncontrollable events.

In sum, our current nuclear policy rests upon a foundation of assumptions, problems, and contradictions that require serious re-examination independent of the threat of a possible nuclear winter effect. Thus the United States now faces many technical and military applications problems which could be as problematic as those posed by a possible nuclear winter threat. Although nuclear weapons techno-logy is available to make possible a force that could threaten Soviet society with complete destruction without causing, in all probability, a nuclear winter, the acquisition of such a force will not resolve the military security dilemmas posed by the existence of nuclear weapons.

A nuclear war that touches the United States—even a very limited one—is likely to be the most terrible thing that the country has ever experienced. While we should not diminish the terrifying prospects of a nuclear winter, neither should we feel comforted about nuclear war *without* nuclear winter. The central question is, and remains, how to avoid a nuclear war.

11

Nuclear Winter Report Excerpts

National Research Council

The National Research Council, a branch of the National Academy of Sciences, issued a report in December 1984 on The Effects on the Atmosphere of a Major Nuclear Exchange. *The 193-page report was commissioned in early 1983 by the U.S. Department of Defense, which wanted both more information about current understanding of the issue and recommendations for further research. The* Bulletin *has followed the varied and expanding discussion of a possible "nuclear winter" from its beginnings. (See "Nuclear Winter" by Anne Ehrlich in April 1984, "Strategic Confusion—with or without Nuclear Winter" by Theodore Postol in February 1985, and Joseph V. Smith's review of* The Cold and the Dark *in January 1985.) In that vein, we present the following excerpts from the "summary and conclusions" section of the National Research Council committee's report. We do so without necessarily endorsing the report's recommendation for a "vigorous research effort" to narrow the scientific uncertainties surrounding the atmospheric effects of a major nuclear exchange. A subject worthy of further discussion is the extent to which scientific resources are being focused on peripheral rather than central arms race issues.—The Editors*

I t is widely understood that any major nuclear exchange would be accompanied by an enormous number of immediate fatalities; nevertheless, a much larger fraction of the human population would survive the immediate effects of a nuclear exchange. This study addresses current knowledge about the nature of the physical environment the survivors would have to face. . . .

. . . Long-term atmospheric consequences imply additional problems that are not easily mitigated by prior preparedness and that are not in harmony with any notion of rapid postwar restoration of social structure. They also create an entirely new threat to populations far removed from target areas, and suggest the possibility of additional major risks for any nation that itself initiates use of nuclear weapons, even if nuclear retaliation should somehow be limited. . . .

. . . The baseline scenario . . . was selected so as to be representative of a general nuclear war: one-half—about 6500 megatons (Mt)—of the estimated total world arsenal would be detonated. Of this, 1500 Mt would be detonated at ground level. Of the other 5000 Mt that would be detonated at altitudes chosen so as to maximize blast damage to structures, 1500 Mt would be directed at military, economic, and political targets that coincidentally lie in or near about 1000 of the largest urban areas. All explosions would occur between 30°N and 70°N latitude. . . .

. . . There are many points in the analysis at which there is a wide range of parameter values that are consistent with the best current scientific knowledge. Any estimate of the overall atmospheric response will involve a compounding of the effects of these uncertainties. Obviously, calculations made under these conditions cannot be read as a scientific prediction of the effects of a nuclear exchange; rather, they represent an interim estimate from which the reader can infer something of the potential seriousness of the atmospheric degradation that might occur. . . .

. . . The committee believes, however, that an appropriately qualified, preliminary quantitative treatment of the problem is warranted on two grounds. First, given the enormous human stakes that may be involved, it may not be advisable to wait until a strong scientific case has been assembled before presenting tentative results; there is a danger that a report that reached no conclusions at all would be misconstrued to be a refutation of the scientific basis for the suggestion that severe atmospheric effects are possible. Second, a quantitative approach to the problem is the best way to ensure that all important factors are systematically considered, and quantification helps distinguish the important factors from the less important ones in the overall analysis. Such results are necessary to the orderly allocation of resources to the most pertinent research questions. . . .

In short: the committee's findings are clearly and emphatically of an interim character.

A vigorous research effort is now needed. Nevertheless, one cannot expect that long-term nuclear effects will be characterized with great precision or confidence in the next few years. Many uncertainties cannot be narrowed because they depend on human decisions that can be made, or changed, long after any particular prediction has been issued. These include, for example, the total yield of the exchange, individual warhead yields, the mix of targets, the mix of altitudes at which the bursts would occur, and the season of the year in which the exchange would occur. In addition, there are obvious limits to the use of large-scale experiments in this field, and the evolution of atmospheric models will require some time.

Many significant uncertainties, however, can be narrowed by further study. In particular, the heights to which smoke is deposited in city-scale fires, the early smoke removal by coagulation and condensation in the fire plume, the extent of continued buoyant rising of sun-heated opaque clouds, and the dynamical response of the atmosphere, first to patchy high-altitude solar absorption and then to the heating of more broadly distributed but still heavy smoke cover, have received only scattered and recent attention.

The general conclusion that the committee draws from this study is the following: a major nuclear exchange would insert significant amounts of smoke, fine dust, and undesirable chemical species into the atmosphere. These depositions could result in dramatic perturbations of the atmosphere lasting over a period of at least a few weeks. Estimation of the amounts, the vertical distributions, and the subsequent fates of these materials involves large uncertainties. Furthermore, accurate detailed accounts of the response of the atmosphere, the redistribution and removal of the depositions, and the duration of a greatly degraded environment lie beyond the present state of knowledge.

Nevertheless, the committee finds that, unless one or more of the effects lie near the less severe end of their uncertainty ranges, or unless some mitigating effect has been overlooked, there is a clear possibility that great portions of the land areas of the northern temperate zone (and, perhaps, a larger segment of the planet) could be severely affected. Possible impacts include major temperature reductions (particularly for an exchange that occurs in the summer) lasting for weeks, with subnormal temperatures persisting for months. The impact of these temperature reductions and associated meteorological changes on the surviving population, and on the biosphere that supports the survivors, could be severe, and deserves careful independent study. . . .

The committee also draws several more specific conclusions:

1. . . . During its tenure in the atmosphere, the smoke would gradually spread and become more uniformly distributed over much of the northern hemisphere, although some patchiness would be likely to persist. Light levels could be reduced by a factor of 100 in regions that were covered with the initial hemispheric average smoke load, causing intense cooling beneath the particular layer and unusually intense heating of the upper layer. While large uncertainties currently attend the estimates of smoke emissions, and of their optical and physical consequences, the baseline case implies severe atmospheric consequences.

2. The production of smoke from fires, and the implied effects on the atmosphere, is more directly linked to the extent of detonation over urban areas than to the aggregate yield of a nuclear exchange. . . . Any war scenario that subjects . . . city centers to nuclear attack, even one employing a very small fraction of the existing nuclear arsenal, could generate nearly as much smoke as in the 6500-Mt baseline war scenario. . . .

3. . . . The lifetime of soot is highly uncertain, particularly in the upper troposphere. . . . Although the lofted soot (and dust) would rapidly spread around the latitude band of injection, the distribution could be uneven for several months, with continent-size patches of lesser and greater density, particularly near the southern edge of the affected zones. . . .

4. . . . A significant fraction of the dust consisting of particles with radii less than one micron . . . would be expected to remain aloft for months. About one-half of these submicron particles would be injected into the stratosphere and would produce some long-term reduction of sunlight at the earth's surface, even after smoke and dust at lower altitudes were removed. This stratospheric dust alone would lead to perceptible reductions in average light intensities, and continental surface temperatures would fall measurably. In a plausible scenario that involves more ground burst attacks against very hard targets than are assumed in the baseline case, the possible dust effects are several times larger. . . .

5. . . . A baseline attack during the summer might decrease mean continental temperatures in the northern temperate zone by as much as 10° to 25°C, with temperatures along the coasts of the continents decreasing by much smaller amounts. In contrast, an attack of the same size during the winter, according to these [general circulation model] simulations, might produce little change in temperature in the northern temperate zone, although there could be a significant drop in temperatures at more southern latitudes. . . .

6. ... The northern hemisphere ozone reduction could become substantial several months after the war. Estimates based on current stratospheric structure suggest that the amount of ozone reduction would decrease by one-half after about 2 years. At the time of maximum ozone reduction, the biologically effective ultraviolet intensity ... at the ground would be approximately one and one-half times the normal levels. Initially, the presence of dust and smoke particles in the atmosphere would provide a measure of protection at the surface from the enhanced ultraviolet radiation. This protection would gradually diminish as the particles were removed. ...

7. ... Although southern hemisphere effects would be much less extensive, significant amounts of dust and smoke could drift to and across the equator as early as a few weeks after a nuclear exchange. A large rate of transport across the equator driven by heating in the debris cloud cannot be ruled out. Indeed, such heating-enhanced cross-equatorial circulation has been found for spring and summer months in computer simulations.

8. ... Prehistoric volcanic eruptions and impacts from extraterrestrial bodies [do not provide] a useful direct analog to the nuclear case because neither type involved the production of highly absorbing soot particles. Furthermore, the atmospheric consequences of prehistoric natural events of these proportions are not known, and their effects on the fossil record, if any, have not been sought in any systematic way. Accordingly, available knowledge about prehistoric volcanic and impact events provides neither support nor refutation of the committee's conclusions.

9. All calculations of the atmospheric effects of a major nuclear war require quantitative assumptions about uncertain physical parameters. ... The larger uncertainties include the following: (a) the quantity and absorption properties of the smoke produced in very large fires; (b) the initial distribution in altitude of smoke produced in large fires; (c) the mechanisms and rate of early scavenging of smoke from fire plumes, and aging of the smoke in the first few days; (d) the induced rate of vertical and horizontal transport of smoke and dust in the upper troposphere and stratosphere; (e) the resulting perturbations in atmospheric processes such as cloud formation, precipitation, storminess, and wind patterns; and (f) the adequacy of current and projected atmospheric response models to reliably predict changes that are caused by a massive, high-altitude, and irregularly distributed injection of particulate matter.

The United States

1

A Militarized Society

Jerome B. Wiesner

In his famous message to Congress on December 1, 1862, Abraham Lincoln wrote: "The dogmas of the quiet past are inadequate to the stormy present. The occasion is piled high with difficulty, and we must rise with the occasion. As our case is new, so we must think anew and act anew. We must disenthrall ourselves."

Lincoln's advice is relevant today, when nuclear weapons have the same desperate meaning for our times as the issues of slavery and freedom had for his. Disenthrall ourselves we must, from the dogmas that account for our fatalistic acceptance of the arms race. In doing so, we must recognize the extent to which the United States has been running an arms race with itself and in the process has become a military culture.

Despite President Dwight Eisenhower's 1961 warning about the growing influence of the military–industrial complex in our society, it has grown even more powerful in the years since. Eisenhower's message reflected his frustration with his inability to control the combined pressures from the military, industry, Congress, journalists, and veterans' organizations for procuring more weapons and against his efforts to seek accommodations with the Soviets.

As a member of Eisenhower's Science Advisory Committee, I saw firsthand how individuals from government and military industries collaborated with members of Congress to defeat the president's efforts. They killed the nuclear-test-ban negotiations with arguments ranging from the need for the neutron bomb and peaceful nuclear explosions to the possibility of Soviet cheating by testing behind the moon or even the sun. Eisenhower cancelled the B–70 bomber and then reinstated it after being subjected to enormous pressure by the political leaders of the Republican Party. Exaggerated estimates of the Soviet nuclear bomb stockpile and delivery system strength were also used several times to justify unneeded U.S. strategic forces.

President John Kennedy had to contend with similar opposition when he continued Eisenhower's efforts to achieve a halt to nuclear testing. In fact, opposition to his efforts was much more intense than that faced by Eisenhower, because it appeared that Kennedy's efforts just might succeed. As Kennedy's special assistant for science and technology, I also saw how pressure from Congress, the Defense Department, and outside groups caused Kennedy to build a much larger Minuteman missile force than was necessary, even after reconnaissance made it clear that the suspected missile gap did not exist.

The pressures continued on subsequent presidents. For example, President Lyndon Johnson decided in 1967 to buy a modest-sized anti-ballistic-missile system to protect the country from a Chinese military attack and, incidentally, himself from an increasing attack by Republicans during the 1968 presidential election. I attended a meeting of a special group appointed by Johnson to advise him on the deployment of the Nike Zeus ABM defense system. The group's overwhelming verdict was that the system would not provide much protection and therefore would be a waste of money. Johnson accepted that advice but decided to build the cheaper anti-Chinese system to blunt political attacks on the earlier decision.

President Gerald Ford and his secretary of defense, James Schlesinger, proposed, because of military pressures, to produce what they called a "limited, strategic, war-fighting capability" that Schlesinger ultimately admitted to Congress was planned for "a highly unlikely contingency." President Jimmy Carter gave up his opposition to the MX missile in the hope of getting the SALT II Treaty through Congress.

Such pressure groups no longer need to operate on the president. President Ronald Reagan not only accepts the ideas of the groups that Eisenhower warned against, he has become their most articulate spokesman, espousing an enormous buildup in U.S. military power—especially nuclear fighting power—while making a shambles of arms control efforts. Reagan's reelection is an indication that the militarization of U.S. society is proceeding with the complicity, if not the overt support, of ordinary citizens.

The history of the B-1 bomber is another case in point. After the project was shut off by the Carter Administration, funds from the space shuttle and other government projects were fraudulently diverted to keep the B-1 alive. A story in the April 7, 1984, *San Francisco Examiner* details how the manufacturer then scattered contracts so widely that almost every state and hamlet in the country had a stake in the B-1's future. Even though it is generally agreed that the B-1 is unnecessary, the campaign succeeded.

The contracts were worth an average of $700 million per state. The states of the 20 senators who lobbied hardest for the aircraft were scheduled to get sums ranging from $1 billion to $9 billion. Even more disturbing is the fact that labor unions and chambers of commerce lobbied vigorously for this marginally useful aircraft at a time when budget deficits were destroying the U.S. economy and the infrastructure of American society. This irrational behavior is only possible because we, the citizens of the nation, permit it. It is no longer a question of controlling a military-industrial complex, but rather of keeping the United States from becoming a totally military culture.

More than 35 years of Cold War language and politics have created a situation in which it is difficult to talk rationally about how we arrived at the present impasse. A combination of Newspeak words, false information, half-baked ideas about successful preemptive attacks and winning nuclear wars, and clairvoyant projections of Soviet forces and objectives have obscured rational alternatives to the arms race. In particular, the use of worst-case analysis, supported by controlled leaks of secret information, has manipulated Americans into denying responsibility for the arms race and believing that the Soviets are relentless and reckless aggressors. As a result, ordinary citizens conclude that they can do nothing to stop the catastrophe they see coming.

A classic case is the "bomber gap" of the 1950s. Shortly after the United States adopted Secretary of State John Foster Dulles's 1954 policy of massive retaliation, the U.S. intelligence community began to suspect that the Soviet Union was building a large intercontinental bomber force, and it sounded an alert. It predicted that the Soviet Union would have several hundred intercontinental and shorter-range bombers, a force that could easily reach overseas U.S. bases and possibly even the continental United States in one-way missions. In response to this, the United States began producing a truly intercontinental bomber, the B-52.

In fact, however, while the Soviet Union did have a substantial force of TU4 medium-range bombers, it lacked an overseas base-complex from which to stage them. Its nuclear bomb supply was also small. In addition, it became evident in the mid-1950s that the Soviet Union was not creating a long-range bomber force on the scale previously feared, and the estimates of its threat began to shrink. By 1958 more sophisticated U.S. reconnaissance showed the Soviet force to be very small, about 100.

I used to believe that this misestimate of Soviet bomber capability was the result of faulty intelligence. Careful examination of the facts now makes it seem more likely a case of deliberate deception. In 1950, a report to President Harry Truman by his Air Policy Commission, headed by Thomas Finletter, concluded that the aircraft industry would have to produce 13 million pounds more aircraft than it had in 1948 and 30 million pounds more than in 1949 in order to maintain adequate military production readiness. Shortly thereafter, in April 1951, Air Force Secretary Stuart Symington introduced the supposed Soviet threat in testimony to Congress. "The Russians possess air equipment capable of delivering a surprise attack against any part of the United States," he said, "and this country has no adequate defense against such an assault." He testified that the Soviet Union "has an air force whose strength in nearly all categories is now the largest in the world and growing larger month by month." Such statements mobilized many scientists to work on U.S. defenses.

On July 14 of that year, a Senate appropriations subcommittee was urged to drive toward a 150-group Air Force in three years, instead of the 87 groups it had already approved. These numbers required precisely the aircraft-production capacity recommended by the Finletter Commission. Finletter, now the new Air Force secretary, not only supported the buildup but urged a major increase in the production of fissionable material, which the United States did undertake.

Of these subcommittee hearings the Congressional Record reported: "The testimony of all witnesses except those speaking for the Department of the Navy was so uniformly of a classified nature that it does not lend itself to publication in any form." Yet somehow most of the testimony on the Soviet threat quickly found its way into the *New York Times* and *Washington Post*.

Interestingly, at no time after the truth was discovered did the creators of those distorted predictions show any concern about the unnecessary buildup they had stimulated or propose that the United States revise its objectives. Recently I spoke to an individual who had been one of the most articulate alarmists about the bomber gap and asked him why he had not revised his view of the Soviet threat when the facts became known. He answered that he had always been certain that they would eventually present a nuclear threat to the United States, and he didn't want to make it too easy for them. Even now he is not willing to admit that our enormous buildup caused the Soviets to follow suit.

A more recent example of this kind of duplicity and distortion is the "window of vulnerability" scare which served as the Reagan Administration's first rationale for building the MX missile. The concept was put forth by the Committee on the Present Danger, a private group organized to defeat the SALT II Treaty and to press for a U.S. military buildup. The Committee's scenario was faulty in many ways. For one thing, its members concerned themselves only with the vulnerability of the land-based portion of the U.S. strategic triad. Furthermore, they assumed that a massive Soviet first strike involving the accurate coordination of hundreds of missiles and thousands of warheads in an attack that had never been practiced would work as predicted. Anyone who conducts experiments knows how unlikely that would be.

But the crowning absurdity of the scenario is that the Soviets would actually lose more than they would gain by such an attack. The Committee presumed that two Soviet warheads would be required to destroy each of the U.S. land-based missile sites, or 2,200 warheads for 1,100 sites. If the attack were entirely successful, only about 2,000 U.S. weapons would be destroyed. Aside from the fact that some 7,000 U.S. weapons on aircraft and at sea would be available for retaliation, the Soviets would have set themselves back in the weapons balance.

The nuclear bomb stubbornly remains the terror weapon wise men saw it to be at its birth. The default solution of the so-called experts has been to continue the arms race in the futile hope that a magic solution will appear. Einstein once said that God would not play dice with the universe. Humankind should not play such games either. That is why we need so desperately to rethink our premises, why we need to stop amassing nuclear destructive power.

Our truly democratic nation has been overtaken by a social cancer from which only mass understanding and action can save it. Only through the continuing involvement of great numbers of informed and dedicated individuals do we have any hope of rescuing ourselves and the rest of humanity from ultimate destruction.

I am often told that this subject is too complicated for average people to understand, and so even though they are frightened by what they see and hear, they have no choice but to accept what the "experts" say. These people are wrong. These issues can indeed be understood by anyone who is willing to make a sustained effort to do so. Just a few hours of study and discussion a week can make a person knowledgeable, if not expert, and a truly knowledgeable citizenry will lead to sounder national policies.

It is even more important to realize that there are no experts on nuclear war. No one knows how to use nuclear weapons. While there are thousands of experts on technical matters and on military hardware, on the critical issues of strategy, tactics, deterrence, and war-winning there are truly no experts. *None!* No one knows for sure about the actual field-performance of missiles, their reliability, or their accuracy. Because it is impossible to test nuclear weapons in realistic conditions, the uncertainty about their performance in combat is even greater than the uncertainty about the performance of their individual components.

There has never been a war, even a tiny one, in which tactical or strategic weapons were used by both sides. Planners are, therefore, completely dependent on theory to support their strategies. Analysts and military officers who plan for the use of conventional weapons can draw on experience. They can conduct more or less realistic field exercises to test their ideas about the use of new weapons or tactics. But because there has never been a nuclear war, or even one nuclear weapon fired at another, all scenarios discussed with such solemnity by so-called experts are based entirely on speculation.

To be sure, the analysts use computer models as a substitute for real experience, but the predictions from such models are totally dependent on the assumptions—guesses —put into the models by the analysts. There are many unknowable factors, such as the reliability of missiles when operated by soldiers instead of trained technicians and fired by the hundreds or thousands instead of singly, the reliability of the command and control system, the accuracy of guidance systems, the precise locations of targets, and exact estimates of target vulnerability.

Even when computers are used to design comparatively simple physical systems such as power systems or aircraft, a certain amount of trial and error is necessary to correct for unanticipated deficiencies. But how can this technique be applied to modeling a massive nuclear war? I doubt that anyone would agree to re-run a nuclear war in order to take advantage of the lessons learned the first time.

It is often suggested that secret information exists that would argue against a nuclear freeze or a test ban or some other logical arms-limitation measure. But there are no secrets on the vital issues that determine the course of the arms race. Each citizen should realize that on such critical issues as what constitutes a deterrent and how many nuclear weapons are enough his or her judgments are as good as those of a president or secretary of defense, perhaps even better since the layperson is not subject to all of the confusing pressures that influence people in official positions. It is important for citizens to realize that their government has no monopoly on wisdom or special knowledge that changes the common-sense conclusion that nuclear weapons have only one purpose—to prevent their use—and that can be accomplished with a small number of secure weapons on each side.

But realization is not enough. It must become informed conviction based on personal study. It is encouraging to see that a large number of people recognize this. In recent years there has been a growing involvement of people in all walks of life in the efforts to find alternate national security measures. There is an explosion of antinuclear groups whose strength flows from an inner conviction that the present course is wrong and dangerous. Perhaps most important of all, we are witnessing the emergence, as dissenters, of increasing numbers of former insiders and experts whose professional loyalty to the Establishment has, until recently, made them reluctant to speak out against policies that worried them. More and more civilian and military officials of the past are expressing disagreement with current national defense policies. This development is very important. Concerned citizens need the information and intellectual support for their own common sense and intuitions that such insiders provide.

Survival is not at all a primarily technological story, even though we recognize that the problems began with technological challenges, the nuclear bomb, and intercontinental delivery systems. If we are going to get out of the appalling situation which we and the Soviets have created for ourselves and all of our companions on the globe, we must change our mode of thinking to include issues that lie at the root of human behavior and are basically social, cultural, historic, moral, ethical, economic, and psychological.

It is the responsibility of Americans in particular to disenthrall ourselves of our false innocence and realize the extent to which our combination of fears and overwhelming technical and economic strength have caused our country to be the leading force in the arms race. And we must find ways of using these same strengths and energies to take the lead in ending it. Doing this, as difficult and unpopular as it may be, represents the ultimate test of dedication to American ideals.

2

History of the Nuclear Stockpile

Robert S. Norris, Thomas B. Cochran, and William M. Arkin

T he United States since 1945 has manufactured some 60,000 nuclear warheads in 71 types configured for 116 weapon systems costing some $750 billion. This amounts to an average production rate of about four warheads per day for 40 years. With the current rate of spending on warhead production exceeding that of the Manhattan Project, the present stockpile of some 25,500 warheads is once again on the rise.

That the most basic facts about the stockpile are shrouded in secrecy and difficult to discover is troubling, given their importance. Absent from the voluminous literature about the nuclear age is any serious treatment of the history of the warhead stockpile. "Gadget," "Little Boy," and "Fat Man" have been the central characters in chronicles of the dawn of the nuclear era, but a history of their many successors remains to be written. Only preliminary data can be offered here, but a full analysis is likely to lead to new insights about the Cold War, the dynamics of the arms race, and features of the contemporary debate.[1]

The nuclear warhead stockpile grew slowly at first. Because of a scarcity of materials and laborious production methods there were only seven hundred by 1950. But by the mid-1950s, with the production complex in place, the stockpile began growing by thousands of warheads per year until it reached its peak in 1967 at just under 32,000. By 1970– 1971 the stockpile had dipped to 27,000, then

then increased slightly over four years with the deployment of MIRVed Poseidon and Minuteman missiles. From 1974 it gradually declined before again starting upward in 1982.

The character of the present nuclear buildup is that huge numbers of warheads produced during the 1950s and 1960s are planned to be retired and replaced with larger numbers of new warheads. Although expenditures are at near-record highs, production rates are not. From fiscal 1984 through 1988 the stockpile will increase, under current plans, by an average of some 650 warheads per year, reaching an estimated level of over 28,000. Production rates of new warheads are in the 1,800-per-year range—five a day—with retirements at some 1,100 a year—three a day—averaging a net addition of approximately two a day.

STIMULANTS TO GROWTH AND DIVERSITY

Service rivalry. In the immediate aftermath of World War II, civilian and military officials were unsure of the exact role that nuclear weapons would play within the armed forces. Clarification of some issues, such as civilian control, began with the passage of the Atomic Energy Act of 1946; new agencies, offices, and bureaucracies were created. Most pronounced in defining a specific military role were the Strategic Air Command (SAC), established as a combat command of the Army Air Corps on March 21, 1946, and the Air Force, created in September 1947. This tradition of strategic bombing and the crucial role of the atomic bomb in ending World War II led Air Force and SAC generals to assume that they would control postwar atomic policy. But the other services "desperately wanted a role in the future use of weapons and strongly resented the de facto Air Force monopoly of the means of delivering such weapons."[2] By the 1960s each service had an expansive panoply of warheads, weapons, and plans.

Many warhead types have been adapted for more than one weapon system and deployed with more than one service. In 40 years the Air Force has made use of 43 warhead types, the Navy and Marine Corps 34 types, and the Army 21. Jointly, the Air Force, Navy, and Marines have deployed 29 types of bombs (18 of them thermonuclear) on 53 kinds of U.S. and Allied aircraft.

Thirty-four warhead types have been configured for 43 missile systems, including 23 surface-to-surface, six surface-to-air, six underwater-to-surface, four air-to-surface, two air-to-air, one surface-to-underwater and one underwater-to-underwater missiles. Six warhead types have been used for 13 kinds of artillery guns in five calibers. Among the more bizarre of these have been a jeep- or tripod-mounted nuclear bazooka (Davy Crockett), a nuclear torpedo (ASTOR), and four kinds of atomic land mines (atomic demolition munitions).

As was no doubt intended, the competition between the two design laboratories, Los Alamos and Livermore, has stimulated stockpile growth and diversity. The former, with its longer history, has designed 53 warheads, while Livermore has designed 18. Of the 30 types in the current stockpile Los Alamos is responsible for 18 and Livermore for 12.[3]

Technological developments. From the outset, technological developments have profoundly influenced the composition and size of the stockpile. An immediate postwar objective was to re-engineer the Fat Man plutonium bomb of the type dropped over Nagasaki to make production easier, but critical components were in short supply, particularly high-explosive castings and initiators. Acceptable new castings finally became available in April 1947 and were incorporated into the Mark III, and the first production model Fat Man entered the stockpile the same month. By the end of June 1947 there were 13 warheads in the stockpile, including at least nine Fat Man models stockpiled through June 30, 1946; the rest were Mark IIIs. But the Mark III was judged to be deficient as an operational weapon: it was too large and heavy, with an awkward shape and overly complex fusing and firing mechanisms. It also required lengthy assembly procedures and had aeronautical and structural weaknesses of the tail assembly.

One significant early technological improvement was the use of fissile cores made of a composite of plutonium and uranium. These cores, which used the plentiful and cheaper stocks of highly enriched uranium more effectively were stockpiled for use in Mark III bombs by the end of 1947. The next major technological innovation was the development of the levitated core. Levitation made for greater efficiency, increasing the yield by 75 percent for the same quantity of fissile material. Levitation and composite cores were tested in Operation Sandstone in April and May of 1948 and were incorporated in the Mark IV, the first mass-produced bomb to be built, starting in March 1949 and continuing in production until April 1951.

In May 1948 Los Alamos began development engineering on the Mark 5, the first lightweight (3,000-pound) bomb intended for "tactical" use. Its entry into the stockpile in May 1952 was followed closely by five additional tactical nuclear warheads, including the versatile Mark 7, which served as the warhead for the Bureau of Ordnance Atomic Rocket (BOAR); a Navy depth bomb, nicknamed "Betty"; the Army's Corporal and Honest John missiles; and the first atomic demolition munition (ADM). Also in this initial flurry of tactical nuclear weapons development was the first atomic artillery shell, the Mark 9, for the Army's 280- millimeter howitzer.

In the early 1950s as part of its strategic weapons program the Atomic Energy Commission pursued parallel development of fission warheads with yields up to several hundred kilotons and fusion warheads with yields from one to 40 megatons.[4] The principle of boosting fission weapons with deuterium and tritium was first recognized as early as November 1945. A boosted device was tested on May 24, 1951 in shot "Item" of the Greenhouse test series, producing a yield of 45.5 kilotons. Full-scale development of the B18, a high-yield fission bomb, was initiated at Los Alamos in August 1952, and the warhead entered the stockpile in July 1953. These high-yield fission warheads were retired in less than three years, being quickly replaced by the more efficient, multistage thermonuclear designs.

Attention to the specifics of the stockpile provides more detail and chronology of the beginnings of the thermonuclear era. Shot "George," on May 8, 1951, which preceded "Item," was the first significant U.S. thermonuclear reaction. The first successful test of a thermonuclear device was the 10.4-megaton "Mike" shot at Eniwetok, on October 31, 1952.

Before "Mike" two candidate warheads (the B16 and B14) entered development engineering in June and August 1952 as part of an effort to provide an emergency capability of bombs and modified B-36 bombers to deliver them.[5] In October 1953 three other thermonuclear warheads entered development engineering, the B15, B17, and B24. Just prior to the beginning of the Castle test series (with shot "Bravo" on February 28, 1954) the first thermonuclear warhead, the B14, entered the stockpile on an "emergency" basis. In March, April, and May, concurrently with the Castle series, the B16, 17, and 24 were also produced in small numbers, providing the planned-for emergency capability. Castle test results led to decisions to produce the 21-ton, high-yield (10-to-20 megaton) B17 and B24 (from October 1954 to November 1955) and the lighter, lower-yield B15 (from April 1955 to February 1957); and to cancel and dismantle the B14 and B16.

After the B21 and B36 bombs entered the stockpile, between December 1955 and April 1956, the total yield of the nuclear arsenal grew exponentially, reaching its peak, at approximately 20,000 megatons, by 1960. It is noteworthy that approximately half the megatonnage of the entire stockpile was concentrated in some 2 or 3 percent of the warheads, as evidenced by the sudden reduction of some 9,400 megatons with the retirement of B36 bombs between August 1961 and January 1962. Over the next two and a half years the megaton-nage rose again by 5,400 megatons, primarily because of the pro-duction of thousands of B29s and W28s, and hundreds of B53s and W53s. From that second peak the megatonnage began a 20-year decline to its present level of approximately 5,500 megatons.

Reagan Administration officials often imply that this decline is evidence of the "decade of neglect" and "unilateral disarmament" of past administrations. They know better. What they fail to tell the public is why and how the arsenal has in fact become more lethal and capable.

In mid-1960 the Strategic Air Command inventory included ap-proximately 1,800 bombers to which some 6,000 bombs were allocated. As ballistic missiles came to dominate strategic forces, the number of bombers declined. Those remaining in the force were allocated a larger number of lower variable-yield bombs and new air-to-surface missiles as technological advances provided more versatility and capability. Improved guidance systems gave greater accuracy, thus allowing MIRVing and a reduction in warhead yields. During the MIRVing of the ICBMs (from mid-1970 to mid-1975) and the SLBMs (from March 1971 to September 1978) the combined megatonnage continued to decline.

Knowledge of the dynamics and composition of the stockpile may provide new insight into the principal milestones of the arms race and certain events of the Cold War. An example of the former is a generally overlooked consequence of the "bomber gap" of the mid-1950s. Most accounts emphasize that the United States responded to its inflated estimates of Soviet bombers with a significant bomber program of its own. This is true, but what is overlooked is the great growth in nuclear air-defense weapons, including Genie and Falcon air-to-air missiles; and Nike Hercules, Bomarc, Talos, and Terrier surface-to-air missiles.

A huge infrastructure was built, and by the early 1960s the con-tinental part alone included 2,612 interceptor aircraft, 274 Nike Her-cules batteries, 439 Bomarc missiles, and hundreds of radars manned by 207,000 personnel.[6] All of this was to counter the Soviet threat of 100 propeller-driven Bear and 60 jet-powered Bison bombers. Combined production of warheads for air-defense missiles totaled some 7,000—a significant percentage of the stockpile. But no sooner had they been produced than they began to be withdrawn. The infra-structure was eventually dismantled and the warheads retired. New threats were substituted for old ones as the "missile gap" crowded out the "bomber gap."

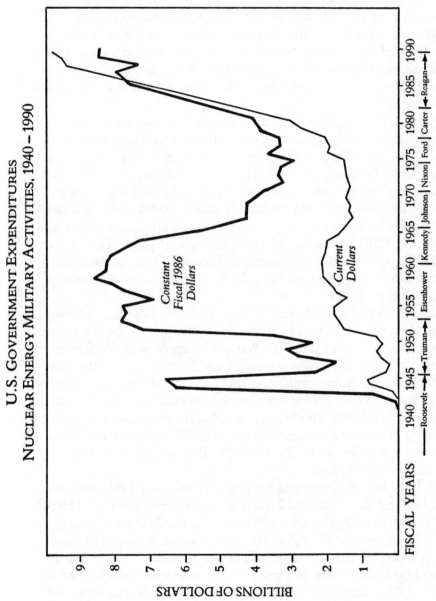

U.S. GOVERNMENT EXPENDITURES
NUCLEAR ENERGY MILITARY ACTIVITIES, 1940–1990

Sources: Figures from the Office of Management and Budget; Manhattan Engineering Division; Atomic Energy Commission; Energy Research and Development Administration; and the Department of Energy.

COST OF THE STOCKPILE

The United States has spent a total of almost $82 billion on nuclear warheads ($209 billion in fiscal 1986 dollars) from 1940 through 1985 (see figure). And these amounts represent only the Department of Energy's (and predecessor agencies') share of the total nuclear weapons bill. The Department of Defense has spent an additional $650 billion ($1.7 trillion in fiscal 1986 dollars) since the end of World War II on nuclear delivery systems (missiles, planes, and so on) and other support costs.

The data show that the United States is currently spending for nuclear warheads at a greater rate than it was during the Manhattan Project.[7] From 1940 to mid-1946, the expenditure was $2.05 billion, equivalent to $16.14 billion in fiscal 1986 dollars. In budgetary terms several Manhattan Project-size programs are currently going forward. The initial research effort of the Strategic Defense Initiative (SDI) alone will double that figure. MX missile costs will be over $30 billion, and the combined Trident submarine and missile programs could be over $100 billion, though both programs are spread over several years.

The data also show that the highest expenditure rates were attained during the first nuclear buildup, from fiscal 1952 to 1964. During this period the production complex was built to mass-produce nuclear warheads. The Manhattan Engineer District facilities at Los Alamos, Oak Ridge, and Hanford were expanded and supplemented by a second design laboratory at Livermore, California. There were also a second production reactor site at Aiken, South Carolina; a continental test site; gaseous diffusion and feed-processing plants; and specialized warhead component and assembly facilities.

With the infusion of $24.3 billion in those 13 years, ($101.4 billion in constant fiscal 1986 dollars) the production rate and the size of the stockpile increased dramatically. The average annual production rate jumped from a range of 200 to 400 warheads per year in the early 1950s to a range of 2,000 to 6,000 warheads per year in the early 1960s. The record number of types simultaneously in production was 17 (for 23 weapons systems) occurring between June and December of 1964. By contrast, at several points between 1976 and 1979 there was only one type being produced.

Currently there are eight types in production with a total of 30 in the stockpile.[8] The first of over 1,000 W87 warheads designed at Livermore will begin production in the spring or summer of 1986; three years later the first of over 3,000 Los Alamos-designed W88 Trident II warheads will begin production. In terms of average annual budgets President Reagan's is third—only slightly behind those of Eisenhower and Kennedy, and outstripping those of Johnson, Truman, Carter, Nixon, and Ford.[9] Reagan's rates are almost double those of Carter. And when future constant- dollar conversions are done, it is possible that the Reagan budget might move into first place.

Stockpiles past and present reflect a variety of factors. Advocates of new weapons always justify them as a necessary response to present and future interpretations of "the threat." As the air-defense story shows, however, several types of warheads owe their existence to faulty interpretations.

As more of the secret nuclear history is revealed, the clearer the perspective becomes with regard to current decisions and events. Bureaucratic competition and inertia have led to nuclear warheads for every conceivable military mission, arm of service, and geographic theater—all compounded by a technological momentum that overwhelmed what should have been a more sober analysis of what was enough for deterrence. The result is a gigantic nuclear weapons system —laboratories, production facilities, forces, and so on—that has become self-perpetuating, conducting its business out of public view and with little accountability.

While there is no single key to understanding the present complex situation, a better knowledge of the stockpile can, at the very least, provoke the asking of new questions.

1. See Thomas B. Cochran, William M. Arkin, Milton M. Hoenig, Robert S. Norris, *Nuclear Weapons Databook II, U.S. Nuclear Warhead Production* (Cambridge, Mass.: Ballinger, forthcoming).

2. Steven L. Rearden, *The Formative Years, 1947–1950: History of the Office of the Secretary of Defense* (Washington, D.C.: Government Printing Office, 1984), p. 423.

3. Lawrence Livermore Laboratory's first stockpile warheads were the W27 for the Regulus II missile (September 1958) and the B27 Navy bomb (November 1958). In addition to the 71 types deployed, another 30 were cancelled or suspended before development was complete.

4. The largest U.S. test was the 15-megaton shot "BRAVO," Feb. 28, 1954.

5. Lee Bowen, *History of the Air Force Atomic Energy Program: The Development of Weapons* (Washington, D.C.: U.S. Air Force Historical Division History, 1955; declassified with deletions June 1981), pp. 211–24.

6. House Armed Services Committee, *Continental Air Defense, Hearing* (July 22, 1981), p. 25.

7. The two peak years for the Manhattan Project were fiscal 1944 and 1945 when spending was $6.24 and $6.60 billion (in fiscal 1986 dollars). This compares with current budgets of $6.63, $7.27, $7.70, $8.06, $7.32, $8.47, and $8.44 billion for fiscal 1984–1990.

8. They are: B61 bomb, Mods 3 and 4, W76 Trident I, W79 8-inch artillery, W80 Mod 0 and 1 sea- and air-launched cruise missiles, B83 bomb, W84 ground-launched cruise missile, W85 Pershing II. The 30 types include the W66 Sprint and W71

Spartan, none of which had been retired as of Dec. 31, 1983. The most recent retirement is the W25/Genie in 1984.

9. Using constant fiscal 1986 dollars, the annual averages are (in millions): Eisenhower—$7,904; Kennedy—$7,690; Reagan—$7,552; Johnson —$4,747; Truman—$3,920; Carter—$3,834; Nixon—$3,505; Ford— $3,317.

3

Erosion of U.S. Foreign Relations

George W. Ball

During the past 40 years, the United States' relations with both the Soviet Union and the noncommunist nations have developed unevenly. At the end of the first two decades after World War II, both sets of relations appeared to be improving; now, 20 years later, they show a substantial decline. As the *Bulletin* celebrates its arrival at middle age, it seems appropriate to look briefly at the evolution of U.S. policies and what may be foreseen for the future.

The event that inspired the creation of the *Bulletin* was the emergence of atomic weapons, and throughout the magazine's 40 years of existence humanity has continued to suffer the brooding threat of nuclear disaster. In that environment the United States has tried to maintain a precarious balance between itself and the Soviet Union, the other great nuclear power, largely by limiting the expansion of Soviet influence and assisting noncommunist countries to improve their economies and resist political and military pressure. From time to time the U.S. government has sought, although without much coherence or consistency, to develop a more systematic *modus vivendi* with Moscow.

The nature of the rivalry between the two superpowers was progressively defined after 1945 as Americans became increasingly aware that the conclusion of World War II had meant not the end of conflict but merely the substitution of one adversary for another. Not only did the Soviet Union command greater military resources than the

245

Axis, but it also offered an ideology seductively attractive to some of the nations emerging from colonialism. For a time many Americans persisted in thinking of the Soviets merely as prickly allies—as they had been during the war. But when Stalin's aggressiveness and persistent bellicosity revealed the dimensions of Soviet ambitions, the United States reacted with ugly excesses such as McCarthyism.

Then, beginning in 1956, when Khrushchev's speech at the Twentieth Party Congress started a progressive destalinization, relations with the United States acquired a more civil tone. In the wake of the Cuban missile crisis—a climactic test of will—the Kennedy Administration negotiated the Partial Test Ban Treaty. Ten years later, in 1972, by laying the foundation of a new relationship with China, President Nixon exorcised the specter of a monolithic Communist bloc. All this led to the brief Indian summer of détente.

As they appeared in 1972, relations between the two superpowers seemed destined for further improvement, and there was reason to hope that we might achieve a safer world. SALT I put a cap on the buildup of offensive weapons and restricted the deployment of anti-ballistic-missile (ABM) systems. Meanwhile, the United States began to develop a network of ties and contacts with the Soviet Union at various levels in a variety of cultural, technical, professional, and commercial areas.

If U.S.-Soviet relations showed improvement during the first 20 years, U.S. relations with the noncommunist nations also developed and matured. Since the United States was the only major power to emerge strengthened rather than weakened by World War II, it was compelled abruptly to revise long-established parochial attitudes and to adjust to a new leadership role. And before long the United States began to enjoy the yeasty experience of world power and responsibility. Since all the world seemed to depend on the United States, it is not hard to see why, in the exuberance of new-felt importance, Americans failed to comprehend the limits of their nation's power or to appraise the priority of its interests.

In the exercise of leadership the United States drew strength not only from its physical, financial, and military resources but also from its moral authority as a democratic power guided by a body of principles and practices that reflect a respect for human rights and the rule of law. To be sure, the country sometimes compromised those principles, as when it launched the Bay of Pigs fiasco. But, during those first 20 years, successive administrations usually practiced what they preached, behaving with a magnanimity and a spacious vision which commanded world respect. The United States devised the Marshall Plan to rebuild Europe and later the Point Four programs that led to some sharing of its wealth with Third World countries. It organized Western defenses through NATO, encouraged Europe to unite, undertook negotiations to untangle the obstructions to the free flow of goods and capital that arose from the war and the interwar period, and established international institutions to stabilize commercial and financial relations. Finally—and by no means the least important—the United States took the lead in creating the United Nations, which provided the essential mechanism for helping a billion people move from colonial dependence to some kind of juridical independence. It is no wonder that many now look back on those two decades as golden years.

Détente unfortunately survived only for a brief period, and, since it had been oversold, the disillusionment as it faded was stronger than events justified. As a result of the Carter Administration's clumsy approach to arms control and its overreaction to the 1979 Soviet invasion of Afghanistan, U.S. relations with the Soviet Union began to deteriorate. With the advent of the Reagan Administration, relations between the superpowers were systemically chilled by a reversion to incivility and the injection of a manichean antipathy. Today those relations are at a dangerously low point.

Paradoxically, just when much of the gas has escaped from the Soviets' ideological balloon, the U.S. government is pursuing a more ideological line than at any time since John Foster Dulles was the secretary of state, 30 years ago. President Reagan, in his actions and attitude, has denied the hope of achieving a more stable and pacific relationship with the Soviet Union. Indeed he has frequently asserted that the United States cannot bargain with a godless country. "How," he has asked, "do you compromise between good and evil? . . . How do you compromise with men who say . . . there is no God?"

In basing security solely on physical means while rejecting diplomatic efforts to exploit a common interest in survival, President Reagan has insisted on an enormous buildup of offensive military power. Consistent with his reliance on mechanistic means for security, he put forward his "Star Wars" program. Regardless of the ultimate findings of the intensive research program he proposes, the president's decision will almost certainly mean acceleration in the massive buildup of weapons on both sides, since it will force the Soviet Union to concentrate on countering or overwhelming U.S. defenses with a greater number of ICBMs and cruise missiles, and on developing its own Star Wars program.

The Star Wars decision will also inevitably weaken U.S. credibility in an already skeptical international environment. Once other nations fully comprehend the president's expressed—if unrealistic—hope to create a world resembling one in which nuclear weapons never existed, they will feel betrayed. Rightly or wrongly, Europeans count on the U.S. nuclear umbrella as the one hope for halting the continuous cycle of wars they have known for generations. And Third World countries will look with dismay at what appears to be an effective abandonment by the nuclear powers of any serious intention to achieve arms control through agreement. That, it should never be forgotten, was the explicit condition on which many of them signed the Nuclear Non-Proliferation Treaty.

Here arises another paradox: while Americans are preoccupied as never before with the nuclear menace, the President is urging a project that—while purporting to gratify the antinuclear movement by promising an end to nuclear weapons—will result in an enormous escalation of both offensive and defensive nuclear arms and may well halt serious efforts to contain the arms spiral.

But if U.S. relations with the Soviet Union are now worse than they were a decade or so ago, so also is U.S. influence with the noncommunist nations. Until disenchanted by the Vietnam War, most Americans uncritically accepted the worldwide scope of U.S. responsibilities. The Truman Doctrine had declared that "it must be the policy of the United States to support free peoples who are resisting attempted subjugation by armed minorities or by outside pressure." And John F. Kennedy had announced in his inaugural address that the United States would "pay any price, bear any burden, meet any handicap, support any friend, oppose any foe to assure the survival and the success of liberty."

In the light of the present U.S. mood, it may be difficult to understand why few Americans initially challenged the need to try to prevent the National Liberation Front and North Vietnamese from overrunning South Vietnam. But the United States' leaders at that time tended to believe that the country's interests were affected by almost any major development in almost any part of the world—particularly when that development might even remotely advance communist influence. The United States had fought for three years in Korea to throw back first the North Koreans and then the Chinese, and the progressive involvement in Vietnam seemed merely another chapter in the continuous effort to prevent the spread of communist power. Any suggestion that Hanoi and the NLF might be more than instruments of Moscow and Peking was dismissed as reflecting a soft-headed attitude toward the communist menace. The defense of the ersatz government of South Vietnam was declared to be "vital" to U.S. interests — and that ended the argument.

The Vietnam ordeal was an exorbitant way to learn the limitations of U.S. capabilities, and the country is still paying heavily for that long, agonizing aberration and its demoralizing effect on national life. Perhaps an even larger cost of the war has been its effect in weakening the moral and psychological authority of U.S. leadership, for it raised questions in the minds of many otherwise friendly nations as to the United States' continued fidelity to democratic principles and reputation for international decency and good sense.

Nor was the Vietnamese imbroglio the only reason for U.S. loss of standing. In two additional geographical areas — the Middle East and Central America — the United States for the past two decades has also pursued policies not supported by most other nations. Indeed, the U.S. government's persistent practice of giving uncritical support to almost any Israeli actions — even when they violated the principles of international law and the U.N. Charter — and the insistence on blocking the efforts of the other Security Council members to uphold those principles have done more than anything else to impair the U.S. reputation for justice and fair-mindedness and have seriously damaged the effectiveness of the United Nations itself.

Prior to the Six-Day Arab-Israeli War in 1967, the United States had sought to maintain a relatively impartial policy toward the Middle East. In pursuance of the Tripartite Agreement [the 1950 agreement among the United States, the United Kingdom, and France guaranteeing the territorial integrity of all Middle Eastern states], it refused to supply arms to nations in the area, including Israel, in order to forestall an arms buildup on both sides. In 1956 President Eisenhower effectively demonstrated his support for the United Nations and the principles it represented by compelling Israel to withdraw its forces from the Sinai, just as the United States had forced the French and British to do.

But after the 1967 war, President Lyndon Johnson reversed the established policy. Instead of seeking to maintain an arms balance, he concentrated on making Israel militarily stronger than any potential combination of its Arab neighbors. The practical consequence was, of course, to accelerate the arms race, leading the Arab nations to augment their military expenditures so that today the Arab states lying to the east of Suez have more soldiers, guns, tanks, and planes than NATO. At the same time, bowing to pressure from pro-Israeli interests, the United States has refused to sell arms to friendly Arab nations.

Meanwhile, the United States has increased its annual subsidy to Israel to unprecedented levels for a country with roughly the population of Los Angeles. And that assistance is not limited to the economic and military spheres. Equally important, the United States has faithfully run political interference to defend even Israel's most extreme actions from U.N. censure or sanctions. In 1967, the United States sat by while Israel annexed East Jerusalem and opposed any U.N. action that might force it to reverse that seizure. And it protested only weakly when, in December 1981, Israel annexed the Golan Heights and then went on to invade Lebanon. The United States continued to increase its subsidy to Israel even after that country had commenced systematically preempting the land and water supply of the West Bank through its settlement program in order, as Israeli leaders frankly admitted, to create "new facts" that would preclude the return of territory as called for under Security Council Resolution 242.

Nor did the United States merely avert its eyes from violations of established international legal principles and the Geneva conventions, but during the 1982 Israeli invasion of Lebanon, it meekly accepted Israel's violations of contractual obligations restricting use of U.S.-provided military equipment strictly to self-defense purposes. That was unconscionable discrimination since we had earlier applied heavy sanctions against Turkey for a similar violation.

The price the United States has paid for its uncritical support of Israel cannot be measured only in terms of the $30 billion of assistance provided so far; even more costly has been the destruction of the U.S. reputation as a nation that stands for and supports established principles of international decency and conduct. That loss of authority is dramatically revealed by the deteriorating U.S. position in U.N. councils. For 25 years, from the establishment of the United Nations in 1945 until 1970, the United States was able to defend and advance its policies through persuasion, friendship, and moral authority. During that period the United States not only refrained from exercising the veto it possessed as a permanent member of the Security Council, but regarded the use of the veto as, in effect, a rejection of the central concept of the United Nations. Indeed, during my days in the State Department, we took pride in pointing out that the Soviets had cast 103 vetoes while the U.S. had cast none — a sure sign of which side held the allegiance and respect of other members of the world community.

But in shifting its Middle East policies after the 1967 War, the United States became so out of step with the opinions of other nations that it could no longer prevail by persuasion. Having once cast a veto in 1970, the United States became hooked on the habit. Thus, since 1970, the United States has cast 40 vetoes, of which 16 have been to prevent censure of, or sanction against, Israel; five to prevent the expulsion of or sanctions against South Africa; five on the issue of Namibian independence; and five to defend positions regarding Vietnam. During that same period, the Soviet Union has cast only nine vetoes—fewer than one-fourth as many.

The United States' improvident use of its veto powers has not only disclosed the degree to which its prestige and influence have diminished. But the fact that the most powerful nation constantly thwarts the will of other Security Council nations has greatly diminished that body's authority, while infusing many Americans with a childish sense of outrage because their nation can no longer command the support of others for its policies. That frustration has led many—even some diplomats accredited to the United Nations—to mount an unseemly and irrational attack on that world institution; thus, instead of supporting the body it helped to create, the United States is mindlessly tearing it down.

The list of international principles the United States has abandoned is distressingly long. By use of its veto, the United States has sanctioned the retention of territory taken by force. It has opposed extending even the basic right of self-determination to the Palestinians, despite the fact that it insisted on writing that principle into the U.N. Charter, and the president regularly espouses it in political speeches. To be sure, the president has offered to support a "Jordanian solution." But since he specifically rejects an independent Palestinian state, that solution recalls Henry Ford's assurance that the American people could buy a Ford car of any color, provided it was black. President Reagan has gone even further than his predecessors in refusing to acknowledge the illegality of Israel's settlement program on the West Bank even though those settlements plainly violate Articles 47, 49, and 53 of the Geneva Convention of 1949, and have been declared illegal by the State Department's own legal adviser.

Principles have integrity only if they are uniformly and impartially applied, and it is likely that the United States' progressive transgression of principle with respect to Vietnam and Israel has contributed to the general disdain for the rule of law expressed in the reversion to gunboat diplomacy in Central America and the Caribbean. Applying what is, in effect, an American Brezhnev doctrine, the United States has already committed such outrages as mining Nicaraguan harbors, assisting in the bombing of Nicaraguan targets, and instructing the insurgents in the odious arts of assassination. These are acts of war, taken with the approval of Congress, and no plausible justification has been forthcoming. Finally, the United States—out of guilt and desperation—has demonstrated a total disrespect for the rule of law by refusing to submit to the arbitrament of the World Court.

Thus, as a result of this creeping attrition of its principles, the United States finds itself today more and more tempted to lower its standards and to pursue the same sordid practices as the Soviets. Indeed, the process of moral deterioration the United States is suffering seems to prove the old French adage that one tends to acquire the visage of one's adversary.

The *Bulletin* is observing its fortieth anniversary at a critical point in the evolution of U.S. policy toward other governments and the rest of humanity. U.S. representatives are just beginning a negotiation which the president has probably already doomed to failure by abruptly announcing his Star Wars project and insisting on its irrevocable nature. Barring a congressional refusal to fund it, this extravagant and reckless scheme may well mean the end of any serious efforts to gain control of the nuclear arms spiral, for, once the rhythm of negotiation is again broken, it may prove impossible to restore—particularly as the buildup of new types of nuclear weapons defeats the possibilities of verification.

At the same time that the United States has let its relations with the Soviet Union dangerously deteriorate, it has lost substantial support among the other noncommunist nations. It is not a happy moment in this nation's history. Let us hope it is only a passing phase.

4

Secrecy and National Security

Morton H. Halperin

The first amendment, with its commitment to robust public debate on all public issues, was viewed by conservatives and liberals alike as one of the likely casualties of the atomic age. Conservatives argued that we could no longer tolerate the lack of discipline in keeping secrets which characterized American politics, and pushed successfully for the draconian secrecy provisions in the Atomic Energy Act. Liberals voiced despair about the possibility of effective public debate when the president could plunge us into total war in seconds.

As with so many other predictions about the consequences of splitting the atom, these observations about secrecy turned out to be exaggerations. The relatively open system of public debate in the United States has been remarkably little changed by the development and deployment of nuclear weapons.

What has changed, of course, are the consequences of a bad decision. When the world can be destroyed in minutes, it is essential that decisions relating to war and peace be made after full and informed public debate.

All of our presidents in the atomic age have resisted such debate and sought to control the process by which information on national security matters is released to the public. They have believed that they knew what needed to be done and that public access to information could only complicate their task. The responsibility for preventing nuclear destruction has led them to seek to tighten the circle rather than to reach out to the public.

If all of our presidents have decried "leaks" and sought to control access to information, only in the last dozen years have they sought to enlist the courts in this effort. This involvement of the judiciary in the enforcement of the executive branch's decisions about what national security information must be kept secret is an extraordinarily ominous development. It poses a threat not only to the structure of the First Amendment, but also to rational debate about national security matters.

Yet most people concerned about arms control and the prevention of nuclear war have barely noticed—and far fewer have been willing to become involved in—the struggle to preserve the right to and the means for public debate on issues of nuclear war.

The First Amendment is a remarkably brief if revolutionary limit on governmental power. Congress may not, it says, pass any law limiting freedom of speech or of the press. When it was written, the great danger was that the government would punish those who spoke out against its policies. The Amendment provided, in short, for the right of all persons to dissent from the policies of the day and to present their views without fear of prosecution for political heresy.

The Amendment did not guarantee the right of access to information. In those simpler days it was assumed that the issues could be debated on the basis of information that was available to all. In modern times the courts have come to see that the right to acquire information is an essential component of the First Amendment. Congress gave added weight to that view when in 1966 it enacted, and in 1974 amended, the Freedom of Information Act to create a public right of access to governmental information relating to national security. However, at the same time that the Congress was recognizing the need for public access to government information and for judicial review of denials of release of information, the executive branch was acting to enlist the courts in the far more troublesome task of enforcing its secrecy decisions.

Until the *New York Times* began publication of the Pentagon Papers, no U.S. administration had ever sought to enlist the aid of the courts in enforcing its view of what should be kept secret. Successive administrations—through Executive Orders on Classification, accompanied by threats of criminal indictments and administrative action—have sought to prevent leaks. If information reached the press, they would, by appeals to patriotism and threats of ostracism, seek to prevent its publication.

Until that day in June 1971, however, that was as far as it went. When the government went to court in an effort to get a judge to tell the *Times* to stop publishing the Pentagon Papers, it shattered a 200-year-old tradition of settling these issues in the political arena. The case and the Supreme Court decision, hailed at the time as a great victory for the First Amendment, in fact set a dangerous precedent whose consequences we are only beginning to see.

The government asked a district court trial judge to issue a legally binding order to a newspaper to stop publishing information in its possession on penalty of prison for contempt of court—something that had never been done before. Only one judge, Gerhard A. Gesell, in the string of judges in New York and Washington who were to hear aspects of the case, did what the U.S. Constitution mandates: he told the government that the purpose of the First Amendment was precisely to take from the government the power to stop a citizen from publishing that which he knew. He gave the government a half hour to get relief from a higher court.

Unfortunately, the appeals court to which the government went, and every other court, took the position that in the right circumstances the government was entitled to enjoin, in the name of national security, information that was in the possession of a private citizen. What made the case seem a victory to most observers is that the Supreme Court ruled, six to three, that the government had not met the standard of proof necessary to secure an injunction. Far more important was the fact that at least six of the judges believed that, given the right facts, the courts did have the authority to order a newspaper to stop printing information relevant to a public-policy issue.

Undaunted by its apparent failure in the Pentagon Papers civil case, the government was soon back in court, twice more seeking the aid of the judicial branch in enforcing its view of what should be kept secret. Each of these efforts was as unprecedented as the attempt to halt the *Times* presses, and each was to set as dangerous a precedent.

Soon after the *New York Times* and other newspapers were permitted to continue publishing the history of the war in Vietnam, the Justice Department brought a criminal prosecution against Daniel Ellsberg who, it believed, had given the study to the *Times*. This action marked the first time that the government had sought to use the espionage laws to convict someone for actions intended to lead to publication of information in the U.S. press, rather than to the covert transfer of information to a hostile foreign government.

The criminal case, like the civil case before it, ended in apparent defeat for the government. The suit was ultimately dismissed in 1973 because of monumental governmental misconduct, but not before Ellsberg was forced to stand trial for months and the trial judge had upheld the constitutionality of the statute.

The third case involved a former CIA official named Victor Marchetti. The government learned through its sources in the publishing world that Marchetti was planning to write a book revealing intelligence secrets. It went to court in 1971 seeking an order requiring Marchetti to show his manuscript to government officials in advance and to permit them to censor any material that they considered classified.

This time the government was totally successful with its unprecedented legal theory. The court ordered Marchetti to submit his manuscript, and in 1972 upheld the government's right to decide what information could not be published.

These three cases taken together established the fundamental principle that, in the right circumstances, the courts would assist the government in enforcing its view of what needed to be kept secret in the name of national security. It would prevent publication, it would criminally punish those who sought to publish, and it would require former government officials to submit to censorship.

Many saw each of these cases as an aberration. And even so, in two of them the First Amendment seemed to have won. Yet they provided potential power to shape public debate that subsequent administrations have found, and will continue to find, irresistible.

In the court case most directly related to nuclear weapons, the government sought in 1979 to prevent the *Progressive* magazine from publishing an article which described how a hydrogen bomb works. The government presented two theories of why it should be allowed to prevent publication: First, it argued that it had met the standard established in the Pentagon Papers case by demonstrating that publication would result in grave and immediate damage to the nation. Second, it claimed that the Atomic Energy Act authorized such prior restraint on publication and that the statute was constitutional.

Once again, while the magazine was eventually able to publish the article—because the basic information had already been published elsewhere—the First Amendment took a terrible beating. For one thing, the article was delayed for weeks. For another, the reasoning applied to the Pentagon Papers case was affirmed in a different context and with the courts showing far more deference to government claims of probable injury to the national security.

Perhaps as disturbing was the attitude of much of the scientific and arms control community. With few exceptions, most scientists refused to help the lawyers representing the *Progressive* and its editors. Some simply shied away from the legal process, but others expressed the view that the article should not be published. They failed to understand that the question of whether publishing the "secret of the H-bomb" would help or hinder nonproliferation efforts was beside the point. The real question was whether the government had the right to decide what information should be published. If the government could stop publication of Howard Morland's article, it could, in theory, prevent publication of any other material that it thought would stimulate proliferation.

The District Court judge who ordered that the article not be published, at least temporarily, noted that he did not want to bear the responsibility for nuclear war. The government, his ruling suggested, need only warn that publication would increase the risk of nuclear devastation for a court to stop publication, no matter how farfetched the argument.

The government's authority to require intelligence officials to submit all their writings for prepublication review was upheld in 1980 by the Supreme Court in the *Snepp* case which established the government's right to collect all of the profits of such publication. The Court's sweeping decision broadened the government's authority to determine the degree of secrecy necessary to protect national security and the deference which lower courts were instructed to give the claims of national security.

The language of the opinion clearly indicated that the government could impose the same requirements on other officials. The Reagan Administration took up this invitation and issued an order that would have required all senior officials to submit all of their writings for life. Had the order been implemented, it is difficult to exaggerate the impact it would have had on public debate about issues of war and peace, including those related to nuclear weapons and arms control.

As the pages of the *Bulletin* demonstrate, much of the writing on nuclear issues is by former government officials and by those with government clearances. Testimony before Congress challenging Administration arms control policies often comes from former senior officials. Under the proposed order, whatever government was in office would be empowered to remove any information from such writing that it considered "classified." Of course, a great deal of the information which is widely discussed on these issues is considered "classified" by the government and thus would be subject to deletion. Although judicial review of such censorship is theoretically available, the time involved would often be fatal to effective public debate, and judges are, in any case, very reluctant to second-guess the government on what needs to be kept secret.

Congress forced the president to delay implementation of the prepublication review order, and the White House promised not to use it in the future without giving Congress several months' notice. However, the authority of the president to impose such a procedure remains intact.

The Administration also relied on the Ellsberg precedent to bring a criminal prosecution in 1984 for actions leading to the publication of information. This indictment poses a serious threat to effective public debate on national security issues.

The case involves a government employee, Samuel L. Morison (grandson of historian Samuel Eliot Morison). He was charged with giving U.S. government photographs of a Soviet aircraft carrier under construction in a Black Sea shipyard to a magazine, which printed them. The government said that it would demonstrate that the photographs relate to national defense because they reveal U.S. intelligence-gathering capabilities and targeting priorities. If the government's view of the statute involved is sustained by the courts and found to be constitutional, then the daily practice of "leaking" to the media, by which the public learns most of what it knows about national security policy, would be drastically curtailed.

In its case against Morison, the government took the position that unauthorized retention of a classified document relating to national defense is a violation of the law. Under this reading, anyone—including a member of the press—who fits the government's interpretation presumably could be prosecuted. The government asserted that it need not even prove that the person transferring the information intended to harm national security or that the information was given to a foreign government—hostile or friendly.

On March 12, 1985 the District Court judge hearing the case upheld the government's interpretation of the law and Morison was subsequently convicted in October. If his conviction is upheld and the higher courts adopt the same view, then the United States will have an official secrets act which could be used to deter publication of any information on nuclear war that the government asserted to be classified.

In addition to enlisting the courts in efforts to enforce its views on what should be made public, the Reagan Administration is seeking to cut back on access to information provided under the Freedom of Information Act. In this, as in other areas, it is following in the footsteps of previous administrations.

Lyndon Johnson threatened to veto the original bill in 1966; he signed it only when its scope was considerably reduced. Gerald Ford vetoed the 1974 amendments when Congress insisted on making national security information available under the Act. The Carter Administration prepared amendments to the Act which would have cut back on access to classified information.

The Reagan Administration initially sought amendments that would have gutted the Act completely as it relates to national security information. When this effort failed, it sought separate statutes giving it authority to withhold unclassified defense information and took administrative actions designed to make it more difficult to use the Act. The courts have continued to defer to government assertions of what must be kept secret and have been unwilling to use the power given to them by the Congress to order release of information which the government holds to be classified.

There is no doubt that much information about issues of war and peace is publicly available today. Indeed, foreigners marvel at the degree of openness in the United States and rely on information made public here for debates in their own countries. Yet much information important to public debate is kept secret, and much of the information that becomes public does so through statements by former officials or by "leaks" rather than official disclosure.

Clearly, the president has vast potential power to prevent or limit various forms of unauthorized disclosure of information related to nuclear war. He is unlikely to exercise that power unless public debate threatens to interfere seriously with the executive branch's view of what the national security requires. In a crisis, when there is extensive public opposition to administration policy, the temptation to use these powers might well be irresistible.

Consider, for example, an administration plan to initiate the use of tactical nuclear weapons in a local conflict or to renounce the ABM Treaty. In the face of strong public opposition, the president might use his powers to prevent the further release of information that would serve to increase the opposition's credibility. Given the current state of the law, the courts might well uphold injunctions against publication of information in the possession of the press or public. Lawyers for former officials would tell their clients that threats of legal action for refusal to clear statements might well be upheld in the courts. Threats of criminal penalties against officials, former officials, and members of the press would be very credible.

This is the time to act, and the only possible arena is the Congress. Groups and individuals concerned about preventing nuclear war must recognize that the fight to prevent greater secrecy and to restrain the threat of draconian measures against public debate in a nuclear crisis is their battle. Only an informed public, free to engage in open debate and armed with adequate information, can keep the Administration from pursuing dangerous policies. The power of the president to prevent public debate must be circumscribed now. In a crisis it will be too late.

5

The Media: Playing the Government's Game

William A. Dorman

N
o democratic institution struggling under the weight of the nuclear age has undergone a more troubling and profound transformation than the news media. Before the atomic bomb, journalism never hesitated to march off to war, but the news media usually were eager to demobilize once victory seemed at hand—not unlike American society as a whole.

In many significant ways, however, the return to peacetime assumptions and practices did not occur after 1945. Instead, the mass media came to embrace the nuclear confrontation's fundamental assumption that the United States now faced a permanent, ruthless and intractable enemy. Given such a presupposition, not surprisingly, the mainstream news media—those print and broadcast organizations considered the dominant sources of information for the general public—have performed during the Cold War as they always have during hot ones.

What has taken shape 40 years after Hiroshima, therefore, can best be described as a journalism of deference to the national-security state. The free marketplace of ideas, if it ever existed, has given way to an arena of limited popular discourse, whose parameters are set in the "national interest" as defined by official Washington. Seemingly absent in post-World War II society is even the possibility of a forum for robust debate over foreign policy and defense issues. As a result, for nearly four decades political elites have been permitted to indulge their global fantasies without serious challenge.

The sense of permanent crisis that grips most Americans and makes possible a continuing obsession with nuclear weapons is, to be sure, not wholly the doing of mainstream journalism. However, the news media have played a decidedly necessary if not sufficient role. For the pictures about foreign affairs in the heads of most Americans are largely put there by the news media, and these pictures throughout the Cold War have been neither reassuring nor substantively at odds with official Washington's dark vision of the world. As a result of living in a mental garrison state that feeds on the media's stark imagery of the forces arrayed against us, most Americans have been only too willing to turn over large parts of their good fortune to preparations for war in general and nuclear war in particular.

Certainly, there are journalists working for specialized publications or in the alternative and opinion media who exercise independent judgment about U.S. defense policy. And there are guerrilla-types within the mainstream who, despite obstacles and at risk to their reputations for "objectivity," question and challenge the statist perspective on the nuclear story. But their work, hopeful as it may be, is more an indication of what might and could be done than representative of what is done routinely. Patterns and not exceptions, finally, are what matter, and the dominant journalistic paradigm remains one that tends to share the state's fixations rather than to question them.

The nuclear obsession, of course, is bound up almost wholly with the Soviet Union: when Americans think of nuclear war, they have only one enemy in mind. It is with the representation of the Soviet Union, then—its motives, behavior, and intentions—that the U.S. media have most effectively and devastatingly served the logic of the nuclear regime. This service has been rendered not through lies, but rather through the routine interpretation of demonstrable truths in relentlessly negative terms. In this regard, the media have not so much created hostile images of the Soviets out of whole cloth as they have tailored them according to a pattern cut in Washington.

There is compelling evidence that the news media have consistently gone along with Washington's overstatements of Soviet strength and military spending, generally supported increases in U.S. military spending, and usually questioned the deployment of new weapons systems only on the basis of whether they are sound investments. Soviet leadership is routinely portrayed in the darkest of terms, and the bleakest motives are habitually ascribed to Soviet behavior. There is also ample evidence of the media's reluctance to dispute U.S. interventions abroad until *after* significant elites begin to defect from a policy consensus—which usually is far too late. Finally, the news media have invariably interpreted the particulars of arms negotiations in ways that are favorable to official Washington and decidedly hostile to the Soviet Union.

This record has prompted George Kennan, the architect of containment, to write of the news media's "endless series of distortions and oversimplifications," "systematic dehumanization of the leadership of another great country," and the "monotonous misrepresentation of the nature and attitudes of another great people." According to Kennan, "the view of the Soviet Union that prevails today in large portions of our governmental and journalistic establishments [is] so extreme, so subjective, so far removed from what any sober scrutiny of external reality would reveal, that it is not only ineffective but dangerous as a guide to political action."[1]

While the news media's frightening picture of the external threat significantly contributes to the difficulty of organizing a sustained challenge to the nuclear regime, their portrayal of internal political dissent from official U.S. policy frequently makes such a task nearly impossible. At best, those who have questioned the state's assumptions and policies have been depicted by the mainstream media as naive romantics, while at worst they have been portrayed as dupes or subversives. Moreover, the media have done little to oppose the suppression of dissent during periodic "red scares," more often than not adding to the fires instead of dousing them. Here again, journalism has too often enforced the limits on public discourse established by the state rather than extended them.

Press behavior since 1945 is probably best understood within the context of the general psychological revolution that has been a major feature of the atomic age. Since Hiroshima, journalism, like most other aspects of society, has been held in nuclear thrall. The prospect of absolute warfare against the homeland (and species) created the national-security state, and journalism has proved no more independent of it than national government, education, the church, or business. Yet it is the news media that should sound the alarm at abuses of state power. Aside from an occasional atavistic twitch, like the Pentagon Papers affair, the media have moved further and further away from the watchdog role democratic theory assumed they would play in affairs of state where national defense and foreign policy are concerned.

The journalistic response to a sense of permanent emergency developed, over a period of years, in ways parallel to the state's. Foreign and defense policy came to be seen only through the lens of superpower confrontation. Statist concerns for containment, deterrence,

and credibility crowded out traditional democratic and journalistic
assumptions about open politics and the dangers of secrecy. In this
latter regard, even when the news media publicize matters the nuclear
regime would prefer kept from public view, journalism usually justifies
its performance by arguing that the material is not really secret within
the *state's* definition of the term.

For instance, as William M. Arkin has pointed out, the *Washington
Post* editorially answered critics in late 1984 by arguing that virtually
all of the information it had published about a space shuttle carrying
a new military intelligence satellite had been "unclassified" by the
government.[2]

A similar case in early 1985 involved publication in the *New York
Times* of information that the United States had unilaterally devised
wartime contingency plans to deploy nuclear depth charges in Canada,
among other places, news which had already appeared in newspapers
abroad. As it turned out, the *Times* story had been prepared with the
help of a State Department official whose assistance had been authorized by the head of the National Security Council. It is a reasonable
assumption that such cooperation was forthcoming in the hope of
exerting damage control on the story.

The tactic appears to have worked: according to the newspaper's
national security correspondent Leslie H. Gelb, who wrote the piece,
"The *Times* editors and I were concerned about genuine national
security as well as news. Therefore, we agreed at the outset to limit
the story to those four countries where the contingency plans had
already been publicly disclosed." And even though Gelb said he had
more sensitive information in his possession, such information has
not been made public.[3] It bears mention that Gelb formerly held high
posts in the State and Defense Departments.

Gradually, then, the U.S. mainstream news media have psycholo-
gized and routinized the needs and strategies of the national security
state in permanent emergency. The result has been a vastly diminished
civil voice in journalism. Editor and journalist Robert Karl Manoff,
in his landmark discussion of the subject, has defined such a voice
as one "with proud recourse to moral authority, dependence on un-
mediated expression, respect for individual opinion and independent
journalistic judgment."[4] In its place has emerged the *statist* voice, with
its reliance on official sources, its preoccupation with Washington
policy debates, and its acceptance of the terms in which these debates
are couched. Even when journalists have seemed to soften their view of
the Soviet Union—during the détente years of Nixon and Kissinger,
for example—or in the spring of 1985 and the ascendancy to power

of Mikhail Gorbachev, the shifts in perspective have originated in Washington, not as a result of a change in the judgments of reporters.

Nowhere are the consequences of a predominantly statist voice clearer than in the media's seeming passivity in covering the specific strategic policies that govern the development, deployment, and use of the nuclear arsenal. Nuclear strategy for the past four decades has received little more than perfunctory attention, with the boundaries of debate being set in Washington instead of in newsrooms. Too, such reporting as there has been on strategic doctrine has largely accepted policy declarations at face value. Coverage has tended to ignore the fact that declared policy represents only the façade of a complex strategic agenda.

Perhaps the news media are at the height of their statism in covering the process of nuclear arms negotiations, when they reflexively assume the posture of the U.S. government. Again to cite Manoff: "The press may reflect and give vent to domestic differences over negotiating strategies, but when it comes to discussing the details and rationales of the other side's position, independent reporting stops at the water's edge."[5]

The willingness of the news media to defer to the national security state is not limited to nuclear matters. Mixed in with nuclear anxiety since World War II has been national ambition to achieve what publisher Henry Luce labeled "the American Century," a time when the United States would be dominant and the world would be a better place for it. In this regard, throughout the Cold War, the news media have usually allowed Washington to define political situations abroad. Too, mainstream journalism has tended to accept uncritically the notion that Third World countries cannot have politics, only fates, and it is best for all concerned if the United States ultimately determines what those fates are to be.

This acquiescence has led the news media to withhold information about U.S. interventions, sometimes knowingly, as was the case in the Bay of Pigs; or, more frequently, to interpret them favorably, as with the interventions in the Congo, Dominican Republic, and Grenada, while routinely lending support to the contention that the world's problems, such as they are, usually result only from Soviet subversion.[6]

Journalism's consistent willingness to suspend independent judgment and to accept Washington's frames, labels, and assessments has had predictable consequences. Thus Cuban involvement in Angola received sustained media attention while U.S. involvement was downplayed; the absence of popular support for Polish martial law was made plain, but the illegitimacy of the Shah of Iran went unnoticed; a pronouncement by the Philippines' Ferdinand Marcos two years ago that antigovernment agitators and publishers who allowed their facilities to print "propaganda" could be executed received only passing mention in the national news. It is not difficult to imagine the tone and scope of press coverage if a similar statement were to be made by the Sandinista government in Nicaragua.[7]

Vietnam, it should be noted, was not the grand exception to the media's statist inclination, as many observers have assumed. This reality has been confirmed by several prominent journalists, whose retrospective comments suggest that the journalistic establishment was at odds with Washington more because of concern over how effectively the war was being fought than with whether it should have been fought at all.[8]

The reasons for media behavior are far more complex and subtle than those usually advanced by critics of the statist orientation. Cronyism, careerism, sheer ignorance, or unconscionable pursuit of profit all play their roles. But nothing that is said here should be interpreted to mean that journalists are part of a planned conspiracy or that their editors act on instructions directly received from the State Department or the Pentagon. Rather, my argument is that the process by which journalism generally tends to reflect official policies is a function of both the media *system's* ideological orientation and Cold War conditioning. It is reflexive instead of deliberate.

Such behavior is deeply rooted in nuclear anxiety, but it also stems from acceptance of the idea of a paramount Soviet threat, plus the profound suspicion that mature capitalist entities hold for Third World revolutions, which involve people instead of technology. Finally this behavior incorporates an intuitive assumption that for corporate journalism to reach a mass audience, it must rule out taking a strong adversary stand against the state.

Most mainstream journalists, of course, reject out of hand the notion that the news media serve as an instrument of the state. Steeped in the ethical rhetoric of a democratic press, they genuinely see themselves as tough-minded practitioners of a well-defined craft, with clearcut rules to eliminate personal bias. To the extent that they see a problem, they perceive it largely as the result of government lies, half-truths, and official deceptions, or of having to cope with the impersonal economic realities of the marketplace. In this latter regard, the journalistic fraternity engages in a form of intellectual plea bargaining. Rather than admit operating under the influence of ideology—a felony—

journalists cop a plea and admit only the pursuit of profit, which in American society is a misdemeanor at worst.

In their personal beliefs, most journalists see themselves as being deeply worried about nuclear catastrophe, like anyone else. A late-1983 Gallup survey of journalistic convictions, indeed, revealed that 81 percent of the journalists polled favored an agreement between the United States and the Soviet Union for an immediate and verifiable freeze on the testing, production, and deployment of nuclear weapons. However, only 4 percent of the same journalists answered "the nuclear arms race" when asked what they thought was the most important problem facing the country. And they split down the middle when asked which of two courses of action would be most likely to increase the likelihood of nuclear war: 49 percent replied that continuing the arms race would be more likely to do so, 45 percent that "falling behind the Soviet Union in nuclear weaponry" was more likely to cause a conflict.

Finally and most important, because journalists know they do not consciously lie, they assume they have written or spoken the truth. They believe devoutly in the first tenet of the journalistic faith: the U.S. news media are nonideological. Thus many journalists are alternatively bewildered and outraged when critics assert that they are serving the national security state. They tend to interpret such criticism as slander, an attack on their personal integrity, and dismiss it as the mean-spirited work of ideologues who can face neither the truth about the Soviet Union nor the nature of a world hostile to U.S. interests. Their self-image, in short, is well protected.

A major clue to understanding the journalistic mindset can be found in the media's professional model. American journalism prides itself on having developed a fairly rigid set of conventions and rules to guide performance. These rules are believed to produce objectivity, being predicated on the notion that if verifiable truths are reported even-handedly, objectivity will result. These rules also put a high premium on passivity. At a national conference on war, peace, and the news media, Judith Miller of the *New York Times* argued: "Our job is not to make the news, or to put forth controversial ideas that will affect the news. Our mission is to cover those ideas and events as they come up."[9]

In particular, the basic tenets of journalism are strongly biased toward established authority, since the authority itself can be readily verified, if not the information it provides. A charmed circle of "credible" news sources which is difficult to break into results, particularly in the area of nuclear arms. In answer to a question about the universal hostility to the nuclear freeze in Washington and in official circles, Judith Miller responded: "It has not been only the Reagan administration that has many problems with the nuclear freeze. It is also those people in Washington who have traditionally been on the side of arms control. I speak of the arms control community, *the professionals.*" Similarly, William Beecher of the *Boston Globe*, a former *New York Times* correspondent and yet another former Pentagon official, added: "It really hasn't been a matter of taking on the coloration . . . of a particular administration. Rather, a lot of reporters in Washington . . . looked at the freeze issue . . . [and] concluded the freeze proponents are a lot of very well meaning, naive people who don't understand how to get anything done; therefore, this is not a serious movement. . . . It had nothing to do with a Republican sitting in the White House."[10]

Secure in the belief that their personal partisan biases are firmly under control, many journalists conclude that they are nonideological. Yet what matters in a discussion of a dominant ideology—here defined as a well-ordered world view shaped by the requirements of the national security state—are shared biases, not individual opinions. To be sure, a journalist's personal opinions may not correspond to society's dominant ideology, but the orientation of the system in which journalists work certainly does. And as with work in any industrial bureaucracy, the individual reporter's preference is not likely to prevail. More important, it is precisely because a worldview is so widely shared inside and outside the journalistic system that it appears nonprejudicial. As one former correspondent remarked, "Is a fish aware of water?" Thus, the major ideological hurdle for journalists to overcome is the belief that they are nonideological.

However, proper emphasis should not be on individual journalists but rather on the system in which they operate. In the United States, most of the dominant frames for defense issues are established by the prestige print media of the Washington–New York axis, including the *New York Times,* the *Washington Post,* the *Wall Street Journal,* and others. Together with the wire services, they provide a sort of trickle-down journalism for the rest of the country.

Such media are mature, highly capitalized corporations whose main product happens to be perceptions. Ownership in the industry as a whole is among the most concentrated in the United States. The owners and decision-makers are important members of what journalist and author Sidney Zion, cited in *Harper's* magazine, termed the "League of Gentlemen," his phrase for the establishment. According to Zion: "Even when the press attacks a particular administration, its owners and managers still belong to that League of Gentlemen, and still consider the government to be basically right." In agreeing with Zion about the "League" and its nature, columnist Tom Wicker, an associate editor of the *New York Times*, added in the same issue: "Sure, someone could write a two-line memo tomorrow and change the news policy of the [*Times*] to be more skeptical and challenging of established institutions. But they won't do it, not because they don't have the power to do it, but because they don't want to suffer more than the minimal necessary disapproval of the League of Gentlemen."[11]

Beyond a range of pressures to conform ideologically that can be exerted on a reporter by a complex set of bureaucratic checks and balances, there is also the reality that the profit-oriented news media find independent journalism "costly." While there is no evidence to indicate that media profits and a nonconfrontational relationship with the Soviets are incompatible, it remains that specialists are expensive, generalists less so. In this sense, to leave the conventional Washington wisdom unchallenged happens also to be economical for contemporary bottom-line journalism. False economy though this may be in the long run, corporate journalism has yet to discover the assumptions of more enlightened business entities, such as those that comprise the American Committee on East-West Accord.

One final force at work on the news media demands mention. In the past five years, a major campaign from the political right has been directed against them. The right argues that the media are antidefense, soft on the Soviet Union, and antinuclear. While these conservatives say that they are interested in an open press, their analysis can only lead to a more closed system, in which the statist perspective is *totally* dominant. How seriously the media are taking this assault is difficult to gauge, but there are some disturbing indications.

For example, the NBC television network invited Terry Dolan, executive director of the National Conservative Political Action Committee, to present a two-minute piece for the March 20, 1985 "Today" show. Dolan chose to do an alternative profile of Mikhail Gorbachev. According to Steve Friedman, the program's producer, Dolan's invitation had "nothing to do with the conservative onslaught on the media, nothing to do with any complaints. We're just trying to do some different television."

Besides the possibility of intimidating the media into an even less objective stance than it usually takes, such a campaign works to the detriment of antistatist critics in two other equally significant, if more subtle, ways:

The right's criticism tends to reinforce the journalists' self-image of being independent from the state. How could journalism be serving the interests of the nuclear regime, such reasoning goes, if the political right is upset? But this view fails to comprehend that the right's basic quarrel with the media, in addition to being based on a fantasy view of Cold War history, is more an argument over degree than kind. That is to say, the mainstream media usually tend to conclude that the United States ought to use less force to pursue its aims than the political right believes necessary. There is no fundamental disagreement, however, about the United States' role in the world.

The current wave of conservative criticism makes it appear to the thoughtful observer that the question of media performance is merely a right-versus-left argument, when instead the debate ought to focus on what journalistic model best serves an open society.[12]

Because of the onslaught from the pronuclear right, it is all the more imperative that those concerned about the nuclear dilemma begin to pay careful and sustained attention to the role the media play, and can play, in the crisis at hand. Up to now, activists in the campaign to confront the nuclear regime seem to have approached the media problem as simply one of getting more publicity for their activities. Yet such a strategy fails to go to the roots of journalistic behavior.

The central fact remains that there is an undeniable need, some 40 years after Hiroshima, to reinvent American journalism, a task for which the media seem unprepared, unwilling, or both. The peace community, it would appear, has little choice but to take on the chore.

1. George F. Kennan, "On Nuclear War," *New York Review of Books* (Jan. 21, 1982), pp. 21–22.

2. William M. Arkin, "Waging Secrecy," *Bulletin* (March 1985), pp. 5–6.

3. Gerald M. Boyd, "White House Role in Article is Cited," *New York Times* (March 3, 1985), p. 3.

4. Robert K. Manoff, "Covering the Bomb: Press and State in the Shadow of Nuclear War," in *War, Peace and the News Media:* Proceedings, David Rubin and Ann Marie Cunningham, eds. (New York: Department of Journalism and Mass Communication, New York University, 1983), p. 202.

5. Robert K. Manoff, "The Media's Nuclear War," *PSR* [Physicians for Social Responsibility] *Newsletter* (Fall 1984), p. 2.

6. See Jonathan Kwitny, *Endless Enemies* (New York: Congdon and Weed, 1984).

7. Recent coverage of events in Central and Latin America has occasionally demonstrated a willingness to challenge official Washington. But these flashes of independent news judgment do not yet constitute a sustained departure from the journalism of deference.

8. Phillip Knightley, *The First Casualty* (New York: Harcourt Brace Jovanovich, 1975), pp. 380–81.

9. Rubin and Cunningham, op. cit., p. 193.

10. Ibid., pp. 194–95.

11. "Can the Press Tell the Truth," *Harper's* (Jan. 1985), pp. 48, 50.

12. For the most comprehensive analysis available of the political right's attack on the news media, see Walter Schneir and Miriam Schneir, "Beyond Westmoreland: The Right's Attack on the Press," *The Nation* (March 30, 1985), pp. 361–67.

6

Lobbying for Arms Control

Christopher E. Paine

Organized popular resistance to the nuclear arms race in the United States is fragmented among a wide array of religious, scientific, professional, environmental, government reform, and grass-roots peace activist organizations. Despite their varying orientations, these groups have managed to form national coalitions to achieve specific legislative objectives, as well as local coalitions to conduct educational events and organize demonstrations.

The unprecedented intensity of the movement, along with its modest achievements, give cause for hope, if not for optimism. The following developments have been particularly encouraging:

A broad coalition of nongovernmental organizations opposing the new MX intercontinental ballistic missile has forced a drastic curtailment of the program. The Carter Administration's original proposal was to spread 200 semimobile missiles over thousands of square miles of the American West. Today, the program has been reduced to probably no more than 50 missiles, based in existing Minuteman silos. This seven-year legislative battle has set new standards of tenacity and political sophistication for the U.S. peace movement, which in the past was rarely able to mount concentrated and effective political pressure on the Congress. Unfortunately, however, the prolonged struggle over a single weapons system has also entailed an "opportunity cost" that the U.S. peace movement can no longer afford to ignore.

The new "arms control lobby" has repeatedly turned back Reagan's requests to begin binary nerve gas production, and in 1984 it prompted the House of Representatives to respond to a Soviet unilateral moratorium on antisatellite (ASAT) testing by sidestepping the president and legislating a reciprocal ban. The House action charts an obvious path for further citizen action to slow down the arms race bilaterally, even in the face of concerted Administration attempts to prolong negotiations and open new areas of military competition.

In November 1982, millions of Americans—in eight out of nine states and in 28 cities and counties—supported the passage of ballot initiatives calling on the president to negotiate a bilateral nuclear weapons freeze with the Soviet Union. Six months later, after the longest debate in the history of the House, the freeze concept was endorsed by a vote of 278 to 149. However, this resolution, festooned with qualifying amendments, supported the freeze solely as an "immediate objective" of arms control negotiations which legislators knew to be under the control of an Administration hostile to arms control.

For the first time in the nuclear age, the public's desire to end the nuclear arms race has become a major motivating factor for citizen involvement in grassroots electoral activity. During 1984, the national Freeze Voter political action committee (PAC), along with Freeze Voter PACs in 38 states, raised a total of $3.4 million to finance some 260 grass-roots organizers working in 244 House and 20 Senate races, coordinating the efforts of some 25,000 volunteers. Political action affiliates of the four other peace organizations doing electoral work raised an additional $2.2 million.

While these figures far exceed sums raised in the past, they barely offset the $3.6 million contributed directly to reelection campaigns by PACs affiliated with the nation's top 20 defense contractors, and do not begin to match the more than $14 million raised by the National Conservative Political Action Committee and Senator Jesse Helms's National Congressional Club. The result of these fledgling electoral efforts, however, was that despite Reagan's nationwide win, five of the seven new senators elected in 1984 promised voters they would support a nuclear freeze, and most of the representatives who had led the opposition to the Reagan Administration's nuclear buildup were returned to office.

During Reagan's first term, the educational efforts of Physicians for Social Responsibility and other local and national organizations, augmented by extensive media coverage, gave millions of Americans a refresher course in the destructive effects of a single nuclear bomb and in the grotesque accumulation of destructive power in the superpowers' arsenals. Religious leaders and groups, most

prominently the Catholic bishops, by questioning the moral underpinnings of the nuclear arms race and deterrence theory based on the
threat of deliberate escalation, have also contributed significantly to
public awareness.

*A recent survey by the Public Agenda Foundation suggests that public discus-
sion of the nuclear issue has convinced a significant segment of the American
people that a nuclear war could not be limited, survived, or won, and that new
nuclear weaponry will not make them more secure.* But this reassertion of
common sense coexists with — and is often submerged by — longstanding public perceptions about the importance of "bargaining with the
Soviets from a position of strength." These contradictory impulses
apparently leave a majority of citizens without a clear sense of the
specific policy initiatives they should support to reduce the threat of
nuclear war.

The recent upsurge antinuclear activism in the United States and
around the globe suggests both a fundamental change in public attitudes toward the nuclear arms race and a quantum leap in individual
and organizational commitments to oppose it. But the American antinuclear movement is still a long way from developing the combination
of political strategy, skilled leadership, and awareness of historic responsibility that characterized earlier struggles to end such deeply
ingrained abuses as slavery and colonialism.

Unlike the European situation, where both ideology and party discipline limit the individual legislator's room for maneuver, the comparatively nonideological and issue-oriented nature of the U.S. political
system encourages and occasionally rewards a short-term pragmatic
approach. But the same factors impede the development of a broad-
based, long-term strategy for changing the overall direction of U.S.
nuclear policy.

American legislative politics has often been compared to a floating
crap game, with all the attributes of easy access and ephemeral activity
this analogy implies. Thus, while the American peace movement has
experienced occasional success in controlling specific outputs and activities of the military-industrial complex, it has not even attempted
to mount a sustained attack on the ideological hegemony and institutional prerogatives of the complex itself. The much strengthened arms
control lobby which has grown up under the Reagan presidency relies
on a kind of political and analytical eclecticism which is both the key
to its present success, and a major barrier to future progress.

The movement's efforts to organize support around a coherent set
of policy alternatives to the status quo are made more difficult by

the endemic "faddism" of U.S. political life. In the news media the set of serious interlocking arms control proposals known as "the freeze" was treated like the political equivalent of the hula hoop: the sudden feast of coverage was matched only by the instant famine when the media-pack moved on, leaving behind the partially digested remains of an issue and a movement struggling to recover from a drastically "oversold" condition.

An avalanche of news coverage can be disorienting to activists, leading them to mistake their own reflections in the media for a mass of converts. Inevitably this tacit media-activist collaboration arouses expectations which it cannot possibly fulfill. When the balloon pops, pundits left and right declare the issue "dead," when in fact it may still be gaining political strength, as measured by real indices that have been corrected for journalistic hyperinflation. The freeze movement, for example, reached its peak of organization, expenditure, and political influence during the 1984 election, long after the media had lost interest in it.

The lesson here is that the American peace movement should not, and need not, be completely vulnerable to the media's capricious "hot issue" syndrome. Fluctuations in coverage are inevitable, but the movement must develop a conscious long-term strategy for shaping its message in the press.

The absence of a consistent, principled foundation for public opposition to the nuclear arms race has been felt in the protracted campaigns against the MX and the B-1 bomber, as well as in the debates over "no-first-use" and the role of past and present bilateral superpower negotiations.

While the current legislative deadlock over the MX must be counted as a historic success, it has been achieved primarily by manipulating contradictions within the established doctrinal framework. The arms control lobbying coalition has relied on the argument that the MX is a dangerous, wasteful, destabilizing weapon because it will be a highly accurate MIRVed missile deployed in fixed silos vulnerable to a Soviet first strike. But this argument implicitly leaves the door open to a whole host of weapons that do not fit this narrow criterion: "Midgetman" missiles are not MIRVed and need not be "fixed"; Trident II missiles deployed aboard submarines will be accurate and MIRVed, but invulnerable. Some leading legislative opponents of the MX are, in fact, enthusiastic proponents of Trident II.

The weaknesses of the current "target of opportunity" approach pursued by the Washington arms control lobby coalition is epitomized by its flip-flop on the ICBM "vulnerability" problem. When the MX opponents were focusing on defeating the Carter Administration's solution—turning the Western Great Basin region into an environmental catastrophe of MX "racetracks" and concrete "garages"—they drove home all the sound reasons why the Soviet first-strike scenario was really just another instance of worst-case planning run amok. This is precisely the kind of self-serving paranoid fantasy unleashed routinely by the Pentagon at critical junctures in the weapons acquisition process.

These same objections to ICBM vulnerability were sufficiently persuasive to be appropriated in subsequent testimony by members and counselors of the Reagan-appointed "blue-ribbon" Scowcroft Commission. Former Secretary of Defense James Schlesinger, for example, has explained to Congress on several recent occasions why the coordination problems and operational uncertainties of a first strike on U.S. missile silos are so severe that the "window of vulnerability" was never really open after all. These same arguments were now being used to bolster the case for deployment of 100 MX missiles in Minuteman silos, but MX opponents failed to use the opportunity for a coherent debate, based on a common set of facts. Instead, they replayed the old tune about silo vulnerability to a Soviet "first strike."

Thus, an opportunity was lost to clarify the nuclear debate and address the fundamental strategic and psychological premises of U.S. nuclear policy. The real case for the MX, and strategic "force modernization" in general, was laid out in some detail in the April 1983 Report of the President's Commission on Strategic Forces; it remained, for the most part, unacknowledged and unopposed by the anti-MX coalition.

The Scowcroft Report's authors argue that the relative balance of U.S.-Soviet nuclear weaponry cannot be "set apart from all other calculations about relations between nations"—a premise of the nuclear freeze—because trends in the nuclear balance purportedly "heavily influence the vigor with which they [Soviet leaders] exercise their power." We are told that the United States cannot afford the "delusion" that Soviet leaders are going to be deterred by the normal human concerns that dissuade American leaders from undertaking agressive, risky ventures overseas.

U.S. strategy must, in this view, focus on persuading Soviet leaders that the United States has both the will and the capability to initiate the use of nuclear weapons against those targets "which the Soviet leaders . . . value most"—a list which the report says includes "military command bunkers" and "missile silos" but not Moscow or Leningrad. "A credible capability for controlled, prompt, limited [nuclear] attack on hard targets" would "cast a shadow over the calculus of Soviet

Soviet risk-taking at any level of confrontation with the West." And in the short term, the report stated, this capability for nuclear intimidation could be provided only by the MX.

Such is the justification not only for the MX, but for Pershing II, Trident II, and the whole gamut of new nuclear weapons systems. It represents the archetypal but seldom articulated "psycho-military" case for continuing the nuclear arms race, yet the U.S. peace movement has failed for the most part to mount a sustained public campaign to discredit this orthodoxy.

Many Americans—perhaps a majority—seem to support, at least passively, the Scowcroft Report's recommended strategy of threatening nuclear war in order to deter conventional conflict with the Soviet Union on U.S. terms. That is, they support the utility of the nuclear bluff. But what little public opinion polling that has been done on the question suggests a public belief that the president should never be the first actually to use nuclear weapons.

Without a much clearer public debate over the role of nuclear threats in U.S. military strategy, it appears that majority opinion will tolerate a president who brandishes threats of nuclear escalation at the battle-front and of a stepped-up arms race at the bargaining table. But widespread public opposition to nuclear civil defense planning, and general disbelief in the prospect that a nuclear war would remain limited, indicate that the public does not subscribe to the "nuclear-warfighting" dimension of current strategy. As might be expected, the public wants to enjoy the purported benefits of a fierce nuclear posture while rejecting its attendant risks. The freeze movement, unfortunately, was unable to bridge this dichotomy in public consciousness.

The history of the B-1 strategic bomber is a painful reminder of another persistent weakness in U.S. peace movement strategy: the confusion between "cost-effectiveness" and arms control. Politicians from all parts of the political spectrum have a tendency to delude themselves and their constituents with the notion that they are helping to achieve the latter by insisting on the former. Regrettably, "more bang for the buck" rarely translates into "less bucks for the bang."

In the mid-1970s antinuclear and human-needs groups formed a tacit alliance with a coterie of defense-minded systems analysts in the Carter Administration to turn back production of the B-1 in favor of converting the existing B-52 bomber force to carry air-launched cruise missiles (ALCMs). Today, almost everyone recognizes that from the perspective of limiting the arms race, this was a temporary victory for "cost-effectiveness" but a political blunder for arms control. General

Dynamics, which lost in the competition to build the ALCM, was awarded contracts to build ground- and sea-launched variants, creating a new SALT limitation and verification problem, and a new dimension for superpower military competition.

Cancellation of the B-1 added fuel to the fires of conservative opposition to SALT II and created an irredentist cause for the military-industrial complex which Reagan was able to tap effectively during the 1980 election. Not only was the B-1 revived and put into production (as the B-1B), but the steady attacks on its "cost-effectiveness" against "anticipated growth in the Soviet air-defense threat" paved the way for development of an entirely new radar-evading "stealth" bomber which is likely to cost even more than the B-1. In the meantime, cruise missiles are moving into their "second generation," and there is even talk of a B-1C.

When divorced from broader political objectives, debates about cost-effectiveness can do little to help arms control, but they seem to have some potential to subvert it. A similar confusion is pervading the MX debate, with the "better weapon" role of the cruise missile now being played by the "Midgetman" single-warhead ICBM.

The various organizations which comprise the active U.S. constituency for arms control and disarmament measures support different combinations of goals and pursue disparate and sometimes politically contradictory strategies for achieving them. Current efforts range from Harvard University's modest proposal to avoid nuclear war through better management of crises and more rational procurement of "stabilizing" nuclear weapons to the visionary efforts of activist religious organizations to abolish all types of warfare and establish economic justice and universal human rights.

A clear premise of the Nuclear Weapons Freeze Campaign over the past four years has been that a halt to the nuclear arms race can be pursued, and possibly achieved, with only a tangential connection to the success or failure of more far-reaching efforts to transform the international system.

This is certainly true at the level of dispassionate analysis. But some progress toward other goals—particularly a reduced reliance on the threat of conventional war—is probably indispensable for establishing the political and psychological preconditions for acceptance of the "general nuclear settlement" envisioned by the freeze movement. In other words, the freeze could be the logical outcome to a classical arms control process of "agreements between adversaries," but the extent to which the Soviet Union and the United States actually remain adversaries will probably determine the fate of the freeze.

Implicit differences in fundamental goals, or a lack of clarity about what ultimate goals their policies are designed to support, can lead organizations to radically different prescriptions for policy even though they share the same short-term objectives. For example, most groups working on nuclear arms control issues favor a "no-first-use" policy for the United States. Some organizations, such as the Union of Concerned Scientists, have suggested that this transition be facilitated by augmentation and improvement of conventional forces, permitting them to shoulder the deterrent burden now being carried by tactical nuclear forces. Other organizations—such as SANE, Coalition for a New Foreign and Military Policy, and Mobilization for Survival—whose primary concerns include foreign intervention and the military budget, argue that the suggested improvements in the mobility and firepower of U.S. conventional forces will merely elicit similar Soviet improvements and make both superpowers even more combative and intervention-prone. An enhanced capacity in conventional forces must not be accepted as the price for gradual denuclearization, they argue, because such off-setting capacities for intervention could become the main agents of a superpower confrontation leading to nuclear war.

The NATO-Warsaw Pact confrontation is truly the primal case of conventional power projection from which much of the current arms race has grown. Much greater trans-Atlantic contact will surely be necessary if the U.S. movement, and its allies in Congress, are to make a positive contribution to European security. In particular, the arms control lobbying coalition, by working more closely with its European counterparts, must find a way to short-circuit the Pentagon's practice of wrapping its nuclear weapons programs in the endorsements of allied governments to protect them from congressional opposition.

In the usual discourse of intra-alliance politics, NATO governments respond to critical inquiries about new nuclear weapons programs by saying, in essence, "Nothing has been decided," while in Washington these same programs are presented as the "requests" of beleaguered U.S. allies. Alleged NATO "resolve" to deploy new tactical and inter-mediate-range weapons is then used to coerce wavering U.S. legislators into demonstrating comparable U.S. "will" by deploying new *strategic* nuclear weapons. Increased international cooperation between peace movements and parliamentary partisans of nuclear arms control can do much to penetrate this trans-Atlantic fog.

Perhaps the most vital task facing current peace movement strategy is that of overcoming the inevitable tension between the *political* role of arms control agreements as symbols of mutual superpower accommodation, and their *substantive* role in controlling and possibly ending the nuclear arms competition. Since substance is routinely sacrificed for symbolism in superpower negotiations, the peace movement is caught in a dilemma. It must choose between a de facto alliance with the right to denounce the agreement and grudging support for ratification of a superpower compact to continue the arms race.

Ironically, arms control talks provide a useful adversarial context for a process which, absent Geneva, is increasingly seen by the public as a dead end of mutual vulnerability, overkill, and diminishing returns. It is no accident that the U.S. peace movement made its greatest gains in 1984, the year the Soviet Union stayed away from the bargaining table.

But critics must tread carefully here. The political importance of arms control negotiations for both sides, and the public's feeling of reassurance when Soviet and U.S. leaders hold a summit meeting, means that little political gain for genuine arms control can come from angry denunciations of the "SALT process." That task is better left to the radical right.

Still, governments must not be allowed to use the Geneva talks as a means to disarm the peace movement. To the contrary, the peace movement must learn how to use the Geneva talks as a means to disarm the governments: by constantly raising expectations about what could be accomplished with a modicum of competence and good will; by defining arms control opportunities more clearly in the public and congressional consciousness; and by using the legislative process to precipitate areas of mutual nuclear restraint, which can then be codified in lasting agreements.

The overall policy which the antinuclear movement seeks to change is both formulated and implemented, however, by vast and only marginally accountable bureaucracies in the executive branch. The same goes for negotiation of the international agreements that will be necessary to bring the nuclear arms race to an end.

A further obstacle to arms control progress resides in the constitutional requirement for Senate consent to treaty ratification by a two-thirds majority. This has given the political right and its military-industrial allies what amounts to a "minority veto" over nuclear arms control agreements. The president's historical willingness to placate this conservative minority in advance so as to assure Senate ratification virtually guarantees that the treaty will impinge as little as possible on U.S.—and hence Soviet—nuclear force modernization. On the other hand, battles to force *unilateral* cancellation of particular nuclear weapons programs can plant the seeds of a political right-wing "boomerang effect" as Soviet programs proceed apace.

Overcoming these obstacles would seem to require nothing less than an expansion of the historically—but not legally—determined boundaries of congressional action in foreign affairs. There is nothing in the Constitution to bar Congress from taking direct account of the prospect for Soviet reciprocal restraint when that body exercises its right to authorize and appropriate funds for the nation's defense. Congress could undertake a simple, verifiable arms control initiative— such as a moratorium on MIRVed ballistic-missile flight testing, or on underground nuclear explosive testing above the long-range detection threshold—with the explicit provision that its continuation after a certain period would be contingent on reciprocal Soviet restraint.

Finally, the diverse grouping of nuclear arms control organizations must come to the collective realization that no irreversible progress is likely without major institutional reforms to loosen the grip of the military-industrial complex on U.S. security policy. New laws are needed: to increase congressional control over the military budget; to drastically curb official secrecy; to limit contractor campaign contributions; to lock the revolving door between the Pentagon and its contractors; and to withdraw from the defense industry the task of evaluating potential new weapons systems. Such legislation is essential to any long-run strategy to end the nuclear arms race and reduce the threat of nuclear war.

The nuclear arms race will not succumb to a movement bogged down in contradictions over short-term objectives and tactics. To build upon its considerable success in changing public opinion and attitudes, the U.S. antinuclear movement must now develop both the inclination and the institutional mechanisms for advancing a broadly shared political strategy which can move national policy steadily in the direction of ending the nuclear arms race.

Futures

1

Uncertainty of the Status Quo

Michael Mandelbaum

In the four decades since Hiroshima the arrangements, both formal and informal, that govern the world's nuclear weapons have assumed a settled shape. There is a nuclear status quo.

Its most basic feature is the existence of weapons of unprecedented and collectively almost unimaginable destructive power. There are now tens of thousands of explosives descended from the two that struck Hiroshima and Nagasaki in August 1945, most of them many times more potent than the originals.

These weapons are chiefly in the hands of two great powers, the United States and the Soviet Union, but other countries have them as well. The British nuclear arsenal, however, is for most purposes part of the U.S. arsenal. The French acquired their own bomb to distinguish themselves from the Americans, but its independent political effect is modest. China, the fifth nuclear power, is more like an independent pole in international affairs, but its stockpile of nuclear weapons is much smaller than those of the two superpowers. It is not inconsequential, especially for the Soviet Union, at which it is aimed; but like its French counterpart it has had, so far, a very modest impact on international politics. The distribution of nuclear weapons may still be described, with rough accuracy, as "bipolar."

Both the United States and the Soviet Union are vulnerable to a punishing attack by the other. Each can devastate the other even after absorbing a massive attack. The common term for their relationship, "mutual assured destruction," is often denoted by the appropriately grim acronym MAD. Their mutual vulnerability is a condition of the nuclear age, the consequence of two other principles of the status quo:

The first is the supremacy of offense over defense in nuclear weaponry. Both great powers can attack successfully; neither can defend itself against the other's attack. The supremacy of offense has its roots in the physical properties of nuclear weapons, the abundance of bombs, and their individual explosive force. Each bomb is powerful enough to destroy a city by itself, and the United States and the Soviet Union have so many that both are certain of their ability to destroy a targeted city, indeed many cities, whatever defenses they might encounter.

The other principle is that the two great powers confront each other with large nuclear arsenals, finally, because they are political rivals. Their rivalry is the heart of their relationship. It is as important for the world's present nuclear arrangements as the physical characteristics of the armaments themselves.

The enormous explosive power that nuclear weapons represent, their concentration in the hands of the governments of two great sovereign states, the dominance of the offense, and the political conflict between the United States and the Soviet Union are fundamental to the status quo in this sense: the nations of the world have developed policies to cope with the dangers and opportunities that these weapons present. If any of these four factors were to change, the policies would change as well. They are also fundamental in that changes would affect the prospects for nuclear war—the way one might begin, the feasibility of fighting it, the likelihood that such a war would occur. What, then, are the prospects for these four basic arrangements for nuclear weapons that have evolved over the past 40 years?

The first will not change. Nuclear weapons will not disappear; in some form they will be part of human affairs forever. They cannot be disinvented. If somehow all existing weapons were to be abolished, the knowledge of how to make them would remain. Even if, through some unimagined series of events, the knowledge were forgotten, as the learning of antiquity was lost in the Middle Ages, it would probably be rediscovered by the ongoing process of systematic investigation of the natural world. Nuclear weapons are, in this most basic sense, the products of science itself.

There is no guarantee, however, that the United States and the Soviet Union will monopolize the world's nuclear firepower in the future as they do at present. An effort to prevent precisely what has happened was in fact launched at the outset of the nuclear age. The Baruch Plan, the initial U.S. proposal for controlling nuclear weapons, and the schemes that followed it provided for the creation of a global supra-national authority to take custody of the means for making nuclear explosives. The purpose of these various plans was to deny the bomb to any particular sovereign state.

None of these early proposals, or similar ones advanced by the Soviet Union and other countries, came close to being adopted.[1] Adherence to national control of the means of defense—the core of national sovereignty—has for 40 years consistently proved powerful enough to override all efforts to dilute it. Neither the United States nor the Soviet Union has shown the slightest inclination to surrender its weapons to what would be an embryonic world government.

Neither, however, have they wished to see other states acquire the bomb. Their common interest in sustaining their nuclear "duopoly" was expressed in the Non-Proliferation Treaty, which they jointly devised and then persuaded most, although not all, other states to adopt.

There has been relatively little nuclear proliferation since 1945. Certainly fewer states now have the bomb than was expected, and feared, 25 years ago when the issue moved to the forefront of official concern in the United States. This is partly the result of a happy coincidence of circumstances. The requirements for having nuclear weapons are both technical and political. A state must have the requisite scientific and engineering talent, since there is almost no international commerce in weapons technology; and it must, of course, decide that getting the bomb will serve its interests. Many of the countries that are technically able to make nuclear weapons have not been politically disposed to do so.

Many of them have been members of the Western alliance and have considered the U.S. nuclear arsenal powerful enough to protect their territories, as well as the continental United States, from Soviet attack. It is possible, of course, that the necessary condition for their confidence has been the size of the U.S. arsenal and that a more modest U.S. nuclear stockpile, although sufficient to deter a Soviet attack on North America, might not seem to the Europeans or the Japanese adequate to *their* needs and would kindle their interest in nuclear weapons of their own.

It is impossible to know which countries, if any, that do not already have them will acquire nuclear weapons, when this will happen, and how many explosives these putative nuclear powers will get. It is unlikely that *no* other country will ever acquire its own bomb, or even that the number of nuclear-weapons states will be the same at the end of the first eight decades of the nuclear age as it is at the end of the first four. The worldwide pool of scientists and engineers who can design and construct bombs and the amount of fissionable material available grows larger with each passing year.

Nor is it easy to say what effects nuclear proliferation will have. It may bring stability to places previously consumed by war. Nuclear weapons may serve as pacifiers of regional conflict. But their spread could also have the opposite effect. As they come into the hands of more and more governments, and perhaps even into the possession of people who do not exercise governmental authority, the odds may shorten that one or more of them will be used. The fear that this is so has animated U.S. and Soviet policies toward nuclear proliferation, and those of other countries as well. Thus, unlike the first feature of the status quo the second is not immutable, and a change in the distribution of nuclear weapons will not necessarily be a change for the better.[2]

President Reagan has challenged the third basic feature of the world's nuclear arrangements, the dominance of offense. He has called for a program of research and development to produce and deploy a system of defense against attack that would render nuclear weapons "impotent and obsolete." He has given official voice to the aspiration to rid the world, if not of nuclear weapons, then of the dangers that they pose. The aspiration is understandable. A world in which armed forces perform their traditional task of defending the citizenry by warding off enemy ataks would be preferable by far to the present world, in which the defense of both great powers rests on the threat to annihilate or poison millions of civilians—which remains a possible, perhaps the probable, outcome of a nuclear exchange even if it is not explicitly threatened—in response to a nuclear attack in which a comparable number of people have been similarly massacred.

As an aspiration, it is irresistible, but can it be fulfilled? It calls to mind the moment in Shakespeare's *Henry IV, Part I* when the Welsh magician Glendower boasts, "I can call forth spirits from the vasty deep," and the cynical warrior Hotspur replies, "So can I. So can any man. But will they come?"

Will it come? Can a defense be built that will protect the citizens of the United States or the Soviet Union from attack by the forces of the other great power? (It seems almost certain that defenses could be built to guard each side's missiles and quite probable that reasonable protection could be provided against a few bombs hurled by some third party. Both may prove appealing in the decades ahead; neither would alter the status quo in the way that population defense would.) The question is a technical one. Paul Nitze, Reagan's special adviser on arms control, has set down two criteria that any defensive system must meet before being deployed: it must be able to survive attack, and it must be "cost-effective at the margin," so that the opponent cannot easily and cheaply defeat it by adding offensive forces.

Can machinery be made that will meet these criteria? For the long term, of course, no one can say; it is impossible to predict what the march of science and engineering will bring. There are those who assert that viable defensive systems are feasible now, or at least visible on the technical horizon. Others vigorously dispute the assertion. At the very least it remains to be proven that techniques for the effective defense of cities are at hand.

The task of defense becomes easier the fewer offensive weapons there are. The president, apparently recognizing this, calls for the progressive reduction of offensive forces while defenses are being developed and put in place. The logical end point of this process, if it occurs, is the absence of any offensive weapons at all, in combination with full-scale defenses — a state of affairs suggested by physicist Freeman Dyson in his recent book *Weapons and Hope*.[3] His proposal for future nuclear arrangements includes both defense and disarmament. Indeed, it may be argued that the two are more than compatible, they are complementary; that in fact, each requires the other, with neither being possible alone.

Disarmament makes defense possible because defense cannot be reliably effective (if it can be effective at all) against any but the most modest offensive salvo: the punier the offense the better the defense, and defense is best of all when there is no offense. Conversely, defense makes disarmament possible because without it neither side could be persuaded to give up all of its armaments. Without defenses each side would fear that, while pretending to disarm, the other would conceal a few weapons or discard them all but then secretly rearm, and so gain a decisive political advantage. With defenses, a few bombs would not be decisive. In this sense defense serves as a hedge against cheating on or breakout from a disarmament agreement.

To create a world of defense dominance, both sides would have to be willing to give up their offensive armaments, which would require considerable trust and cooperation. This would have to be voluntary; neither could force the other side to do it. (The attraction for each of discarding its weapons would also depend on the policies of third countries: Soviet leaders would certainly not agree to abandon their armaments without assurances that they would not then be at the mercy of Germany, Japan, China, Britain, or France—assurances that the United States would not be able to give.) The chances for reductions that would change the third basic feature of the nuclear status quo, therefore, depend on the fourth, the political relationship between the United States and the Soviet Union.

The size and shape of the two great nuclear arsenals have ultimately been determined by political considerations. The modest restraints imposed by negotiated arms control agreements since 1945 have required a certain minimal level of political accommodation between the United States and the Soviet Union, but those restraints are exceptional. What is more striking over the last 40 years is the competitive accumulation of weaponry. The arms race is the expression, and the result, of the essence of the political relationship between the two. And this is conflict, not cooperation.[4]

The degree of political cooperation necessary for drastic reductions in nuclear weaponry, and especially for the complete abolition of offensive armaments, seems, from the vantage point of mid-1985, quite beyond the realm of possibility. There is no technical obstacle to such reductions; they would not transgress the laws of physics. But politics has its laws as well, or at least its deeply rooted and powerfully persistent trends, and it is on these trends that the hostility between the Soviet Union and the United States rests, a hostility so solidly grounded in them as almost to warrant being called "natural."

One of the bases of the conflict is the tendency for great powers to define their spheres of interest broadly, to wish to expand their influence, and to bump up against each other, a tendency that dates back at least to the mortal rivalry between Athens and Sparta in the fifth century B.C. To this, in the case of the two great nuclear powers, have been added differences of political and economic organization and belief. The United States is the bearer of one kind of civic culture, while the Soviet leaders are the partisans and beneficiaries of a different and opposed system of social and political order. Historians have carefully scrutinized the origins of the Cold War, in the first years of the nuclear age, with an eye to discovering the fatal moment when the possibility for U.S.-Soviet harmony was lost. Their labors often have served instead to demonstrate that the possibility never really existed. The forces behind the rivalry were powerful and pervasive then and remain so now.

The degree of hostility between the two great powers has varied, with some periods less bitter than others. In the early years of the 1970s, the political climate was cordial enough to produce the ABM

Treaty and a ceiling on offensive missiles. Whatever the prospect at the moment, a return to comparably amicable relations is not out of the question over the course of the next several decades.

Even arms control agreements more sweeping than those of 1972, however—even reductions by half, as some have proposed, of each nuclear arsenal—would leave both the United States and the Soviet Union in the same fundamental predicament. Each would remain at the mercy of the other, vulnerable to a crushing attack.

In the sense that reductions in the levels of armaments, even large ones, would not matter very much, neither would increases. From this perspective the arms race has not been especially dangerous— because it has not disturbed existing nuclear arrangements. It is true that as weapons on one side become more accurate those on the other become more vulnerable to preemptive attack, and it is this process which has the effect of degrading the supremacy of the offense. But the simultaneous increase in the *numbers* of weapons on both sides has had a compensating effect, insuring that enough weapons to launch a retaliatory salvo will survive any attack on either great nuclear power. It has become easier for each side to hit targets, but there are also many more targets at which each must aim.

Even the most extensive arms control agreements that are remotely feasible, therefore, would not alter the first three features of the world's present nuclear arrangements. But they would affect the fourth.

Arms control accords bespeak, because they both require and contribute to, an improvement, a warming, in U.S.-Soviet relations. The status of the political relations between the two nuclear superpowers is of crucial importance because so long as they are poised to annihilate each other—as long as the first three features of the status quo remain in place—it is on the fourth, on a minimally tolerable political relationship between them, that their safety depends.

The public obsession with arms control talks that has developed in the United States and Western Europe in the last few years is misplaced insofar as it is based on the expectation that the negotiations are likely to lead to the abolition of nuclear weapons and the end of all danger. But it is well grounded insofar as it reflects an understanding of the political salience of agreements.

The movements of the *Bulletin*'s "doomsday clock" have been based on the recognition of the political significance of arms control. If the United States and the Soviet Union were to reach agreement on limits to their weaponry comparable to the provisions of SALT I or SALT II, the editors would probably turn the clock back a few more minutes from midnight, and they would be right to do so.

Since 1945 political relations between the two great nuclear powers have not approached the intimacy and trust that would be necessary for disarmament, or even for major offensive weapons reductions. Neither, however, have relations deteriorated into open warfare. Although the United States and the Soviet Union have accumulated tens of thousands of nuclear weapons, none has been fired in anger. The most important by-product of the world's nuclear arrangements is the four-decade nuclear peace that the world has enjoyed since August 1945. The prospects for these arrangements are important not for their own sake but for their bearing on the chances that this one great accomplishment of the status quo will endure.

War remains possible. Nor does the foregoing survey suggest that basic changes lie ahead that will make it less likely. The changes that would make the world dramatically less prone to nuclear conflict— the disappearance of these weapons, reversal of the balance between offense and defense, political reconciliation between the United States and the Soviet Union—are not at all likely. The more likely changes, such as the spread of nuclear weapons, will not, in all probability, make the world safer.

This is not to say that war will be dramatically more likely during the next four decades than it has been in the last four. The status quo has within it the seeds of its own restraint. One of its basic features— the political rivalry between the Soviet Union and the United States— promotes conflict; but another—the enormous explosive power of nuclear weapons—keeps the conflict from sliding into open warfare. The elementary physical properties of nuclear weapons have enforced a measure of prudence upon the policies of both great powers.

Like the rest of us, policymakers on both sides carry with them an image of the world after nuclear warfare that is horrible beyond precedent. They understand that a thermonuclear exchange would leave large stretches of what had once been civilization looking like the rubble-strewn desolation of Hiroshima, photographs of which are among the most important legacies of the only nuclear war that has thus far been fought. The image is sobering. It induces caution in even the most adventuresome soul. Its effects are not likely to fade as the world moves farther away from August 1945.

So if there are not grounds for complete confidence, there is at least reason for hope that over the next four decades peace will be compatible with the arrangements for nuclear weapons that have come into being over the last four. Given the probable future of those arrangements, given the likely persistence of the status quo, it had better be.

1. Michael Mandelbaum, *The Nuclear Question: The United States and Nuclear Weapons, 1946-1976* (New York: Cambridge University Press, 1979), Chap. 2.

2. Michael Mandelbaum, *The Nuclear Future* (Ithaca, New York: Cornell University Press, 1983), Chap. 3.

3. Freeman Dyson, *Weapons and Hope* (New York: Harper and Row, 1984), especially Chap. 22.

4. On the nuclear arms race see Michael Mandelbaum, *The Nuclear Revolution: International Politics before and after Hiroshima* (New York: Cambridge University Press, 1981), Chaps. 4, 5.

2

Liberation from Military Logic

Richard Falk

Ever since the atomic bombs were exploded at the end of World War II, there have been demands, proposals, and policy adjustments aimed at reducing the nuclear threat. For whatever reason, including good fortune, this series of efforts has at least managed to avoid World War III, as well as any subsequent use of a weapon of mass destruction, despite intense political rivalry, various battlefield temptations, and several global crises.

Yet such achievements have not produced any durable sense of geopolitical serenity. Periodically, international developments have aroused acute public anxiety. Fears for human survival at such times become explicit, widespread, and almost unbearable. Nuclear threats have been made, although never executed and usually in secret, suggesting how close the world has come on several occasions to the reality of nuclear war. Enormous resources have been wasted in the production of weapons whose use in any role would be catastrophic. Religious and cultural authorities have passed harsh judgments upon governments that continue to base their security on threats to initiate nuclear war or to use nuclear weapons indiscriminately.

Perhaps a fair summary of the situation would be that deterrence is the best that can be done in a world of sovereign states, but deterrence cannot last forever, and nothing less than unconditional assurance is acceptable when survival is at stake. To accumulate more or better weapons tends to accelerate the arms race, raise tension levels, and produce insecurity. And yet to get rid of weapons by unilateral or even agreed means tends to tempt international adventurism, to arouse fears about vulnerability and weakness, and thus to produce insecurity.

As a result, an uneasy compromise has evolved since Nagasaki. Its components are a continuous flow of new weapons systems, more or less matched by a continuous effort to manage risks in various ways including arms control arrangements, summit meetings, and various efforts at command and control. One of the most massive efforts at reassurance has been associated in the last few years with the Strategic Defense Initiative (SDI), the ideal war-maker's approach to nuclearism by way of the most elaborate technological fix ever conceived.

Whether it is the champions of "Star Wars" or the advocates of total disarmament who seize the podium, most of us realize in our hearts that we are trapped in a tragic situation for which there are no satisfactory answers. The essence of the tragedy is the connection between war and the state. The logic of war is associated with prevailing over enemies by any means possible. As Clausewitz has taught the leaders of the modern world, war is an absolute whose only ethic is victory. The state has been the custodian of this military logic, creating new technologies of violence to gain an upper hand on the hypothetical battlefields of the future.

It is inconceivable that a major modern state will forego any technological development that might give it a military advantage, or give up war-making as a mode of securing its existence. As this dynamic has unfolded, the militarist roots of the state have dug deeper and deeper into such support structures as science and technology, mainstream political parties, the mass media, and even the educational environment. Serious national debate presupposes the constraints of this military logic. As a result, the political imagination of policy-makers is severely disciplined by militarist orthodoxy.

Throughout the nuclear age, peacetime has been an extended rehearsal for global nuclear war. The technology of mass destruction and perpetual mobilization induces constant preparations to fight an ultimate war even if the one and only purpose of these preparations is to diminish the prospect of war itself. Yet the real possibility of such a catastrophe cannot be ruled out; it remains only minutes away even in periods of apparent geopolitical relaxation. Anxiety arises from the continuous possibility that the other side might launch a surprise attack or secretly gain the upper hand by some technological breakthrough. And this situation guarantees that the more militarized sectors of government will enjoy easy and preferred access to top political leaders and to vast resources, building up huge entrenched bureaucratic and economic interests that insist upon the inevitability and normalcy of an endless nuclear arms race.

Given the structure and ideology of the leading states, this set of circumstances unavoidably produces a series of rehearsals for nuclear war, either as responses to actual war-threatening situations or as plans for dealing with an array of imagined scenarios of danger. Every approach to the threat of nuclear war that does not break this iron link between war and the state is in the end delusionary.

Global war-making with nuclear weapons is, of course, irrational and self-destructive, but reason is a weak instrument of reform, except in the hands of the powerful. Deterrence has become so entrenched as an approach, not because it has objective merit as the best means to avoid war, but because it alone reconciles nuclearism and the state system in an age of technophilia. Its hyper-rationality is, in the last analysis, an ingenious rationalization for the international status quo.

The conventional wisdom holds that deterrence is more than just an approach; it is a fact of life emerging from the interplay between technology and distrust. As long as these weapons exist, there is no way to get rid of them except by exposing one's own country to attack. There is no way to be sure that other states will do what they say. Indeed, the uncertainty that would follow on deep weapons cuts can be understood as actually increasing the risks that now attend a nuclear standoff, reinforced by enormous offsetting arsenals of warheads and missiles.

Verification procedures, even if greatly improved by advances in satellite observation, as well as by sensing and surveillance capabilities, can never give real confidence that the determined cheater has not found a way to exploit the vulnerability of others to attack or blackmail. So long as we understand security in terms of threat and counter-threat, it seems true that there is no way to lift the curse of nuclearism.

Can this way of conceiving security continue to be valid? It has certainly been the dominant mode of thinking during the several centuries of international political life which have culminated in the nuclear age. But it is not the way that families or many pre-industrial communities understand security. Their sense of solidarity, although broken at times, generally avoids the psychology of war-making, if not of conflict. The possibility of any decisive shift in what security entails for political communities largely depends on whether the globalist dimensions of today's world will eventually produce new types of beliefs, attitudes, and behaviors.

The process of adjusting to this globalist context could take several centuries, or perhaps only a few decades. If the planet were to come under a credible threat from an enemy elsewhere in the galaxy or if a partial breakdown of order should follow a limited nuclear exchange, then one could imagine an irresistible push for political unification, demilitarization at the national level, and some kind of international police mechanism.

World government is one possible outcome of such traumatic challenge, but it is not the only one. The breakdown of nations into smaller units — a kind of reemergence of feudal-scale principalities with only local war-making capabilities — could also result from an incomplete breakdown of present structures. The challenge is whether we can hasten this process of globalizing our political existence without inviting imperial conquest or inducing catastrophic collapse.

Is it possible to escape from these structures? And should we, as citizens concerned with peace, justice, survival, and a hopeful future, commit ourselves to such a project? My responses are guardedly affirmative to both questions. It is not possible, however, to plan an escape with the warden's cooperation. This, ultimately, is the fallacy that underlies placing one's bets on either the United Nations or arms control negotiations.

So long as the structures of state power are oriented around the military logic of war, apparent official efforts to build an alternative system of security based upon international cooperation, a global identity, and nonviolence in human affairs will come to nothing. They will function mainly as a species of propaganda designed to appease public concerns. No more than a Buddhist monk pledged to nonviolence can seize arms to deal with danger, can leaders of modern sovereign states seriously undertake to throw them away. And even if the leaders should miraculously be so inclined, their bureaucratic underlings would effectively rebel to "save" the militarized state.

To rid the world of the nuclear threat we need to focus on transforming the modern state. Without such transformation, proposals for weaponless deterrence or defensive postures of security, however well-intended, will always be brushed aside by those more formidable energies devoted to gaining the upper hand over potential rivals. To challenge this form of political control requires a social movement that is at least as committed to militant struggle on behalf of a new world order as were earlier movements against slavery, royalism, and colonialism.

These movements succeeded despite their seeming weakness. Militant struggle was not enough. Leadership with a vision of a promised land was necessary, along with great perseverance. Also vital were circumstances that discredited the old order and made its retention seem both impractical and indecent. If we inquire into how Christianity moved from the catacombs to the imperial palaces of ancient Rome, or how Zionism proceeded from an intense vision to the establishment of a strong independent state, we begin to gain insight into the kind of political process that is required to rid ourselves decisively of the nuclear threat.

Such past developments are encouraging, not because they are analogous to the challenge of the war system but because they illustrate how shifts in social consciousness and historical context can rapidly and fundamentally change our sense of what is possible. There is no doubt that the Nazi phenomenon created a new set of political possibilities for Zionist leaders. These leaders were then able to establish and sustain Israel as a state among states, an undertaking that would have been impossible without the waves of Jewish settlement caused by Hitler's policies and the sense of guilt and responsibility felt by leading diplomats of the time who were inclined to solve their moral and political problems at the expense of the Arab nations.

We cannot project the scenario that would translate an emergent global consciousness and situation into new political forms and ideologies, but there are historical justifications for being receptive to such developments even if they appear unrealistic from our present standpoint in time and space. Deterrence, along with its institutional and ideological supports, dominates the realist imagination today, but this does not mean that it exhausts the range of future possibilities.

At this stage, blueprints of alternative world order systems are not very important. What is most needed is a new tradition of citizenship based on the values of peace, economic well-being, human rights, and ecological balance. Such a citizen will challenge the logic of war and seek to reinvigorate democracy so that society can control the state rather than the other way around. The image of a citizen-pilgrim devoted to a different future for society and species responds to the historical challenge in the only realistic way open to us. Embarking on such a pilgrimage does not, of course, promise dramatic, quick, or assured results; but as every profound political leader has understood, imparting a sense of urgency is no substitute for perseverance. Patience is the greatest of revolutionary virtues.

The pursuit of a new world order should not be a sentimental journey guided by wishful thinking. There are actual economic, cultural, and technological forces reshaping the context within which war-making and international politics occur. The net effect of these forces is to turn strategic warfare, including its preparation, into an irrational form of behavior even for the strong; means cannot be related to ends.

Such an objective condition generates a variety of responses, including what psychologists call "denial" or "numbing"—shielding our awareness of a destructive situation, especially when no alternative has been devised. But there are other more hopeful responses, including a variety of ways to affirm species identity as transcending the various partial or subspecies identities associated with nation, race, class, and gender. There is, in particular, a new appreciation of holistic thinking in science and religion, as well as the rise of an ecological consciousness stressing the maintenance of living systems at all levels of complexity. Similarly, the outlooks of pre-industrial peoples, with their emphasis on survival and harmony, are exerting a growing influence. In effect, the *mental* preconditions for a new politics are beginning to be satisfied.

Even on the political plane there are some favorable developments. At this stage they are marginal and perhaps without lasting consequence, but possibly they are part of the slow birth process of something quite new in human affairs. Such developments because of space constraints can be mentioned only as illustrations; each may be interpreted in a variety of ways.

One important area is the emergence of religion as a source of judgment and resistance. The U.S. Catholic bishops' Pastoral Letter on nuclear weapons policy is one expression of this role, while another is the increase in nuclear resistance by individuals who regard it as a religious duty to stop the nuclear arms race by symbolic or exemplary acts of disobedience.

Another dimension concerns efforts of smaller nations to separate themselves from nuclearism: New Zealand and Greece have both taken strong stands against allowing their ports to be used by naval vessels carrying nuclear warheads. More generally, there are various efforts underway to enable neutral or nonaligned governments to challenge the legality of nuclear weapons in the World Court at The Hague. Along a similar path in the United States, a recent civil disobedience case—*Keller and others v. the State of Vermont*— involving opposition to the CIA role in Central America gave judicial support to the view that citizens have a legal right to a lawful foreign policy. The symbolic demand for a Magna Carta in the area of war and peace is an indication that patriotism might take a globalist turn in the future. Developments among independent peace groups and churches in Eastern Europe and the Soviet Union suggest similar gropings, although carried on at great risk, given the oppressive character of the governments in those countries.

Worldwide, the struggle to achieve democratic control over state power is assuming prominence, although in different forms reflecting local conditions. Increasingly, the state, as now constituted, is being discredited as a problem-solving framework for human affairs, whether the issue is security, economic well-being, political freedom, or environmental safety. Only a global framework seems responsive to the scale and complexity of these problems. Religious and cultural challenges have been mounted more and more insistently, underscoring the moral bankruptcy of nuclearism and sharpening tensions between state and civil society. The exploration of space and the planetary character of economic, ecological, and cybernetic complexity are building the foundations of an inevitable global consciousness.

This consciousness need not lead to a world state or to the negation of government authority at the state level, but it does imply a rejection of statist logic in all of its dimensions, and it suggests new ways to safeguard civil society. The reshaping feature of a globalist orientation is its sense of the whole as predominant, whereas the common feature of every statist logic is to accord unconditional preeminence to the part—that is, to the fragment—even at the risk of survival.

We can never be sure when latent possibilities for profound change in the political order will be realized: almost every revolution in history has taken its leaders by surprise. The old order suppresses all acknowledgements of its fragility through its extensive control over ideological space. The seriousness of challenges is ignored, denied, belittled— especially as they mount against established authorities. Today, we have the opportunity to reinvent democracy, and once more make the state serve the well-being of citizens. We cannot hope to remove the nuclear threat, or even to reduce it drastically, without reconceiving citizenship and revitalizing democracy.

A final cautionary note: these long-term goals are associated with transforming the state by rejecting the logic of military power as the essence of security. Such an undertaking need not displace more immediate efforts to moderate the dangers that this logic produces. It can be useful to work against MX, Star Wars, or Trident II, or on behalf of some forms of arms control. But these activities must not foster the grand illusion that we can get rid of the nuclear threat without liberating the state from militarism. Nor can we achieve these ends without a great new surge of political imagination in the direction of revitalizing democracy through determined initiative expressive of societal demands for a peaceful world.

3

Disengaging Europe from the Superpowers

Mary Kaldor

Mikhail Gorbachev, who was soon to become the new leader of the Soviet Union, visited Britain in December 1984. He was warmly welcomed by the media, and Prime Minister Thatcher announced that she liked him and could "do business with him." The same week, the *New Statesman* disclosed official British regulations which would allow guards at nuclear bases to shoot unarmed antinuclear protestors. Moreover, during 1984, members of the independent peace organization in the Soviet Union, the Moscow Trust Group, had been severely harassed.

How do we explain this paradox? How can these two leaders be so friendly when they are, at the same time, presiding over a momentously dangerous increase in the nuclear weapons pointed at each other's territory? And when both sides are busy suppressing those who oppose this dangerous increase?

The orthodox Western justification for nuclear weapons holds that there exists an inevitable conflict between freedom and totalitarianism. Without the horrifying threat of nuclear weapons, totalitarianism, in the form of the Red Army, would invade the free West. A milder version holds that, without the threat of nuclear weapons, totalitarianism would exert an insidious political pressure. The orthodox Soviet justification for nuclear weapons is not so very different: the inevitable conflict is between socialism and Western imperialism, and only Soviet nuclear and conventional weapons hold in check the expansionist tendencies of Western imperialism. Both sides draw heavily on the experiences of World War II and justify preparedness in terms of the lessons of 1939 and 1941.

These views of the East-West conflict rest unhappily with détente or peaceful coexistence, as it is known in the East. How can we reconcile the easing of East-West tensions and the reality of superpower cooperation with the inevitability of conflict? How can we explain the need not only to maintain but to increase the threat of extinguishing humanity if the enemy no longer appears to embody absolute evil? The notion of mutual vulnerability, on which the premise of détente and arms control is based, presupposes a kind of rationality and stability on the part of the nuclear powers that is completely at variance with the rationales for possessing nuclear weapons.

An alternative explanation of the East-West conflict might more readily account for these puzzles. It would treat these orthodox views as a form of ideology which serves to cement the two spheres of influence established by the superpowers after World War II. The system of permanent armament and the fear of an external enemy can be seen as a way of preserving the kind of social cohesion that the Allied governments experienced in wartime. In a sense, nuclear deterrence could be described as a simulation of war; military exercises, hostile propaganda, and nuclear war scenarios are a kind of psychological spectacle that substitutes for the reality. This is, more or less, what George Orwell described, in stark terms, in *1984*: "War . . . is now a purely internal affair. . . . The object of war is not to make or prevent conquests of territory but to keep the structure of society intact. The very word 'war' has become misleading. It would probably be more accurate to say that by becoming continuous, war has ceased to exist."[1]

Of course, there are important asymmetries between East and West. In the West, NATO is based on voluntary cooperation between the United States and European governments and, at least in northwestern Europe, these governments were popularly elected. It was different, however, in southern countries of Europe. Andreas Papandreou, for example, has described Greece in the 1950s as "almost technically a colony";[2] his father was deputy prime minister, but his signature was not valid unless countersigned by the head of the U.S. economic mission. Today, perhaps the most brutal violations of human rights in Europe are taking place in Turkey, and in the minds of many Turks this repression is aided and abetted by NATO.

The situation in Eastern Europe is much more comparable with that of Southern Europe. The Soviet role is maintained through direct military force, such as the interventions in Hungary and Czechoslovakia, and, especially during the 1950s, through brutal forms of internal repression. Giangiacome Migone has characterized this difference between the U.S. and Soviet roles as a difference between hegemony and domination.[3] Hegemony is based on consent and domination on coercion.

There are also differences in U.S. and Soviet interests. It is probably true that, at least technologically, the West has initiated important new rounds of the arms race. I would argue that this is because the arms race has, in the West, its own autonomous dynamic, stemming from the relationship among the armed services, the laboratories, and the private manufacturers of arms. Likewise, the Western system is *economically* expansionist. Thus the need to provide a framework for the free movement of investment and trade and to prevent the kind of economic warfare experienced in the 1930s was an important factor in the consolidation of the U.S. sphere of influence — an interest shared by West European allies.

Soviet concerns have been much more defensive. There is considerable inertia in the Soviet military system, and therefore considerable resistance to cutbacks or reductions in armaments. (Khrushchev has described this phenomenon in his memoirs.) But by the same token, there is not much pressure for innovation or technological change. New Soviet military technologies are nearly always responses to military technical changes in the West. Also, having experienced the direct consequences of invasion, the Soviets, at least initially, viewed Eastern Europe as a security belt separating their territory from the West.

It is also the case that the Soviet Union was concerned not only about Western armies but also about Western ideas and products. Stalin regarded the creation of a "socialist world market" as one of the most important consequences of World War II because it relieved the Soviet Union, at least for a while, of the necessity of trading with the West, especially for advanced technology. Maintaining control of the security belt has, of course, become a concern in itself, and fears about the spillover effects of internal changes in Eastern Europe are increasingly cited as a reason for the continued Soviet presence. Nevertheless, it is probably correct to describe the Soviet role in Europe as both more defensive or reactive and more coercive than the U.S. role in Western Europe.

The Cold War and détente can be seen as different ways of managing East-West relations on the basis of existing spheres of influence. Détente was seen as a way of reducing the risks of war. Soviet writers have described peaceful co-existence as a way of channeling the conflict into nonmilitary forms of competition. Détente was a kind of mutual guarantee of noninterference in each other's spheres of influence. The Basic Principles of Détente, agreed on by Soviet and U.S. leaders in 1972, stipulated that nations must:

> Prevent the development of situations capable of causing a dangerous exacerbation of their relations,
>
> Do their utmost to avoid military confrontation,
>
> Recognize that efforts to obtain unilateral advantages at the expense of the other, directly or indirectly, are inconsistent with these objectives.[4]

Détente also provided the conditions for arms control, which was seen as quite different from disarmament. It was a way of controlling the most destabilizing aspects of the arms race and channeling it into less dangerous and perhaps mutually advantageous directions. The problem was that precisely because détente removed the immediacy of the threat of war, it was much more difficult to maintain the cohesion of the bloc system in Europe or to justify the continued arms race.

It is no coincidence, in my view, that the height of the Cold War was also the period of McCarthyism in the West and Stalinism in the East. Détente ushered in a period of looser relationships within the blocs. In the West, this allowed for greater independence of West European governments vis-à-vis the U.S. government and for the emergence of new social movements in Europe, of which the most important was the peace movement. By the late 1970s, after the end of the Vietnam War and the signing of the Helsinki agreements, it was much more difficult to believe in the Soviet threat and the necessity for warfighting nuclear weapons in Western Europe.

In Eastern Europe, détente allowed for limited degrees of pluralism. This was not an inevitable consequence of the weakening of external coercion. Rather, it depended on each country's internal conditions. Czechoslovakia, for example, experienced much tighter domestic controls than formerly. Rumania, which took a very independent stance regarding the Warsaw Pact, has one of the most authoritarian and repressive systems within the Pact. On the other hand, in Hungary, Bulgaria, East Germany, and Poland, there were varying internal pressures for change. The emergence of Solidarity in Poland represented the first mass movement in Eastern Europe since World War II. And it was because Solidarity was a mass movement that the Soviet Union did not directly invade Poland, as it had done in Hungary and Czechoslovakia. In those two states it had been a matter of getting rid of the government; getting rid of Solidarity was much more difficult.

Growing understanding of the connections between internal control and external conflict, I believe, was what led to the emergence of independent peace groups in Eastern Europe and the increasing concern of human rights groups—like Charter 77 in Czechoslovakia—with peace questions. "We are more afraid of Cold War than of nuclear war," wrote one young Hungarian peace activist.[5] For him, Reagan Administration nuclear-war-fighting policies could mean a return to the Cold War and to the state terrorism of the 1950s.

The new Cold War of the early 1980s can be viewed as an attempt, albeit unsuccessful, to reestablish cohesion in both blocs. The deployment of cruise and Pershing II missiles in Western Europe was explicitly seen as a way of increasing the "visibility" of the U.S. nuclear presence, and hence "recoupling" Western Europe and the United States. The argument was that deployment would "reassure" Europeans that the United States would come to their aid in the event of a Soviet attack on Western Europe, as it had in 1942. To many Europeans, the implication was that they ought to be worried about the danger of war and should recognize their dependence on the United States and behave more gratefully.

Deployment of cruise and Pershing II and the imposition of martial law in Poland in December 1981 provided a kind of mutual legitimation. Moreover, the so-called Soviet counterdeployment of SS-21s and SS-23s in East Germany and Czechoslovakia provided an excuse to harass independent peace activists. It is worth noting that this was the first time the Soviet Union had publicly announced the presence of nuclear weapons in Eastern Europe. This could represent a shift, in the wake of the Polish events, away from coercion based on direct military force, and toward what might be described as the kind of ideological coercion, based on the fear of nuclear war, that characterizes U.S.-West European relations.

But the new Cold War is simply less convincing than the old Cold War. The memory of World War II and the gratitude to the superpowers for liberating Europe from fascism has faded. Consciousness of the effect of nuclear war has grown. Moreover, opposition movements themselves no longer think in bipolar terms. For the left in Western Europe, the Soviet Union no longer represents a model of socialism; indeed with the growth of movements for peace, ecology, or women's liberation, socialism itself no longer seems so relevant. In Eastern Europe independent groups for peace or human rights increasingly recognize that freedom has been violated in places like Turkey and Central America and do not advocate a return of the capitalist system. What is more, détente has been institutionalized; it is difficult to do away with arms control machinery, East-West trade, and the like.

This is the paradox of the current security system in Europe: the difficulty of simulating a continued war situation and the growing need to do so in order to bypass or overcome internal tensions. The way to deal with those who oppose government policy—antinuclear protestors or miners—is to show that somehow they are undermining national security and that they can be identified, in direct or indirect ways, with the Soviet threat. But where is the Soviet threat? Last December, it was having dinner with Thatcher at Chequers, her country residence.

If we wish to maintain and to deepen détente, in the sense of permanently relaxing the tension between East and West, then, according to my analysis, there must be a gradual erosion of the bloc system in Europe and a disengagement of European nations from the superpowers. If internal cohesion requires external conflict, then overcoming the conflict means less cohesion; it means acceptance of diversity. A useful term to describe this process of disengagement is "dealignment."

Dealignment differs from neutrality in that it is a policy of "beyond the blocs" rather than "between the blocs." Neutrality may depend on the continued existence of the bloc system; some Swiss and Swedish military experts, for example, consider that their security depends on an East-West military balance. Dealignment is more akin to nonalignment, a Third World concept, in that it aims to increase the domestic space for maneuver, to increase the accountability of governments to their citizens, rather than to the superpowers or to multinational organizations like NATO or the Warsaw Pact.

Accountability to the citizenry is currently denied in Europe primarily as a result of military, especially nuclear, relationships. For example, the decision about whether or not to start a nuclear war would be taken in Washington or Moscow. This represents an extraordinary abrogation of national sovereignty, even though European governments may have consented. (Actually, with a few exceptions, the decision to place nuclear weapons on European territory was taken without public knowledge.) The decision to go ahead with the deployment of cruise and Pershing II, despite vociferous and articulate opposition, supported by majority opinion in all five deployment countries, indicated that West European governments felt a greater sense of responsibility toward the requirements of NATO unity than to domestic public opinion.

Dealignment means a cooperative, not confrontative, relationship with the superpowers. It does *not* mean the creation of a new military bloc in Europe, with the substitution of British and French nuclear weapons for U.S. ones, because the cohesion of such a bloc and the legitimacy of nuclear weapons could be maintained only through continued external confrontation. What it does mean is a lessening of the military element in the relationships among nations.

Dealignment does not necessarily mean withdrawal from the formal military alliances, but it does mean changing the *content* of those alliances. Countries like Denmark and Greece which are dissenting from NATO's nuclear policies, or like Rumania and Hungary in the East, may be more dealigned than a country like Switzerland or even France, which is formally outside NATO's military structure. Policies aimed at nuclear disarmament or the withdrawal of foreign troops and bases are fundamentally strategies of dealignment because they challenge the content of the alliances.

In a way, dealignment may be seen as a way of reconceptualizing disarmament strategies. Unilateral nuclear disarmament measures or nuclear-free zones are important—not because they are arms control measures but because they represent a form of abstention from the simulation of war. The original rationale for unilateralism was that, since multinational arms control talks had failed to achieve anything, we should start to reduce arms independently. Today it is increasingly recognized that in case of nuclear war *all* countries will be engulfed.

The usefulness of a disarmament measure depends on whether it can ease the tension that could lead to war. Multinational arms control measures are predicated on the continued existence of the blocs, on the "balance" that exists between the two sides in a simulated war, and on preserving mutual vulnerability. But the point of a unilateral or independent disarmament measure is to get away from the notion of sides. It helps to loosen the relationship with the superpowers and this, in turn, weakens the ritual of East-West confrontation.

The fact that the Soviet relationship with Eastern Europe is both more defensive and more coercive than is the U.S. relationship to Western Europe gives rise to both optimistic and pessimistic assessments of Moscow's reaction to unilateral disarmament measures. Because the Soviet Union is defensive or reactive, it is more likely than not to reciprocate. On the other hand, the fact that it is more coercive means that independent actions on the part of East European countries, and hence the prospects for reciprocal dealignment, are much more tightly circumscribed. Greater pluralism in Eastern Europe—say, the legitimation of independent peace groups—would therefore be a much more meaningful reciprocal response than an equivalent disarmament measure.

Détente cannot be sustained unless the erosion of spheres of influence is allowed to continue. The danger is that the superpowers could resort to more and more extreme ways of reestablishing their positions, to more and more realistic simulations of war. Pressures for internal change are growing in both halves of Europe. The problem is how to accommodate change without threatening war.

Dealignment expresses a process in which disengagement from the superpowers through denuclearization and demilitarization, détente, and self-determination for European nations are mutually reinforcing conceptions. A dealigned Europe would be one in which respect for diversity and tolerance for different political systems replaced the rigid, two-sided, good-bad view of conflict inherited from World War II.

1. George Orwell, *1984* (London: Penguin Books, 1954 edition), p. 160.

2. Interview, *END Journal*, no. 2 (February-March, 1983).

3. Giangiacome Migone, "Understanding Bipolarity," in R. Falk and M. Kaldor, eds. *Dealignment for Western Europe* (forthcoming).

4. Department of State Bulletin (June 26, 1972).

5. Janos Laszlo, "I Do Have the Right to Make My Voice Heard," *END Journal*, no. 3 (April-May, 1983).

4

Reducing U.S. and Soviet Nuclear Arsenals

Harold A. Feiveson, Richard H. Ullman, and
Frank von Hippel

The almost total absence of discussion of alternative futures that has characterized the nuclear weapons debate was first broken by the freeze movement and then by President Reagan's 1983 Strategic Defense Initiative ("Star Wars") proposal. Thus far, six basically different alternative nuclear futures have been discussed:

The abolitionist vision would completely eliminate nuclear weapons.

The president's vision would effect a transition to a "defense-dominated" world in which increasingly effective defenses result in offensive systems' withering away.

An arms race unconstrained by the 1972 Anti-Ballistic Missile (ABM) Treaty would maintain the mutual hostage relationship of the United States and the Soviet Union by the continuing dominance of offensive nuclear weapons systems.

A constrained arms race would proceed more or less along current lines — constrained by the ABM Treaty and by modest SALT II-type limitations on some categories of offensive nuclear weapons.

A tightened arms-control regime or freeze would take SALT II as its starting point to put stringent limits on the strategic arms competition, but would leave both superpowers with nuclear forces not much reduced in quantity or variety from those they now possess.

Finite deterrence would couple very deep reductions in the superpower nuclear arsenals — but not enough to put in doubt their mutual hostage relationship — to severe constraints on the development and deployment of first-strike and ABM technologies.

The first two alternatives would represent radical departures from the current "balance of terror." The third would represent the breakdown that many fear is imminent in the current arms control regime. The last three represent attempts to rationalize the current situation.

Both radical alternatives will remain infeasible for the foreseeable future. Although we hope that abolition will ultimately be feasible, so many difficult issues would have to be dealt with that intermediate goals are required. The president's notion that nuclear weapons can be made "impotent and obsolete" by a unilateral U.S. technical fix is technologically impossible, and the effort to move toward a defense-dominated world will only lead to the third alternative: an all-out offense-defense arms race.

Of the proposals to rationalize the current situation, an interim freeze on new nuclear weapons would probably be an essential prerequisite to a comprehensive scheme of reductions. Beyond that, however, only the finite-deterrence alternative provides a rationale for reducing the current scale of the superpower arsenals. These arsenals, which contain tens of thousands of nuclear weapons, are completely out of correspondence with the reality of the world that nuclear weapons have created: they cannot be used without great risk of triggering the murder-suicide pact that binds East and West together.

The adoption of finite deterrence would make possible a 10-fold reduction of the superpower nuclear arsenals and the elimination of their most destabilizing and dangerous weapons. Thus, it could transform the relationship between the United States and the Soviet Union, reducing the dangerous fantasies and paranoia that feed and are fed by the arms race and making it much easier for them to build the foundations for a more satisfactory *modus vivendi.*[4]

The idea of finite or minimum deterrence goes back at least to the later years of the Eisenhower Administration, when it was advocated by the U.S. Navy. During the Kennedy Administration, Jerome Wiesner, the president's science adviser, argued that the United States required only a few hundred survivable nuclear weapons. And at about the same time, the Soviet Union was offering disarmament proposals which were compatible with this approach.[2]

However, even as the Navy was arguing that 232 survivable Polaris missiles would be "sufficient to destroy all of Russia," the Strategic Air Command was putting on its target list 645 airfields from which Soviet strategic bombers might be launched, and thousands of tactical nuclear weapons were being deployed to Europe. By the mid-1960s, the U.S. arsenal contained approximately 30,000 nuclear weapons —

slightly more than today's. The Soviet arsenal grew to comparable levels during the 1970s.

Neither the United States nor the Soviet Union seriously pursued a finite deterrence posture—on the U.S. side, principally on the grounds that nuclear weapons must be available for counterforce targeting, that is, for striking at military targets as a deterrent to Soviet aggression. Each side has also sought the ability to mount preemptive strikes to reduce the nuclear threat from the other.[3] Finite deterrence has also been criticized for resting upon "incredible" and "immoral" threats to destroy cities in order to deter attacks on other targets. Critics have also raised concerns that if nuclear arsenals were much smaller than those of today, they might be more vulnerable to neutralization by surprise attack or technological breakthrough. These concerns may best be addressed by discussing a concrete example.

The table on the following page shows an illustrative finite deterrence force and compares it with current superpower nuclear arsenals.[4] This may not be the best possible finite deterrence force. A strong argument can be made, for example, that the United States should take advantage of the relative invulnerability of its submarine-based forces and shift *all* of its ballistic missiles to sea. Furthermore, the superpowers might—for organizational or other reasons—choose very different mixes of nuclear weapons within overall arsenals of approximately equal size. (Such questions will be addressed in future studies by the Princeton Project on Finite Deterrence.)

The key changes in the transition from the current nuclear arsenals to the finite-deterrence force in the table are:

Strategic warheads have been reduced by about 80 percent (from about 10,000 to 2,000), in large part by replacing multiple-warhead with single-warhead missiles.

Intermediate-range nuclear weapons have been largely eliminated, although some land-based missiles might be located in Europe.

Tactical nuclear weapons have been eliminated.

The resulting force is therefore quite similar to one that would be obtained by stripping the current force of its most destabilizing elements.

The destructive capacity of the finite-deterrence force is fixed by assuming that each of the warheads in the finite-deterrence arsenal has a yield of 100 kilotons. That yield is at the low end of the range of warhead yields in the current strategic arsenals of the superpowers, but it is approximately eight times larger than the yield of the bomb that destroyed Hiroshima. Such a warhead could destroy, by blast

U.S. AND SOVIET NUCLEAR ARSENALS IN 1985 AND IN AN ILLUSTRATIVE FINITE-DETERRENCE (FD) REGIME

	Missiles or bombers			Warheads		
	United States	Soviet Union	FD (each side)	United States	Soviet Union	FD (each side)
LONG- AND INTERMEDIATE-RANGE						
ICBMs	1,023	1,398		2,126	6,420	
Intermediate-range missiles (land-based ballistic and cruise)	104	534	500[a]	104	1,362	500[a]
Submarine–launched ballistic	690	967	500	5,728	2,887	500
Long-range bombers	297	300	200	3,334	600	1,000
SUBTOTALS	2,114	3,199	1,200	11,292	11,269	2,000
OTHER WARHEADS						
Artillery shells				2,400	900	0
Antisubmarine warheads				2,000	600	0
Antiship cruise missile warheads				0	1,000	0
Battlefield ballistic missile warheads				300	1,600	0
Anti-aircraft missile warheads				200	300[b]	0
Anti-ballistic-missile warheads				0	32	0
Atomic demolition mines				600	some	0
Nonstrategic bombs				4,000	4,000	0
OVERALL TOTAL WARHEADS[b]				20,792	19,701	2,000

and fire, an area of about 50 square kilometers (20 square miles), containing, in a typical large urban area, about 100,000 people. Several such warheads in the illustrative arsenal could be targeted against *every* U.S. and Soviet city with a population of over 50,000.

Figure 1 shows the results of calculations done in 1967 for Secretary of Defense Robert McNamara of the percentage of the estimated 1972 Soviet urban population that could be killed and industrial capacity destroyed as a function of the "equivalent megatonnage" used.[5] The fatalities shown at a given level of equivalent megatonnage are significantly lower than *could* occur. Many effects—including those of radioactive fallout and the impacts of the destruction of the economy on the rural and surviving urban populations—appear to have been neglected. Only about 50 equivalent megatons would be required to destroy by blast and fire about one half of the urban area of the Soviet Union or a comparable area in the United States.[6] Since a 100-kiloton warhead has approximately 0.2 equivalent megatons⋆ destructive power, if each warhead in the 2,000- warhead illustrative finite-deterrence arsenal had a 100-kiloton yield, the arsenal's total destructive power would be almost 400 equivalent megatons.

This article addresses a series of questions about this finite-deter-

---

⋆The area that could be subjected to a certain level of blast overpressure varies as the two-thirds power of the yield (Y) of a nuclear weapon. This fact is captured by measuring the potential area-destructiveness of a nuclear warhead by its "equivalent megatonnage," $Y^{2/3}$. The equivalent megatonnage of a nuclear warhead with less than one-megaton yield is larger than its megatonnage. Above one megaton, the situation is reversed.

---

[a]Some of the 500 land-based missiles in the finite-deterrence arsenal might be intermediate-range ballistic or ground-launched cruise missiles.
[b]Not including reloads

Sources: For strategic weapons: U.S. Department of Defense, *Soviet Military Power, 1984* (Washington, D.C.: Government Printing Office, 1984), pp. 24, 26; U.S. Department of Defense, *Report of the Secretary of Defense, Caspar W. Weinberger, to the Congress, 1986* (Washington, D.C.: Government Printing Office, 1985), Chart III.E.4 and Appendix C. For U.S. forces, we assume 10 warheads per Poseidon, eight per Trident I, eight bombs and short-range attack missiles on all 241 B-52G/Hs and six on each of the 56 FB-111s, and 12 air-launched cruise missiles on each of the 90 B-52G bombers. For Soviet forces, we assume four warheads per SS-17, 10 per SS-18, six per SS-19, seven per SS-N-18, nine per SS-N-20. We do not include Soviet bombers assigned to naval aviation, and we assume an average of two bombs and/or attack missiles per bomber, based on Senate Committee on Armed Forces, *Department of Defense Authorizations for Appropriations for FY 1985: Hearings*, 98th Cong., 2d sess., Feb. 1, 1984, p. 123.

For intermediate-range missiles: *New York Times*, April 14, 1985, p. E1.

For other nuclear weapons: Nuclear Weapons Databook Staff, in *World Armaments and Disarmament: SIPRI Yearbook, 1985* (London: Taylor and Francis, 1985).

FIGURE 1. POTENTIAL CONSEQUENCES FROM BLAST ALONE IN AN ALL-OUT ATTACK AGAINST SOVIET CITIES

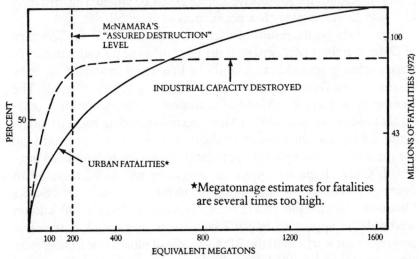

The fatality levels shown could result from a much lower level of equivalent megatonnage.

Sources: Robert S. McNamara, *The Fiscal Year 1969-73 Defense Program and the 1969 Defense Budget* (Washington, D.C.: Department of Defense, 1969). The fatality levels shown could result from a much lower level of equivalent megatonnage: see Frank von Hippel, "The Effects of Nuclear War," in David W. Hafemeister and Dietrich Schroeer, eds., *Physics, Technology and the Nuclear Arms Race* (New York: American Institute of Physics, 1983).

rence force: Would a commitment to finite deterrence brake the arms race dynamic? Is it moral? Would it deter? Would it be stable? Would it be adequately verifiable? And is it realistically achievable?

The nuclear arms race is driven largely by attempts to make nuclear weapons more "usable" and to develop combinations of first-strike and defensive capabilities that would make possible escape from the mutual hostage relationship. But no matter how technically sophisticated nuclear weapons systems have become, the mutual hostage relationship has made them unusable and that relationship itself has proved to be very robust.

Figure 2 illustrates this situation dramatically. Despite the recent U.S. scare about a "window of vulnerability," during a crisis neither superpower could reduce the other's strategic arsenal by more than about half—far from the hundred-fold reduction required even to begin to loosen the grip of the mutual hostage relationship. Efforts to escape from hostage through defense appear similarly hopeless—so much so that the superpowers agreed in the 1972 ABM Treaty not even to try. And few independent analysts see any escape through new generations of counterforce weapons or the proposed Star Wars defenses.

Adoption of finite deterrence would require acceptance of the implications of the mutual hostage relationship and therefore a surrender of the illusions that drive the arms race. As Admiral Arleigh Burke, then chief of naval operations, argued almost three decades ago: if the superpowers abandoned the false hopes of "winning" through new counterforce or defensive systems, the rationale for new weapons would be greatly weakened.[7]

Mutual deterrence depends fundamentally on the possibility that any large-scale direct confrontation between the United States and the Soviet Union could lead to untold destruction. This is true both for current nuclear arsenals and for the finite-deterrence arsenal proposed in the table. In terms of this immense destruction, the threats implicit in both postures must be viewed as immoral. Nevertheless, some have argued that a finite-deterrence posture would be particularly immoral because its smaller size implicitly emphasizes the threat to cities.

To acknowledge that threat, however, is not to insist that cities be targeted in the event of a nuclear war. Nothing in the configuration of the illustrative finite-deterrence arsenal would require the targeting of population centers rather than, for example, military installations. Nuclear strategists currently can fantasize that thousands of nuclear weapons could be so used, but by the time even hundreds of them had been used against, for example, military targets in Central Europe, civilian fatalities would number in the millions, command and control networks would be collapsing, and the chances of limiting the war would be rapidly vanishing.[8] Under these circumstances, the moral distinction between targeting military facilities and targeting cities would have become nearly irrelevant.

Therefore, adoption of a finite-deterrence posture would in no way reduce the superpowers' abilities—if they so wished—to avoid mass slaughter in a nuclear war. It would simply strip away the dangerous self-deception that a war could be fought with thousands of nuclear warheads without destroying civilization. This realization is a moral *advantage* of the finite-deterrence posture. Moreover, to the extent that a finite-deterrence posture would reduce the probability of accidental nuclear war and, in the event of all-out nuclear war, would inflict less overall destruction—especially on noncombatant nations—it also has a moral advantage. The superpower allies would be attacked by many fewer warheads, noncombatant nations would receive much less radioactive fallout, and the global environment would be less severely altered by the effects of ozone destruction and smoke. (Such advantages, however, must not be offset by increasing the average yield of the smaller number of warheads.)

Political leaders understand that the mere possibility of catastrophe inherent in the mutual hostage relationship—not the details of the arsenals or the plans for targeting them—is what deters each superpower from threatening the vital interests of the other. McGeorge Bundy has termed this "existential deterrence."[9] As Bundy wrote during the great debate over anti-ballistic-missile systems in the late 1960s:

> Think-tank analysts can set levels of 'acceptable' damage well up in the tens of millions of lives. They can assume that the loss of dozens of great cities is somehow a real choice for sane men. They are in an unreal world. In the real world of real political leaders— whether here or in the Soviet Union—a decision that would bring even one hydrogen bomb on one city of one's own country would be recognized in advance as a catastrophic blunder; ten bombs on ten cities would be a disaster beyond history; and a hundred bombs on a hundred cities are unthinkable.[10]

The destructive capacity in the illustrative superpower finite deterrence arsenal, although one-tenth the size of today's, is, nevertheless, many times greater than that required to accomplish even an "unthinkable" level of destruction.

Of course, existential deterrence would also exist for what has come to be termed "extended deterrence"—that is, not merely of nuclear attacks against the United States, but also of non-nuclear attacks against U.S. allies, particularly in Europe. For its entire history, NATO has relied upon the threat posed by U.S. nuclear weapons to make up for what has always appeared to be an imbalance of conventional forces in favor of the Warsaw Pact. Indeed, most of the U.S. nuclear arsenal is justified ultimately not by the need to protect the United States itself against nuclear attack, but as a deterrent to Soviet aggression in areas of U.S. vital interest.

Yet, ever since the Soviet Union achieved a secure second-strike capability in the early 1970s, extended deterrence has been largely a matter of doctrine and faith. Indeed, the desire to make plausible the U.S. willingness to risk American cities for the sake of the European allies has been a powerful motive in the constant search for additional credible "nuclear options" and more "usable" nuclear forces.

Despite the elaboration of nuclear options, however, extended deterrence seems no more (and, indeed, no less) plausible today than it did, say, two decades ago. Now, as then, extended deterrence depends not upon any imbalance in nuclear capabilities but upon perceptions of relative willingness to risk nuclear war. If Moscow is now deterred from launching a conventional war in Europe because of its inherent uncertainty about whether the West would attempt to stem the tide with nuclear weapons, there is no demonstrable reason why the same deterrence would not apply if each side possessed 2,000 warheads.

The character and size of the illustrative superpower forces have been largely determined by the design requirement that the current degree of stability should exist after deep reductions. Despite the 90 percent reduction in the total number of warheads shown in the table, the number of U.S. "delivery vehicles" has only been reduced by about one-third. Assuming that Soviet nuclear forces would be reduced similarly, the U.S. finite-deterrence arsenal would be *less* vulnerable than the current arsenal because the Soviet Union would have available many fewer warheads per target for counterforce attacks. In addition, because of the deMIRVing, more than one ballistic missile warhead would be required to destroy one ICBM warhead on the other side.

Calculations such as those done for Figure 2 show that about half of the 2,000 warheads in the finite deterrence arsenal would survive a first strike. This result depends primarily on assumptions made about the percentages of bombers that would be on alert during a crisis and of ballistic missile submarines that would be at sea, not on the number of warheads used in the attack. Thus, even the great reductions envisioned here are not enough to destabilize the superpower strategic balance. That *would* occur if further reductions reached the point where such details as, for example, which side struck first or had more capable non-nuclear forces once again began to matter.

The survivability of the illustrative finite-deterrence arsenal could be further enhanced by making the single-warhead, land-based missiles mobile (if this could be done without making their numbers inadequately verifiable) and by distributing the single-warhead, submarine-launched missiles among a larger number of smaller submarines.

To discourage new threats to the stability of this situation, the establishment of a finite-deterrence regime should be accompanied by verifiable bans on the development of new types of weapons such as reentry vehicles that could "home in" on bombers in flight. Strict limitations on ballistic missile flight tests would severely hamper the development of such weapons and the pursuit of counterforce stra-

320   *Harold A. Feiveson, Richard H. Ullman, and Frank von Hippel*

FIGURE 2. THE FUTILITY OF COUNTERFORCE: CALCULATED RESULTS OF STRATEGIC COUNTERFORCE EXCHANGES, 1985 FORCES

These calculations assume that in a first strike the Soviet Union assigns two ICBM warheads to each U.S. Minuteman silo, that the United States assigns two Minuteman III warheads to each Soviet silo containing a MIRVed ICBM, and that 80 percent of the missiles so attacked are destroyed. It is also assumed that both sides are on generated alert with as many bombers on alert and ballistic-missile submarines at sea as possible. This figure is an update of one whose derivation is explained in greater detail in Harold A. Feiveson and Frank von Hippel, "The Freeze and the Counterforce Race," *Physics Today* (Jan. 1983), p. 36.

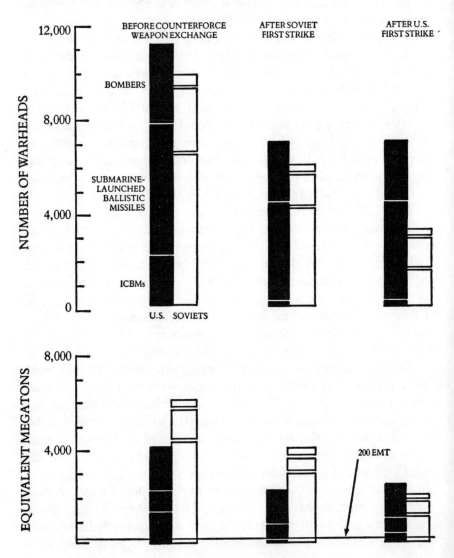

tegies more generally. Placing restrictions on the deployment of antisubmarine-warfare technologies would also be valuable.

Because the number of ballistic missile reentry vehicles that defenses would have to deal with would be greatly reduced, the importance of restraining defensive technologies would be increased. Therefore, the ABM Treaty should be strengthened in the gray areas where anti-tactical-ballistic missile and anti-aircraft defense capabilities overlap with anti-strategic-ballistic missile capabilities.

More worrisome than the vulnerability of nuclear weapons is the vulnerability of the superpower nuclear command-and-control systems. Even after completion of the current ambitious upgrade of the U.S.-command-and-control system, its designers believe that it could, at best, withstand an attack involving "a few hundred" nuclear warheads before losing positive control over the U.S. arsenal.[11] This mismatch between the number of weapons in the superpower nuclear arsenals and the survivability of the systems that direct them could raise pressures for preemptive use of the weapons before centralized control was lost, and would also encourage excessive decentralization of control during a crisis. "Decapitation" of either superpower's nuclear weapons system could well result in a globally catastrophic reflexive "spasm" attack: Deep reductions would not eliminate the vulnerability of command-and-control systems, but they would limit the number of warheads both that are available to attack them and that these fragile systems currently control.

Elimination of tactical nuclear weapons would also contribute to stability. The superpower armies and navies are now so thoroughly equipped with nuclear weapons for every purpose (about one nuclear warhead per one hundred military personnel on average) that there would be enormous risk of crossing the nuclear threshold in the event of any large-scale confrontation between the two militaries. This would derive from the myriad ambiguities and complexities inherent in the intermingling of conventional and nuclear forces on both sides, from the temptation to preemptively attack concentrations of nuclear arms, and from appeals from units about to be overcome to higher authorities to authorize use of their nuclear weapons.

The above discussion can be turned around to argue that the fragility of command and control and the nuclearization of tactical forces enhance deterrence by increasing the danger that any military confrontation between the United States and the Soviet Union might result in nuclear war. Such a prospect, no doubt, does help to instill caution on both sides. But beyond a certain point, rationalizing brittleness in this way becomes the irresponsible advocacy of deterrence by an all-purpose doomsday machine.

Another key criterion for the illustrative finite-deterrence force was that no credible level of undetected cheating could allow either super-power to remove itself from hostage. If the forces are as large as those suggested and are adequately survivable, then even the secret doubling of the strategic weapons available to one side would not significantly alter the mutual hostage relationship.

It appears that the most critical changes in the transition to a finite-deterrence regime—reductions in the numbers of long-range bombers and replacement of large multiple-warhead missiles by smaller single-warhead missiles—could be verified by nonintrusive means such as satellites. A ban on testing MIRVed missiles would be verifiable by long-range monitoring techniques and would, over time, erode confidence in the usability of any hidden stockpile of MIRVed missiles, especially for a first strike.

Although a 100-kiloton limit on the yield of nuclear warheads may not be verifiable (in this range, each additional kilogram of warhead weight can result in an additional yield of about one kiloton[12]), a limit in the range of a few hundred kilotons—a typical yield for the individual warheads on current multiple-warhead ICBMs—ought to be enforceable. This could be done by limiting the throw-weights of the new single-warhead ballistic missiles and the sizes of cruise missiles.

Some aspects of a finite-deterrence regime, however, would be more difficult to verify and would probably require cooperative verification arrangements. For example, on-site monitoring will be necessary to verify the dismantling of nuclear weapons and the "burning" of the recovered fissile material in nuclear power reactors and to ensure that nuclear power installations are not being used to produce fissile material for new warheads.

Small, mobile missiles could present serious verification problems since they would be much more difficult to count than current missiles which are relatively large and fixed in massive silos. This tradeoff has been left unresolved in the illustrative force. Sea-launched cruise missiles (SLCMs) pose a similar dilemma. Putting them on attack sub-marines would greatly increase the number of submarines armed with long-range nuclear delivery systems that would have to be destroyed in a disarming first strike. Their location and small size, however, would make them virtually impossible to count. As long as SLCMs are deployed, all attack-submarines and major surface ships will have to be assumed to be nuclear cruise-missile carriers.

The "denuclearization" of short-range systems such as fighter-bombers, sea-based and ground-launched cruise missiles, short-range ballistic missiles, and artillery would also be relatively difficult to verify. The systems themselves would still exist to fire conventional munitions, and the nuclear warheads, which are quite small, could be quickly delivered from secret stockpiles. Successful concealment of some nuclear warheads for short-range delivery systems would not, however, threaten the mutual hostage relationship.

A superpower transition to a finite-deterrence regime would affect other nations. Indeed, it would be critical to make the transition in a way that did not disrupt international relationships. For example, withdrawal of nuclear weapons from Europe would have to be done in a way that would give maximum reassurance to the Europeans. In fact, the accompanying table allows for the possibility that some intermediate-range land-based missiles might be based in Europe.

Complications would also arise in dealing with the "medium" nuclear powers—France, the United Kingdom, and China. Although the superpower arsenals—measured by numbers of delivery vehicles—would still be an order of magnitude larger than those of the medium powers, if France and the United Kingdom completed MIRVing their submarine-launched ballistic missiles (SLBMs), the Soviets would find arrayed against them a number of warheads far exceeding their own. Even if 2,000 warheads are enough to pose an effective deterrent against all these forces, the political appearance of such an imbalance might be unacceptable. For that reason it would almost certainly be necessary to induce these medium nuclear powers to limit the size of their forces. The Chinese government has stated that it would consider constraints on its nuclear forces if the United States and the Soviet Union cut back their nuclear forces by 50 percent.[13]

Such difficulties and the tremendous inertia of the arms race would have to be overcome if drastic reductions of the superpower nuclear arsenals are to be achieved. As a result of the debates over the nuclear weapons freeze and Star Wars proposals, however, the political conditions for a radical change in the current postures may be more favorable than they have ever been. The finite-deterrence proposal would also represent a solution to the problems that are stalemating current U.S.-Soviet arms control negotiations. The United States has been insisting upon reductions in the numbers of Soviet MIRVed land-based missiles, and the Soviet Union has been insisting that the United States not proceed with its Star Wars program. The finite-deterrence proposal, by eliminating MIRVed missiles and maintaining stringent limitations on anti-ballistic-missile systems, would meet both of these concerns.

The arsenal described here should be about as effective and survivable a deterrent as the current superpower arsenals. It should therefore be *technically* possible for either superpower to adopt a finite-deterrence position unilaterally. This would seem unrealistic *politically*, but, given the superpowers' vast excess of available nuclear forces, many of the steps toward a finite-deterrence regime could be taken independently. For example, NATO could unilaterally denuclearize a large part of its artillery and short-range missiles. Since the military value of these area-destruction weapons is increasingly being seen as marginal in an era of precision-guided munitions, there is already broad support for such a move.

Therefore while a transition to a finite-deterrence regime would be difficult, it should not be impossible. The result would still be a balance of terror with the same caution-inducing characteristics as the current regime—but with some of its overkill and its dangerous and mind-twisting complexity stripped away.

1. Richard H. Ullman, "Denuclearizing International Politics," *Ethics*, 95 (1985), pp. 567–88.

2. U.N. General Assembly, "Revised Draft Treaty on General and Complete Disarmament under Strict International Control," in *Documents on Disarmament, 1962*, p. 913.

3. Desmond Ball, *Targeting for Strategic Deterrence*, Adelphi Paper 185 (London: International Institute for Strategic Studies, 1983); David Holloway, *The Soviet Union and the Arms Race* (New Haven, Conn.: Yale University Press, 1983).

4. In a number of his talks, Richard L. Garwin has described finite-deterrence forces similar to the one discussed here.

5. Robert S. McNamara, *The Fiscal Year 1969–73 Defense Program and the 1969 Defense Budget* (Washington, D.C.: Department of Defense, 1968), pp. 50, 57.

6. Frank von Hippel, "The Effects of Nuclear War," in David W. Hafemeister and Dietrich Schroeer, eds., *Physics, Technology and the Nuclear Arms Race* (New York: American Institute of Physics, 1983), p. 1.

7. See, for example, David Alan Rosenberg, "The Origins of Overkill," *International Security* (Spring 1983), p. 3.

8. William M. Arkin, Frank von Hippel, and Barbara G. Levi, "The Consequences of a 'Limited' Nuclear War in East and West Germany," *Ambio* (June 1982), p. 163.

9. McGeorge Bundy, "Existential Deterrence and Its Consequences," in Douglas Maclean, ed., *The Security Gamble: Deterrence Dilemmas in the Nuclear Age* (Totowa, N.J.: Rowman and Allanheld, 1984), pp. 3–13.

10. McGeorge Bundy, "To Cap the Volcano," *Foreign Affairs* (Oct. 1969), p. 2.

11. Charles A. Zraket, "Strategic Command, Control, Communications, and Intelligence," *Science*, 224 (1984), p. 1306.

12. Thomas B. Cochran, William M. Arkin, and Milton M. Hoenig, *U.S. Nuclear Forces and Capabilities* (Cambridge, Mass.: Ballinger, 1984).

13. *New York Times*, June 22, 1983, p. 2.

5

Parallel Cuts in Nuclear and Conventional Forces

Randall Forsberg

For three decades, ardent arms controllers have urged the superpowers to widen the firebreak between nuclear and conventional war. For three decades, the superpowers have done just the opposite. They have maintained large "nuclear warfighting" forces: diverse nuclear arms, numbering in the tens of thousands, aimed at the opponent's nuclear and conventional forces, and threatening massive attacks on those forces in the event of an East-West conventional war.

Over half the superpower nuclear arsenals are allotted to naval, battlefield, tactical air, and intermediate-range systems. Dispersed among U.S., Soviet, and allied conventional forces, these weapons make it virtually impossible for the big powers to fight a conventional war without "going nuclear." Battlefield and naval nuclear arms strewn along the front lines of East-West confrontation in Europe, the Middle East, and Asia make small probes with conventional weapons risky. Tactical air and intermediate-range nuclear systems threaten deep strikes behind enemy lines in an all-out conventional war. Even strategic intercontinental nuclear weapons pose an escalatory threat. Aimed at nuclear forces and other military targets on superpower territory, they signal that the superpower homelands are not immune to nuclear attack in an escalating conventional war.

No U.S. administration or sizable fraction of the Congress has ever sought to create a firebreak between conventional and nuclear war, either unilaterally or jointly with the Soviet Union. The way to do so would be to adopt a minimum-deterrence strategy by renouncing the first use of nuclear weapons, abolishing the 30,000 shorter-range nuclear arms, and reducing the 20,000 strategic intercontinental weapons to a few thousand or less. Such cuts in the superpower arsenals, minimizing the risk of escalation, have been rejected in the United States by Democrats as well as Republicans and by their counterparts in other Western countries.

In response, arms controllers have tried to reduce the enormous arsenals gradually, with procurement restraints and bilateral arms agreements. Yet these efforts have also failed because there is no consensus on widening the firebreak. Robert McNamara, secretary of defense in the Kennedy and Johnson Administrations, limited U.S. ICBMs and SLBMs but approved development of MIRVs; President Jimmy Carter stopped the B-1 bomber by supporting cruise missiles. These and other programs have steadily increased U.S. and Soviet nuclear war-fighting options since 1960. They have provided growing numbers of increasingly accurate, low-yield, missile-carried weapons, which put more military targets at risk, with relatively less potential injury to populations.

If, as recent history suggests, it is impossible to build a consensus to widen the firebreak, there is only one other way to reverse the nuclear arms race: to make conventional war so unlikely that those who support large nuclear forces for conventional deterrence will no longer consider them necessary.

Most people think that the risk of conventional war among the big powers (the United States, the Soviet Union, the United Kingdom, France, West Germany, China, and Japan) is already extremely low. Many doubt, however, that it would remain low if nuclear weapons were greatly reduced. They fear an erosion of restraint, which would lead ultimately to World War II-type aggression, or to World War I-type unplanned escalation from a smaller conflict to a big-power conventional war.

Whether or not nuclear arms are actually needed to prevent big-power war, there is no doubt that they have made such a war not just unlikely but unthinkable as a deliberate policy choice. The risk of global destruction obliges the big powers to dismiss all thought of aggression against each other and to prevent escalation of crises. In the span of human history, this is an enormous change. People do not want to go back to devastating conventional wars every generation or so. Of course everyone would prefer to keep the peace without living under the shadow of a nuclear holocaust. But can conventional war be avoided if nuclear annihilation is not its likely penalty?

Minimum-deterrrence advocates believe that if nuclear weapons are needed at all to deter conventional war among the big powers, small nuclear forces would be adequate. Large nuclear forces do little more than small ones to deter conventional war, they argue, since the threat of a large-scale nuclear attack on military targets is not credible; no sane leader would order such an attack because it poses too high a risk of all-out nuclear war. Most important, moving toward minimum deterrence would reduce the risk of war by gradually replacing fear and hostility with a truly stable peace through nuclear cuts, conventional confidence-building steps, and increased trade, travel, and scientific and cultural exchanges.

Advocates of nuclear war-fighting forces disagree. Suppose that after theater nuclear arms are abolished and strategic forces are reduced to, say, 2,000 for each superpower (a 90 percent cut in the arsenals), East-West relations deteriorate, a crisis develops, and conventional war breaks out. That would be terrible in itself, they say; even worse, it could lead to nuclear war, for the losing side would try to use its nuclear arms to avoid defeat. Moreover, the loser would do so even if superpower arsenals were reduced to truly minimal levels — say, 200 each (a 99 percent cut). In fact, they continue, a conventional war or a crisis that could precipitate such a war is the most likely origin of a nuclear war. A few nuclear weapons might be exploded in peacetime as a result of human error, technical failure, terrorist action, or third-country war. But with diverse systems to prevent simultaneous false alarm or massive loss of control, it is hard to imagine hundreds or thousands of nuclear weapons ever being used except as the result of a deliberate order given during a war or when war seemed imminent.

Thus, they argue, to avoid nuclear war we must avoid both big-power conventional war, which would create enormous pressure to use nuclear arms, and a seemingly "war-winning" combination of nuclear offenses and defenses, which would invite preemptive nuclear attack by either side.

It is true, advocates of nuclear war-fighting forces say, that nuclear attacks on military targets could lead to the destruction of the attacker's society. But this simply means that the risk posed by large nuclear war-fighting forces is only slightly greater than the risk posed by small forces. Since nuclear war cannot be won, there is little incentive to use nuclear weapons in attacks on military targets; and the fact that such attacks could lead to all-out war is a strong barrier to them. In fact, they conclude, the risk of escalation posed by large war-fighting (but not war-winning) forces is just right for avoiding both routes to nuclear war: it is great enough to deter conventional war, yet limited enough not to invite preemptive nuclear attack.

Minimum-deterrence advocates respond that it would be much safer to deter conventional war with conventional forces. Advocates of war-fighting forces reply that since conventional forces already absorb 80 percent of U.S. and Soviet military spending (including overhead), nuclear cuts offset by stronger conventional forces would raise military spending. Moreover, if NATO strengthened its conventional forces, the Soviets would respond in kind, leading to an even more expensive conventional arms race. Most important, while stronger conventional forces might deter outright aggression, they would increase the risk of unplanned escalation from smaller conflicts to big-power conventional war.

Politicians in power and military and arms control experts tend to support nuclear war-fighting forces, while minimum deterrence advocates tend to be politicians out of power, retired officials, peace activists, and members of the public. Assuming that the reason for this is that the policy-makers are in the grip of vested interests, minimum- deterrence advocates try to create enough public pressure to outweigh these interests. This, they believe, will make the policy-makers support new policies, which professional analysts will then develop in detail.

This strategy keeps failing because it ignores factors other than vested interests which work to perpetuate the status quo. Members of the public are ambivalent about the choice between minimal and nuclear war-fighting forces. On the one hand, people are convinced that nuclear war cannot be survived, and they agree with critiques of vested interests, overconfidence in crisis control, and overkill. On the other hand, people do not want to make any changes that would increase the risk of war with the Soviet Union or reintroduce devastating conventional wars every generation.

Meanwhile, policy-makers and their advisers convince themselves that perpetuating the status quo is the safest course. Those in power are naturally reluctant to change nuclear policy. If retaining war-fighting forces leads to nuclear war, the responsibility is shared by many leaders in many countries over many years; if moving toward minimum deterrence leads to nuclear war, however, the innovator alone bears the burden. Policy-makers exaggerate their own ability and that of other leaders to maintain control in crises—inherently so, since it takes only one failure to prove the judgment wrong. Analysts reassure the policymakers that nuclear war-fighting policy is the moderate road between even more dangerous extremes: the war-winning extreme (supported by Colin Gray and Edward Teller), which increases the risk of preemptive nuclear attack; and the minimum-deterrence extreme, which increases the risk of conventional war and, indirectly, the risk of nuclear war. Policy-makers support arms control talks as added insurance against preemptive nuclear attack. The talks keep the superpowers away from the brink of war by underlining their mutual interest in avoiding nuclear war, maintaining dialogue, and insuring that neither side moves too close to war-winning forces.

The public's ambivalence and the policy-makers' rationalizations constantly reinforce each other. Members of the public, easily roused to oppose the arms race, are just as easily quieted by allusions to the need to be cautious in reversing it, so as not to raise the risk of conventional war or, as it is usually expressed, "encourage Soviet adventurism." Politicians fear that if they support steps to widen the firebreak, they will be labeled "weak on defense"—that is, weak on deterring conventional war with the Soviets. Convinced that preserving nuclear war-fighting forces is the safest course, especially if accompanied by regular arms control talks, both liberal and conservative politicians send the public a conservative message: policies that perpetuate the arms race with slight limits are the only safe choice for the near future. The frequent repetition of this message by leaders and experts of both parties deflates the public's hope for change, and the rapidity with which popular demands for change subside makes it risky for politicians to advocate change and safe to advise caution.

In order to break this cycle and mobilize sustained popular pressure for change, the benefits of a new military policy must greatly outweigh the benefits of the current policy in the minds of both the public and the policy-makers. In addition, many politicians and professional military and arms control experts must sincerely support the popular demand for change and vigorously reinforce it in the national media.

The experience of the last 30 years suggests that steps to widen the firebreak and move toward minimum deterrence cannot command the degree of public and political support needed to prevail. Such steps would offer one main benefit: they would reduce the risk of nuclear war in the event of a conventional war or a severe crisis. Against this point for change are three points for the status quo: it is probably cheaper, since nuclear cuts offset by conventional increases would raise military spending; it does more to deter big-power conventional war; and by deterring conventional war, it may do more to avoid nuclear war. Moreover, the idea of widening the firebreak implies that we may fail to avoid conventional war. People do not want to hear this. They want to believe that we can avoid both conventional and nuclear war.

Compared with widening the firebreak, an effort to make deep cuts in conventional forces before or simultaneously with reducing nuclear arms offers a far stronger case for change: it would greatly reduce military spending, the risk of conventional war, and the risk of nuclear war. Against this approach is just one serious obstacle: deep cuts in conventional forces would end the interventionary use of force. For wielders of power, ending intervention would entail a certain loss of power or control. For average citizens, however, this represents a benefit; those in large nations would not be sent to war in smaller ones, and those in small nations would be allowed to determine their own futures.

Both government policy and public behavior imply that the deepest roots of the nuclear arms race lie in the desire to avoid conventional war. If this is so, then to abolish nuclear war-fighting forces we must find other ways to make big-power conventional war unthinkable.

As long as NATO and Warsaw Pact countries maintain large conventional forces, it will be easy to imagine crises that could grow into an East-West conventional war. To make conventional war unthinkable, big-power conventional forces, with their threatening long-range potential, must be converted to small border guards with short-range, defensive (antitank, antiaircraft, and antiship) weaponry, suitable for defending national territory but not for aggression.

Conventional force reductions alone, however, are not the answer. Many people fear that during or after such cuts, one nation or another might rearm, either clandestinely or in an abrupt, overt "breakout." To build the trust needed even to begin reductions in conventional forces, the big powers, especially the United States and the Soviet Union, must end large-scale, unilateral military intervention in smaller countries. As long as the superpowers plan to retain conventional forces for intervention, they will not move toward deep cuts in these forces. Equally important, the practice of intervention precludes confidence in the conventional peace among the big powers. In fact, as long as the superpowers continue to intervene in areas where they do not risk escalation to nuclear war, they provide the strongest possible evidence for the conservative view that if it were not for the risk of a nuclear holocaust, sooner or later they would go to war with each other, as big powers have done throughout recorded history.

Ending superpower military intervention in smaller nations seems very difficult, but there are strong reasons to believe that it is possible:

The utility of force as a tool of power has been declining throughout the twentieth century, as populations have increasingly refused to be beaten, coerced, or intimidated into submission. Witness the end of colonialism, the failure of the superpower interventions in Vietnam and Afghanistan, the non-violent overthrow of the Shah of Iran, and the reluctance of the Soviet Union to send its troops into Poland. Ending big-power military intervention in Third World conflicts in particular would complete and formalize this trend.

If the United States and the Soviet Union renounced intervention, they and the other big powers could reduce their conventional forces to border guards, eventually abolish nuclear weapons, convert $700 billion a year to constructive human ends, and promote self-determination in the South and civil liberties in the North. From the point of view of real U.S. and Soviet interests, there is no comparison between these benefits and the trivial rewards of treating the world as a political chessboard.

Distinguishing between Europe and the Third World makes it possible to chart a politically feasible course to ending intervention. Since Moscow considers control of Eastern Europe vital to its defense, it will not renounce intervention there at an early stage in the process of building trust; and as long as the Soviets use force to dominate Eastern Europe, the West will retain the armed forces that feed Soviet fears, in a self-perpetuating cycle. This cycle can be broken by ending superpower intervention in the Third World, where the issues are not vital to the superpowers. If the United States and the Soviet Union renounce direct military intervention in the developing countries of Latin America, Africa, the Middle East, South Asia, and the Far East, the Soviets must withdraw from Afghanistan and U.S. troops must stay out of Central America and the Persian Gulf. Renouncing intervention as a way to control governments in these and other Third World regions would not put any truly vital interests at risk and would have a powerful effect in building trust.

Renouncing Third World intervention alone probably will not create enough trust for the Soviet Union to withdraw from Eastern Europe. Two additional steps could be taken, however, without prior trust and then sustained for 10 to 20 years, while trust builds, without increasing the risk of conventional war: a nuclear freeze, which would end advances in nuclear war-fighting capability, and a moratorium on production of large conventional weapons systems— long-range missiles, combat aircraft, naval ships, and tanks —with threatening long-range capability.

If the superpowers adopt a nuclear freeze and nonintervention policy, then over a decade the stability created by these steps should build enough trust to permit initial cuts in NATO and Warsaw Pact forces of, say, 10 to 20 percent. Over another decade, these cuts plus the freeze and nonintervention should build enough trust for the Soviets to restrict the grounds for their intervention in Eastern Europe to acts which pose a direct military threat, such as an alliance with the West.

When this degree of East-West trust and Soviet restraint has been established, NATO and Warsaw Pact conventional forces could be reduced to perhaps half their present size, and a 10-year moratorium could be placed on production of long-range conventional weapons systems. (The industries that produce such weapons would be put on standby and limited to the production of spare parts.) By keeping to the nuclear and conventional freeze and the nonintervention regime for another decade, NATO and Warsaw Pact nations should build enough trust to be able to replace their remaining long-range conventional forces with small border guards, equipped with short-range weaponry.

Throughout the process, as NATO and Warsaw Pact nuclear-capable guns, missiles, and aircraft are reduced, the stocks of nuclear munitions dispersed among the conventional forces would be drawn down. In the last step, when conventional forces are converted to border guards, the remaining theater nuclear arms would be abolished and strategic weapons reduced to minimum-deterrence forces. Eventually, when more years of peace have made big-power conventional war truly unthinkable, nuclear weapons could be abolished altogether.

Reducing both nuclear and conventional forces in a phased, long-term process differs from past approaches to arms control and disarmament in several important ways. Unlike arms control efforts, this approach offers many powerful incentives for change: not just reduced risk of nuclear war, but less incidence of conventional war, a way to abolish nuclear arms, global savings of $700 billion a year, self-determination for the Third World, and advances in civil liberties in both East and West.

Moreover, all parts of the world would gain something at each step in the process. The nuclear freeze would benefit both superpowers as well as the rest of the world by forestalling weapons that pull the nuclear tripwire tighter. Nonintervention would benefit both East and West by keeping the forces of both out of the Third World; and it would benefit Third World nations by promoting self-determination. NATO and Warsaw Pact conventional force reductions would promote civil liberties, decrease the risk of war, and release huge sums of money for domestic and Third World development. These powerful and diverse benefits can build a powerful political coalition, one sufficiently broad, committed, and sustained to overcome the vested interests that perpetuate the arms race.

Unlike past disarmament schemes, this approach adopts conservative assumptions about the tendency of the big powers to go to war and the use of nuclear arms in deterring conventional war. Before any arms reductions, it requires two extraordinary, confidence-building steps by the superpowers: a halt in the production of nuclear arms, and an end to intervention in the Third World. These initial measures reflect the judgment that steps toward deep cuts in nuclear arms will never be taken while the two sides continue to compete in producing improved types; and similarly that steps toward deep cuts in conventional forces oriented to Europe—a region of vital interest and the scene of wars for a millenium—will never be taken while the superpowers continue to use conventional forces in the Third World.

In addressing the East-West confrontation in Europe, this approach does not follow the traditional firebreak-widening recipe of ending "first use" policy, reducing or eliminating theater nuclear arms, and strengthening conventional forces. Instead, it proposes steps to reduce nuclear and conventional forces in parallel. Its final conservative or cautious aspect is to provide for the abolition of strategic and theater nuclear war-fighting forces only when there is enough trust and stability to limit NATO and Warsaw Pact conventional forces to border guards.

In addition to maximizing the benefits and minimizing the risks of policy change, this approach provides a way to change popular attitudes, so that a stable, disarmed peace will be possible. Each step in the process—the nuclear freeze, nonintervention, and confidence-building steps in Europe—requires a major public debate, leading to a decision to shrink the accepted roles of force in some way. Thus, the successive steps would gradually strengthen internalized constraints against the use of force. Eventually, the only use of force widely considered to be legitimate would be for national defense against external aggression. The spread and strengthening of internalized constraints against other uses of armed force are essential to making conventional war unthinkable.

The main obstacle to cuts in nuclear and conventional forces is the interventionary use of force. This remnant of imperialism makes the big powers rely on nuclear arms to keep the peace among themselves.

Ending it would pave the way to a more peaceful, productive, democratic world—and let us lift the shadow of nuclear war from our lives.

6

Prospects for Conventional Deterrence in Europe

John J. Mearsheimer

There has been peace in Europe for 40 years now. No crisis in Europe during that period, except possibly in Berlin, threatened to lead to war. Moreover, it is commonplace to hear defense experts of different political persuasions claim that they find it difficult to imagine circumstances under which the Soviets would strike into Western Europe.

Either of two general explanations can account for this remarkable stability. First, there has been and continues to be no political reason why the Soviets would even consider attacking. The second explanation rejects the notion that there has been no political rationale for Soviet aggression and argues instead that the Soviets have been deterred by the potential costs and risks of military action.

Considering how little we know about the Soviet Union, it is difficult to determine which explanation is the more apt. Nevertheless, NATO has a formidable military posture, well-suited to deterring the Soviets, should they think about moving against the Alliance. That deterrent posture is comprised of both nuclear and conventional forces, and, as I have argued elsewhere, NATO's powerful conventional forces could presumably thwart a Soviet blitzkrieg.[1]

NATO should be able to prevent the Soviets from winning a quick and decisive victory and then turn the conflict into a protracted war of attrition—in which the Soviets could not be confident of success. When one assesses the risks that the Soviets would face in a conven-

335

tional war against the Western alliance, as well as the tremendous threat associated with the presence of thousands of nuclear weapons in Europe, there is good reason to be highly confident about NATO's deterrent posture.

There is, to be sure, an influential body of opinion which argues that NATO's deterrent posture is flawed , with criticism directed at both the nuclear and conventional elements of that deterrent force. There appears to be, however, a widespread belief that there is a favorable outlook for improving NATO's conventional forces. This would be especially good news for those who support reduced reliance on nuclear weapons, although enthusiasm for improving the conventional balance is certainly not restricted to opponents of nuclear deterrence.

My purpose here is to examine the prospects for improving NATO's conventional deterrent. The analysis will not include an assessment of likely trends in the Warsaw Pact's force structure, the assumption being that the future will mirror the present. This assumption, however, should not ignore the possibility that the Soviets and their allies might find it difficult to maintain their present force levels. My principal conclusion is that it is very unlikely that there will be any improvement in NATO's conventional deterrent. In fact, there is reason to think that the conventional balance might shift against NATO in the decades ahead.

To determine what is necessary to improve NATO's conventional deterrent, one must have a theory of conventional deterrence, that is, a clear conception of the conditions under which an adversary is likely to go to war. Then, one can determine how to improve the conventional deterrent.

Deterrence is most likely to fail in a crisis if a potential attacker thinks that it is possible to win a quick and decisive victory.[2] It is unlikely that a state's decision-makers will opt for war if they envision a lengthy war of attrition—even if they believe that they will ultimately prevail. Rapid and decisive victories on the modern armored battlefield are the result of implementing a specific military strategy, the blitzkrieg. An examination of the principal armored wars of the past half century illustrates this point.

Consider, for example, the German victory against the Allies in May 1940 and the Israeli triumph in the Sinai in 1967—two of the most widely heralded military operations of the twentieth century. Both the Germans and the Israelis employed a blitzkrieg strategy. Most importantly for deterrence purposes, it was the *belief* that they could effect a blitzkrieg that led in each case to the decision to launch an offensive.[3] It seems reasonable to assume that the Soviets, who would be fighting on an armored battlefield that markedly resembles the battlefields of 1940 and 1967, would face basically the same calculations that confronted German and Israeli decision-makers.

The blitzkrieg is predicated on the assumption that the opponent's army is a large and complex machine, geared to fighting along a well-established defensive line. In that army's rear lies a vulnerable network, comprised of numerous lines of communication along which supplies as well as information move, and key nodal points at which the various lines intersect. Destruction of this central nervous system is tantamount to destruction of the army and is therefore the principal aim of the attacking forces.

Thus, a blitzkrieg is comprised of essentially two operations: the *breakthrough battle*, where the attacking forces pierce the defender's forward positions, and the *deep strategic penetration*, where the attacking forces wreak havoc in the defender's rear support network. To accomplish the first task, the attacker concentrates his armored forces at one or two specific points along the defender's front, hoping to achieve an overwhelming force advantage that will allow him to pierce the defender's forward line. Once the breakthrough is accomplished, the attacker seeks to avoid further contact with the defender's main body of forces and instead concentrates on driving as rapidly as possible into the defender's rear, severing lines of communication and destroying key junctures in the defender's command and control network.

The key question for our purposes is: how can NATO significantly improve its prospects of thwarting a Soviet blitzkrieg? There is only one answer: increase the number of its fighting units on the central front. NATO must build a larger force structure if it hopes to improve its conventional deterrent in other than marginal ways. This becomes clear when one considers what NATO must do to thwart a blitzkrieg:

First, the Soviets must not be allowed to pierce NATO's forward defenses. NATO's ability to prevent the adversary from winning a breakthrough battle will be largely a function of force-to-space ratios plus the ratio of opposing forces at those points of main attack. NATO's forward positions, in other words, must be manned by large numbers of units, so that individual units have to cover only small portions of the front, and so that the opponent cannot achieve decisive force advantages on the main avenues of attack. There is reason to believe that NATO is now in good shape on these counts.[4] Nevertheless, to achieve a truly robust conventional deterrent, NATO must increase the number of divisions it has deployed along the intra-German and Czech-German borders.

Second, if the Warsaw Pact should rupture NATO's forward positions, NATO needs powerful operational reserves that can prevent the Pact forces from effecting a deep strategic penetration. NATO must have units at the rear that can be moved forward to contain those attacking forces that pierce the forward defensive positions. Today, NATO has only small operational reserves; these must be significantly augmented if the prospects of halting a blitzkrieg are to be improved.

The outlook for increasing the number of NATO's fighting units, however, is not promising. In fact, there is good reason to believe that the size of NATO's standing forces will decrease in the years ahead. The principal reason is demographics. Virtually all of our European allies are facing very sharp drops in the size of their manpower pools.[5]

Consider the West German case. The *Bundeswehr,* which provides approximately 50 percent of NATO's ground forces on the central front, numbers 495,000 men. To support that force with the present conscription system, 225,000 conscripts are needed each year. There were 290,000 men available for conscription in 1982, thus creating a surplus of manpower. That figure, however, will drop to 225,000 by 1987 and will plummet to 140,000 by 1994.[6] These staggering figures mean that in a little over 20 years the size of the draft-age cohort in Germany will have been halved. Official German studies predict that with the present conscription system the *Bundeswehr* will shrink from 495,000 to 290,000 by 1995.

Germany can pursue a variety of measures that will enable it to maintain present force levels, but these steps will involve significant political and economic costs. The recent acrimonious debate over increasing the term of service for conscripts from 15 to 18 months highlights this point. It is difficult to imagine circumstances under which Germany will increase its force levels; it is much easier to envision at least some reduction.

Diminution of the *Bundeswehr* will undoubtedly have an adverse impact on the attitudes of the other West European countries which have severe demographic—not to mention economic—problems of their own. The Belgians, the British, and the Dutch will in all likelihood use any case of German reductions to justify scaling back their own force levels on the central front. The French, who are presently *reducing* the size of their conventional forces, are hardly likely to compensate for reductions by others.

That leaves the Americans, but if anything, there appears to be a growing sentiment in the United States to pull forces out of Europe.

The principal reason for this attitude is the belief that Europeans are not contributing enough to the NATO effort. Of course, any reductions in the size of the *Bundeswehr* or other European military forces is likely to exacerbate the problem by fueling that sentiment for "bringing the boys home." The reductions would probably not motivate Americans to come to the rescue of their beleaguered allies.

In sum, there seems little hope of increasing force levels in the decades ahead. Yet, in my view, this is the only way to improve significantly NATO's conventional deterrent. It is not surprising, in light of this depressing situation, that almost all of the proposals to enhance the conventional force posture in Europe focus on either changes in NATO strategy or technological solutions. These panaceas unfortunately hold little promise of improving NATO's prospects of thwarting a Soviet blitzkrieg.

NATO currently employs a strategy of forward defense. This calls for placing the majority of its forces along West Germany's eastern border, with the aim of preventing Warsaw Pact units from penetrating into West Germany. Many analysts argue that this is not the optimum strategy for defending against a blitzkrieg and that adopting one of three different strategies would markedly improve NATO's prospects of thwarting a Soviet blitzkrieg. Strategy, in effect, can be used as a cheap force multiplier. The three alternatives under debate are maneuver defense, area defense, and offense.

A maneuver defense calls for placing the majority of NATO forces in large operational reserves deployed in the depths of Germany. A small number of NATO units are deployed in forward positions to serve as a screening force and, in effect, to "escort" the attackers into the heart of Germany, where they are destroyed in large-scale mobile battles by NATO's powerful operational reserves. This defensive strategy is most clearly identified with the self-styled "military reform movement."

Area defense, sometimes referred to as "nonprovocative defense," calls for breaking up NATO's large-scale armored units and dispersing the manpower in small groups armed with precision-guided munitions and heavily supported by "smart" artillery. These very small units are then spread out across a wide belt of West German territory. The objective is to wear down the attacking forces as they attempt to drive through this heavily defended belt. Some variants of this strategy allow for a small number of armored forces, which can be used for limited counterattacks. This defensive strategy is most clearly identified with the German political left, which finds it attractive because it is virtually impossible to launch an offensive with an army comprised essentially of small bands of infantry.

Both of these alternative strategies have significant military drawbacks.[7] There is no need to outline them here, however, because both are unacceptable to the West Germans and therefore are not likely to be adopted. Specifically, successive West German governments have made it unequivocally clear that they will not countenance any strategy that allows the attacking forces to penetrate their territory. Obviously, the Germans want to stop a Warsaw Pact offensive right at their eastern border, and thus remain firmly wedded to forward defense.[8]

The third alternative—adopting an offensive strategy—certainly does not involve giving up German territory, at least in theory. The objective instead is for NATO to launch an attack deep into Eastern bloc territory immediately after the Pact begins its attack, on the theory that the best defense is a good offense. The military utility of this strategy is highly questionable, but again, there is no need to consider it in detail since it is also politically unacceptable to the West Europeans. They are firmly wedded to a defensive posture and categorically reject adopting an offensive strategy, which they see as highly destabilizing. NATO will thus have to make do with its strategy of forward defense.

There is considerable interest in relying on sophisticated new military technologies to shift the conventional balance in NATO's favor. Substituting technology for manpower is a time-honored solution which certainly has a rich tradition in the United States. Certain technologies, which have attracted a great deal of attention, are to be employed as part of a strategy commonly referred to as "deep strike." This strategy calls for NATO to develop and deploy esoteric new weapons which will enable it to strike at the Pact's second-echelon forces, far behind the battle front. Proponents assume that destroying the Pact's second-echelon forces will eliminate a critical element of the attacking force. Specifically, the key to success is to deny the Pact the reinforcements that it will need to exploit its initial victories along the forward edge of the battle area.

For a number of reasons, it is doubtful that the proposed technological solution can shift the balance in NATO's favor or compensate for any future shrinkage in NATO's fighting forces. First, there is the matter of technological feasibility. Proponents of this option tend to give the impression that the weaponry is effectively "sitting on the shelf" and that NATO only has to find the political will and economic resources to purchase it. In fact, the sophisticated weapons needed to implement a deep-strike strategy have not been developed yet. Moreover, almost all of these new technologies have experienced significant problems in the research and development process, so it is not at all certain that NATO will have the option of procuring this panoply of weapons.

Further, there is the question of how much the deep-strike option will cost. If the past is any guide, this sophisticated weaponry will carry a very expensive price tag. The United States, which is expected to be the principal producer (a point that is likely to cause significant political problems) has been plagued by cost overruns in its weapons acquisition process over the past decade.

Finally, there are reasons to doubt the military utility of a deep-strike approach. First, the Soviets will undoubtedly take measures to counter these new technologies, and the cost-exchange ratios that will attend this mini-arms race may not favor NATO. Second, a careful look at the historical record on deep interdiction reveals that it is a very complex undertaking where the *actual* results are usually not the *predicted* results. As a Rand study notes:

> One of the most important conclusions to be drawn from an unbiased examination of interdiction experience is that the outcomes seldom came close to the expectations of the interdiction planners. Even when an interdiction effort has been judged successful, the achievement has not infrequently been quite different from the original objective.[9]

Third, and perhaps most important, there is evidence that the Pact's second-echelon forces would not be very important for effecting a blitzkrieg. A study of successful armored offensives shows that the first-echelon forces conducted both the breakthrough battles and the deep strategic penetration. In the German victory of May 1940, for example, a mass of armored units under General von Kleist made the breakthrough in the Ardennes, and those same forces then immediately drove deep into the Allies' rear to immobilize the French and British forces.[10]

The Germans did not wait for a second echelon to exploit the breakthrough. Such a move would have wasted valuable time, during which the Allies would have shifted forces to cover the hole ripped in their line at Sedan.

If the Soviets are to score a quick and decisive victory in Europe, which will certainly be their objective, it will have to be accomplished by units massed at the breakthrough points. These are the first-echelon forces, and NATO should be primarily concerned with stopping them.

In short, these various panaceas hold little promise for NATO. There is only one way that the Western Allies can markedly improve the conventional balance, and that is by increasing the number of their fighting units. That will not happen, and, in fact, NATO is going to have a very difficult time merely maintaining its present size in the decades ahead.

Another reason why NATO is not likely to shift the burden of deterrence from nuclear to conventional forces is resistance from the European national security establishments, especially the Germans. European elites have long maintained that the best way to prevent a war in Europe is to insure that Soviet and U.S. decision-makers recognize the strong likelihood that a European conflict will escalate into a general thermonuclear war.

The Europeans fear a situation where the superpowers think it is possible to fight a conventional war or a limited nuclear war in Europe. Deterrence, they maintain, would then be greatly weakened because the superpowers could engage in a conflict that would spare their homelands. This is why the Europeans were so adamantly opposed, in the early 1960s, to abandoning massive retaliation and adopting flexible response. Thus the Europeans have a long-standing interest in "coupling" the U.S. nuclear deterrent to the defense of Europe.

The matter of coupling is especially vital to the Germans, whose territory will be the battleground in a European conflict and who have no nuclear weapons of their own that can serve as a deterrent. Instead, they rely on the U.S. "nuclear umbrella." Conventional deterrence is invariably seen by the Germans as a codeword for decoupling the U.S. nuclear deterrent from the defense of their homeland. They would undoubtedly accept some enhancement of conventional NATO forces, if it could be done at a reasonable price. But it is very unlikely that they would support an effort to improve markedly the conventional posture, simply because this would be seen as leading to decoupling. Other Europeans, as well as many Americans, would also resist a large buildup of conventional forces.

One might argue that since the uproar over the 1979 NATO decision to deploy Pershing II and cruise missiles in Europe, traditional European thinking about the great deterrent value of nuclear weapons is undergoing a radical transformation. The result would be European, and particularly German, willingness to do as much as possible to excise nuclear weapons from the deterrence equation.

This should mean that there will be support in Europe for conventional deterrence, but this is not a likely scenario. Although there is much unhappiness with NATO's deterrent posture, there does not appear to be enough dissatisfaction to overturn the status quo. Moreover, the status quo has many defenders, whose momentary silence should not be allowed to obscure their formidable political power. Finally, a move away from reliance on nuclear weapons will require NATO to strengthen its conventional forces so that they will be better able to assume their increased responsibilities. As previously emphasized, there appears to be no feasible way of accomplishing this goal.

It is difficult to see how NATO will be able to decrease its reliance on nuclear weapons in the remaining years of the twentieth century. In fact, if one accepts the purport of this analysis, it is likely that NATO will have to rely more heavily on nuclear deterrence in the years ahead.

1. John J. Mearsheimer, "Why the Soviets Can't Win Quickly in Central Europe," *International Security* (Summer 1982), pp. 3–39; Barry R. Posen, "Measuring the Conventional Balance: Coping with Complexity in Threat Assessment," *International Security* (Winter 1984–1985), pp. 47–88.

2. For a more extensive discussion of conventional deterrence, see John J. Mearsheimer, *Conventional Deterrence* (Ithaca: Cornell University Press, 1983), esp. chapter 2.

3. Ibid., chapters 4–5.

4. See works cited in note 1.

5. Gilbert Kutscher, "The Impact of Population Development on Military Manpower Problems: An International Comparison," *Armed Forces and Society* (Winter 1983), pp. 265–73. The Soviet Union and especially the East Germans also face demographic problems, but the Poles and the Czechs do not.

6. Commission on Long-Term Planning for the Federal Armed Forces, *Final Report* (Bonn: Federal Minister of Defense, June 21, 1982).

7. John J. Mearsheimer, "Maneuver, Mobile Defense and the NATO Central Front," *International Security* (Winter 1981–1982), pp. 104–22; Hew Strachan, "Conventional Defense in Europe," *International Affairs* (Winter 1984–1985), pp. 27–43. The latter article contains an excellent critique of area defense.

8. For a good example of West Germany's deep attachment to forward defense, see *White Paper 1983: The Security of the Federal Republic of Germany and the Development of the Federal Armed Forces* (Bonn: Federal Minister of Defense, 1983), esp. pp. 142–45, 158–62.

9. Edmund Dews and Felix Kozaczka, *Air Interdiction: Lessons from Past Campaigns,* Rand Note N-1743-PA and E (Santa Monica: Rand Corporation, Sept. 1981).

10. See Hans-Adolf Jacobsen, "Dunkirk 1940," trans. Edward Fitzgerald, in H.A. Jacobsen and J. Rohwer, eds., *Decisive Battles of World War II* (New York: Putnam, 1965), pp. 29–68.

7

Arms Control and the Year 2000

John H. Barton

Fourteen years ago President Nixon and Premier Brezhnev signed the SALT I strategic arms control agreement. In the year 2000, 14 years from now, we will look back at today's arms control negotiations from the same perspective. That future year is close enough to reflect trends now at work, yet distant enough to be shaped by unanticipated effects.

THE STRATEGIC MILITARY EVOLUTION

The strategic effects are the most predictable. Today's arms control negotiations will be seen as a success or a failure depending on whether they prevent the extension of the arms race into space.

Other possible accomplishments are relatively unimportant or unachievable; the negotiations can have little effect on overall force levels or expenditures by the year 2000. Under the most favorable conditions, there might be two arms control agreements in the next 15 years, each one reducing strategic forces by about 30 percent. At best, then, strategic force levels in 2000 might be half those of today. Conventional forces make up the largest part of the defense budget and are unlikely to be reduced equivalently. Hence, the largest possible defense budget savings are 15 to 25 percent, the number depending on one's degree of pessimism in projecting a non-arms-control budget. Even the largest of these reductions would not change the U.S.-Soviet relationship in any fundamental strategic or economic way.

345

What will be important is the future of the space technologies: anti-satellite weaponry (ASAT) and the Strategic Defense Initiative (SDI). Just as today's strategists look back at SALT I and regret the failure to control MIRVs, tomorrow's strategists will look back and see space as today's central issue. The space technologies, like MIRVs, are most effectively verified at the testing phase; they risk inducing strategic instability, thus making future arms control even more difficult.

It may already be too late. The Soviets have moved toward limited ASAT weaponry, and the United States has since moved toward more advanced ASAT weaponry. Because the United States is heavily dependent on satellites, it must be very confident of the verification of an ASAT agreement. Even existing ASAT systems may be advanced enough so that enormously intrusive and difficult verification would be needed to provide adequate confidence.

If it is not too late, both ASAT and SDI technologies should be controlled. ASAT is the riskier technology and the more immediate concern, because it threatens space-based reconnaissance, early warning, and communication systems. It therefore favors a first strike against these sensitive systems and greatly complicates strategic forces' command and control as well as the negotiation of future arms control agreements.

The SDI arguments depend on whether, as President Reagan urges, SDI can be a way to maintain nuclear peace by protection rather than by the threat of retaliation. If Reagan is right, SDI might be deployed sometime during the 1990s and, in the best of all worlds, the two superpowers could negotiate a smooth transition to strategic defense dominance around the year 2000. Another optimistic outcome would be for SDI to work only well enough to allow an effective defense of missile fields and thus to support the stability of traditional deterrence in the face of increasing missile accuracy.

Technologically, however, it is most likely that SDI will in fact work just well enough to create uncertainty about traditional deterrence, but not to create the new confidence of defense dominance. It would certainly reduce the decision time available in a strategic crisis. And it would also favor a first strike in space.

Moreover, neither system is likely to be built alone. In response to ASAT development, the two nations will protect their satellites with space-based defense systems, using technology similar to that of the SDI. And it is hard to imagine a space-based SDI system not provoking the construction of ASATs in response. Thus, unless *both* these areas of technology are controlled, future deterrence will almost certainly be more sensitive to crisis and less stable than has been the deterrence of the last several decades.

ASAT and SDI would also complicate strategic policy for Europe and Japan. The greater riskiness of deterrence, together with the underlying failure to achieve an arms control agreement, would strengthen European and Japanese political movements against U.S. nuclear policy. At the same time, should SDI be designed to defend only U.S. territory, America's allies will feel vulnerable and isolated. This may lead to strong political movements to build or increase national nuclear forces. Which political movements will prevail is not easy to say, but to avoid creating the sense of isolation, the United States might seek to extend the SDI system's protection to Europe and Japan. This would permit and require a new level of alliance collaboration in building and operating the system, but planning for the decision to use SDI would be even harder than today's planning for the decision to use NATO nuclear weapons.

THE POLITICS OF ARMS CONTROL

Political issues are always more important than military questions, and the real political issues are much more profound than the atmospheric effects. Success in arms control is likely to help the mood, but in the years before 2000, there will be at least one major change in mood and atmosphere. No one today takes much comfort in the era of good feeling surrounding the arms control agreement of 1972.

The real political issues are those of internal political balance. Although one must be very careful about attributing U.S. strategic theories to the Soviet Union, long-term insecurity in the strategic balance seems likely to strengthen hard-line Soviet positions and to slow political change in that nation. One can be much more confident in estimating that the failure of arms control would polarize U.S. politics over nuclear issues and, unless the strategic community acts very wisely, leave arms control improbable for another generation.

This last point deserves emphasis. The failure of strategic arms control would turn many "outside" strategists against the government—but would also intensify the need for them to communicate with the government. Ideas from outside the Administration will be essential to help solve the difficult task of maintaining strategic stability as space technology moves toward strategic vulnerability. Moreover, should outside strategists leave the issue to partisan politics, they will lose—unless they work very hard to educate the public. The political trend in the United States is toward the South and the West—constituencies which in 1985 gave the MX its 55 to 45 vote in the Senate, and which will support arms control only if they are absolutely confident that U.S. security is protected.

From World War II until the Vietnam War, policy thinkers inside and outside the government worked cooperatively in a way that is needed again. The initial nuclear arms control proposals were prepared by the scientists who had actually invented the weapons. The test ban debates in the late 1950s and early 1960s were conducted by a combination of government and academic scientists and analysts who paid much attention to informing the public and gave great credit to that public's intelligence and responsibility.

This changed in the late 1960s, primarily because the insiders and the outsiders differed so sharply over the government's policy toward Vietnam. Outside analysts, particularly those in the universities, deliberately broke ties with the defense and internal arms control communities. The government also isolated itself, building up its own internal bureaucracy for arms control negotiations, and weakening communications with those on the outside. When President Reagan shifted the inside rhetoric sharply to the right, many of the outsiders shifted to the left and sought to focus public debate on the freeze rather than on what Leslie Gelb has called a "middle," a strategically feasible alternative to the Administration's policy.

The public has been the greatest loser, both because policy has been less well made and because the information readily available has been more propagandistic than thoughtful. Those who had paid so much attention to public information in the 1950s failed during the 1960s and 1970s to provide comparable public education on deterrence theory and its limitations, or on the weapons involved and their limitations. It became easy for one side to play on fear of the Soviet Union and for the other to play on fear of nuclear war.

If arms control fails, then new dialogue will be needed to develop the ideas and find the subtle balances necessary to stabilize a more sensitive deterrence—ideas and balances unlikely to come from the inside bureaucracy without responsible outside criticism and communication. This will require the academic and governmental strategic communities to be more open with each other, to listen to each other, and to weigh and evaluate arguments with the responsibility incumbent on those who share power. One of today's hopeful signs is that arguments are increasingly sought from both sides for public presentations on topics ranging from SDI to Nicaraguan policy.

THE SIDE DEALS OF ARMS CONTROL

No major U.S.-Soviet arms control agreement can be visualized without side deals and side effects that rival the central agreement in importance. The Limited Test-Ban Treaty of 1963 proved more important in sharpening the Sino-Soviet split than in controlling nuclear weapons technology. In 1972, the Soviets were intensely interested in recognition as equals and in access to Western technology and sought these goals as an implicit part of the SALT I package. The 1975 Helsinki package combined confidence-building measures, human rights, and recognition of the division of Europe. After the ASAT-SDI issue, such a side agenda will be the most important aspect of arms control in the 1980s; it deserves to be thought out with great care.

In 1972 the Soviet Union gained recognition as an equal. It did not, however, gain the technology it thought it would, and its economy is now even worse off than it was in the early 1970s. Hence technology may still be a Soviet goal, particularly in light of Gorbachev's apparent interest in internal reform. The technology and trade pattern of former Secretary of State Henry Kissinger's détente, however, is unlikely to appeal to President Reagan, who has strongly resisted the flow of technology to the Soviet Union and is clearly interested in encouraging change in that society. One is therefore inclined to look in new directions.

At least two seem plausible. One is to encourage each nation to invest in the other, with the recognition that U.S. investment in the Soviet Union would be much larger. Choosing industries that would transfer useful, but not sensitive, technology may appeal to both U.S. and Soviet leadership. It could provide a broader and more intense contact than the cultural and scientific contacts of the 1950s that paved the way for the arms control and détente of the 1960s and early 1970s. Consider the long-term benefits of manager-to-manager and engineer-to-engineer cooperation in areas like agriculture and nuclear safety.

The other possibility, which could again build on a combination of motives, would be to expand educational exchanges. An immediate program to exchange 10,000 students a year (about the number of foreign students from Hong Kong) would cost each nation under $200 million a year. In 15 years, 150,000 people in each nation would have a better understanding of the other nation, and the oldest would be in their early forties and nearing leadership positions.

THE DEVELOPING WORLD—THE REAL ISSUE

By the year 2000, the developing nations will increase their strength, relative to the industrialized countries. Those nations that are now developing will make up about four-fifths of the world's population instead of three-quarters as they do now, or two-thirds as they did

in 1960. The very rapid developing-world military force increases of
the early 1970s have slowed down, but this slowdown is essentially
confined to the Middle East. Growth rates in most other areas are
at least comparable to those in the developed world. There will also
be qualitative military changes favoring the developing nations, such
as the spread of precision-guided weaponry like that used against
British ships in the Falklands (Malvinas) war. And there may be several
new Southern nuclear nations.

In the face of such a military balance, the North may continue its
disengagement from any military role in the South, even when a strong
Southern nation takes advantage of its neighbors. However, the United
States is beginning to lose its fear of another Vietnam and will almost
certainly have changed to a new mood by 2000. The Soviet Union
will probably lag in such changes. Consider that in the year 2000,
Afghanistan veterans will be in their late thirties, Vietnam veterans
in their fifties.

Whether there will be political disengagement is even less clear.
In spite of current budgetary pressures and declining political support
for foreign assistance, the United States may be forced into engagement as a result of events in Mexico and Central America. By contrast,
in nonmilitary respects, the Soviet Union has never been seriously
engaged in the developing world. Domestic politics will also play
a major role: What will be the position of the refugee communities
in the United States? Of the U.S. sunbelt, more conservative than the
frostbelt but more internationalist in its economics? Of the Muslim
community straddling the southern Soviet border?

Failure of U.S.-Soviet arms control would intensify Third World
criticism of the two nations and make it less likely that the Non-
Proliferation Treaty will be renewed when it is voted on in 1995.
Nevertheless, for many nations, confidence in the actual strategic
balance and in the stability of defense commitments will continue
to be the most important factors against acquiring nuclear weapons.
Nuclear programs like those of Israel and South Korea tend to proceed
at a rate inversely proportional to confidence in the military commitment of the United States. By the turn of the century, many West
European nations, Japan, and perhaps a large number of nations in
South Asia and Latin America will be considering whether their
security is enhanced or decreased by building nuclear weapons.

The risks are clear if the United States and Soviet Union retreat
into strategic isolation, as they may, particularly should SDI be deployed. SDI could become a self-justifying weapon. Just as the United
States looked to missile defense in the 1960s as a protection against

a nuclear China that was thought to be too irrational to be deterred, the two superpowers might begin to look to SDI to protect themselves against a new generation of proliferation.

Even with arms control and without SDI, there will be North-South tensions. Demography, economics, and ecology make it inevitable. Bringing the South into formal arms control is unlikely by 2000; the question is rather whether the Non-Proliferation Treaty will survive.

Fortunately, international contacts and communications are growing at the same time. It is easy to cite statistics about trade or multinational corporations, or the number of international migrants, or the number of families with members working abroad, or the explosive growth of television throughout the world. But the most important of the evolutions cannot be quantified—that of ideas flowing readily from nation to nation, political concepts like arms control and peace or environmental movements, the spectrum of religious concepts, styles like blue jeans and rock music. The short-wave radio, audio- and video-tape recorders, and—by 2000—the direct-broadcast satellite make effective censorship nearly impossible.

Much of this communication is superficial. It has not only failed to surmount nationalism; it has sometimes even strengthened it. Yet it is hard to believe that we can long communicate without creating a stronger global community and ultimately bringing our political institutions along with us. As these institutions evolve, they will attract the pressure and conflict that now shape domestic politics.

Hence the key challenge and opportunity for the next generation is to encourage and harness this communication toward engagement in the North and justice in the South, and to ensure that those conflicts which arise are dealt with politically rather than militarily. There are many barriers, ranging from the North's frustration at the sweep of the South's demands, to the Southern governments' postcolonial sensitivity to anything that weakens their power.

The side deals with the Soviet Union, as we have seen, appear minor at first but can grow to become the most important parts of a new arrangement. Similarly, we must look for new approaches and institutions which may appear weak at first but can build on growing international communication. Educational exchange, one of our few new options for the Soviet Union, already occurs with developing nations but needs to be expanded and protected from budgetary cutbacks.

Institutions should be created that can reflect citizens' views and transcend national governments, differing from the United Nations approach, which overemphasizes national sovereignty. Consider the possibility of international cooperation like that among the various European Socialist or Christian Democratic parties; of new international functional cooperation in areas like the environment, labor standards, human rights, and narcotics control; or ultimately of international parliaments of representatives chosen (like the European Parliament in Strasbourg) by people rather than by governments.

These mechanisms appear to work slowly, and they work best with democracies. Yet it was just 12 years from the end of World War II to the construction of the European Economic Community. The Community is far from a complete success, but within that time a new Franco-German war was made essentially impossible, and the ground was laid for the Community to encourage democracy—and ultimately membership—for once-dictatorial Greece, Portugal, and Spain.

Analysts in the year 2000 will look back and evaluate our work today by whether we have negotiated peace in space; whether we have built a domestic politics that can deal realistically with strategic weaponry; and, most of all, whether we have invested in the international education, communications, and institutions that will provide expanded opportunities for both diplomats and citizens.

8

Toward a Nuclear-Age Ethos

Robert Jay Lifton

We are in the midst of a significant but tortured shift in consciousness concerning the nuclear threat. At precisely such a time, we would do well to consider what might be an appropriate set of convictions—appropriate psychologically and in terms of life enhancement. The 10 principles I wish to elaborate are simple ones, already adopted by a growing number of people.

We face a new dimension of destruction—not a matter of disaster or even of a war—but rather of an end: an end to human civilization and perhaps humankind.

This concept violates our ingrained mental constructs concerning human continuity: though we can imagine particular cultures being impaired or even destroyed, we expect humankind to heal itself sufficiently to survive. But the findings of a possible "nuclear winter" effect concretize the idea of a nuclear end, and, however grim, serve the imagination in the difficult task of looking into the abyss in order to see beyond it.

The image of the nuclear end includes not only death and suffering on the most massive scale but, beyond that, nothingness. Two relatively recent historical events, the Nazi holocaust and the atomic bombings of Hiroshima and Nagasaki, assist that kind of imaginative act.

In visiting Auschwitz in connection with research on Nazi doctors, I saw many exhibits suggesting the extraordinary cruelties human

beings are capable of inflicting on other human beings. But the exhibit
that left the most powerful impression on me was a very simple one:
a room full of shoes, mostly baby shoes. Nothing more.

Similarly, I spoke to a Hiroshima survivor who was on the outskirts
of the city when the bomb fell, and he told me how he climbed a
hill and looked down at the city to discover, to his amazement, that
"Hiroshima had disappeared," and "just didn't exist." In our discussion, he expressed the view that Hiroshima should be memorialized
by leaving completely empty a large area around the hypocenter, the
spot where the bomb hit, and that on August 6, no one would stir
in the city, and the doors of all homes and shops should be closed.
Then all could understand that "such a weapon has the power to make
everything into nothing."

The "nothingness" portrayed in both cases forces one to do the
psychological work of imagining the missing people. We come closer,
in Martin Buber's phrase, to "imagining the real." Just as we must
imaginatively confront our own death in order to live fully, so must
we begin to imagine the end of the world in order to maintain the
world.

*That nuclear end must be rejected. We must commit ourselves to the flow
and continuity of human life and to the products of the human imagination.*

There is little solace, for instance, in the idea of a "divine spirit"
or a "Buddha mind" continuing after a nuclear war. However sublime
these images, they are expressions of the human imagination.
Theologians of all religions must question the morality of asserting
any principle of spiritual survival in the event of the annihilation of
humankind.

To reject the nuclear end, we need to experience the nurturing vibra-
tions and affirmations of everyday human life as well as to concep-
tualize the psychological significance of larger human continuity. As
creatures who know that we die, we need a sense of immortality: of
living on in our children and in an endless chain of attachment that
can come to include group, tribe, organization, people, nation, or even
species; in human influence and work or "works"; in some form of
spiritual attainment; in relation to nature; or in association with psychic
states so intense that within them time and death disappear. To contribute to maintaining the world, we need to affirm our connection with
that which has gone on before and that which will go on after what
we know to be our finite individual life-span.

*We either survive or die as a species. Nuclear weapons create a universally
shared fate—a technologically imposed unity of all humankind.*

The message of this shared fate, from any American to a Soviet counterpart, is simple and primal: If I die, you die; if you survive, I survive. The principle of shared fate applies to nations no less than to individuals. The United States and the Soviet Union are simultaneously terrorists and hostages. As in the case of an airplane hijacked in flight, the terrorist's use of his own weaponry will kill him as certainly as it will his hostages.

This shared fate highlights as nothing else does the pragmatic dimension of nuclear-weapons issues and of survival itself. At the same time it can throw us back on not just individual but collective humanity, on an evolving ethic of mutual responsibility, again as both individuals and nations, for shared life. As pragmatism and moral imagination combine, the United States and the Soviet Union may be able to think less in terms of "the enemy"—the real enemy to both is nuclear extinction—and more in terms of committed partnership in survival.

Collective human power can bring about change, awareness, and ultimately human survival.

If one looks only at expanding nuclear stockpiles and dubious mutual assumptions supporting that buildup, the image of collective human power on behalf of survival grows dim indeed. But on the other hand there has been an extraordinary and unanticipated recent shift in world consciousness to revulsion toward nuclear weapons, awareness of their destructive power, and demand for their radical reduction.

This protest is a form of collective human rights: the right not to be extinguished as a species, the right to bring up children without nuclear fear and futurelessness, and the right to reclaim from the nuclear priesthood—those who make decisions of ultimate life-and-death consequence—a reasonable degree of control over one's own destiny, which in the United States could be thought of as a return to Jeffersonian democratic principles.

This struggle incorporates different dimensions of the human repertoire. It requires a capacity for reflection and rigorous thought to produce new ideas for coping with unprecedented combinations of threat. It requires passion, which may include some of the emotions of the traditional warrior spirit transmuted into militant actions against the nuclear threat and on behalf of nonviolence and human survival. Above all a spirit of healing is required, to draw an ever-broadening spectrum of people into the struggle and to keep attitudes and actions commensurate with life-enhancing goals.

The human insistence upon imagining a future gives powerful psychobiological support to this protest. Indeed precisely the capacity to do so contributed centrally to the evolutionary emergence of our species. Imagining a future was crucial to our becoming human and continues to prod us toward efforts to maintain collective human life.

We need be neither optimistic nor pessimistic about that human future; rather, we must hope. Hope means a sense of possibility and includes desire, anticipation, and vitality. It is a psychological necessity and a theological virtue, a state that must itself be nurtured, shared, mutually enhanced.

A key to that life-power lies in the renunciation of nuclearism—of the dependency upon, and even worship of, nuclear weapons.

Psychologically, nuclearism includes so great an attachment to the weapons as to count on them for safety or "security"; for solving strategic, political, and social dilemmas; even for keeping the world going. It is the ultimate human irony that we embrace our potential agents of extinction as a means of maintaining human life.

Nuclearism is an ideology which requires a series of deadly illusions: the illusion that one can manage nuclear-weapons use and circumscribe the effects; the illusion that nuclear attack can be prepared for by fabulous evacuation plans and shelters (which would be, if one got there, crematoria); the illusion of stoic behavior under attack, substituting images of boy-scout-like cooperation for the immobilized death-like state of the few who might temporarily survive; and the illusion of recovery.

Nuclearism derives from both our general tendency to demand the "technological fix" in situations requiring human solutions, and even more importantly from the awesome power of ultimate destruction the weapons actually possess. The tendency of strong advocates of nuclearism to reverse themselves at the moment of retirement—what I call "retirement wisdom"—indicates the strength of institutional nuclearism. A recent exemplar has been Admiral Hyman Rickover, but the tendency goes back to the famous memo of Henry Stimson, the man most concerned with decisions about use of the first atomic weapons, upon resigning from his post of secretary of war; to J. Robert Oppenheimer in his critique of attitudes concerning the hydrogen bomb after having so strongly committed himself to atomic-bomb use and subsequent military control of nuclear energy; and includes President Eisenhower's wise warning about the dangers of the military-industrial complex, along with retirement statements and attitudes of a significant number of other leading political and military figures. The pattern suggests that prior doubts had been suppressed by group tendencies, while in office, to view the world through a nuclearistic lens. These doubts could be permitted to surface when leaders were released from pressures of institutional power, resulting in (or psychologically requiring) expressions of conscience that could be eloquent in their reflection of personal experience and inside knowledge.

A consequence of the expanding public awareness of the destructive power of nuclear weapons, buttressed by the findings of nuclear winter, is a profound contradiction affecting both policy and mind-set of nuclear strategists. While acknowledging that any nuclear exchange is likely to produce a nuclear end with neither victory nor survival, they have structured the nuclear-weapons buildup to include a nuclear war-fighting option. Many strategists struggle with this inner contradiction, as the research of Steven Kull demonstrates ("Nuclear Nonsense," *Foreign Policy*, no. 58 [Spring 1985], pp. 28–52). Given the world-destroying power of existing stockpiles, strategists recognize claims of survivability or of the need for added nuclear weaponry as illusory, and yet may publicly defend those very illusions. Kull points out that they may do so because they think the illusions are required by either the American people or the Soviet leaders or both. But I believe that there may be a less rational psychological process involved: an inner division I speak of as "doubling." In response to extremity, a second self may take shape and function relatively autonomously from the still-existing prior self, and thereby adapt to situations of extreme contradiction, including those involving a potential for mass killing or genocide.

Generally, however, the rejection of nuclearism and recognition of its dangers has become widespread. Ordinary people in both nuclear superpowers reject, and indeed consider absurd, the nuclear illusion promulgated by their governments. To renounce nuclearism is to renounce the nuclear illusions of limit and control, preparation, protection, stoic behavior under attack, and recovery, and to recognize nuclear weapons as instruments of genocide and that the continuity of human life—hope itself—lies only in prevention.

A world without nuclear weapons is possible—a world that directs its energies toward more humane goals and looks to more genuine human security.

To be sure, from the standpoint of the present situation, this conviction sounds utopian. But as a goal to be achieved gradually and incrementally it is more realistic than the present course. That goal, and the general process by which it can be achieved, must first be agreed upon so that nuclear arms control or disarmament is not viewed as a sporadic, disorganized process controlled by "bargaining chips" or "positions of strength." The initial agreement could become part of a continuous process in which there is a sequence of agreed-upon

steps toward nuclear disarmament, with very active third-party participation, and continuous monitoring and exchange of information. The
nuclear superpowers and the various participating governments could
then have a much better chance of exerting pressure on other actual or
potential possessors of nuclear weapons to become involved in a similar process. The stance we must take, then, includes both an address to
our immediate nuclear-weapons-dominated world and the elaboration
of images, plans, and policies beyond present arrangements. This is
very different from a stance of "living with nuclear weapons" and
from accepting longstanding patterns of nuclear buildup.

To contribute to a climate that makes genuine nuclear disarmament
possible, ideas about it must be more widely exchanged among Americans. Activists, students, and scholars from among minority groups
may be ready to enter the process more energetically now, if they
can see it to be connected, as it surely is, to questions of social justice.
There are also means by which these ideas cross over barriers between
the United States and the Soviet Union. The process could come to
include reductions in conventional weapons and even explorations
of ways to rid the world of the institution of war as such. Shared
fate can be the beginning of wisdom.

*The step must be taken away from resignation—from "waiting for the
bomb"—toward commitment to combatting it.*

Each person, at some level of consciousness, realizes that there is
no individual escape from the question, if only because the bomb
envelops all as potential victims. In making the decision to do something of this kind in one's life, however modest, there can be a considerable sense of relief, even liberation. For a great deal of psychological
work goes into the conflict over whether or not one can or should
do anything in connection with nuclear threat.

The step toward commitment may be small, from the stance of
having been a sympathetic spectator, or an enormous, conversion-
like recognition of what is involved from having permitted oneself
to see into the nuclear abyss. Taking that step relieves one from self-
deception even as one assumes new responsibilities. In overcoming
resistance and admitting to our minds knowledge we wish we did
not possess, that knowledge, rather than remaining only the darkest of
shadows, becomes a basis for truthful thought and constructive action.

*In these personal, individual efforts, one's everyday working professional exis-
tence and creative concerns may be connected with the struggle against nuclear
weapons.*

People need no longer be workers, teachers, or students from nine to
five Monday through Friday and antinuclear people on an occasional

evening or weekend. They are at all times both. Professional activity of any kind should be informed by the nature of the nuclear threat, and approaches to that threat require whatever professional knowledge can be mustered. More than that, each in this way can proceed toward unification of the self.

Just as scientists and doctors have attempted to draw from their professional knowledge and experience to inform and deepen the antinuclear movement, so can every profession, academic discipline, or working tradition do the same. Architects, workers on assembly lines, medieval historians, policemen, and ministers—all can bring significant aspects of their experience and tradition to the struggle to maintain human life.

Indeed one of the great scandals of our time is the paucity of human and material resources mobilized to cope with the absolute question of our time. That is beginning to change, though ever so slightly. There are stirrings of a more general, extraordinarily overdue, cultural response from the sciences, the arts, academia, the professions, and popular cultural sources.

This struggle does not call one to embrace hopelessness and despair, but rather a fuller existence.

In confronting a genuine threat, rather than numbing ourselves to it, we experience greater vitality. We feel stronger human ties. We turn to beauty, love, spirituality, and sensuality.

There is a distinction between depression and despair. Depression is usually reactive, having to do with a sense of loss, or in this case threatened loss. Depression has a certain symptom complex: one slows down, has less energy, withdraws from people, and may have varying degrees of guilt and anger. Yet depressed people, as studies have shown, are not necessarily hopeless about the future, and may in fact anticipate recovery and a return of vitality. Despair, on the other hand, involves hopelessness and absence of larger human connection. Moments of depression are inevitable; they are part of being human. Despair can be more serious and can be managed only by reasserting human ties, both in immediate life relationships and in shared antinuclear struggle. Despair is overcome when we begin once more to believe in, and act on, a human future.

The struggle to preserve humankind lends a renewed sense of human possibility; one feels part of prospective historical and evolutionary achievements.

A culmination of this overall ethos is a higher self-regard. We feel more authentic in our life and work—as physicians or clergy, as scientists or artists, as teachers or students, as human beings alive to ultimate threat and hopeful in working toward a future beyond that threat.

Thomas Merton, a great spiritual antiwar warrior, has posed the
question: "We cannot give an irresponsible and unchristian consent
to the demonic use of power for the destruction of a whole nation,
a whole continent, or even the whole human race. Or can we? The
question is now being asked." And Theodore Roethke has provided
an answer: "In a dark time the eye begins to see."

Contributors

William M. Arkin is the director of the Arms Race and Nuclear Weapons Research Project at the Institute for Policy Studies in Washington, D.C. He is coauthor, with Richard W. Fieldhouse, of *Nuclear Battlefields: Global Links in the Arms Race* (1985), from which the essay "Nuclear Infrastructure" in this book is adapted.

George W. Ball, deputy secretary of state from 1961 to 1966, is the author of *Error and Betrayal in Lebanon* (1984) and the forthcoming book, *The Passionate Attachment,* an analysis of U.S. policy in the Middle East.

John H. Barton, a consultant with his own firm, International Technology Management, is on leave from Stanford Law School. He is the author of *The Politics of Peace* (1981).

Hans A. Bethe, an emeritus professor of physics at Cornell University, received the Nobel Prize in physics in 1967. He was the leader of the theoretical division of the Los Alamos Laboratory during World War II and a member of the President's Scientific Advisory Committee 1957–1959. He has long worked for and written about arms control.

Harrison Brown, editor in chief of the *Bulletin of the Atomic Scientists,* has worked extensively in geochemistry, on energy and resources, and on the problems of economic development, hunger, and population. A chemist on the Manhattan Project, he was most recently director of the Resource Systems Institute at the East-West Center in Hawaii.

Thomas B. Cochran, a physicist, is senior staff scientist and director of the Nuclear Weapons Databook project at the Natural Resources Defense Council.

Hugh E. DeWitt is a theoretical physicist at the Lawrence Livermore National Laboratory in Livermore, California.

William A. Dorman is a research associate in the Adlai E. Stevenson Program on Nuclear Policy at the University of California, Santa Cruz, and at the Center for the Study of War, Peace and the News Media at New York University.

Jack F. Evernden is a research geophysicist with the U.S. Geological Survey in Menlo Park, California, and has been a consultant for the Arms Control and Disarmament Agency for a number of years. He is the coauthor of a chapter in *Arms Control Verification: The Technologies That Make It Possible,* edited by Kosta Tsipis (1986).

Richard Falk is the Albert G. Milbank Professor of International Law and Practice at Princeton University. He is the author of *The End of World Order* (1983) and co-editor of *International Law: A Contemporary Perspective* (1985).

Harold Feiveson is a research political scientist at Princeton University's Center for Energy and Environmental Studies and coauthor of *Nuclear Proliferation* (1977).

Bernard T. Feld, former editor in chief of the *Bulletin* and a professor of physics at the Massachusetts Institute of Technology, received the Council for a Livable World's Leo Szilard Annual Peace Award in December 1984.

Richard W. Fieldhouse is a visiting scholar at the Stockholm International Peace Research Institute and is a research associate at the Institute for Policy Studies in Washington, D.C. He is the coauthor, with William M. Arkin, of *Nuclear Battlefields: Global Links in the Arms Race* (1985), from which the essay "Nuclear Infrastructure" in this book is adapted.

Randall Forsberg, founder and director of the Institute for Defense and Disarmament Studies in Brookline, Massachusetts, is the author of the 1980 "Call to Halt the Nuclear Arms Race," which launched the nuclear weapons freeze campaign. She is a coauthor of *Winding Down* (1986) and of the *Peace Resource Book 1986.*

Alexander L. George is Graham H. Stuart Professor of International Relations and fellow at the Stanford Center for International Security and Arms Control at Stanford University. His essay is adapted from a paper presented at a meeting sponsored by the Soviet Academy of

Sciences, Moscow, in May 1983.

Charles L. Glaser is a research associate at the Defense and Arms Control Studies Program of the Center for International Studies at the Massachusetts Institute of Technology. A longer, more complete version of the essay in this book appeared in the Fall 1984 issue of *International Security.*

Morton H. Halperin, a former deputy assistant secretary of defense and National Security Council staff member, directs the Washington office of the American Civil Liberties Union.

David A. Hamburg is chairman of the board of the American Association for the Advancement of Science in Washington, D.C., and president of the Carnegie Corporation of New York. His essay is adapted from a paper presented at a meeting sponsored by the Soviet Academy of Sciences, Moscow, in May 1983.

John P. Holdren is a professor of energy and resources at the University of California, Berkeley, chairman of the Federation of American Scientists, and a member of the executive committee of the Pugwash Conferences on Science and World Affairs.

David Holloway, a senior research associate at the Center for International Security and Arms Control at Stanford University and reader in politics at the University of Edinburgh, is the author of *The Soviet Union and the Arms Race* (1983) and coauthor of *The Reagan Strategic Defense Initiative: A Technical, Political, and Arms Control Assessment* (1984).

Jerry F. Hough is J.B. Duke Professor of Political Science at Duke University in Durham, North Carolina, and a staff member of the Brookings Institution in Washington, D.C. He is the author of *The Struggle for the Third World: Soviet Debate and American Options* (1986).

Mary Kaldor is a senior fellow at the Science Policy Research Unit, University of Sussex in the United Kingdom, editor of the *END Journal,* and author of *Baroque Arsenal* (1982).

Michael Krepon is a senior associate at the Carnegie Endowment for International Peace in Washington, D.C., where he directs a verification project. He is the author of *Strategic Stalemate: Nuclear Weapons and Arms Control in American Politics* (1984).

Paul Leventhal, founder and president of the Nuclear Control Institute in Washington, D.C., was a congressional observer at the 1975 Nuclear Non-Proliferation Treaty review conference and was an observer for the Institute at the 1985 meeting.

Robert Jay Lifton is Distinguished Professor of Psychiatry and Psychology, the City University of New York at John Jay College of Criminal Justice. His most recent book, with Nicholas Humphrey, is *In a Dark Time* (1984).

Alan P. Lightman is a physicist at the Smithsonian Astrophysical Observatory and teaches at Harvard University. He is the author of *Time Travel and Papa Joe's Pipe* (1984), a collection of essays on science.

Michael Mandelbaum, research and editorial director at the Lehrman Institute in New York City, is the author of three books on nuclear weapons, most recently *The Nuclear Future.*

Michael M. May is associate director at large of the Lawrence Livermore National Laboratory in Livermore, California.

John J. Mearsheimer is an associate professor in the political science department at the University of Chicago. He is the author of *Conventional Deterrence,* which won the 1983 Edgar S. Furniss, Jr., Award.

Robert L. Messer, an associate professor of history at the University of Illinois at Chicago, is the author of *The End of an Alliance: James F. Byrnes, Roosevelt, Truman and the Origins of the Cold War* (1982). He is currently working on a book on Truman's nuclear weapons policy.

Robert S. Norris is a senior research associate with the Natural Resources Defense Council in Washington, D.C.

Christopher E. Paine is a consultant on nuclear nonproliferation policy to Princeton University's Center for Energy and Environmental Studies and the House Subcommittee on Energy Conservation and Power.

Sir Rudolf Peierls, a theoretical physicist, retired in 1974 from a chair at the University of Oxford.

Theodore A. Postol, a physicist, is a senior research associate at the

Center for International Security and Arms Control at Stanford University. As an assistant for weapons technology at the Pentagon (1982–1984) and an analyst at the congressional Office of Technology Assessment, he was involved in technical and policy issues of both strategic weapons systems and arms control negotiations.

The late *David J. Rose* was a professor of nuclear engineering at the Massachusetts Institute of Technology and one of the originators of fusion engineering as a university discipline.

Joseph Rotblat is emeritus professor of physics at the University of London, St. Bartholomew's Hospital Medical College. A founder of the Pugwash Conferences on Science and World Affairs, he was its secretary general for 17 years and is currently chairman of the British Pugwash Group.

Martin J. Sherwin is Walter S. Dickson Professor of History at Tufts University in Medford, Massachusetts, and author of *A World Destroyed: The Atomic Bomb and the Grand Alliance* (1975). He is currently writing a biography of J. Robert Oppenheimer.

John Steinbruner, a specialist in U.S. strategic policy and decision theory, is the director of the Foreign Policy Studies program at the Brookings Institution in Washington, D.C. His chapter in this book is adapted from one that first appeared in *U.S.-Soviet Relations: Perspectives for the Future,* a Center for National Policy publication.

Toshiyuki Toyoda is a professor of physics at Meiji Gakuin University in Tokyo and co-editor of *Is It Possible to Abolish Nuclear Weapons?* (1984).

Richard Ullman is a professor of political science in Princeton University's Woodrow Wilson School of Public and International Affairs.

Frank von Hippel, a theoretical physicist, is a professor in Princeton University's Woodrow Wilson School of Public and International Affairs.

Victor F. Weisskopf, Institute Professor of Physics, emeritus, at the Massachusetts Institute of Technology, was deputy chairman of the theoretical division at the Los Alamos Scientific Laboratory and director general of the European Center for Nuclear Research in Geneva.

Jerome B. Wiesner is president emeritus and Institute Professor at the Massachusetts Institute of Technology in Cambridge.

Spencer R. Weart is the director of the Center for History of Physics at the American Institute of Physics in New York City and author of the forthcoming *Nuclear Fear: A History of Images.*

Robert R. Wilson, emeritus professor of physics at Cornell University in Ithaca, New York, was head of the Research Division at Los Alamos from 1944 to 1946. He has been the director of the Laboratory of Nuclear Studies at Cornell University (1947–1967) and was director of Fermilab in Illinois from 1967 to 1978.

Len Ackland and *Steven McGuire* are, respectively, editor and managing editor of the *Bulletin of the Atomic Scientists.*

Bibliography

The following bibliography presents a selection of books and periodicals that treat in greater detail the individual subjects covered in this book. The selections were made in an effort to represent various aspects of and perspectives on the problems posed by nuclear weapons and the arms race. The list does not, however, make any pretense to being complete or definitive; many of the works included offer more detailed references and resources.

BOOKS

Adams, Gordon. *The Politics of Defense Contracting: The Iron Triangle.* New Brunswick, N.J.: Council on Economic Priorities, 1981. A study of the relationships linking defense contractors, the military, and Congress. It identifies abuses facilitated by present arrangements and suggests directions for reform.

Adams, Ruth, and Susan Cullen, eds. *The Final Epidemic: Physicians and Scientists on Nuclear War.* Chicago: Bulletin of the Atomic Scientists, 1981. A reader covering medical consequences of nuclear war and psychological and economic aspects of the arms race.

Alperovitz, Gar. *Atomic Diplomacy: Hiroshima and Potsdam.* New York: Penguin, 1985. An expanded and updated version of the controversial 1965 revisionist examination of the beginnings of the nuclear age.

Alternative Defence Commission. *Defense without the Bomb.* London: Taylor and Francis, 1983. Detailed examination of how Britain might defend itself if it abandoned reliance on a nuclear deterrent.

Arkin, William M. *Nuclear Battlefields: Global Links in the Arms Race.* Cambridge, Mass.: Ballinger, 1985. Describes the global infrastructure supporting the nuclear forces of the major powers: bases, storage depots, early-warning systems, communications linkages, and so forth.

Arms Control and Disarmament Agency, U.S. *Arms Control and Disarmament Agreements: Texts and Histories of Negotiations.* Washington, D.C.: Government Printing Office, 1982. Contains the Geneva Protocol of 1925 and all major arms control agreements since World War II in which the United States has been a participant.

———. *World Military Expenditures and Arms Transfers.* Washington, D.C.: Government Printing Office, annual. Statistics on arms expenditures, sizes of armed forces, and arms transfers, plus various social indicators, for nearly all countries.

Barnet, Richard J. *Real Security: Restoring American Power in a Dangerous Decade.* New York: Simon and Schuster, 1981. A realistic appraisal of the U.S.-Soviet balance of power—military, economic, and political—and the policy implications.

Blair, Bruce G. *Strategic Command and Control: Redefining the Nuclear Threat.* Washington, D.C.: Brookings Institution, 1985. The author, a former Minuteman launch control officer, traces the evolution of U.S. strategic command-and-control arrangements over the past 25 years and recommends improvements.

Bracken, Paul. *The Command and Control of Nuclear Forces.* New Haven, Conn.: Yale University Press, 1983. An accessible introduction to how the systems and techniques by which nuclear forces would receive orders to fire affect the stability of the nuclear stalemate and the chances of nuclear war by mistake.

Brodie, Bernard. *Strategy in the Missile Age.* Princeton, N.J.: Princeton University Press, 1965. One of the original works on deterrence theory.

Burns, Grant. *The Atomic Papers.* Metuchen, N.J.: Scarecrow Press, 1984. Annotates over 800 books published since 1945 and over 300 articles published since 1980 on nuclear issues.

Calder, Nigel. *Nuclear Nightmares.* New York: Penguin, 1981. Compact introduction to the main concepts and issues in deterrence and nuclear warfighting, dwelling particularly on some plausible ways a nuclear war could start and escalate.

Carter, Ashton B., and David N. Schwartz, eds. *Ballistic Missile Defense.* Washington, D.C.; Brookings Institution, 1984. A detailed and comprehensive treatment of the topic for the general reader.

Cochran, Thomas B., and William M. Arkin and Milton M. Hoenig. *Nuclear Weapons Databook: Vol. 1: U.S. Nuclear Forces and Capabilities.* Cambridge, Mass.: Ballinger, 1983. The most comprehensive compendium of data on U.S. nuclear bombs, warheads, and delivery vehicles.

Committee for the Compilation of Materials on Damage Caused by the Atomic Bombs. *Hiroshima and Nagasaki: The Physical, Medical, and Social Effects of the Bombings.* New York: Basic Books, 1981. A thorough summary and analysis of the events and their aftermath by leading Japanese physicists, physicians, and social scientists.

Cracraft, James, ed. *The Soviet Union Today.* Chicago: Bulletin of the Atomic Scientists, 1983. A collection of essays covering most aspects of Soviet society.

Dennis, Jack, ed. *The Nuclear Almanac.* Reading, Mass.: Addison-Wesley, 1984. Collection of essays by well-known scholars and authors on nuclear weapons, strategy, and effects.

Drell, Sidney D., and Philip J. Farley and David Holloway. *The Reagan Strategic Defense Initiative: A Technical, Political, and Arms Control Assessment.* Cambridge, Mass.: Ballinger, 1985. A rounded analysis of the issue, explaining technical intricacies and exploring likely Soviet reactions.

Dyson, Freeman. *Weapons and Hope.* New York: Harper and Row, 1984. Exploration of the nature of military activities and popular hope, a review of approaches to arms control and disarmament, and a proposed route to disarmament.

Ehrlich, Paul R. *The Cold and the Dark: The World after Nuclear War.* New York: W.W. Norton, 1984. Contains the edited proceedings of the Washington conference where the results of two major studies on the climatological and ecological consequences of nuclear war were made public.

Falk, Richard A., and Samuel S. Kim, eds. *The War System: An Interdisciplinary Approach.* Boulder, Colo.: Westview Press, 1980. A rather massive anthology containing essays on the origins of war from a wide variety of disciplinary approaches.

Fallows, James. *National Defense.* New York: Random House, 1981. Not mainly about nuclear war, this book documents how the defense industry and the military waste money and undermine real military capability. The key message is that we could have more military capability (particularly non-nuclear) for less money.

Federation of American Scientists. *Seeds of Promise: The First Real Hearings on the Nuclear Arms Freeze.* Andover, Mass.: Brick House Publishers, 1983. Testimony by Randall Forsberg, Richard Garwin, Paul Warnke, and Robert Dean, with cross-examination by other experts.

Ford, Daniel. *The Button: The Pentagon's Command and Control System—Does It Work?* New York: Simon and Schuster, 1985. Contains a wealth of descriptive information about the U.S. command-and-control system and its shortcomings, but its overall conclusion that the shortcomings imply an intention to strike first is not persuasive.

Freedman, Lawrence. *The Evolution of Nuclear Strategy.* New York: St. Martin's, 1981. A thorough history of the twists and turns of nuclear strategy over three and a half decades.

Garthoff, Raymond L. *Détente and Confrontation: American-Soviet Relations from Nixon to Reagan.* Washington, D.C.: Brookings Institution, 1985. A monumental, thoroughly documented history of U.S.-Soviet relations in the period 1969–1984.

Ground Zero. *What about the Russians—and Nuclear War?* Pocket Books/Simon and Schuster, 1983. A great deal of information about the Soviet Union—history, government, armed forces, economy, and more—crammed into a compact format.

Haley, P. Edward, and David M. Keithly and Jack Merritt, eds. *Nuclear Strategy, Arms Control, and the Future.* Boulder, Colo.: Westview, 1985. Contains many of the seminal documents and articles on nuclear weapons, strategy, and doctrine.

Harvard Nuclear Study Group. *Living with Nuclear Weapons.* Cambridge, Mass.: Harvard University Press, 1983. An introduction to some aspects of the history and problems of arms control. The book disappointingly concludes that since we have to live with nuclear weapons, their management should be left to experts.

Herken, Gregg. *The Winning Weapon: The Atomic Bomb in the Cold War, 1945–50.* New York: Vintage/Random House, 1981. A history of the period of U.S. monopoly on nuclear weaponry, this book emphasizes the political struggles over how the monopoly was to be managed, preserved, and exploited.

Hersey, John. *Hiroshima.* New York: Bantam Books, 1946. Vivid eyewitness accounts of six survivors immediately after the bombing; reissued by Bantam in 1985 with a new introduction.

Holloway, David. *The Soviet Union and the Arms Race.* 2d ed. New Haven, Conn.: Yale University Press, 1984. A study of the evolution of Soviet strategic thinking and programs.

Howard, Michael. *The Causes of Wars.* Cambridge, Mass.: Harvard University Press, 1983. A series of thoughtful essays by the Regius Professor of History at Oxford University.

Independent Commission on Disarmament and Security Issues. *Common Security: A Programme for Disarmament.* London: Pan, 1982. Examines the dangers of the current situation and offers measures for disarmament and security-building measures, such as a nuclear-weapons-free zone in Central Europe.

International Institute for Strategic Studies. *The Military Balance.* London: International Institute for Strategic Studies, annual. Less detailed coverage than SIPRI's of nuclear forces, but more detailed coverage of conventional forces. IISS leans somewhat toward more pessimistic estimates of Soviet capabilities—that is, when in doubt, chooses higher estimates.

Jervis, Robert. *The Illogic of American Nuclear Strategy.* Ithaca, N.Y.: Cornell University Press, 1984. A persuasive tour of some of the dilemmas and logical traps in nuclear doctrine.

Kahn, Herman. *On Thermonuclear War.* Princeton, N.J.: Princeton University Press, 1960. A "classic" in the theory of nuclear war, it was widely derided for advocating the usefulness of preparing for nuclear war, but it was very influential and was the precursor of many current debates on the subject.

————. *Thinking about the Unthinkable.* New York: Horizon, 1962. The benefits of deterrence, the feasibility of civil defense, and the possibility of controlled nuclear war; a popularized version of the author's *On Thermonuclear War.*

Kaplan, Fred. *The Wizards of Armageddon.* New York: Simon and Schuster, 1983. An account of the influence of "defense intellectuals" in the RAND Corporation, the Department of Defense, and elsewhere on the development of thinking about nuclear strategy.

Kendall, Henry, and Daniel Ford. *Beyond the Freeze: The Road to Nuclear Sanity.* Boston: Beacon, 1982. Analyzes key arms race issues and presents a long-term disarmament program, including a freeze and economic conversion.

Kennan, George F. *The Nuclear Delusion: Soviet-American Relations in the Atomic*

Age. New York: Pantheon, 1982. A collection of essays from 1950 to 1982 by a former ambassador to the Soviet Union.

Kissinger, Henry A. *Nuclear Weapons and Foreign Policy.* New York: W.W. Norton, 1969 (abridged ed.). An early (originally published in 1957) and influential view on the usefulness of various kinds of nuclear threats and on limited nuclear war.

Krepon, Michael. *Arms Control: Verification and Compliance.* New York: Foreign Policy Association, 1984. Covers the basic concepts of verification, Soviet views of verification, and treaty compliance; contains a glossary.

Leaning, Jennifer, and Langley Keyes, eds. *The Counterfeit Ark: Crisis Relocation for Nuclear War.* Cambridge, Mass.: Ballinger, 1983. Explores the dangers and fallacies of civil defense programs.

Lifton, Robert Jay. *Death in Life: Survivors of Hiroshima:* New York: Random House, 1971. Describes the psychological as well as the physical effects of the bombings on survivors.

Lifton, Robert Jay, and Nicholas Humphrey, eds. *In a Dark Time.* Cambridge, Mass.: Harvard University Press, 1984. Poetry and prose anthology on war and nuclear weapons, from authors ancient and modern.

Longstreth, Thomas K., and John E. Pike and John B. Rhinelander. *The Impact of the U.S. and Soviet Missile Defense Programs on the ABM Treaty.* Washington, D.C.: National Campaign to Save the ABM Treaty, 1985. A cogent analysis of the nature, timing, and implications of threats to the ABM Treaty.

Mapes, Deborah, and Elizabeth Bernstein and Peter M. Steven, eds. *Peace Resource Book 1986.* Cambridge, Mass.: Ballinger, 1985. Guide to numerous national and local peace groups, extensive bibliography on weapons and disarmament, listing of college and university educational programs. Also contains an introduction to issues of weapons, strategy, and arms control.

Mearsheimer, John J. *Conventional Deterrence.* Ithaca, N.Y.: Cornell University Press, 1983. Argues that the prospects for conventional deterrence in Europe are good: even without improvements in NATO's conventional posture, the Warsaw Pact could not count on overrunning Western defenses.

Myrdal, Alva. *The Game of Disarmament.* New York: Pantheon, 1976. A denunciation of the folly of the superpowers and a prescription for serious arms control.

Office of Technology Assessment, Congress of the United States. *Antisatellite Weapons, Countermeasures, and Arms Control.* Washington, D.C.: Government Printing Office, 1985. A companion volume to the following one.

———. *Ballistic Missile Defense Technologies.* Washington, D.C.: Government Printing Office, 1985. Extensive and well-illustrated coverage of technological options and their strategic implications. Includes many references, a glossary, and appendices containing several of the relevant official documents.

———. *The Effects of Nuclear War.* Washington, D.C.: Government Printing Office, 1979. Detailed analyses of the consequences of nuclear attacks of various sizes on the United States and the Soviet Union. Includes a fictional account of the aftermath of an attack on the United States.

Organization of the Joint Chiefs of Staff. *United States Military Posture.* Washington, D.C.: Government Printing Office, annual. Provides a wealth of up-to-date detail on various measures of U.S. and Soviet military capabilities.

Pringle, Peter, and William M. Arkin. *SIOP: The Secret U.S. Plan for Nuclear War.* New York: W.W. Norton, 1983. Description and critique of the Defense Department's Single Integrated Operational Plan for use of nuclear weapons in wartime and of the U.S. nuclear warfighting posture.

Ramberg, Bennett. *Nuclear Power Plants as Weapons for the Enemy: An Unrecognized Military Peril.* Berkeley, Cal.: University of California Press, 1984. Focuses on the radiological risks posed by the possibility of nuclear power plants being bombed by hostile military forces.

Rochlin, Gene I. *Plutonium, Power, and Politics: International Arrangements for the Disposition of Spent Nuclear Fuel.* Berkeley, Cal.: University of California Press, 1979. A thorough presentation of the technical characteristics of the problem and the political impediments to its solution.

Rotblat, Joseph, and Sven Hellman, eds. *Nuclear Strategy and World Security.* London: MacMillan, 1985. Essays and background papers from conferences, symposiums, and workshops organized by Pugwash in 1984. Covers current issues, including militarization of space, chemical weapons, European security, and Third World crises.

Russet, Bruce. *Prisoners of Insecurity: Nuclear Deterrence, The Arms Race, and Arms Control.* New York: W.H. Freeman, 1983. Brief treatment of the history of the nuclear arms race and arms control, including such topics as deterrence theory, crisis stability, and the causes of war.

Sampson, Anthony. *The Arms Bazaar.* New York: Viking/Bantam, 1977. An account of the corporate maneuvering behind the international arms trade, going back to Alfred Nobel and the invention of dynamite.

Scheer, Robert. *With Enough Shovels: Reagan, Bush, and Nuclear War.* New York: Random House, 1982. Journalist Scheer examines the beliefs and rhetoric of some members of the Reagan Administration about nuclear war.

Schell, Jonathan. *The Abolition.* New York: Knopf, 1984. Explores the links between nuclear weapons and the political uses of force and offers a comprehensive proposal for nuclear disarmament.

———. *The Fate of the Earth.* New York: Knopf, 1982. An impassioned exposition of the physical and social destruction that would be caused by nuclear war and a call for disarmament.

SCOPE (Scientific Committee on Problems of the Environment), International Conference of Scientific Unions. *The Environmental Consequences of Nuclear War.* New York: John Wiley and Sons, 1985. The most comprehensive study to date on the nuclear winter theory, confirming the potential for severe impacts on climate and ecosystems.

Scoville, Herbert. *MX: Prescription for Disaster.* Cambridge, Mass.: MIT Press,

1981. Tells more about the MX than most readers will want to know, as well as giving a penetrating view of the dangers of the arms race.

Scowcroft, Brent, chairman. *Report of the President's Commission on Strategic Forces.* Washington, D.C.: Government Printing Office, 1983. This report persuaded Congress in mid-1983 to continue funding the MX missile, although it contends that the "window of vulnerability"—the rationale for the MX—had never been open.

Scribner, Richard, and William Metz and Theodore Ralston. *The Verification Challenge: Problems and Promise of Strategic Nuclear Arms Control Verification.* Boston: Birkhauser, 1985. This book, the result of an American Association for the Advancement of Science project, sketches the political and technical aspects of verification in a way that is accessible to the general reader.

Seaborg, Glenn T. *Kennedy, Khrushchev, and the Test Ban.* Berkeley, Cal.: University of California Press, 1981. As former chairman of the Atomic Energy Commission, the author provides a behind-the-scenes account of the domestic infighting and international negotiation that led to the Limited Test Ban Treaty.

Sherwin, Martin J. *A World Destroyed: The Atomic Bomb and the Grand Alliance.* New York: Knopf, 1975. The best account of the political and diplomatic circumstances surrounding the development and use of the first atomic bomb, covering the 1939–1945 period.

Sivard, Ruth Leger. *World Military and Social Expenditures.* Leesburg, Va.: World Priorities, annual. Provides detailed statistics on arms spending compared to social expenditures for nearly all countries, military bases on foreign soil, status of arms control agreements, and so forth.

Smith, Alice Kimball. *A Peril and a Hope: The Scientists' Movement in America, 1945–47.* Chicago: University of Chicago Press, 1965. History of atomic scientists' involvement in building the first atomic bomb and their subsequent efforts to control the arms race.

Smith, Gerard. *Doubletalk: The Story of SALT I.* New York: Doubleday, 1980. A revealing history by the chief U.S. SALT negotiator from 1969 to 1972.

Soviet Ministry of Defense. *Whence the Threat to Peace.* Moscow: Military Publishing House, 1982. Issued as a rebuttal to the 1981 Department of Defense *Soviet Military Power,* this booklet uses rhetorical techniques and selective presentation of data to reach the conclusion that the United States and NATO are striving to achieve military superiority over the Soviet Union.

Spector, Leonard S. *Nuclear Proliferation Today.* New York: Vintage/Random House, 1984. A region-by-region guide to proliferation prospects around the world.

Stares, Paul B. *The Militarization of Space: U.S. Policy, 1945–1984.* Ithaca, N.Y.: Cornell University Press, 1985. Provides perspective on the long history of the militarization of space.

Steinbruner, John D., and Leon V. Sigal, eds. *Alliance Security: NATO and the*

No-First-Use Question. Washington, D.C.: Brookings Institution, 1983. Detailed exploration of the requirements for and implications of a declaration of no first use of nuclear weapons by the NATO alliance.

Stockholm International Peace Research Institute. *The Arms Race and Arms Control*. London: Taylor and Francis, annual. This softcover book contains some of the best material from the SIPRI yearbook in a more affordable and compact form. Coverage includes statistics about nuclear forces, arms transfers, and military spending, plus recent developments in weaponry, testing, and arms control.

————. *World Armaments and Disarmament: The SIPRI Yearbook*. London: Taylor and Francis, annual. Up-to-date information on military expenditures, weapons systems deployed and under development, arms trade, nuclear weapons tests, arms control treaties, and current strategic doctrines.

Talbott, Strobe. *Deadly Gambits*. New York: Knopf, 1984. This detailed account of the behind-the-scenes struggle over arms control in the Reagan Administration has been called into question by some who criticize the author's sources and methodologies.

Thompson, E.P., and Dan Smith, eds. *Protest and Survive*. New York: Monthly Review Press, 1981. Essays on the European antiwar movement.

Tsipis, Kosta. *Arsenal: Understanding Weapons in the Nuclear Age*. New York: Simon and Schuster, 1983. Readable introduction to nuclear weapons and delivery systems from a physicist's point of view.

Union of Concerned Scientists. *The Fallacy of Star Wars*. New York: Vintage/Random House, 1984. Introduction to the technology and arms race implications of space-based defenses against ballistic missiles.

U.S. Department of Defense. *Soviet Military Power*. Washington, D.C.: Government Printing Office, annual. A large-format, well-illustrated catalogue of Soviet nuclear and conventional forces, arguing that the Soviet Union is striving for superiority over the United States and that the United States must continue its own military buildup.

Ury, William Langer, and Richard Smoke. *Beyond the Hotline: Controlling a Nuclear Crisis*. Cambridge, Mass.: Nuclear Negotiating Project of the Harvard Law School, 1984. A compact presentation of the problem of crisis control and a number of partial solutions.

Wasserman, Harvey, and Norman Soloman. *Killing Our Own: The Disaster of America's Experience with Atomic Radiation*. New York: Dell, 1983. The impact of radiation from nuclear power plants, weapons testing, and waste disposal on U.S. citizens.

Yergin, Daniel, and Martin Hillenbrand, eds. *Global Insecurity*. Boston: Houghton Mifflin, 1982. A politically oriented collection of essays from the Harvard Business School.

York, Herbert. *Race to Oblivion: A Participant's View of the Arms Race*. New York: Simon and Schuster, 1970. Rich with the insights of a participant in many key decisions, this book illuminates the interplay of the military, the defense industry, and the government in generating the U.S. side of the arms race from 1945 to 1969.

Zuckerman, Solly. *Nuclear Illusion and Reality.* New York: Viking, 1982. A former scientific adviser to the British government, the author argues that nuclear war can neither be limited nor won and illuminates the role that weapons technologists have played in driving the arms race.

PERIODICALS

Arms Control Today. 11 issues/year. The Arms Control Association, 11 Dupont Circle, N.W., Washington, D.C. 20036. Analyses of current arms-control issues with summaries of the state of ongoing negotiations and extensive current bibliographies on defense issues.

Bulletin of the Atomic Scientists. 10 issues/year. 5801 S. Kenwood, Chicago, Ill. 60637. The oldest general journal emphasizing the nuclear arms race, arms control, and interrelated issues of science and technology.

Defense Monitor. 10 issues/year. Center for Defense Information, 303 Capitol Gallery West, 600 Maryland Avenue, S.W., Washington, D.C. 20024. Newsletter of a research organization run by retired military officers and noted as an authoritative alternative to Pentagon information.

Detente. 4 issues/year. Ann Hegelson, Centre for Russian and East European Studies, University of Birmingham, P.O. Box 363, Birmingham B15 2TT, United Kingdom. This journal devoted to understanding the Soviet Union is a cooperative project of a number of British Sovietologists.

F.A.S. Public Interest Report. 10 issues/year. Federation of American Scientists, 307 Massachusetts Avenue, N.W., Washington, D.C. 20002. Newsletter emphasizing analysis and opinion by prominent advocates of arms control.

Foreign Affairs. 5 issues/year. Council on Foreign Relations, 58 East 68th Street, New York, N.Y. 10021. Forum for major articles by senior foreign-relations analysts, includes a section with capsule summaries of recent books on international relations.

Foreign Policy. 4 issues/year. Subscription Department, Box 984, Farmingdale, N.Y. 11737. Coverage similar to *Foreign Affairs,* with somewhat less emphasis on the seniority of authors.

International Security. 6 issues/year. MIT Press Journals, 28 Carleton Street, Cambridge, Mass. 02142. Publication of Harvard's Center for Science and International Affairs includes articles on military and arms control strategy, theory, and implications.

Nuclear Times. 6 issues/year. Room 512, 298 Fifth Avenue, New York, N.Y. 10001. Newsmagazine of the antinuclear movement, with sections on resources and organizing ideas.

Science. 51 issues/year. American Association for the Advancement of Science, 1333 H Street, N.W., Washington, D.C. 20005. Newsmagazine of the scientific community often contains first reports of emerging nuclear-weapons issues.

Scientific American. 12 issues/year. Subscription Manager, P.O. Box 5969, New York, N.Y. 10017. Forum for major science and science-policy articles, including such issues as verification, Star Wars, and weapons systems. The nuclear weapons and arms control articles are periodically published in reprint collections by W.H. Freeman.

Survival. 6 issues/year. The International Institute for Strategic Studies, 23 Tavistock Street, London, WC2E 7NQ United Kingdom. In addition to articles on a range of international security issues, this journal publishes current documents on selected themes in each issue.

Index